Industrializing Financial Services with DevOps

Proven 360° DevOps operating model practices for enabling a multi-speed bank

Spyridon Maniotis

BIRMINGHAM—MUMBAI

Industrializing Financial Services with DevOps

Copyright © 2022 Packt Publishing

Group Product Manager: Rahul Nair
Publishing Product Manager: Yashashree Hardikar
Senior Editor: Athikho Sapuni Rishana
Technical Editor: Rajat Sharma
Language Support Editing: Safis Editing
Copy Editor: Safis Editing
Project Coordinator: Ashwin Kharwa
Proofreader: Safis Editing
Indexer: Pratik Shirodkar
Production Designer: Sinhayna Bais
Senior Marketing Coordinator: Nimisha Dua
Marketing Coordinator: Gaurav Christian

First published: December 2022
Production reference: 1101122

Published by Packt Publishing Ltd.
Livery Place
35 Livery Street
Birmingham
B3 2PB, UK.

ISBN 978-1-80461-434-1

www.packt.com

Contributors

About the author

Spyridon Maniotis is an experienced DevOps professional based in London, UK. In recent years, his career focus has been on working with enterprise DevOps transformations in the financial services industry. His financial services DevOps experience includes Nordic, British, and French incumbent banks, as well as European payments and pension fund corporations. He has worked for more than 10 years with financial services technology at Nordea Bank, Danske Bank, Deloitte Consulting, Capco, and Ericsson, serving in several DevOps leadership positions. He is a well-rounded and seasoned practitioner of DevOps, SRE, SDLC, technology strategy, regulatory compliance, as well as agile methodologies. He holds a BSc in computer science, an MSc in software engineering, and an MBA degree.

About the reviewers

Aleksandras Artemjevas worked at an incumbent bank for 4 years. His last role there was DevOps engineer in the DevOps center of excellence. He was part of a team driving the DevOps adoption at scale. Currently, he is working at a banking infrastructure provider as a service reliability engineer.

Michał Gryko has been tinkering with electronics and computers since he was a kid. This led to a career in computer science and eventually various SysAdmin/DevOps/SRE roles. He is always focused on taking code from developers to production as quickly as possible while keeping the company running in the meantime.

Katarzyna Bieszk has 20 years of IT experience in program and project management, leading cross-functional teams to successful implementation according to SAFe/Agile, waterfall, or hybrid standards. Since 2020, she has been acting as a DevOps driver implementing DevOps Health Radar and Value Stream Mapping. She has been a trainer for SAFe DevOps courses as a SAFe Program Consultant. Katarzyna is currently employed by Nordea full time, where she heads the software development team within Group Functions Technology and focuses on increasing cloud maturity.

Table of Contents

Part 2: The 360° DevOps Operating Model, Governance, and Orchestration Mechanisms

3

4

Enterprise Architecture and the DevOps Center of Excellence   69

5

Business Enterprise Agility and DevOps Ways of Working Reconciliation   95

Part 3: Capability Engineering, Enablement, and Launch

6

DevOps Software Development Life Cycle 360° Evolution and Engineering   131

7

The DevOps 360° Technological Ecosystem as a Service   155

8

360° Regulatory Compliance as Code   183

Part 4: Adopt, Scale, and Sustain

9

The DevOps Portfolio Classification and Governance   211

10

Tactical and Organic Enterprise Portfolio Planning and Adoption   235

13

14

Preface

In recent years, large financial services institutions have been embracing the concept of DevOps at the core of their digital transformation strategies.

This book is inspired by real enterprise DevOps adoptions in the financial services industry and provides a comprehensive and proven practical guide on how large corporate organizations can evolve their DevOps operating model. The three main themes underpinning the book's approach are the ones of *360°*, *at relevance*, and *speeds*. Starting with how a bank's corporate and technology strategy links to its enterprise DevOps evolution, we provide a rich array of proven practices for designing and creating a harmonious 360° DevOps operating model that should be enabled and adopted *at relevance in a multi-speed context*.

The book is packed with real case studies and examples from the financial services industry, as we have learned lessons and used tools that the reader can adopt in their organization and context.

Who this book is for

This book is for DevOps practitioners, banking technologists, technology managers, business directors, and transformation leads. Readers should have knowledge and experience of fundamental DevOps terminology and concepts and ideally have been involved in practicing DevOps in large organizations.

What this book covers

Chapter 1, The Banking Context and DevOps Value Proposition, provides an introduction to the main actor of the book, which is an incumbent bank. Its external and internal contexts in relation to DevOps are discussed in depth. In this chapter, we also provide our DevOps definition and the banking value proposition. Two important elements of the book are also introduced: **relevance** and **360°**.

Chapter 2, The DevOps Multi-Speed Context, Vision, Objectives, and Change Nature, presents the concept of multi-speed in banking, with examples. The importance of understanding the DevOps context will also be discussed with representative examples from incumbents. Afterward, we will discuss how DevOps is linked to the enterprise vision and strategic corporate and technological objectives, and how enterprise DevOps OKRs can be created. We will also outline elements of the nature of DevOps change.

Chapter 3, The 360° DevOps Operating Model Pillars and Governance Model, proposes a governance model for defining the 360° operating model and its enablement and launch mechanisms. Governance bodies such as vision and design authorities as well as workstreams will be defined and their roles discussed in detail. The governing dynamics of those bodies will be discussed based on the influence that they can have on the DevOps evolution. Closing the chapter, we will focus on three industry use cases that will reveal how organizational structures can potentially influence the DevOps evolution.

Chapter 4, Enterprise Architecture and the DevOps Center of Excellence, discusses the vital role of enterprise architecture, anchored to banking business domains and critical flows, as well as modernization strategies and reference architectures. The various roles that the DevOps CoE can have in the evolution along with potential operating and service models will be outlined. At the end of the chapter, we will provide four use cases of incumbent banks that have deployed DevOps CoEs in different ways.

Chapter 5, Business Enterprise Agility and DevOps Ways of Working Reconciliation, analyzes the relation of DevOps with Enterprise Agility overall and their points of reconciliation. We will deep dive and discuss how DevOps can be reconciled in an agnostic way with business enterprise agility models. The business enterprise agility models we will use are *basic agile, the Spotify model, value streams*, and *the Scaled Agile Framework*, as they have been adopted by several incumbents. In the second part of the chapter, a proven and detailed technique will be provided on how to design the DevOps organizing principles *at relevance* in your agile DevOps teams. Several complementary recommendations are embedded in the technique.

Chapter 6, DevOps Software Development Life Cycle 360° Evolution and Engineering, focuses on defining the heart of the DevOps model, which is the engineered and evolved software development life cycle. We will start by analyzing the SDLC anatomy in terms of phases, frameworks, and capabilities. A technique of collecting and consolidating capabilities will be presented, along with how to engage the relevant stakeholder and eventually, through value stream mapping and flows, define the future way of designing, building, deploying, and running software. This chapter will provide a proven step-by-step technique to define your future SDLC.

Chapter 7, The DevOps 360° Technological Ecosystem as a Service, focuses on the main parts of the technological ecosystem that will contribute to the adoption. We will discuss the relationship between DevOps and technology and make a case for technology standardization. The main focus in the chapter will be the DevOps platform teams, which we will cover from an operating and service model perspective. Special reference will be made to specific platform teams that incumbents establish.

Chapter 8, 360° Regulatory Compliance as Code, discusses the regulatory environment around DevOps, taking a globally systemically important bank's point of view. The compliance value proposition for DevOps will be discussed through four real industry stories. These four stories will serve as a justification for the book's argument that compliance is a DevOps enabler and vice versa. Special focus will be placed on discussing the topics of DevOps controls and segregation/separation of duties. We will also provide several tips in the chapter on how to manage the relationship with your regulator.

Chapter 9, The DevOps Portfolio Classification and Governance, discusses methods to classify your DevOps portfolio based on *criticality and impact* and *technology and architecture*. We will also examine how speeds are shaped based on those categories and how concepts such as licenses to continuously deliver can help certain parts of your portfolio to move faster. In the second part of the chapter, we will discuss important aspects of portfolio governance, placing special focus on application DevOps attributes and the mechanism of the production readiness assessment.

Chapter 10, Tactical and Organic Enterprise Portfolio Planning and Adoption, discusses how the adoption will be embedded in the enterprise's annual and quarterly portfolio planning, from the corporate strategy to the Enterprise DevOps OKRs, to initiatives, epics, and stories in the backlogs of the enablement and adoption teams. Special reference will be made to the concepts of tactical and organic adoption, which must be balanced. A core part of the book that is included in this chapter is the concept of DevOps minimum viable adoption.

Chapter 11, Benefit Measurement and Realization, focuses on recommendations for how to measure and realize the benefits of the evolution. We will introduce the concepts of key performance targets and metrics and why it is important to distinguish the two. Afterward, we will provide practical recommendations on how to define your KPTs and metrics, providing some practical inspiration. The rest of the chapter will be full of advice that you can consider during the process.

Chapter 12, People Hiring, Incubation, and Mobility, focuses on DevOps hiring, incubation, and mobility. The initial focus will be on the importance of Π-shaped DevOps professionals. Key aspects to consider in your hiring strategy will be outlined by real lessons learned. Moving to incubation, we will discuss several recommendations on how to make it more effective. We will close the chapter by making a case for people mobility.

Chapter 13, Site Reliability Engineering in the FSI, starts by defining SRE and relating it to DevOps. Afterward, we will outline the fundamental SRE responsibilities as we propose them to be defined based on real industry experiences. We will make several *at relevance* recommendations focusing on SRE eligibility, engagement models, and reconciliation with ITIL. Closing the chapter, we will outline four industry use cases on how different incumbents have adopted SRE.

Chapter 14, 360° Recap, Staying Relevant, and Final Remarks, recaps the core DevOps operating model aspects, focusing on the relevant elements that we highlighted in each chapter. Some final concluding remarks will be provided.

Download the color images

We also provide a PDF file that has color images of the screenshots and diagrams used in this book. You can download it here: `https://packt.link/FckEw`.

Conventions used

Following is the text convention used throughout this book.

> **Tips or important notes**
> Appear like this.

Get in touch

Feedback from our readers is always welcome.

General feedback: If you have questions about any aspect of this book, email us at customercare@ packtpub.com and mention the book title in the subject of your message.

Errata: Although we have taken every care to ensure the accuracy of our content, mistakes do happen. If you have found a mistake in this book, we would be grateful if you would report this to us. Please visit www.packtpub.com/support/errata and fill in the form.

Piracy: If you come across any illegal copies of our works in any form on the internet, we would be grateful if you would provide us with the location address or website name. Please contact us at copyright@packt.com with a link to the material.

If you are interested in becoming an author: If there is a topic that you have expertise in and you are interested in either writing or contributing to a book, please visit authors.packtpub.com.

Share Your Thoughts

Once you've read *Industrializing Financial Services with DevOps*, we'd love to hear your thoughts! Scan the QR code below to go straight to the Amazon review page for this book and share your feedback.

https://packt.link/r/1804614343

Your review is important to us and the tech community and will help us make sure we're delivering excellent quality content.

Download a free PDF copy of this book

Thanks for purchasing this book!

Do you like to read on the go but are unable to carry your print books everywhere? Is your eBook purchase not compatible with the device of your choice?

Don't worry, now with every Packt book you get a DRM-free PDF version of that book at no cost.

Read anywhere, any place, on any device. Search, copy, and paste code from your favorite technical books directly into your application.

The perks don't stop there, you can get exclusive access to discounts, newsletters, and great free content in your inbox daily

Follow these simple steps to get the benefits:

1. Scan the QR code or visit the link below

https://packt.link/free-ebook/9781804614341

2. Submit your proof of purchase

3. That's it! We'll send your free PDF and other benefits to your email directly

Part 1: Introduction, Value Proposition, and Foundation

This part provides an introduction to the value proposition of DevOps in banking and introduces three core elements of the book: DevOps 360° qualities, relevance, and multi-speeds. It also provides an overview of how the corporate and technology strategies of an incumbent bank can be reconciled and how enterprise DevOps OKRs can be defined.

This part of the book comprises the following chapters:

- *Chapter 1, The Banking Context and DevOps Value Proposition*
- *Chapter 2, The DevOps Multi-Speed Context, Vision, Objectives, and Change Nature*

1

The Banking Context and DevOps Value Proposition

This chapter starts by introducing the main actor of the book, which is an incumbent bank, and defines its key characteristics. The internal and external environments of the bank will be discussed, aiming to present a detailed overview of its key external and internal context determinants in relation to DevOps. Continuing, the book's tailor-made DevOps definition is presented and mapped to the DevOps value proposed for banking, using a mobile banking application as an example. The rest of the chapter focuses on introducing two important concepts and perspectives that are at the core of adopting DevOps at scale in a banking context. Starting with the concept of relevance, we discuss why context and situation are key parameters for consideration. In concluding the chapter, we discuss why enterprise DevOps adoptions should cater to a 360° perspective through the enablement of four qualities.

In this chapter, we're going to cover the following main topics:

- The main actor of the book, and its characteristics and ecosystem
- Examining the incumbent's external and internal context at a glance
- Defining DevOps and its value proposition for banking
- What is the importance of adopting DevOps at relevance?
- Why take a 360° perspective when adopting DevOps?

Introducing the main actor of the book

Starting this book, it is important to introduce our main actor. Understanding who is the subject of focus at this early stage is important so you are in a better position to understand our actor's nature and context, as well as how DevOps as a concept is related. This chapter introduces and outlines the characteristics of the main actor, but also makes reference to other actors that operate in the same industry and ecosystem and have a role to play in the book.

Our main actor is an **incumbent bank**, representing a sample of global and regional incumbent banks. The incumbent bank in focus is a large institution, well established in the financial services industry, which has the objective of advancing its DevOps adoption on an enterprise level, as part of implementing its new corporate and technology strategy.

Our incumbent is characterized by the following specifications:

- It runs global operations in multiple regions of the world.

- It offers a rich variety of products and services across the banking, payments, and capital markets, asset and wealth management, and the insurance and pension domains.

- It is of regional and global systemic importance.

- It is exposed to different macroeconomic conditions and customer behaviors in the different markets in which it operates.

- Its market share position varies per operating market.

- It has a long history in the industry and is a result of several mergers and acquisitions.

- It historically started to adopt DevOps in several of its units but has not attempted enterprise and at-scale adoption before.

The largest world banks you can think of are represented by our incumbent.

> **Bonus Information**
>
> As a global, systemically important financial services institution, we've defined a bank whose failure could result in triggering a global financial crisis. There were 30 such banks in total across the globe in 2021, which we also refer to as *too big to fail*. Being systemically important indicates that as an institution, you are subject to higher supervisory expectations by the Financial Stability Board.

The incumbent bank operates in the same ecosystem and markets as **challenger banks**, **neobanks**, as well as **banking infrastructure providers**. The challenger banks, neo banks, and banking infrastructure providers are relatively **new entrants** in the financial services industry, with the following characteristics:

- **Challenger banks**: New, fully digital, online and mobile banks, without a physical presence, that offer banking products and services under a banking license. Revolut, Monzo, N26, and Lunar belong to this category.

- **Neobanks**: New, fully digital, online and mobile banks, without a physical presence, that offer limited banking products and services compared to incumbents and challengers without a banking license. Yolt and Chime belong to this category.

- **Banking infrastructure and platform providers**: These are companies that offer financial infrastructure services through platform integration to both incumbents and challenger banks. Mambu, Banking Circle, Klarna, and Nets belong to this category.

Our incumbent bank's has relationship to challenger banks and neo banks is characterized by competition, while its relationship with banking infrastructure and platform providers, in most scenarios, is that of a service consumer.

It is important to make reference to another category that is closely related to our incumbent bank – **beta banks**. These are subsidiaries of incumbents operating under the banking license of the parent bank, or by using licenses of partner banks in specific countries. The business case behind those banks is the fast launch, experimentation, and expansion of new services and products to either existing or new markets. Mettle by NatWest and BforBank by Crédit Agricole are two examples.

Speaking of terminology, it is important to clarify an approach taken in this book. We will refrain from using the term *FinTech* to identify new entrants in the industry, as we perceive the term **FinTech** as standing for **Financial Technology**, which is equally used both by incumbents and new entrants.

Examining the incumbent's external and internal context at a glance

When understanding the conditions and circumstances under which the incumbent operates, it is important to examine the financial services industry's external and internal environments, seen from the perspective of our main actor. Getting this contextual understanding will serve as a fundamental awareness element for the rest of the book, especially when relating the industry's context with that of DevOps. Context is of vital importance in adopting DevOps, as we will also see later in the book, and the financial services context is indeed evolving at a very dynamic pace.

What does an incumbent bank's external context look like?

The term **external context** is used to refer to the external environment within which the bank operates. As our bank operates in global markets, we are taking a global average and as representative as possible a snapshot, while of course, we remain conscious that factors such as specific regions, countries, market conditions, regulatory frameworks, and economic factors force our bank to be faced in its reality with more dynamic and versatile circumstances and conditions than our snapshot presents.

As this is not an economics book, we will refrain from discussing economic concepts such as interest rates, inflation, gross domestic product, and industrial production indexes when examining the external environment. We will exclusively focus on the external environmental factors that do have a direct and/or indirect relation to how our incumbent's DevOps enterprise adoption will be designed and will evolve.

Regulatory focus due to the 2008 financial crisis

Let's attempt a flashback and go back to the years after 2008 and the global financial crisis. The aftermath of the crisis for large incumbent banks was characterized by waves of heavy regulatory requirements (Basel, EMIR, MiFID, Dodd-Frank, PSD, SCI, and T2S, to mention a few), which were complemented by extremely rigorous audit assessments, especially for globally systemically important institutions. Those audit assessments, apart from traditionally assessing the compliance and maturity levels of business operations, activities, and resiliency, were complemented by a significant focus on IT infrastructure and the related service domain. Technology operations and IT risk management came into strong focus with the supervisory authorities somewhere around 2015. By coincidence, around that time was the period that DevOps started to be known as a concept in the industry.

Licenses to operate came at risk, and capital was set aside to cover potential fines due to foreseeable challenges in complying with legislation on time. Inevitably, that situation forced incumbent banks to deploy significant amounts of their capital and resources to regulatory work, while in parallel they were struggling with profitability due to the volatile macroeconomic conditions of that period. Digital innovation agendas were compromised or put on hold for some time.

Obviously, the circumstances did not totally hold incumbents back from innovating during those years. Some indeed took advantage of the regulatory demand and capital set aside for those purposes to promote their digital innovation agendas, which was an intelligent tactic indeed. To some extent, it was also inevitable to not invest in new technologies, in order to close old audit remarks, as new regulations could not be met with legacy applications, infrastructure, and tools. Therefore, deploying innovative technologies to effectively respond to the continuously evolving regulatory environment, in certain cases, was the only sustainable way. Nevertheless, despite the creative mindset and approaches of several incumbent banks, their digital innovation plans were jeopardized, or at least slowed down.

Technology industrialized rapidly in the meantime

That *turbulent* period for the industry was at the same time a period of rapid advancement for technological utilities and concepts globally. Technologies such as APIs, cloud services, machine learning, artificial intelligence, and data analytics were proliferating and maturing, while concepts such as enterprise agility, DevOps, and SRE created new means and enablers for digital innovation and new **ways of working (WoW)** in the industry. Digital services have become mainstream in recent years, hybrid cloud has become the dominant infrastructure model, cyber security is evolving on top of the risk factors agenda, regulators are becoming more tech-savvy, the challenger banks' business model delivers, and investment in digital customer journeys and intelligence has become one of the top profitability sources. The adaptation of such technologies and concepts challenges the traditional technology operating models of incumbents, requiring a generous shift toward modern WoW and advanced engineering capabilities. Concepts that the industry used to call "another nice thing to have" have become "another necessary capability we need to build."

In recent years, and after that decade of global economic volatility and high focus on responding to regulatory demand, incumbents have entered an era of financial growth, characterized by increased profitability, which, in combination with technological advancements, allows capital and resources to be strategically deployed on digital innovation, materializing what some in the industry call **the long-awaited transformation**. Technology has started not only to be considered a key business enabler but the business itself.

Which are the forces that shape the financial services industry?

On providing a more detailed and rounded picture of the incumbent's external environment, Porter's Five Forces model is used to identify and analyze the industry's main five competitive forces and reveal its respective strengths and weaknesses. The results of this method can be used by companies to support the evolution of their corporate strategy, which influences their technology strategy and consequently their DevOps adoption, as we will discuss in the next chapter.

A representative Five Forces analysis of our incumbent bank is presented as follows:

- **Bargaining power of customers – Pressure level: Moderate**: This force is very much client segment dependent, as well as operating markets and business domain related. A small daily banking client holding a bank account with a deposit of 1,000 euros has close to zero purchasing power if they decide to move to another bank. In contrast, a wealthy private or corporate banking client with a diversified portfolio of assets with a value of 500 million euros has significant purchasing power, as they could cause financial and reputational loss. The former is the one who is most likely to leave our incumbent for a challenger or neobank and the latter to another incumbent.

- **Bargaining power of suppliers – Pressure level: Moderate**: The two major suppliers of an incumbent bank are capital and people. The ability of the bank to compete in its markets, generate strong revenue, and maintain a high credit score rating, as well as meeting its return of equity and cost/income ratio targets, can attract clients and investors. Nevertheless, even though incumbents have returned to strong profitability, presently corporate investors' interest in expanding their investments beyond incumbents toward challengers through funding rounds is increasing. On the people side, technological advancements, people skill scarcity in the market, talent competition, as well as the new flexible working conditions brought about by the Covid pandemic increase the challenge of maintaining and hiring talented people, primarily in technological domains. In addition, challengers and neobanks look appealing in the eyes of young talent, due to better career prospects through the usage of the latest technologies.

- **Competition from industry rivals – Pressure level: High**: The industry is traditionally very competitive, driven by aggressive profitability targets and ratios, backed by a digitalization *time-to-market race* for new products and services. The relatively low cost of switching from one incumbent to another or from an incumbent to a challenger intensifies an already competitive landscape. This rivalry, though, apart from bringing competition, also generates opportunities for joint ventures. The motto *if you can't beat them, join them* is becoming part of corporate strategies across the industry and domain-specific ecosystems, through increased **merger and acquisition (M&A)** activities, vertical integrations, and FinTech incubation hubs. Banco Santander is a great example of an incumbent that is very active in pursuing joint ventures.

- **Threat of substitute products and services – Pressure level: High**: The incumbent's monopoly is undoubtedly in decline. The industry is threatened by substitutions arising from the proliferation of new players within its ecosystem (challengers, neobanks, and infrastructure providers), as well as technological giants such as Google and Apple (in association with incumbents such as Goldman Sachs) that have entered the financial services industry. Changing customer behaviors, which is driven by the high technological literacy of new generations on one hand and on the other hand by sharing economic factors, generate demand for new substitute services. As the COO of a bank, I used to work on the basis of the saying *Most customers now have smartphones and many options. What they do not have is time and patience.* However, a competitive advantage that incumbents still maintain is that they offer the most complete service and product offerings across financial services domains, including financial advice.

- **New entrants – Pressure level: High**: The new entrants, after an initial period of facing high obstacles to penetrate the market and compete with incumbents, due to certain entry barriers such as regulatory frameworks, capital and license requirements, legacy bonds of clients with traditional institutions, and reputation establishment, have eventually made a significant breakthrough in the industry. Many of these new entrants have managed to build trust in the industry's clients and attract funds from investors, as well as talented people. Their advantage is not only fully digital services, with reduced costs, but also new business models, improved customer experience, and technology service reliability. The effect that new entrants have varies across operating markets, business domains, and ecosystems, primarily due to factors such as regulatory frameworks, the resiliency and robustness of incumbents, as well as their market position, along with customer relations and behaviors.

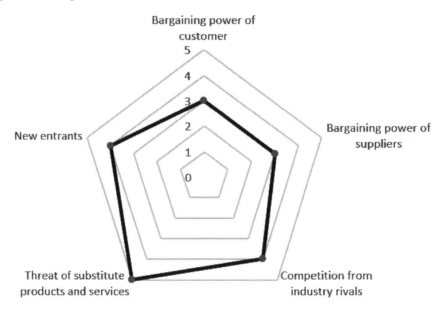

Figure 1.1 – Porter's Five Forces (1979) adapted to the financial services industry

What does an incumbent's internal context look like?

The internal context of our representative incumbent bank is subject to more differences per incumbent compared to the external context, one can argue. There are, though, certain commonalities characterizing the internal context of globally and regionally systemically important banks. As we did with the external context, we will not cover the complete spectrum of internal conditions and will focus only on internal forces that have a direct or indirect foreseeable impact on enterprise DevOps adoption.

Persistent pressure on cost/income ratio

Incumbent banks, to remain competitive, need to continuously improve their cost/income ratio. This can either be achieved by reducing operating costs while keeping revenue relatively flat, or by keeping operating costs relatively flat and increasing revenue, or the *happy days* scenario, which combines operating cost reduction and revenue increase in parallel. Obviously, there is a *convenient solution* available, which is to bravely reduce the operating costs of the bank, as revenue increase is an exercise that requires great effort, and it is also affected by several external factors. In addition, focusing primarily on operating cost reduction can have an immediate effect on the bank's balance sheet, while revenue increase is more of a long-term impact. Therefore, incumbents are extremely cost-conscious.

> **Bonus Information**
>
> The cost/income ratio is a major metric that determines the profitability of a bank. Its measurement analyzes the operating costs of running the bank against its operating income. The lower the cost/income, the more efficient and profitable a bank is. The mathematical formula used is *operating cost / operating income = cost/income ratio.*

Operational efficiency focus

Incumbents strive to produce more with less in improving their operational efficiency through the utilization of resources. Aiming to maintain a competitive advantage and create a first-mover advantage through the delivery of more innovative services and products, incumbents continuously examine possibilities to extend their production possibilities frontier through resource utilization. Their production possibilities frontier can be increased either with extra people and capital deployed, which is not the ideal strategy due to cost constraints, as we explained earlier, or by deploying technological advancements as their means of delivering new products and services. The latter sounds optimal and is the only sustainable possibility. In distinguishing this internal context factor from the cost-income ratio factor, we need to clarify that producing more does not necessarily mean more revenue, and the deployment of new technologies will also not necessarily come with a cost reduction in technology operating expenses. Your new products might not sell, and the utilization of new technologies does not come for free.

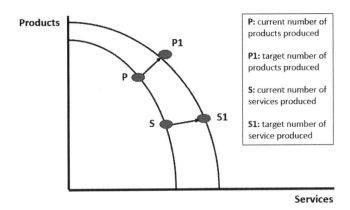

Figure 1.2 – Production possibilities frontier, adapted to incumbent banks

New ways of working

New, in this case, does not mean newly invented in the industry, but new in the sense of enabling new ways of doing things in a banking context. Concepts such as Agile, DevOps, scaled Agile delivery, modern software delivery, and site reliability engineering have been around for many years but very few incumbents have found solid steps in adopting them in a harmonious and scaled way, characterized by continuous organic evolution and not back-to-back transformation programs. You will often hear stories such as Bank A just started its Agile Transformation v3 or that Bank B started its DevOps Industrialization v2. I always remember a saying from an ex-peer of mine: *Banks get transformation programs done so they can start another transformation program to transform the results of the previous one.* This is of course not representative of every incumbent, but it does hold lots of truth in it. Another present challenge is the difficulty for incumbents to fit all the new WoW concepts under one operating model that is characterized by harmony and reconciliation. Often, also, as we will see later in the book, the adoption of new WoW concepts is complemented by organization structure changes that in many cases defeat the new WoW method's purpose. All of this results in a confused and misaligned modus operandi, characterized by internal variations, an ineffective blend of old and new ways of doing things, and resistance, under the mentality that if it is not invented here, it cannot be implemented here.

Organizational debt

In IT, we often use the term **technical debt**, referring to software solutions that have been deployed to production that are characterized by low quality and in the future will result in functional and non-function abnormalities. Looking at the broader context, incumbents are faced with what I prefer to call **organizational debt**, which spans horizontally and vertically across their organizations, from outdated people skills to coupled legacy platforms, and from bureaucratic policies to complex and cumbersome manual processes, backed by a deep-rooted old-school mentality on WoW, based on silos and fragmentation. All these elements have multidimensional and domino-effect consequences for an incumbent's internal operations and its ability to transform and advance. Such conditions not only increase the cost and complexity of delivering and running technological solutions but also impose high operational and regulatory risk, slow down the adoption of new WoW and radical digitalization initiatives, as well as impose a great risk on an incumbent's ability to attract and maintain talented people.

Digitalization and platformization

Banking as a service is becoming the new business model norm and a vehicle for *staying relevant*, enabled by significant investment in digitalization and platformization. The focus is not only narrowed on how clients interact with banks but also on how internal business units interact with IT, as well as IT-to-IT interaction. However, in many cases, banks face significant challenges on that digitalization and platformization journey, primarily due to heavy reliance on legacy technological platforms. The situation is characterized by old untenable platforms, with unknown technical debt, *black-box* business logic implementations, expiring maintenance contracts, poor documentation, monolithic architectures, lack of integration, high customization, difficulty upgrading, unreliability, and scarcity of people with deep knowledge. What is often called in the industry a *legacy dilemma* is still to be solved for most incumbents, with some bombs ticking as we speak (borrowing an expression of an ex-CIO of mine).

Corporate and technology strategy objective misalignment

Technology is there to enable the business and the other way around, you could rightly claim. That statement indicates that corporate and technology strategies need to therefore be in close alignment and evolve together. This condition of alignment is challenging to achieve, especially in very large incumbents. Organizational structures, siloed business domain thinking, a lack of collective strategic initiatives, conflicting performance indicators, ambiguous benefit realization procedures, a lack of technological literacy on the business side, as well as a lack of business literacy on the technological side, in combination with middle management being the transmitter of priorities and direction, creates a condition of misalignment and misunderstandings. On the technological side, this misalignment in many cases goes deeper between the business IT areas and the core infrastructure teams. One of the situation's consequences is the occurrence of extreme variations in the adoption of different technologies and concepts. Another consequence is the inability of teams to understand how they are supposed to contribute to materializing the incumbent's strategic objectives, the motivation behind those objectives, as well as what their position is and their role in the delivery value stream.

Defining DevOps and its value proposition for banking

"DevOps is what you make out of it!" you could claim with confidence. In this section, we will examine what incumbent banks can potentially make out of DevOps. But before we start discussing the DevOps value proposition for banking, let me ask you a question. Have you ever thought that DevOps literally and technically is not attributed to a single definition and interpretation?

Some define DevOps plainly as a combination of software development and operations. Others define it as a value-driven approach, combining software development and operations, in an agile context. Amazon Web Services defines it as the combination of cultural philosophies, practices, and technologies that increase an organization's ability to deliver services at high velocity, while Google describes it as a set of practices, guidelines, and culture designed to break down silos in software development and operations, with the DevOps Handbook referring to DevOps as the concept that enables development and operations teams to work toward common goals, enabling a fast workflow while achieving reliability.

In my opinion, there are four main reasons for this variety of definitions. The first one is the broadness of the concept. It is very difficult to define it in only two sentences. The second is people's various perceptions of DevOps based on their experiences, background, and convenience. The third one has to do with the term not being descriptive enough. See, DevOps stands for development and operations, but it is not only about development and operations, as we will also discuss later in the book. Last but not least, the essence of DevOps is that an organization should decide what it wants to make out of it and define it accordingly. We will get back to this point later in the book.

Despite the lack of one DevOps definition, we need to make sure that we understand it the same when we use the term in this book. Therefore, we will take advantage of this absence of a universal definition of DevOps and create our own definition.

The DevOps definition that will guide this book is as follows:

A set of practices, frameworks, and technologies that enable flows, continuity, and collaboration across the **Software Development Life Cycle (SDLC)**, to materialize common objectives while achieving an equilibrium of time to market, reliability, and compliance of services.

> **Tip**
> Randomly select 10 people from different backgrounds and seniority within your organization and ask them about their individual definitions of DevOps. You will be surprised by the versatility and variety of the answers.

Having our definition outlined, let us cross-reference it with the value proposition of DevOps for incumbent banks, looking into some core aspects and using a mobile banking application as an example.

Time to market, reliability, and compliance

This is what I call the *triptych* of DevOps outcomes. Before you question why security is omitted, this is to inform you that it is covered under reliability, as security in my mind is a reliability aspect.

Utilizing DevOps, incumbent banks can firstly improve the time to market of services. With *time to market*, we define the length of time it takes for a product or service to go from the phase of ideation to the phase of being released to production and being made available to customers. In simple words,

DevOps enables the fast delivery and release of software to the market. In our example, the value proposition is that DevOps practices such as automation across the SDLC can minimize the time required between the mobile banking product owner coming up with a new feature idea of a drag-and-drop account aggregation functionality and the feature being made available through an update and upgrade to the bank's clients.

Secondly, DevOps practices can improve the *reliability* of services. With reliability, we define the ability of a service to fulfill its non-functional criteria, such as availability, performance, security, and so on. In our example, a mobile banking application is expected to be available 99.99% of the time and respond within 0.2 seconds when the customer wants to see their deposit account. DevOps practices such as *performance*, *testing*, and *self-healing* can support reliability.

The third aspect of our triptych that can be improved is *compliance*. With compliance, we define the practice of obeying the rules of a higher authority. The higher authority in our context is the banking regulatory and supervisory bodies. Back to our example, regulatory bodies require a mobile banking application to keep an audit trail of unauthorized login attempts as part of security logging. **Compliance as code** DevOps practices can support the utilization of security logging mechanisms.

Equilibrium

This is one of my favorite terms to be used in a DevOps context. The Oxford dictionary defines *equilibrium* as the state of balance between different forces or influencers. In our context, the main forces or influencers are the outcomes of the following:

- Time to market
- Reliability
- Compliance

We have all had experiences where one of the three objectives had to be compromised in favor of the others. Achieving a DevOps equilibrium in our example means that we can achieve time-to-market targets for the new account aggregation functionality without impacting the performance of the application, as well as having a security logging mechanism implemented. **Site Reliability Engineering** (**SRE**) practices such as **production readiness reviews** can support that objective.

Common objectives

This indicates that all the stakeholders in the mobile banking application – product owners, developers, operations, DevOps engineers, and so on – share and understand the **common goals** of the service and their organization's objectives and consequently work in alignment toward them. This goes from an understanding of the mobile banking business domain and customer behaviors and needs to why the service is of high business criticality, and from why feature A is prioritized over feature B to the importance of moving from weekly to *on-demand* release cycles.

The SDLC

DevOps, to deliver its ultimate potential, needs to be applied across all phases of the SDLC: from ideation and planning to development and testing, and from staging to production and deployment to its operations and maintenance, and eventually sunsetting. But by saying across the SDLC, we do not only refer to the phases themselves, but also to the people involved across the value stream. Those at the top of the core mobile banking business, development, and operations teams include the incumbent's core infrastructure teams, enterprise architecture, and the command-and-control center. Yes, indeed, everything I just mentioned is also part of the SDLC.

Flows, continuity, and collaboration

We will bundle the definitions of flow and continuity, due to the strong interrelation of the two concepts, and define them as the steady and continuous movement of something, in one direction, without interruption. Flows and continuity are core principals enabling DevOps and are actually symbolized in the loop of infinity characterizing DevOps. Practices and methods such as **value streams**, **engineering**, and **capabilities as a service** can support the elimination of lead times and waste across the SDLC of our mobile banking application. For example, removing bottlenecks of manual approvals in the release management process, through value streaming techniques, speeding up the quality assurance process through **test automation**, and provisioning **infrastructure as code** within seconds will all contribute to a flawless and continuous mobile banking application delivery model. Inevitably, flows and continuity are empowered by strong collaboration across the actors of the SDLC; **shared objectives**, **feedback loops**, **common benefit measurement realization**, and **collapsed silos** are all factors supporting a better team and client experience in our mobile banking application.

Practices, frameworks, and technologies

This part of our DevOps definition indicates that the adoption of DevOps requires certain capabilities to be enabled and consumed in the organization, with multidimensional sources. They, as we will also see later in the book, are at the heart of adopting DevOps, as they provide the necessary materialization and enablement means. In our example, a *shift left practice* can support the reliability of the mobile banking application by focusing on the quality and operations of the services early in the SDLC. An **observability framework** can support the time to market via the assurance of production environment readiness, reliability through proactive service monitoring, as well as compliance through the implementation of a logging as a service capability, parts of which will be security logging. Last but not least, technology can, for example, be deployed through *continuous integration and delivery pipelines*, which can speed up the path to production for our account's drag-and-drop aggregation functionality. **Chaos engineering tools**, embedded into **cloud services**, can support resiliency improvements of services, and a **logging as a service telemetry tool** can provide the compliance evidence our regulator requires on security logging. The DevOps practices, frameworks, and technologies that banking services can benefit from are countless.

The mobile banking example that we have used was intended to establish a relationship between DevOps as a concept and its practical value proposition in a banking context. From that specific example, it is quite intuitive to derive the broader DevOps proposition for the entire bank. Faster time to market increases the bank's ability to deliver quickly on new customer needs, which can increase revenue. Service reliability means satisfied customers and lower operational costs. Compliant services mean the license to operate is not in threat and focus shifts to innovation. Increased collaboration toward common goals means aligned implementation of strategic objectives. Investment in technology means the attraction of talent and platform modernization.

But speaking about the broader incumbent bank's perspective, is DevOps equally applicable in all business and technological domains within it? Is the mobile banking context similar or different to the contexts of digital customer engagement, customer resource management, and liquidity reporting, for example? Is the DevOps value proposition equally relevant across the bank? Should business applications and technological platforms be treated in the same way? The upcoming section will introduce us to a concept of vital importance when adopting DevOps in an enterprise and at scale. This concept will dominate the approach of this book in the chapters to come.

What is the importance of adopting DevOps at relevance?

Different definitions and interpretations drive different approaches, solutions, and depth in enterprise DevOps adoption. Despite, though, those differences in approaches, there are certain principles that universally and in any context guide DevOps adoption collaboration, flows, automation, visibility, feedback loops, and so on. On top of them, in this book, we introduce a principle, which we name the *guiding principle*, that not much has been written about in the available literature, and when I use it as an expression in real business contexts, people in most cases ask me *What do you mean? We've never heard of this concept.*

Defining relevance

This guiding principle is one of **relevance**, which in my opinion adds the necessary elements of *sophistication* and *intelligence* to enterprise DevOps adoption. According to the Oxford English Dictionary, the definition of relevance is *a close connection with the subject you are discussing or the situation you are in.* In our case, we will slightly paraphrase that definition and we call relevance *a close connection of the subject discussed with a situation we are in.* In our case, the **subject** we are discussing is obviously DevOps and the **situation** we are in is the context of an incumbent financial services institution. In other words, with relevance, we examine the level of connection required between the situation and the subject.

The relevance of the situation level

The first level of relevance is the **situation** level. What is relevant from a DevOps perspective for an incumbent financial services institution might not be for an aerospace company and vice versa. Let us put that into context. A bank can live with an outage on its core banking application (business-critical system), while an aerospace company cannot on its aviation system (safety-critical system).

This is simply because the potential consequences of the outages are of different severity. In a bank, clients might lose access to their deposits for 10 minutes, while on a plane, passengers might lose their lives. Equally, if Google's services (mission-critical) are down for 30 minutes, the impact is great and reaches every part of the world, with millions unable to perform basic daily operations. Or, think about a scenario of a hospital processing daily end-of-day medical records (security-critical) and facing latency on its data transmission channels. Rolling back the data to *day 1* is not acceptable as patients might need to take new medical prescriptions, while such a practice is a common data latency error handling mechanism in banking on end-of-day reporting activities.

The relevance of sub-situation levels

Normally, a situation consists of several **sub- and sub-sub-situations**. The deeper we go into the levels of a situation, the more subcontexts we discover. Let us examine sub-situations and sub-context layers, using an example from the context of our incumbent bank.

Part of the incumbent's business model is the domain of capital markets (sub-situation). Through that domain, the incumbent offers investment services and products to its clients. Capital markets have several sub-domains (sub-sub-situations) that all support what is called the trade life cycle (see it as a value stream of business activities within capital markets), as in all the phases a trade has to go through, from the time that the client orders its execution till the time that the asset that has been traded has entered the client's portfolio and the corresponding activity commission and investment amount has been settled. Two of the domains under capital markets are equity trading and equity settlement. Despite the fact that both domains belong to capital markets, and also the same value stream, they have some distinct differences. Equity trading is a real-time business where zero latency and service availability of 99.99% are crucial, while equity settlement is not a real-time business, where a little latency is tolerated and service availability of 97.5% is sufficient. In addition, equity trading is high up in the trading activity life cycle (also called front-office trade execution activity), while equity settlement is at the end of the trade life cycle (also called back-office post-trade execution activity). Issues originating in equity trading can generate more severe domino effects than issues occurring in equity settlement. Furthermore, equity trading is a profit-making mechanism for the bank, while equity settlement, as the name indicates, only formally settles the trades. Last but not least, I am certain that those who have worked for an investment bank can relate. Business users in equity trading, called equity traders, are far less tolerant of failures than business users in equity settlement, called settlement officers. Equity traders are also less accessible to people sitting in IT than equity officers.

Another factor that distinguishes the two cases of our example is what we will call in this book **current circumstances**. By circumstance, we mean *one's state*, which subsequently defines what is currently most important from a DevOps adoption perspective. Suppose our equity trading application currently is facing severe stability issues, while its time-to-market numbers exceed expectations. Naturally, improvements in reliability engineering are more important than release velocity in its current situation. On the other hand, equity settlement has been meeting its availability targets back to back for months, but it cannot be released as fast as expected by its product owner. Naturally, equity settlement will focus on release velocity and not reliability engineering.

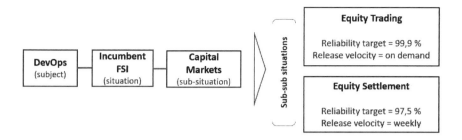

Figure 1.3 – Relevance example

Such combinations can be numerous and not only relevant in applications supporting business domains and processes, but also in internal banking infrastructure service providers, as we will discover later in the book.

The preceding example proves that there are several sub-situations within a situation within the incumbent. Those situations have distinct characteristics that make them vary in many aspects. This variation creates a DevOps constraint. *One DevOps solution must not be applied equally to any context, situation, or circumstance.* Referring to DevOps being applicable based on context, situation, and circumstance, the term *at relevance* will be used to indicate what is relevant to a situation and/or sub-situation and what is not. In other words, while adopting DevOps in an enterprise, only what is relevant in each situation and sub-situation should be adopted. *Who are the ones making this decision on what is relevant, what is not, and to whom?* We will discover this later in the book.

Why have a 360° perspective when adopting DevOps?

As we discovered through the book's DevOps definition, there are several elements that contribute to what DevOps is about for an organization. From practices to people and from technology to shared objectives, all these elements need to come into harmony. In this chapter, we introduce the element of **360° in DevOps**, explaining its value proposition and applicability.

In mathematics, the term 360° indicates a complete trip around the edge of a circle. Take as an example the rotation of the Earth around the Sun, or the rotation of a clock's hands in order to complete 12 hours, or to relate even more to our context, take a look at the symbol of DevOps, *the loop of infinity.* In all these examples, there is a starting point and after a 360° rotation around different phases, we end up again at the starting point. Ending up at the same point where we started does not indicate that we achieved nothing, and we are back at square one. It indicates that we managed to achieve a complete and flawless rotation across DevOps capabilities: complete in terms of we have engaged all necessary capabilities that comprise our DevOps model and flawless in terms of those capabilities were so harmoniously interlinked that it did not interrupt our 360° journey.

In this book, 360° indicates the need to cater to four qualities when adopting DevOps at the enterprise scale (*please note that the definitions of the following terms are taken from the Oxford English Dictionary*):

- **Completeness**: We define completeness as *the fact of including all the parts that are necessary; the fact of being whole*. In our DevOps context, these parts are all the tools, stakeholders, processes, policies, mechanisms, frameworks, metrics, funding, and so on that are necessary in order to perform successful enterprise adoption at scale. The fact of being the *whole* indicates on the one hand the necessity of involvement of the whole organization, or at least the required parts that directly or indirectly have a role to play in DevOps adoption. And on the other hand, the DevOps capabilities that are to be enabled and adopted need to complement each other, as in being the interconnected and interrelated pieces of the broader DevOps adoption puzzle.

- **Continuity**: We define continuity as *the fact of not stopping*. In DevOps, this means going on and on (infinitely) around DevOps phases and the capabilities that enable them, without interruption, but also ensuring that the DevOps adoption is not a *one-off* activity, and it organically becomes part of the organization's DNA, characterized by continuous evolution.

- **Reconcilability**: We define reconcilability as *the ability of a concept to coexist with another*. In our context, this defines the ability of DevOps to coexist in harmony, on the one hand within its sums, meaning harmony and balance across the concepts that are at its core – for instance, compliance controls being in harmony with release velocity. And on the other hand, it means to be in harmony and balance with other concepts that are also adopted in the organizational context, such as Agile and ITIL.

- **Interoperability**: We define interoperability as *the ability of entities in a network to connect with each other and carry out their functions*. In our context, we refer to the ability of the DevOps technological ecosystem and corresponding enabled capabilities being perceived as the backbone of DevOps adoption, to achieve a high level of interconnectedness through full stack engineering. In addition, we refer to the ability to collect data across the technological ecosystem that can be mapped to the end-to-end SDLC, across the DevOps continuity phases, and be utilized as a source for feedback loops, visibility, and continuous improvements.

The four qualities mentioned do have a relation of interdependence among them, and it is necessary to evolve them in parallel as one cannot deliver its full potential without the others. As an example, if in your DevOps adoption, you do not engage the *complete* set of your infrastructure team's stakeholders, you will never be able to achieve *continuity* in the developers' journey of consuming infrastructure capabilities, which will consequently result in technological solutions' *interoperability* gaps and, moreover, fragmentation in your technological DevOps enablers' *reconciliation*.

Your enterprise 360° DevOps adoption should be characterized by these four qualities, which should eventually be recalled readily by each participant in your organization and guide ideas, discussions, disagreements, decisions, and solutions. Your adherence to them can be checked by asking the following four simple questions:

- Does approach A fulfill the quality of completeness?

- Does solution B fit in the continuity cycle or does it break it?

- Is solution E reconcilable with concept D?

- Is solution C interoperable with the core technological ecosystem?

Summary

As we have seen in this chapter, incumbent banks have certain characteristics and are surrounded by several counterparts operating within the same ecosystem. Those counterparts create an external environment that, along with other factors, puts certain levels of pressure on an incumbent bank and influences its corporate strategy. Incumbent banks, on top of similarities in their external contexts, also have certain similarities in their internal contexts, especially in domains that are relevant to DevOps. The absence of a universal DevOps definition, as we discussed, created the need to establish our own definition for this book, which we have applied to the mobile banking example of outlining the DevOps value proposition for the incumbent. Closing the chapter, we discussed the importance of two elements, relevance and the 360° nature of enterprise DevOps adoptions, through examples. By now, you have built a good understanding of the book's main actor and its context, having defined DevOps and introduced two new core DevOps adoption elements.

In the next chapter, we will discuss the early-stage phases that the incumbent needs to follow in defining and establishing the fundamental direction of its DevOps enterprise adoption.

2

The DevOps Multi-Speed Context, Vision, Objectives, and Change Nature

This chapter starts by introducing the concept of *multi-speed* and discussing its relevance in the DevOps adoption of an incumbent bank. Continuing, we will examine the importance of understanding the *state-of-art* DevOps context of an organization and outline the top 10 DevOps context parameters that represent an average sample of incumbent banks, along with how they are generated and their corresponding implications. After that, we'll set the desired DevOps vision and objectives for this book's main actor, reconciling them with its corporate and technology strategies, both of which are influenced by its external and internal context. Then, we'll outline the possible DevOps approaches to types of change an incumbent can take. We'll do so by proposing the one that we will use throughout this book, along with citing the reasons for doing so. Finally, we will discuss the importance of building an understanding of the forces that are predicted to act in favor of or against your DevOps adoption.

In this chapter, we're going to cover the following main topics:

- Understanding multi-speed banking
- Understanding your state-of-art DevOps context
- Enterprise DevOps vision and objectives
- The potential types of the DevOps change
- A method of capturing the DevOps forces

Understanding multi-speed banking

The term **multi-speed** refers to the capability of a subject to operate at more than one level of speed simultaneously. Multi-speed occurs all around us in real life. We often refer to multi-speed organizations, economies, and sports. Our incumbent is also characterized by the condition of multi-speed. This condition is important to understand in terms of its originating factors and influence on the enterprise's DevOps adoption. It is crucial to take it into consideration when defining your vision, objectives, and implementation approach.

Why multiple speed levels arise out of different situations and ambitions

A multi-speed incumbent bank can be a natural result of situations (remember the equity trading and settlement example in the previous chapter) or an intentional construction driven by vision and ambitions. It is inevitable; being in different situations or being driven by different ambitions creates natural or constructed differing speed levels within the same organization. Factors such as how fast we are required to, how fast we want to, and how fast we can fulfill our objectives determine how we define different speed levels and their evolution.

How multi-speed is enabled by the nature of a business

Let's go back to our equity business example from the previous chapter. Equity trading has to be a milliseconds real-time business; otherwise, the bank risks losing market share in equities, with its stakeholders not having much tolerance for failure. On the other hand, equity settlement does not need to be in real time, with its stakeholders being more tolerant of failure and there being a lower likelihood of losing market share if things fail. These two situations, which are driven by different banking business natures, enable two different speed levels within the capital markets domain. Relating this to a DevOps adoption, perhaps advanced real-time infrastructure monitoring and auto-scaling capabilities being supported by a dedicated reliability engineer is more of a necessity for equity trading than for equity settlement.

How multi-speed is enabled intentionally or organically

How fast you need to be, when driven by banking business nature, is one parameter. But you also need to think about how fast you want to and can be. Certain areas within an incumbent bank have more ambitious product owners, more demanding clients, better technological foundations, better engineers, and a larger budget for innovation, even though situations and banking business nature might require those areas to run at the same speed as others. These areas are characterized by conditions that allow them to be the frontrunners of DevOps adoption and hence enable them to deliver software faster than others, for example. Those areas' situational positions may, for example, require them to release new functionality weekly, but their conditions (ambition and capacity) enable them to deliver *on demand*. They over-achieve their banking business nature objective, even if it's not necessary, thus exceeding expectations. In this case, it is due to their aspirations and the conditions that they operate in, rather than out of natural necessity, that different speed levels arise. This is a common phenomenon that can be observed in incumbent banks, and you will find those areas mostly in the capital markets, wealth management, and digital banking business domains.

What is the role of circumstances in enabling multi-speed?

Circumstances also play a key role in multi-speed environments. Let's look at another example. Two sub-sub-situations of very similar banking business natures, such as equity settlement and equity safekeeping, might be addressed with the same objective of improving their reliability due to high instability. The equity safekeeping system team, with support from their product owner, makes the brave decision to prioritize the hypercaring of the production environment and the resolution of all the preventive measures appointed after P1 incidents, rather than releasing new functionality. In contrast, the securities settlement team has been urgently requested to respond to a compliance readiness request by a large partner incumbent bank to which it provides global custody services. They have only 2 weeks to generate the necessary evidence. Inevitably, due to resource constraints, as well as urgency and product owners' priorities, they cannot focus on reliability. This example proves that circumstances also contribute to the creation of different speed levels. Not every sub-sub-situation will work on their DevOps-related work at the same speed – not because they do not need to, but due to the present condition and circumstances.

The role of individuals in multi-speed

Going back to the incumbent's banking business nature context, principally, not all product teams within it need to release on demand, not all teams need to re-engineer their platforms to be cloud native, and not all teams need to hire site reliability engineers. This is acceptable, so long as they meet the functional and nonfunctional objectives set for them. Do you recall the quality of relevance from the previous chapter? Something that's relevant to equity trading is not necessarily also relevant to equity settlement. But there are some human elements involved: personal ambition and perception. These elements generate yet another factor that defines the levels of speed, and they are quite crucial, as we will see later in this book. Certain people within an incumbent bank define the services' functional and nonfunctional objectives and can influence the conditions that a service finds itself in, along with how those conditions evolve.

Understanding multi-speed banking in a DevOps adoption context

Understanding every aspect of multi-speed within your organization is an impossible task that is not worth the investment. The present factors, sub-situations, conditions, and circumstances are countless and ever-evolving. Therefore, you will never have perfect information on the speed levels that characterize your context, and you must expect them to evolve alongside your DevOps adoption and also be influenced by it. However, understanding your high-level multi-speed context, as well as its drivers and how they shape it, while also having the means to keep track of its evolution, helps determine the vision, objectives, approach, and degree of success of your enterprise's DevOps adoption. Despite the difficulty of precisely capturing the multi-speed context, there are some key parameters, criteria, and factors that can support a *speed-level grouping* of our incumbent's business and application portfolio, with a relative and practical proximity to how the current context is shaped. This kind of grouping can be used as an enterprise DevOps adoption framework for meeting the qualities of relevance and 360°, as well as facilitating the intelligence mechanism behind the adoption's rollout. We will explore this **multi-speed banking** DevOps framework when we discuss **business domains and flows**, **ecosystems**, and **portfolio classification** later in this book.

Understanding your state-of-art DevOps context

In the previous chapter, we discussed the external and internal context of our incumbent bank. In this section, we will deep dive into the third contextual layer, which is the state-of-art DevOps context, by providing an average representative snapshot of how the DevOps context of an incumbent bank looks. We will focus on contextual elements and capabilities that we consider the most important.

> **Important Note**
>
> To avoid misunderstandings, it is important to clarify that with the term "*state-of-art*" in our book, we refer to it as *the level of development reached at a particular time, within a certain organization, as a result of the DevOps methodologies and practices employed.*

Why examining your state-of-art DevOps context is vital

"*Do not start changing something if you do not know it well enough*," an ex-CIO of mine used to say. DevOps is a concept that most incumbents have been adopting for many years. Some have done so in a harmonized and tactical way, while others have done so based on individuals' aspirations; some at scale and some in a more fragmented way. Some have already adopted advanced DevOps enablers, such as public cloud services, while others are still in the proof-of-concept phase of core CI/CD pipeline capabilities; some have already adopted shift-left practices on their CI/CD pipelines, while to others, *shift left* is still a confusing term. However, some common DevOps contextual snapshot characteristics can be found across incumbent financial service institutions.

Having a deep, comprehensive understanding of your state-of-art DevOps context is of vital importance for various reasons:

- It provides input on defining your DevOps vision and objectives. Why focus on implementing CI/CD pipelines across your portfolio if you have already done it?

- It guides your adoption approach. Are you to transform, evolve, or radicalize your DevOps context?

- It allows you to identify foreseeable DevOps adoption forces.

- It provides an understanding of how ready your organization is and identifies the foundation you need to build on top of.

Before we move on to the representative state-of-art DevOps context of an incumbent, let me tell you a story. This will provide insight into why it is possible to capture an average snapshot of some incumbents that can act as a representative picture for the whole industry.

Once upon a time in Berlin

One time, I was at a Fintech conference in Berlin, sitting around the lunch table with people representing incumbent banks across Europe, discussing our organizations' DevOps approaches. At some point, a CI/CD architect of a large incumbent bank said, "*Guys, it seems that we all have the same problems. It feels like we kind of work for the same bank.*" We all laughed at that comment. It was spot on! Another person at the table continued, "*It is true actually. We have all worked for the same banks, read the same books, attended the same conferences, are in the same industry, have the same regulators, and operate in the same markets. It is natural that we follow similar approaches and face the same challenges.*" Everyone around the table agreed with those views.

Why industry imitation is decisive in shaping DevOps adoptions

The reason for telling the Berlin story was to make an important point. Incumbent financial service institutions have, to some degree, depending on the case, been imitating business and technology concepts, DevOps included.

This is not a coincidence and is driven by five main conditions:

- Fear of falling behind the competition and the desire to follow in the steps of others, in an attempt to stay relevant in the industry.

- The belief that the actions of others who are perceived as more innovative and reputable are driven by a high degree of intelligence. See the example of ING and its Spotify model-inspired adoption. ING's success in improving its Agile **Way of Working** (**WoW**) served as an example for Danske Bank, ANZ, and Commerzbank, to mention a few. *Do we know what others have done?* is a typical question asked in strategy meetings.

- Industry synergy purposely creates incentives for imitation. Historically, incumbents have created alliances among themselves, which has influenced the adoption of certain concepts. The domains of public cloud, compliance, and cyber security are good examples.

- Partnerships with technological vendors and management consulting firms have played a significant role in creating incentives for imitation across the industry. We have all seen slides with titles such as *What the big players in the industry do* or *How we helped a UK bank to advance its DevOps practices.*

- People are rotated across incumbent banks, especially at regional or national market levels. It's obvious, right? When you jump to the competitor, literally in the building next door, you take DevOps intellectual assets and insights with you.

Imitating the actions of others is not necessarily a harmful tactic and does not strictly imply that you have identical visions, objectives, implementation approaches, and outcomes, nor that your DevOps context is state-of-art and will eventually look identical to others'. Factors such as your firm's internal context and dynamics are great influencers, and despite certain industry commonalities, conditions such as culture, budgets, leadership, people, and the ability to think and execute quickly differ from institution to institution. Therefore, state-of-art DevOps contexts have certain similarities as well as differences, which require tailor-made approaches due to the nature of DevOps having to balance case **agnosticness** and **sensitivity** – case agnosticness in the sense that certain DevOps approaches can be applicable equally across different contexts (e.g., CI/CD pipelines adoption) and case sensitivity in the sense that certain DevOps approaches should only be applicable to certain cases (e.g., public cloud security for cloud-native applications).

Are there several DevOps "states of the art" within an incumbent's context?

Yes. DevOps varies not only between incumbents but also within them. By conducting a simple internal environment scan, you could find an extreme variation between different DevOps state-of-art within the same firm. Some will be quite different, while others will be quite similar. While you will probably discover areas such as capital markets and digital banking at the forefront of the DevOps journey, you will also discover many areas in your back office or group operations and core infrastructure that are left behind, and maybe have not even set the fundamentals up. At this stage of your adoption, you should only focus on the broader organizational DevOps state of art rather than specific areas of the organization. While you probably do not have the means or the time to do so, you also need to try to get a representative picture of every single area. This will be an exercise that the stakeholders of its sub-situation will have to conduct later in your adoption, as we will see in the coming chapters.

The following figure provides a visual representation of the various contextual layers of an incumbent:

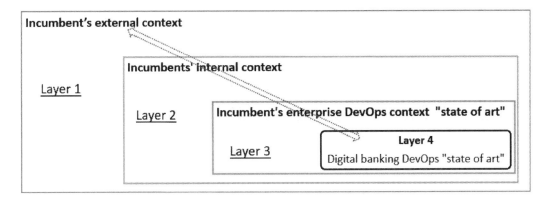

Figure 2.1 – The contextual layers of an incumbent that influence the DevOps adoption

The preceding diagram visualizes the layers of our incumbent that need to be captured while establishing the fundamentals for enterprise DevOps adoption. In the coming sections of this chapter, we will see how that multi-layer contextual understanding is essential in defining the DevOps vision and objectives, as well as deciding on the DevOps change type and approach.

What does a representative state of art DevOps adoption look like for an incumbent bank?

Most incumbents will find that there are several state of art DevOps elements that are repeated quite often across the industry, with some being dominant in representing the average context of most large incumbents.

Your state-of-art snapshot exercise should be targeted at key, core DevOps enablers, capabilities, and organizational aspects, rather than covering every single DevOps aspect and corner of your organization. It would not be humanly possible to cover everything. Also, it is important to mention that when understanding the context, you do not need to measure maturity. We will cover how and when in your adoption you should address maturity aspects later in this book.

Now, let's examine the most common elements of the state-of-art DevOps context of incumbents. You will notice that in attempting to provide a quantified representation, we use the symbol N, borrowed from mathematics, which indicates an infinite number. In our context, an infinite number means that we don't know the actual number and we can't project it with confidence or based on data, which is a common situation that incumbents find themselves in:

- **N unofficial DevOps operating and adoption models**: This indicates the absence of a commonly launched DevOps operating model for the organization, and it's the parameter that defines most of the rest of the contextual elements to some extent. This absence has probably led your organization, with its different organizational units and functions, to define its own DevOps operating model and consequently create a significant variation of DevOps approaches within the same firm. Typical observations of things that have led to this in teams is having their own daily DevOps organizing principles, no streamlined way of measured adoption, the freedom to build their own DevOps capabilities and not consume central ones, the ability to deal with compliance individually, and a lack of alignment with the firm's corporate and technological objectives. This situation results in extreme, unknown, and uncaptured variations in DevOps maturity levels within the same organization.

- **Nonstructured DevOps teams organizing principles and topologies**: The main phenomenon in this parameter is the absence of harmony and alignment in how your teams organize in a DevOps context. For example, in some business IT areas, it is developers who provide production support and have access to production data, while in other areas, there are dedicated operations teams providing production support, with developers' access to production being revoked. There can also be a third flavor of developers performing the operations work and an operations team performing only business support work. In general, a rather anarchical situation is observed in terms of roles and responsibilities, separation of duties, identity and access management, data protection, and more. Note that there is nothing wrong with operating in a hybrid and multi-speed setup, as long as there is alignment and consensus.

- **Organizational structured walls**: Another typical phenomenon, especially in organizations that have implemented a *hardcoded* separation of duties policies, is finding two different operating models characterized by conflict and fragmentation. The software development side of the organization uses advanced software development practices, while the operations and infrastructure side of the organization uses process-driven practices. Such situations violate the core principle of DevOps, shifting the organization toward Dev | Ops | Infra. The | symbol indicates fragmentation and discontinuity within your organization.

- **Lack of trust in central platforms**: Another typical observation is around common DevOps platforms. For various reasons, driven primarily by the lack of a common DevOps operating model and DevOps know-how, as well as conflicting incentives and strategic directions backed up by leadership appetite, in many DevOps adoptions, common platforms have not managed to establish themselves as trustworthy service providers. Common platforms, that is, teams offering central DevOps capabilities, such as CI/CD pipelines, containers, hybrid cloud, and tactical automation, have struggled to find their place in the organization. There are some specific reasons for this phenomenon:

- The business' IT areas are ahead because they have been building their own platforms well in advance of the central teams.

- Lack of collaboration in defining requirements, customer journeys, and experience.

- Central platform teams realizing they are running behind more advanced IT business areas and attempting to catch up leads to them jeopardizing quality, with platforms characterized by reliability issues.

- Traditionally, the core infrastructure teams of incumbents (some refer to those teams as "dark IT"), such as infrastructure provisioning and hosting, network, and storage, have been very slow in responding to DevOps advancements and consequently have held organizations back.

- Lack of domain know-how backed by outdated skills.

- Lack of self-service and automation, backed by infinite hours of lead times.

- Opinionated engineers and architects driving their agendas in business IT areas.

- **N technological capabilities: duplication, fragmentation, proliferation, and omission**: *Shadow IT at its best*, a colleague of mine used to call it. This is the phenomenon of numerous and duplicated solutions across DevOps technological enablers and corresponding frameworks. This includes multiple CI/CD pipelines, test automation and observability tools, cloud-native technologies, and security tools – the list can go on forever. A mild scenario that can be observed is that each business line has solutions but they are streamlined within the business line; this is similar to the asset and wealth management IT teams using their own solutions but standardized across their business lines. An even more problematic situation is that even within the same business line, business domains use their own solutions. For example, within the business line of digital banking and among "sister teams," separate DevOps solutions could be built for the mobile banking applications, compared to the online banking applications, without valid business justification and purely driven by the actions of certain individuals and leadership's dark motives, such as fulfilling personal ambitions. The proliferation of such solutions introduces several implications:

  - Increased operational cost, risk, and maintenance

  - Fragmentation across the technological ecosystem's capabilities

  - DevOps adoption compliance has a lack of visibility

  - Enterprise-level scalability challenges

  - Extreme innovation without tangible business value

  - The data related to the adoption of DevOps is stored in countless home-grown solutions and is not aggregated, resulting in a lack of visibility and transparency

As well as the proliferation of unnecessary capabilities (such as six different application monitoring tools), there are also capabilities that are totally absent. These gaps in capabilities, in certain cases and depending on their nature, can severely restrict incumbents from advancing in their DevOps journey. They are mainly discovered in the domains of public cloud, security, and data.

- **DevOps conceptual reconciliation gaps**: DevOps is not the only concept that's adopted in an incumbent bank. Business and enterprise agility models, enterprise portfolio planning mechanisms, **IT Infrastructure Library** (**ITIL**) processes, IT risk management and controls frameworks, software development methodologies, **Site Reliability Engineering** (**SRE**) models, and more are all part of the enterprise. However, they don't always coexist in harmony. A common phenomenon is gaps in the reconciliation of DevOps concepts and practices with other concepts adopted within an organization, which promotes a conflicting situation from an overall concept adoption and reconciliation perspective. We all know about the DevOps versus ITIL versus SRE dilemma. Reconciliation gaps not only arise from an overarching perspective across different concepts but also during their practical implementation. This includes problem management processes not being reconciled with backlog prioritization, development squads being distant from operations teams, and IT controls not being aligned with DevOps continuity. These reconciliation gaps are primarily created by gaps in understanding concepts and conflicts of interest with stakeholders. Different concepts, the use of different terminology, and a lack of horizontal understanding and ability to connect the dots create misunderstandings. At the same time, different stakeholders pursue their own agendas.

- **Misalignment of performance indicators and measurements**: The main phenomenon that's observed is the lack of a common, structured, and transparent mechanism for outlining the main performance indicators and measurements that are related to DevOps. Typically, you will find that four main DevOps metrics – **time to market**, **change failure rate**, **change frequency**, and **mean time to recover** – are used by incumbents due to their convenience and simplicity. These are considered *industry best practices*. But usually, there is a lack of front-to-back accountability with development and operations directors owning conflicting KPIs, a lack of value chain flow visibility across the SDLC, and a lack of credible data across platforms, with the primary source of data being IT service management tools, representing incidents, problems, changes, and availability management numbers. In addition, time to market is the dominant indicator, which is backed by a **Deploy, Deploy, Deploy** (**DDD**) culture.

- **The "trust me, I am an engineer" approach**: Many incumbents' state-of-art contexts are characterized by a lack of *trust but verify* mechanisms that are embedded in the technological ecosystem by design. The main observations are either that IT controls are not implemented in alignment with various areas within the organization and that there is a lack of strong implementation evidence mechanisms, or the IT controls are complemented by significant manual and bureaucratic overhead on their practical adoption and evidence-generation mechanisms, impacting productivity. Moreover, one-size-fits-all approaches are used to address compliance, without taking their relevance to each case into account.

- **Lack of necessary DevOps experience and expertise**: We are all aware that there is *talent scarcity* in the market for any sort of DevOps engineering profile, from CI/CD engineers to cloud engineers, to security engineers to SREs. As we saw in the previous chapter, the external talent competition for new entrants is aggressive. Also, people within an incumbent's organization tend to move toward more advanced areas, widening the internal DevOps experience and expertise gap. Overall, incumbent banks are observed to not possess the necessary skills, in terms of both quality and quantity, to achieve their DevOps objectives.

- **DevOps is not prioritized**: For many areas of an incumbent, DevOps is not a priority. If a team manages to deliver with acceptable release velocity and be close to its required service reliability numbers, that is just good enough. This area is considered *DevOps done*; no budget becomes available for DevOps activities and the product owner will not prioritize DevOps advancements in the product's backlog.

Understand that your state-of-art DevOps context will never be completely perfect, either because you lack credible data, you have as many approaches to adopting DevOps as you have feature teams, or you do not have the time. An approximate qualitative picture that best characterizes the average practices of the teams in your organization will be sufficient. Where possible, it is advisable to collect indicative quantitative data to be able to best define your enterprise DevOps objectives.

> **Advice**
>
> During this exercise, be gentle in your approach to ensure that you do not generate resistance from people, as they could misunderstand your intentions and feel that they are being judged.

Enterprise DevOps vision and objectives

Now that we've outlined some fundamental aspects that define the foundation of your enterprise's DevOps adoption, such as multi-layer contexts, as well as outlined the qualities and definition of DevOps, the next step is to define what you want to get out of DevOps. In this section, we will define the enterprise DevOps vision of an incumbent bank, as well as the corresponding objectives that can support its materialization.

Recapping the forces and qualities that shape the DevOps vision

The following is a brief recap of the forces that influence how the DevOps vision is shaped:

- **Contextual forces**:

  - **External environment**: Macro factors from the external context

  - **Internal environment**: Micro factors from the internal context

- **DevOps state of art**: The current level of DevOps adoption
  - **Multi-speed**: The condition of running at different speed levels
- **Strategic forces**:
  - **Corporate strategy**: The incumbent's business strategy, which is set by the board of directors
  - **Technology strategy**: The strategy that is set by the technological units to materialize the corporate strategy
- **DevOps qualities**:
  - **At relevance**: The DevOps adoption should consider some specific parameters of different situations when defining and implementing objectives
  - **360°**: The DevOps adoption should be characterized by completeness, continuity, interoperability, and reconcilability
- **DevOps definition**: Your tailor-made DevOps definition, which indicates your vision

Figure 2.2 – Diagram of the main forces and qualities that influence the DevOps vision

The next section is dedicated to the strategic forces that we have discussed so far.

Examining the incumbent's corporate and technology strategies

In this section, we will discuss corporate strategy and technology strategy and outline their strong interrelation, along with the key targets and priorities that underpin them.

Corporate strategy

With the term **corporate strategy**, we are referring to the strategy that sets the firm's overall direction for the future in terms of target destination and objectives. The corporate strategy and the decisions that shape it define the direction that the business should take and are strongly influenced by the external context, while defining how the internal context is shaped. In the following list, we will focus on the most fundamental corporate strategy objectives for incumbents that have a close relation to DevOps. You should be able to intuitively relate these objectives to the incumbent's external and internal context, which we discussed in the previous chapter. Corporate objectives such as increasing return on equity, improving the sustainability footprint, and increasing capital ratios are outside the scope of this book, for obvious reasons:

- **Accelerate digitalization at scale**: The objective of improving the delivery of digital services and the products portfolio to the market

- **Best-in-class customer experience**: The objective of improving customers' digital journeys when dealing with the incumbent's services and products

- **Operational and capital efficiency**: The objective of becoming more effective in delivering products and services while managing costs

- **Preferred partner for customers**: The objective of attracting new customers while also maintaining the current customer base

- **Compliant and secure**: The objective of meeting compliance demands and becoming proactive in addressing security threats

- **Data-driven**: The objective of utilizing data to support business decisions

- **Simplicity and standardization**: The objective of standardizing and streamlining operating models and processes

- **People first**: The objective of investing in the development of employees

> Tip
>
> Are you interested in the corporate strategies of different incumbent banks and want to examine the preceding objectives in terms of their financial performance, societal contribution, and business lines? I propose that you read the latest annual reports of some incumbents.

An important point to make that can influence DevOps adoption is that the different markets that the incumbent operates in create a dynamic *multi-speed corporate strategy* that balances the *play to win* and *play not to lose* tactics. The following table summarizes some of the differences between the two tactics that can impact DevOps adoption for certain domains:

Play to Win (Home Markets)	Play Not to Lose (Challenger and Growth Markets)
First in the market advantage	Second mover advantage
Desire to shape the market	Desire to follow the market
Radical product innovation	Incremental product innovation
Cutting-edge greenfield products	Build on top of legacy products
Acquire new entrants	Collaborate with new entrants
Market share increase	Market share maintenance

Table 2.1 – Play to win versus play not to lose strategy differences

Technology strategy

With the term **technology strategy**, we refer to the strategy being shaped by the various technological units within the firm in responding to the objectives set by the corporate strategy. Again, we are taking a representative sample of incumbents with the difference that this time, we do not need to conduct a **DevOps-relevant** selection, as the totality of the technology strategy objectives has direct or indirect relevance to DevOps.

The following is a complete overview of the representative technology strategy objectives of an incumbent:

- **Run the bank**: Focuses on the ability of the technology to ensure adequate organizational and operational means of supporting production IT services

- **Act commercially**: Relates to optimizing the expenses of building, delivering, and running IT solutions on both the IT application and infrastructure layers

- **Modernize and deal with legacy**: Refers to eliminating or modernizing various legacy components in the organization, such as platforms or processes

- **Improve WoW and efficiency**: Advancements in the WoW models across technology areas and also with the business line partners, as well as eliminating waste and lead time to improve operational efficiency

- **Build or acquire skills**: Acquiring or building the necessary technological skills

- **Compliant and secure by design**: Effectively addressing compliance demands and ensuring security threats are dealt with proactively

- **Plan ahead in alignment**: Ensuring portfolio planning mechanisms are implemented to achieve alignment and synchronization across various teams

- **Simplify and standardize**: Removing complexity and duplications, re-engineering certain processes and policies, and shifting toward streamlining

- **Deliver on commitments**: Meeting the defined targets of **service-level agreements (SLAs)**, security risk profiling, time to market, and recoverability targets

There are several parallels between the corporate and technology strategies, and this is expected, or rather, mandatory. The following figure provides a clear idea of how the corporate and technology strategy objectives are reconciled. Annual and quarterly re-alignment and benefit realization activities should be carried out at the enterprise level, as we will discuss in *Chapter 10, Tactical and Organic Enterprise Portfolio Planning and Adoption*:

Corporate/Technology Strategic Objectives Reconciliation	Run the bank	Act commercially	Modernize and deal with legacy	Improve WoW and efficiency	Build or aquire skills	Compliant and secure by design	Plan ahead in alignment	Simplify and standardize	Deliver on commitments
Accelerate digitalization	R		R	R	R			R	
Best-in-class customer experience	R		R	R		R	R	R	
Operational and capital efficiency	R	R	R	R				R	R
Preferred partner for customers	R					R			R
Compliant and secure	R				R			R	R
Data driven	R	R		R			R	R	
Simplicity and standardization	R	R	R	R				R	R
People first					R				

Figure 2.3 – Corporate and technology strategy objectives reconciliation ("R" stands for reconciliation point)

Shaping the DevOps vision

Having discussed all the factors that contribute to shaping the DevOps vision, we are now ready to start defining it by combining these elements. In this book, we are taking the approach of defining DevOps objectives first, the totality of which will define the broader DevOps vision, which is also expressed by the DevOps definition. We will provide a one-to-many relationship, with many objectives, and define one vision. Such an approach helps you to think about how the vision can be shaped more tangibly as part of a collection of objectives, as well as understanding what the motives behind them are.

> **Advice**
>
> Start by defining the objectives and then summarize the vision in a single line. If you do this the other way around, you will find you are restricted in that the possible objectives from a linguistics and practical perspective (verbally, as in not able to find descriptive words, or conceptually, as in not able to consolidate practical aspects of concepts) do not seem to fit in the vision's single-liner.

Needless to say, the DevOps vision should be tailor made based on the nature of the factors that impact your organization. The people in your organization should find it relevant and be able to find a place for themselves in it, rather than perceiving it as nothing more than high-level DevOps buzzwords with no real meaning.

Defining the DevOps enterprise OKRs

A widely used and very successful practice to follow is **Objectives and Key Results (OKRs)**. Using this approach, you can define an objective and some key results as outcomes. In our case, we will go a little bit further by also appointing the motivating factors for each OKR, which will help with acceptance and realizing the benefits. While doing so, be extra conscious of the following points:

- Create a **sense of urgency** by highlighting not only the value proposition but also the potential consequences.

- Be **careful about how you phrase** the motivating factors. Do not call out issues within specific problem areas and teams; this will create a feeling of blame and discomfort.

- For **transparency and traceability** purposes, link each OKR to the technology and corporate strategies.

Now, let's discover the fundamental DevOps objectives that incumbent banks define.

OKR 1 – improve time to market

Here, we focus on speeding up the path to production for the incumbent's application portfolio:

Objective	Key Results	Strategy Link	Motivating Factors
Improve time to market across the portfolio, especially for core digital services. This includes the following: 1) Mobile banking 2) Online banking 3) Open banking 4) Payments 5) Electronic trading	KR 1: Achieve "on-demand" releases to production for core digital services KR 2: Measure release velocity, reliability, and compliance balance KR 3: 70% of the modern application portfolio is using the standard CI/CD pipeline KR 4: Change management process automation	Accelerate digitalization at scale and deliver on commitments	1. Proliferation of new entrants, which introduces new products faster 2. Loss of customers due to inability to respond fast to demand

Table 2.2 – Sample of the improve time to market enterprise OKR

OKR 2 – improve compliance as code

Here, we must ensure the incumbent's portfolio fulfills its compliance requirements using DevOps practices:

Objective	Key Results	Strategy Link	Motivating Factors
Strive toward compliance as code across our portfolio	KR 1: A minimum viable adherence IT control mechanism is enabled KR 2: Improvements in the policy and evidence engineering mechanisms KR 3: All audit remarks for business-critical applications are closed	Continuous compliance by design	1. Improve our efficiency in addressing the ECB and local FSA's audit remarks on IT risk management, to avoid reputational and capital loss 2. Minimize the compliance impact on time to market and productivity

Table 2.3 – Sample of the improve compliance as code enterprise OKR

OKR 3 – improve reliability through engineering practices

Here, the aim is to improve the reliability of services through reliability engineering practices:

Objective	Key Results	Strategy Link	Motivating Factors
Embed reliability engineering practices in the SDLC	KR 1: The reliability targets across the application portfolio are revised KR 2: Reliability engineering practices are implemented in the top 20 business-critical services KR 3: Reliability engineering practices are implemented in the common DevOps platforms	Create a best-in-class customer experience, run the bank, and deliver on commitments	1. FCA audit remarks on service fragility and domino effects 2. The top 20 business-critical services face instability 3. Fragility in our common DevOps platforms, which disturbs software delivery

Table 2.4 – Sample of the improve reliability through engineering practices OKR

OKR 4 – enable a tactical platform modernization mechanism

Here, we must enable a mechanism for application classification based on its technological nature, as well as enable mechanisms for portfolio modernization and interoperability:

Objective	Key Results	Strategy Link	Motivating Factors
Achieve platform modernization on business applications and their core infrastructure	KR 1: All newly built applications fulfill cloud-native, microservices, APIs, and event-driven architecture principles through reference architectures KR 2: Utilize PaaS in the public cloud and increase IaC utilization in the private cloud KR 3: A portfolio classification and modernization mechanism is defined KR 4: Interoperability issues in the DevOps tech ecosystem are resolved	Accelerate digitalization at scale and deal with the legacy	1. Legacy business applications pose an operational risk 2. Public cloud will require platform re-engineering 3. Lack of clarity on application classification and evolution 4. Interoperability gaps across the technological ecosystem

Table 2.5 – Sample of the tactical platform modernization enterprise OKR

OKR 5 – enable a tactical hiring and incubation mechanism

The aim is to strengthen the incumbent's DevOps engineering capabilities through hiring and incubation:

Objective	Key Results	Strategy Link	Motivating Factors
Focus on people skills and incubation	KR 1: The hiring process is diversified and new near-shore locations are created KR 2: Engineers and developers are trained on our strategic technologies and platforms, enabling Π-shaped profiles KR 3: Internal job mobility is increased	Focus on people by building or acquiring skills	Stay relevant, support the DevOps transformation with the required skills, and retain and attract talent Reduce dependency on consultants

Table 2.6 – Sample of the tactical hiring and incubation enterprise OKR

Π-shaped profiles indicate people who understand the big DevOps picture (the horizontal line on the Greek letter Π), such as the DevOps vision, and have at least two DevOps engineering specializations (the two vertical lines of the letter Π), such as CI/CD pipelines and observability. We will get back to this definition and look at it in more detail in *Chapter 12, People Hiring, Incubation, and Mobility*.

OKR 6 – improve DevOps journeys and experience

Here, the aim is to improve the productivity and experience of the people that are part of the DevOps adoption:

Objective	Key Results	Strategy Link	Motivating Factors
Improve DevOps journeys and experience	KR 1: The DevOps infrastructure and tools service fulfillment and onboarding lead times have been reduced KR 2: The IaC capabilities of the private cloud have been enriched KR 3: Value streams across DevOps platforms are defined KR 4: The public cloud onboarding process is reduced to 2 weeks	Improve operational efficiency and minimize cost	1. Simplify the way we deal with each other at three levels: 1) client to bank, 2) internal business units to IT, and 3) IT to IT 2. Increase DevOps productivity through technological advancements 3. Gain value streams flow visibility across the DevOps journeys, continuity, and experience

Table 2.7 – Sample of the improve DevOps journeys and experience enterprise OKR

OKR 7 – improve the DevOps WoW

Here, the aim is to improve the WoW from the perspective of multidimensional DevOps and other adopted concepts:

Objective	Key Results	Strategy Link	Motivating Factors
New WoW	KR 1: The organizational silos across the SDLC's stakeholders collapse KR 2: Operations shift left on the SDLC KR 3: The business agility, SRE, ITIL, and DevOps models are reconciled KR 4: The daily DevOps organizing principles and topologies are aligned KR 5: The portfolio planning mechanism is advanced KR 6: The SDLC flows are harmonized and advanced	Simplification, collaboration, and operational efficiencies	1. Shift toward common WoW to ensure value streams have end-to-end integration and visibility 2. Eliminate existing continuity gaps among the implemented concepts 3. Modernize our outdated SDLC to stay relevant 4. Ensure alignment on daily operations to stay compliant

Table 2.8 – Sample of the improve the DevOps WoW enterprise OKR

OKR 8 – improve standardization and simplification

Here, the aim is to streamline and standardize 360° across DevOps enabling and adoption capabilities:

Objective	Key Results	Strategy Link	Motivating Factors
Standardize and simplify from a DevOps 360° perspective	KR 1: Common DevOps platforms are standardized through a capability menu and technology radar and shadow IT is eliminated KR 2: The SDLC is simplified for cloud-native apps KR 3: Usage of standard performance mechanism to measure the realization benefits KR 4: DevOps tools, platforms, and processes are examined based on their future purpose KR 5: The service registry mechanism is standardized KR 6: The DevOps capabilities consumption in an "as a service" model is simplified	Standardization, simplification, cost optimization, and operational efficiencies	1. Reduce waste and duplications and improve the economies of scale to achieve operational efficiency 2. Reduce shadow IT and technical debt to reduce operational risk 3. Speed up DevOps adoption by utilizing solution templates and recipes

Table 2.9 – Sample of the improve standardization and simplification enterprise OKR

> **Advice**
>
> Avoid using the words *culture* and *cost* in both the corporate and technology strategic objectives, as well as the DevOps vision and objectives. They simply give the wrong message regarding your motives and can cause unnecessary resistance.

In summary, the following diagram outlines the DevOps enterprise adoption OKRs that define what you want to get out of your DevOps adoption at an enterprise level. With these OKRs and by consulting your DevOps definition, you will find your DevOps vision to be appropriately expressed by the following statement:

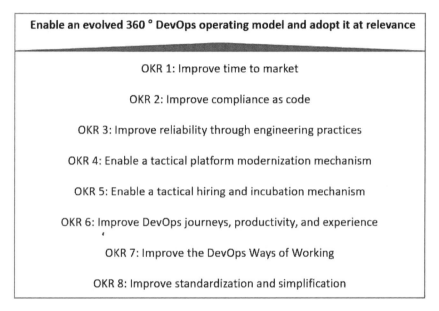

Enable an evolved 360 ° DevOps operating model and adopt it at relevance

OKR 1: Improve time to market

OKR 2: Improve compliance as code

OKR 3: Improve reliability through engineering practices

OKR 4: Enable a tactical platform modernization mechanism

OKR 5: Enable a tactical hiring and incubation mechanism

OKR 6: Improve DevOps journeys, productivity, and experience

OKR 7: Improve the DevOps Ways of Working

OKR 8: Improve standardization and simplification

Figure 2.4 – DevOps enterprise adoption OKRs

We will learn how those enterprise OKRs will eventually become more tangible for the business IT areas and your infrastructure teams later in this book.

What circumstances influence your vision and objectives?

How your enterprise DevOps objectives are formed and their priority, as well as the overall vision, will depend on your current but also short-term foreseeable circumstances. The following factors are key influencers and need to be considered and assessed based on their pressure barometer (also known as **priority level**) in your organization:

- Market competitiveness
- Macroeconomic environment

- Regulatory pressure

- Falling behind digital innovation

- Difficulty to attract talent

- Production services instability

- Cost pressure

- Are you already in the middle of another transformation?

Deciding on the nature and extent of your DevOps adoption

A DevOps enterprise adoption, despite its objectives, vision, or magnitude, is a change management process. Its connection to the corporate and technology strategies constitutes strategic change. You are modifying or replacing certain elements of the way that DevOps has previously been deployed in an organization. Your current state-of-art DevOps context will change during the adoption and will not look the same by the end. In this section, we will discuss a decisive decision that you need to make.

Why you need to decide on the nature and extent of change

A tool that I always find easy and intuitive to use when planning strategic changes is *Types of Change Source* by Balogun and Hope Hailey (2004). Through that, an organization can define its change type approach by looking at it from two dimensions. The first one is the *nature* of change, while the second one is the expected *result*. The nature of the change defines the sequence and speed of it and is divided into *incremental*, referring to gradual changes executed in sequence, and *big bang*, referring to one big change executed in one go. The result of the change defines the magnitude of its scope and is separated into *realignment*, which refers to small adjustments, and *transformation*, which refers to significant adjustments.

The possible combinations of the nature of change and the resulting dimensions define four possible strategic change types, as shown in the following diagram:

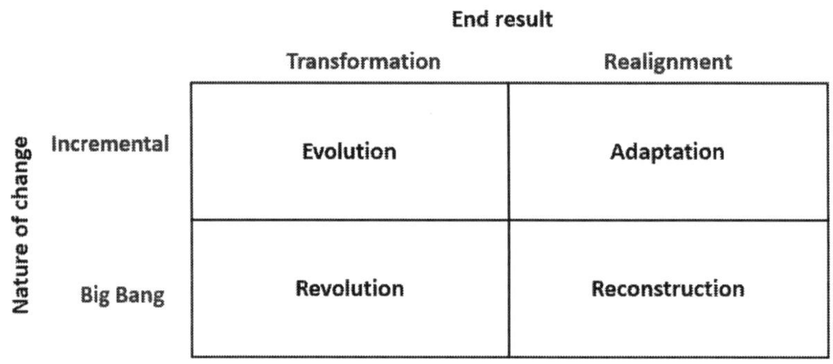

Figure 2.5 – Types of Change Source by Balogun and Hope Hailey (2004)

Let's look at these in more detail:

- **Adaptation**: Primarily used to realign the way DevOps is adopted in the organization and is implemented through incremental steps. Can be executed with the existing culture and applied incrementally across the DevOps capabilities.

- **Reconstruction**: A more foundational approach to realigning the way DevOps is adopted in the organization, with several simultaneous initiatives. Fundamentally, the culture does not change, and the change execution is rapid.

- **Revolution**: A radical approach to changing the way DevOps is adopted with simultaneous radical changes. Fundamentally changes the organization and culture through enforcement.

- **Evolution**: A transformational change approach to the way DevOps is adopted through several simultaneous and interlinked initiatives that are delivered incrementally. Organizational capabilities and cultural advancements are achieved over time.

Which is the most pragmatic approach for an incumbent bank?

Choosing the most suitable and fit-for-purpose change strategy for your DevOps enterprise adoption requires not only strategic planning, design, and execution but also a level of *political correctness* and *fairness* toward your organization. Maybe you have not yet reached the desired state of DevOps in your organization, but you have taken concrete steps and enabled fundamental organizational DevOps capabilities, and some of your teams have gone quite far already. From a change marketing perspective, to ensure that you achieve a status of buy-in and limit resistance to change, demonstrating appreciation with words and actions for what has been already achieved in your DevOps adoption is crucial. Your organization's people will not like hearing that you plan to reconstruct your DevOps adoption, indicating that it is currently broken. You will also need to provide convincing answers to the potential questions raised by the people in your organization. This includes "*We are already doing DevOps, what is this about?*," "*We already have a common CI/CD pipeline*," and "*We already involve the operations team in backlog prioritization.*" In addition, there is probably no need to be radical and boil the DevOps ocean either. The materialization of your objectives can be gradually realized. In this book, by following a pragmatic approach and being inspired by how a representative sample of incumbent banks in a real-life business approaches their DevOps enterprise adoptions, we will propose the evolutionary change type as the most sustainable and pragmatic strategy.

There are some qualities, fundamental aspects, and conditions of an organization that will also support a jump-start of an evolutionary enterprise DevOps approach, as well as increasing the probability of materializing the expected outcomes. You should do a reality check on whether your organization meets any of these:

- Empowerment to make collective decisions in a hybrid manner. Hybrid in this context indicates decision-making taking place both from top to bottom (leadership to employees) and from the bottom up (employees to leadership), with the two directions meeting in the middle.

- A clear strategic vision, aligned between business and technology, must be established.

- Ability to deliver incrementally and experiment with psychological safety conditions.

- Identify interim changes, gradually leading to the end target.

- Sustained top management commitment and emotional intelligence.

- The fundamental DevOps capabilities are already adopted.

- No irrational sense of urgency to deliver in a short and fixed timeframe.

You are free to choose any other change type that possibly better fits your vision, objectives, organizational context, cultural aspects, sense of urgency, and current state-of-art DevOps context. It is also advisable to stick to one change type and not try to combine more than one; this will probably generate feelings of discrimination among your teams, plus it will require that you have variation in your collective strategic objectives, which will create confusion and misalignments.

This section indicates two milestones for the next phase of this book. In the coming chapters and sections, we will no longer refer to the term enterprise DevOps adoption; instead, we will refer to **DevOps enterprise evolution** – or as I enjoy calling it, as inspired by the field of international relations, **DevOps industrialization and globalization**. Here, we are talking about industrialization in the sense of evolutionary advancements in organizational DevOps capabilities and globalization in terms of moving away from a DevOps culture characterized by fragmentation and protectionism and shifting toward interdependency and interconnectedness. This alternative naming indicates the beginning of embedding international relations terms in our DevOps enterprise evolution; I am confident you will find this very interesting.

> **Bonus Information**
>
> International relations is a scientific field of study on how states interact with each other as well as with international organizations in a global context. You will be surprised at how international relations concepts such as law, diplomacy, foreign policy, globalization, and sanctions can apply to the context of an incumbent bank and its DevOps evolution.

Why is it important to define and weigh the forces of your evolution?

Your evolution will most definitely not go as planned, as with everything in life. There will be plenty of challenges in your path, with some creating opportunities, while others being pure obstacles that you will have to overcome. Some of these challenges are very difficult to predict, while others are easier. Certain forces are derived from your internal and external context that will be a source of challenges and opportunities. Identifying them in the early stages of your evolution and taking precautions will be game-changing.

The quality and outcome of this exercise will be impacted by four main factors:

- **Prior change know-how**: The level of know-how from prior change activities that your organization has undergone in its history.

- **DevOps evolution know-how**: Having done a DevOps enterprise evolution before, you can predict the positive and negative operational and organizational forces.

- **Deep awareness of the organizational context**: Context plays a key role in the precision of the prediction. Knowing the organization and its dynamics, as well as having awareness of other change initiatives running in parallel, is an asset.

- **Deep awareness of the DevOps concept**: *Knowing your DevOps* is important. The deeper your DevOps enterprise knowledge, experience, and expertise, the better you can predict what lies ahead in the evolution and be able to act proactively based on know-how.

A method that is commonly used in the industry is *Force Field Analysis*, developed by Lewin (1951). This method provides an efficient tool for capturing the macro and micro forces that influence the change, along with how they evolve. The process is rather simple and intuitive: you need to list all the forces that are perceived to contribute positively to your DevOps evolution, as well as the ones perceived to contribute negatively. Each force is weighed by pressure points from 1 to 3, with 1 being low pressure and 3 being high pressure. The sum of all the negative and positive forces shows you whether the pendulum leans toward supporting your DevOps evolution or not. Using such a method serves as not only a change design tool but also a proactive risk management and decision-making mechanism.

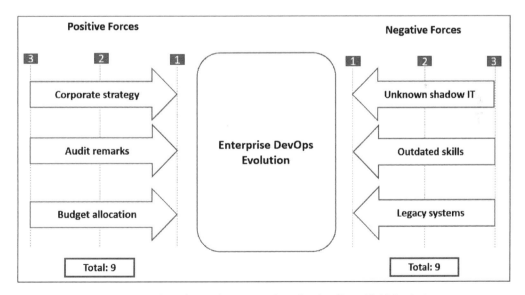

Figure 2.6 – Sample DevOps enterprise adoption Force Field Analysis

When using such tools, you should also be aware of certain limitations that arise that require extra consciousness and effort. The analysis itself, if not complemented by a proactive risk management mechanism, will eventually become a paper exercise. In addition, on achieving the best possible precision, significant environmental scanning is required with attention to organizations' context and DevOps concept details. Moreover, some of the inputs might be subjective based on people's experiences, perceptions, and biases, resulting in a *manipulated* picture. Furthermore, you need to be conscious that certain forces can be double-edged swords – that is, they can have a positive and negative influence at the same time, so they even themselves out. Compliance is one of them as it can be a DevOps enabler but also a distractor. Such an exercise does not need to be perfect, but approximate. However, it is important to have a way to check the evolution's temperature and adapt it accordingly, especially when *DevOps evolution fatigue* kicks in.

Summary

In this chapter, we have seen that multi-speed levels that appear in an incumbent's context can strongly influence a DevOps enterprise's evolution. We also looked at the third contextual layer, the one of DevOps state-of-art, and analyzed the most repeatable and representative contextual elements that we typically find when looking at a representative sample of incumbent banks. The core DevOps-related elements of an incumbent's corporate strategy were defined, followed by the corresponding ones of its technology strategy. As we discovered, the corporate and technology strategic objectives have several similarities, and it is very intuitive to link them to a DevOps enterprise evolution. Then, we explained the importance of defining your DevOps enterprise objectives before your vision and outlined the most dominant and representative objectives of incumbents, the sum of which we used to define our DevOps vision in a single line. Continuing, we stressed the importance of defining your DevOps change type and provided arguments about why your approach should be evolutionary. At that stage, we reached an important milestone in this book and announced that for the remainder of this book, we will be referring to enterprise DevOps adoption as DevOps enterprise evolution. Finally, we provided a sample tool for identifying and measuring the forces toward and against such change.

Now that we've looked at the fundamental and foundational aspects of a DevOps enterprise evolution, in the next chapter, we will focus on further conceptualizing this vision by using an enterprise model. To do so, we will define the core governance elements that will steer and orchestrate this change.

Part 2: The 360° DevOps Operating Model, Governance, and Orchestration Mechanisms

This part introduces the overall DevOps 360° operating model. Following that, it proposes a governance mechanism that could be established in order to facilitate the DevOps evolution. The elements of organizing principles and topologies, reconciliation with enterprise agility, the role of the DevOps center of excellence, and the importance of the enterprise architecture function are discussed.

This part of the book comprises the following chapters:

- *Chapter 3, The DevOps 360° Operating Model Pillars and Governance Model*
- *Chapter 4, Enterprise Architecture and the DevOps Center of Excellence*
- *Chapter 5, Business Enterprise Agility and DevOps Ways of Working Reconciliation*

3

The DevOps 360° Operating Model Pillars and Governance Model

In this chapter, we'll introduce the core pillars that comprise the skeleton of the DevOps 360° operating model and provide an overview of its domains. Then, we will discuss the two main governing bodies that you should establish; that is, a DevOps 360° vision authority group and a 360° design and advocacy group, along with their responsibilities. After that, we will stress the importance of engaging a broad DevOps ecosystem of stakeholders across your organization and provide an overview of the ones we believe are the most important, along with their corresponding DevOps value propositions. Then, we will define the workstreams that should be enabled to support the materialization of DevOps enterprise OKRs. We will use compliance as code as an example to define the workstreams' responsibilities. After that, we will discuss the value of understanding the governing dynamics of your organization and how they can influence its evolution, as well as the need to ensure that you are speaking the same language to all DevOps stakeholders. Finally, we will deep dive into the role that organizational structures and hierarchies have in DevOps evolutions. We will examine organizational structures and hierarchies through the lenses of three real use case examples from different incumbents.

In this chapter, we're going to cover the following main topics:

- The core pillars of the DevOps 360° operating model
- The vital role of the DevOps vision authority
- The need for a DevOps design and advocacy group
- Why you should engage your DevOps enterprise evolution ecosystem
- The evolutions workstreams and scope

- Why you need to understand your governing dynamics

- A simple tool so you speak the same DevOps language

- Three real use cases where organizational structures influenced DevOps evolutions

Defining the DevOps 360° operating model core pillars

In the previous chapter, we discussed the link between DevOps evolution and the strategic objectives of an incumbent, and we defined the core DevOps enterprise OKRs and visions. We will start this chapter by outlining the skeleton of the DevOps 360° operating model and its core pillars. In this and the upcoming chapters of this book, we will explore the model's journey toward completeness.

In the following diagram, you can see the skeleton of the DevOps 360° operating model that will unfold throughout this book. It fulfills the 360° qualities of **completeness**, **continuity**, **interoperability**, and **reconciliation** while enabling **adoption at relevance** in a **multi-speed incumbent bank**:

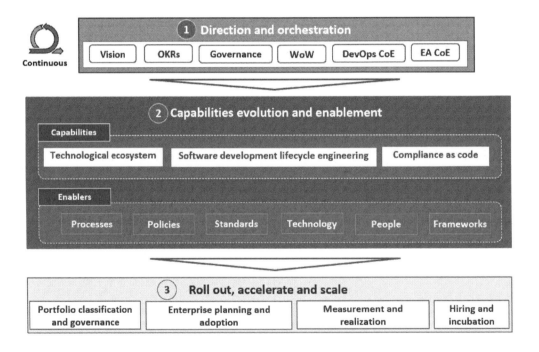

Figure 3.1 – The DevOps evolution 360° operating model skeleton

We can define each of the three pillars around a unique value proposition:

- **Direction and orchestration**: This defines all the mechanisms that will direct, steer, and coordinate the evolution throughout its life cycle, as well as the new WoWs.

- **Evolution and enablement**: This focuses on DevOps capabilities evolution and enablement, ensuring that the four 360° qualities are materialized by engaging the totality of DevOps enablement stakeholders.

- **Roll out, accelerate and scale**: This enables the necessary mechanisms for launching and adopting the evolved DevOps capabilities and achieving a tactical and organic adoption. It is also inevitably characterized by alignment, acceleration, and scale in a multi-speed context.

Tip

In the initial phase of the evolution, keep the 360° operating model as brief and compact as possible so that you don't overwhelm your organization with too many details about the pillars. Presenting the full magnitude of the evolution in this phase is likely to generate resistance.

The evolution's core governance

In this section, we will discuss the core governance bodies and mechanisms that we suggest you establish when governing your evolution. Note that we will intentionally not refer to communication tools, progress and risk reporting, and change management methodologies, as we consider these to be obvious basic hygiene mechanisms that should already be established.

Establishing a DevOps 360° vision authority group

Direction setting, orientation, steering, and sponsorship will be required and strong involvement from senior management will need to be secured. Senior management in our context refers to senior directors from various units, including business, technology, and group functions, that are hierarchically positioned one or two levels below the group COO, depending on your organizational structure. We suggest that those stakeholders become your **DevOps 360° vision authority group** and take on the following responsibilities:

- Reconciling the objectives of the corporate and technology strategies with the DevOps enterprise evolution vision and objectives

- Ownership of the funding, prioritization, and risk management mechanisms

- Ultimate strategic decision-makers who also serve as escalation points

- Delegation to middle management, connecting decision authority with the rest of the organization

- Continuous measurement of the evolution's *temperature* and tempo setting

- Definition of the early adopters as part of the evolution's tactical adoption, as we will see in *Chapter 10, Tactical and Organic Enterprise Portfolio Planning and Adoption.*

- Definition of the evolution's workstreams

- Ultimate ownership of the DevOps 360° operating model

The decisions that are taken by the DevOps 360° vision authority group should be binding and its members should be obliged to fulfill them and be held accountable for the parts of the organization that they represent. Decision and action unilateralism by certain parts of the organization should also be addressed by this group and disciplinary/deterrence actions should be taken by the group to ensure that such actions don't recur. In other words, this group should be the Leviathan that governs and brings order to the evolution so that those involved are able to unleash their creativity in an environment characterized by *DevOps alignment and solidarity.*

Bonus Information

Leviathan (the Leviathan in our case being the DevOps vision authority group) is a masterpiece of political philosophy written by Thomas Hobbes and published in 1651. This book is concerned with the structure of society (or, in our case, the structure and evolution of the DevOps enterprise) and who has the authority to govern. According to Hobbes, in the absence of a Leviathan, life becomes chaotic and people cannot focus on creativity, as they constantly fight for survival.

Ideally, this group should be headed by two people: a senior executive appointed by the group's COO, and someone who can be accountable for the DevOps evolution, who should either be the head of your DevOps CoE, the **Chief Information Officer (CIO)**, or the **Chief Technology Officer (CTO)**. All the core stakeholders' areas should be represented in the group, to ensure the best possible balance. The vision authority group should have permanent members as well as guests based on the agenda to be discussed at its assemblies. The guests should be representatives of the DevOps 360° design and advocacy group and workstreams.

Tips on Managing the Vision Authority Group

Based on my experience of working with such groups, I recommend that you consult the following tips:

- Base the membership of the group on the four qualities of the change forces that we outlined in the last section of *Chapter 2, The DevOps Multi-Speed Context, Vision, Objectives, and Change Nature.*

- When meeting as a broader assembly, ideally, you should meet offsite. Changing scenery will energize things and improve relations.

- Understand the power bases of the group and the overall dynamic.

- When important decisions are to be made, speak to the members in one-to-ones before the session and conduct a psychological scan of them to predict the atmosphere in the room. With the term psychological scanning, we refer to the process of observing their psychological state and reactions when they are presented with the decisions that are to be taken. For instance, are the members energized and confident or do they look confused and uncertain? Does their body language reveal resistance or calmness?

- Always use relevant data (hard and soft) so that educated decisions can be made, along with calculated justifications.

- Study the members' background and personalities to adopt your DevOps vocabulary. As in, you need to adapt the DevOps terminology you use and change how you position it contextually for each stakeholder. As an example, you will have to adjust your wording and practical examples when you explain release engineering to the Head of IT Operations, compared to the Director of Fixed Income Trading.

Establishing a DevOps 360° design and advocacy group

The first thing you should do in order to engage stakeholders outside the vision authority group should be to establish a DevOps 360° vision and advocacy group. It is crucial to hand-pick the members of this group based on a combination of the following characteristics:

- They should have a strong passion for and knowledge about DevOps at enterprise scale.

- They should have championed and practiced DevOps successfully for several years.

- They should belong to the tactical evolution areas you have chosen.

- Their profiles should balance hard (technical) and soft (interpersonal) skills and they should be able to take a collaborative and collective approach.

- They should have good reputations and recognition across the organization.

- They should have proven experience in enterprise initiatives.

Ideally, the composition of this group should be diverse in terms of roles and organizational origin; there should be everyone from developers and architects to infrastructure engineers and middle managers.

These people should be easy to identify as they should have already made their *DevOps name* in your organization. Diversity is very important in ensuring a good range of DevOps skills and experience across the broader DevOps ecosystem, as well as to cover organizational context-specific aspects, requirements, and views. A senior developer from the payments domain would oversee certain aspects of DevOps differently than an Oracle database administrator from the core infrastructure domain. Mixing insiders and outsiders in this group is also important as you will require people that know your state-of-the-art DevOps context and its historical evolution well, but also people who are fresh hires that have seen how DevOps is done elsewhere and can inject fresh ideas, eliminating unconscious bias.

The advocates need to have decision making authority mandated by their line managment and the vision authority group. The vision authority group and the advocacy group's line managers will neither have the time nor the domain expertise to make all of the decisions themselves; they would become bottlenecks or require extensive coaching. Nevertheless, this advocacy group won't be able to make all the decisions as some will be too strategically significant, require political correctness, or be too difficult to come to a collective agreement about. Hence, a clear decision-making and escalation process should also be defined.

The main responsibilities of the group should include the following:

- Accountability for the future design of the DevOps 360° operating model.

- The design and approval of DevOps solutions and frameworks.

- Workstreams coordination and DevOps enterprise catalog definition.

- Acting as a bridge between business IT and core technology.

- Piloting the new DevOps 360° operating model in their respective areas.

- The communication aspects of advocacy for the DevOps evolution, such as awareness sessions and demos. The group must also have the ability to continuously improve the DevOps operating model based on regularly collected feedback.

It will be necessary for this group to think ahead about how the DevOps model should develop, and this vision should be closely aligned with that of the vision authority group. This will help them steer workstreams, be forward-looking when it comes to decision-making, and have the necessary time to prepare the organization for evolution.

> **Be Aware**
>
> There will be *spies* in this group. They will be people that, due to conflicting DevOps agendas, will attempt to spy on what is being planned for the DevOps evolution and bring the information back to their units so that they can prepare their defense plans.
>
> Availability and commitment will be an issue when it comes to the members of this group, either because they are scarce and very important to the business or because they are not dedicated enough to the cause of the group.

Defining your DevOps enterprise evolution ecosystem

Maybe the problem is that it is called DevOps! This is a phrase I have borrowed from a fellow DevOps practitioner who interviewed me once upon a time at a DevOps conference. We were discussing why many organizations often follow a developer-centric approach when adopting DevOps and exclude operations. And is it only operations that they omit? The fact that the concept is called DevOps can make people intentionally or accidentally neglect several other important DevOps stakeholders. As we will see in this section, there is a wide range of stakeholders, each of them bringing a unique value proposition, that are involved in ensuring that all of the four qualities comprising the DevOps 360° operating model are fulfilled.

Who should be considered as key stakeholders?

As different incumbents have different organizational structures, we will focus on DevOps domains rather than unit names. The following tables provide an overview of the primary and secondary domains that you should consider including in your evolution:

DevOps Domain/Stakeholder	Value Proposition
Primary	
Software Development and Operations	Builds and runs software. The primary consumers of technology utilities and DevOps capabilities.
Business Units	Owns and uses products, applications, and services. Manages DevOps priorities for business applications and funding.
Enterprise Architecture	Forms the governing mechanism for architecting your portfolio of applications, services, platforms, domains, and flows.
DevOps CoE or CoP	Sets your organization's DevOps standards.
Control Center	This is the first line of service operations and continuity.
Enterprise Service Desk	Handles business inquiry fulfillment on IT applications.
Process Governance	Owns the service life cycle operational processes.
Common Platforms	Comprises utility teams offering technological DevOps capabilities.
Cyber Security	Enables security policies across your SDLC.
Service Portfolio Governance	Form the application and service registry mechanism.
IT Risk and Controls	Facilitates the implementation of the IT risk management framework.
Business Agility CoE or CoP	Oversees the business agility model of your organization.
Data Governance	Enacts data classification and protection policies.
Quality Assurance	Facilitates the creation of quality assurance strategies and plans.

Core infrastructure	Provides the core technology infrastructure capabilities.
Data Analytics	Provides telemetry and reporting capabilities.
IT Audit	Provides an overview of open IT audit remarks.
Talent Acquisition and HR	Manages recruitment, mobility, incubation, and job descriptions.
User Experience	Facilitates DevOps journeys, experience, and value streams.
Regulators	Manage the alignment of regulatory demand responses.

Table 3.1 – Primary DevOps ecosystem stakeholders

As you can see, the primary stakeholders consist of more than just developers. To some extent, they represent the enterprise as a whole. Now, let's extend the list a bit more by looking into the secondary stakeholders:

DevOps Domain/Stakeholder	Value Proposition
Secondary	
Legal	Supports regulatory negotiations
Vendor Management	Manages the renegotiation of contract terms
Third-Party Vendors	Offer technological foundation utilities
Managed Services	Offshore teams that support development and operations
Friendly Customers	Customers that support the piloting of new products
Partnerships	Partnering incumbent banks, technology innovators, and management consulting firms

Table 3.2 – Secondary DevOps ecosystem stakeholders

The broad stakeholder's ecosystem, as we will see later in this book, is used in several dimensions of the DevOps 360° operating model. As your new model comes to life, each of these stakeholders will not only support its formation but will eventually own parts of it that relate to their domain.

Stakeholder appointment needs to be conducted by people who fulfill the four qualities that we discussed at the end of the previous chapter due to the following reasons:

- For some domains, due to structural ambiguity, it will be difficult to identify the right people.

- Explaining to the broad stakeholders how they are expected to contribute, as well as what's in it for them, will be necessary.

- A cross-capabilities stakeholder dependency matrix will have to be created.

- Knowledge of historical internal dynamics will be vital to overcome the resistance of stakeholders who do not see themselves as a direct part of the DevOps model.

> **Bonus Information**
>
> In a bank I used to work in, we identified 31 different domain areas that had to contribute to creating a new DevOps enterprise operating model. Imagine how far you might have to go and how much effort it might require!

Defining the evolution's workstreams

Each DevOps enterprise OKR and pillar of the DevOps 360° operating model will be enabled through several workstreams running in parallel and delivering incrementally and continuously.

Organizing the workstreams

Your workstreams should be designed in harmony with each other and operate under the same model and principles, as well as having a very close connection to the vision authority group and the design and advocacy group. Each workstream will comprise several stakeholders from the broader ecosystem. They will have different roles, as shown in the following table:

Roles	Description
Owner	A vision authority group member who has expertise in the workstream's domain of focus. This member also represents the business partners of the incumbent.
Lead	A senior member of the design and advocacy group who has expertise in the workstream's domain of focus and who has coordination experience. This member, along with the owner, represents the business units.
Integrator	A person ensuring reconciliation with other workstreams running in parallel.
Squads	Permanent people who are appointed to be part of the workstream and come from the broader DevOps ecosystem. They are fixed for each workstream.
Satellites	Non-permanent members who join only when their domain of expertise comes into focus. They are not permanent and support several workstreams in parallel.

Table 3.3 – Roles within workstreams

Consulting the DevOps enterprise OKRs and vision that we have defined in this book, we propose the following workstreams, accompanied by a one-line value proposition for each:

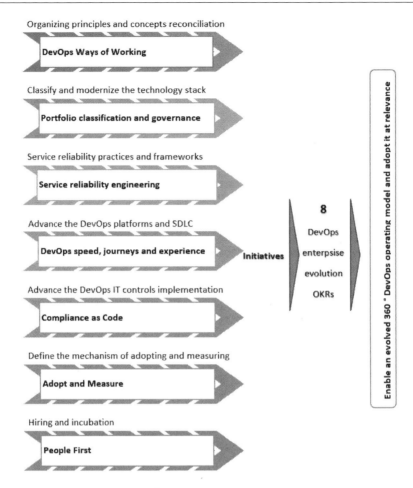

Figure 3.2 – Overview of the DevOps enterprise evolution workstreams

The following sub-section provides a deep dive into the operating model of workstreams.

Defining workstream scopes

The workstreams will be primarily tasked with the following activities; to demonstrate, we will use the **Compliance as Code** workstream as an example:

- Define the starting, intermediate, and target states for the workstream:

    - **Starting**: Bureaucratic DevOps controls policies and inadequate implementation.

    - **Intermediate**: Policy engineering and minimum viable adherence adoption. These are two terms that we will discuss in detail in *Chapter 8, 360° Regulatory Compliance as Code*, and *Chapter 10, Tactical and Organic Enterprise Portfolio Planning and Adoption*.

- **Target**: Policy as code embedded into the tech ecosystem and an automated minimum viable adherence mechanism established.

- Define the key domains across the broader DevOps stakeholder ecosystem that are to be part of the implementation. In our example, we foresee that we will need to involve *security*, *IT audit*, *IT risk and controls*, *common platforms*, and *DevOps teams*.

- Define the core **initiatives** for the enablement teams and support their backlog creation:

  - **I1**: Controls revision and simplification. Assigned to the DevOps CoE.

  - **I2**: Automated evidence generation. Assigned to the common platforms.

  - **I3**: Automated adherence attestation. Assigned to service governance.

- Facilitate the piloting of the teams' part of the tactical evolution, as we will see in *Chapter 10, Tactical and Organic Enterprise Portfolio Planning and Adoption*. For instance, digital banking domain applications would need to be supported while piloting the DevOps controls, which we will further discuss in *Chapter 8, 360° Regulatory Compliance as Code*.

- Reconcile and align its initiatives with those of the other workstreams. For example, align with the DevOps speed, journey, and experience workstream to ensure that the new DevOps controls mechanism is tactically embedded in the new SDLC and can be consumed as a service in the new common CI/CD pipeline for cloud-native applications.

- Support the definition of the DevOps evolution enablement and adoption OKRs.

- Raise decision points for the authority groups. For example, will the control's minimum viable adherence be mandatory across all business applications?

Minding the balance

With the formation and operation of the workstreams and the work that they will generate for the evolution's enablement and adoption teams, a large proportion of your organization will have to be mobilized. Therefore, it is important to find the right balance between business as usual, other change activities, and the DevOps evolution. This will make people feel less distracted, plus it will be easier to institutionalize the evolution and make it organic in the long run. Let's say you were to do enterprise business continuity testing in one month, upgrade the central JIRA instance this weekend, decommission the legacy trade general ledger application next month, and provide an update to your auditor on the progress of controls implementation in the next quarter. Build on those already-planned initiatives and let people continue delivering on what is already planned while injecting the evolution's objectives and outcome incrementally. Overloading the organization or freezing it until you get the planets of your DevOps universe aligned is irrational. Remember that we have chosen the *evolution* type of strategic change to ensure that the organization evolves incrementally through interrelated activities without the need for radical actions and urgency.

Bringing it together

The following diagram summarizes the governing and materialization actors of your DevOps evolution:

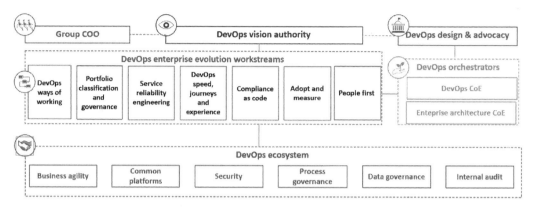

Figure 3.3 – Governance bodies and stakeholders illustration

As you can see, there are two actors labeled as orchestrators that we have not focused on in this chapter. The next chapter will be dedicated to them.

Understanding the governing dynamics

Eventually, you will need to reach an equilibrium across the main governing bodies of the evolution and its executors. By the term equilibrium, we indicate a situation where every stakeholder balances what is best for the part of the organization that they represent with what is best of the organization as a whole. Being inspired by the Nash equilibrium, I borrow the phrase *governing dynamics* and add an element of DevOps to it. One of your aims in your evolution should be to come into a *DevOps equilibrium* across the organization by doing what is best for individual areas and what is best for the broader organization. One of the ways to do that is to ensure that you understand and balance your *DevOps governing dynamics*. *Governing* indicates both the ones that govern (the vision authority) the evolution, but also the ones being governed (the organization's lower levels) in the evolution.

Understanding the balance of power in the governing bodies

Balancing the power of the members of the governing bodies we discussed earlier in this chapter will be a complex yet necessary activity to perform. Typically, and especially among senior stakeholders, you will observe the following types of power that different people possess. Those different types of power should eventually come into a balance-of-power equilibrium:

- **Hierarchical**: The power that comes with a given position
- **Personal**: The power that comes from being influential and persuasive through personal appeal

- **Agenda setting**: The ability to set the agenda for any discussion or decision making

- **Information**: The power that comes from having privileged access to insightful information

- **Knowledge**: The power that comes from deep domain knowledge and expertise

> **Bonus Information**
>
> The balance-of-power theory in international relations suggests that states may secure their safety by preventing any other state from gaining enough power to dominate everyone else. Typically, states choose between two tactics – balancing, by creating alliances with others, and bandwagoning, by aligning themselves with the power that threatens them.

Bringing two different worlds together

Your organization probably runs with two modi operandi that focus on autonomy and alignment. Some teams operate *autonomously*, seeing any centralized decision-making only as a bureaucratic means of controlling them, while others operate in *alignment*, following central decisions and direction. Those two worlds have certain characteristics that you can use to spot and manage them, as you will have to bring them into equilibrium:

The Organizationally Aligned	
Differentiation	Clear segregation of duties and responsibilities in the team
Centralization	Managers are fully aligned with central organizational priorities and decisions
Standardization	Tools, processes, and policies follow central standardization
Supervision	"Do not trust, get evidence and verify"
The Organizationally Autonomous	
De-differentiation	Freedom when it comes to the allocation of tasks and responsibility
De-centralization	People have the space and mandate to go in their own directions
De-standardization	Flexibility in bypassing central tools, processes, and policies
De-supervision	"Trust, do not verify"

Table 3.4 – Organizationally aligned teams versus autonomous teams

These dynamics will have a key role in your evolution as you will see some people that are not in managerial positions, for example, being reluctant to make decisions without their managers' involvement, while with others, it will be the opposite. Also, while you will find people who are used to working in alignment with a central governing body and find it acceptable and desirable to work toward a common model, you will find others who feel that a common model violates their need for freedom, autonomy, and independence.

Speaking the same DevOps language

One of the fundamental aspects of human interaction is language. Due to its versatility, breadth, and lack of universal definitions, DevOps is a source of several misconceptions. Some are due to a lack of literacy, others due to convenience (as in, what they feel more comfortable with is what they will keep understanding, raising resistance to new ideas and concepts), and still others are due to promoting personal agendas within an organization. For everyone to make sense of each other during a DevOps evolution, you need to be able to speak the same *DevOps concepts language*, while killing DevOps misconceptions. Therefore, it is important to align concept definitions and perceptions. We have all been in a DevOps meeting where release velocity was confused with release management and where continuous delivery was considered the same as continuous deployment, while self-healing and auto-healing were implied to be identical.

It is not only a matter of definitions but also of perceptions. For instance, we have all participated in a debate where cloud-native, for some in the room, is perceived as necessarily referring to the adoption of public cloud capabilities and for others is perceived as referring to certain characteristics and qualities of an application and its infrastructure, such as scalability, modularity, and containerization. You should not be surprised to find *conceptual misunderstandings and misperceptions* during a DevOps evolution. While you cannot achieve a perfect understanding overnight, especially considering the fact that conceptual understandings require experience and knowledge, you can start by creating common definitions that get everyone on the same page and tailor them to your context, objectives, and vision:

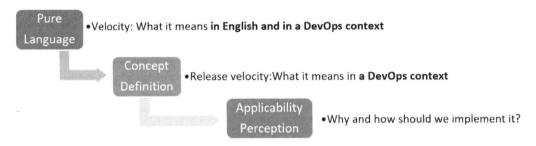

Figure 3.4 – The DevOps language tree

Collectively defining the DevOps enterprise evolution lexicon within your governing bodies can help you set the fundamentals of DevOps communication among those groups and then cascade them to the rest of the organization. You can find plenty of DevOps lexicons by just googling them, and it is advisable to use one of them as a foundation to build on top of, using your organization's understanding and interpretation of certain DevOps concepts as well as your own DevOps definitions and vision. Using the same language will help the DevOps CoE to understand its client and help the core platform teams to align with the enterprise architecture. This will also bring more consistency to your documentation and give you a better understanding across various stakeholders, including your business partners and regulators. However, you should expect that areas with vast contextual and technological differences, such as your core IBM Mainframe z/OS platforms and your cloud-native applications, representing two different generations will never speak the same language. They do not need to.

> **True Story**
>
> Once upon a time, a peer asked me to give a DevOps presentation to their team. They were starting their DevOps journey, balancing between traditional software development and ITIL, and were looking for inspiration from other teams. I made a nice deck, putting together the best of my team's DevOps adoption, and met them. I always keep eye contact while presenting to capture reactions so that I can adjust my presentation style. To my surprise, I mostly observed bewilderment in the room. Ending the presentation, I asked if anyone had any questions and there were none. Then, I asked something to the effect of, *"Did I confuse you?"* One person responded, *"Where can we find the definitions of the DevOps terms you used? This is the first time I've heard of them."*

We all have numerous stories such as the preceding one to tell. Some are quite entertaining, with people getting into conflict situations not because they were disagreeing, but because they were using different terms that meant the same thing. A common DevOps lexicon is a foundational tool that will not solve all your communication and perception challenges, but it is a good start. In the coming chapters, we will discover more tools and frameworks that will get you closer to speaking the same DevOps language.

Understanding your organizational structure dynamics

Organizational structures and hierarchies are core influencers of your DevOps enterprise evolution governance model and execution. Reporting lines, business operating models, and capabilities demarcation not only define your daily operations and dynamics but also establish an optimal governance mechanism. In this section, we will discuss three of the most dominant structural use cases found in incumbents, along with their potential implications. You will notice that we will be using the past tense when describing the use case dynamics that arose as we are observing real situations that occurred in the past.

What to look for in your organizational structure

The purpose of outlining these models is not to deep dive into the reasoning behind banking organizational structures as those are deeply rooted in the internal context and business model of each incumbent. Instead, we aim to highlight the core organizational structure elements that can generate DevOps structural constraints or efficiencies and need to be considered when deciding on a DevOps enterprise evolution governance model. The main elements of focus are as follows:

- DevOps capability concentration and density
- Strategic direction influence

- Decision-making authority
- Power polarity

In each use case, the organizational hierarchy starts with the group's COO for two reasons. Firstly, your DevOps evolution will, to a certain extent, alter the way your organization operates with your group COO as they are the ultimate owner of the organization's operating model. Secondly, the group COO is one of the main executives in your organization who interacts directly with your main regulator and is accessible to your largest and wealthiest clients. It is common in incumbents that regulatory audit reports and corresponding remediation actions are addressed by the respective COOs and also that large and wealthy clients have COOs on speed dial. Keep in mind these common characteristics of the COOs as we will return to them later in this book.

Use case 1 – segregated business technology lines and group technology

In this use case, we have several business technology lines, each one having a dedicated COO and CIO, with the application development teams being embedded. Those business technology lines are segregated by group technology, where the application operations and common platform teams are located, and are headed by the group CIO or CTO:

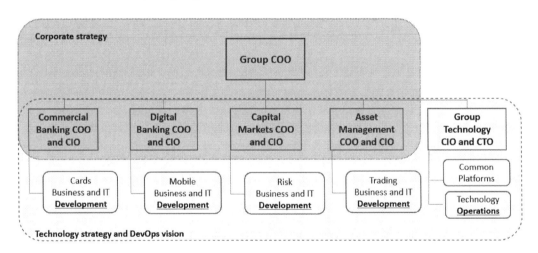

Figure 3.5 – Segregated business technology lines and group technology structure

Assessing the situation against the four main elements of focus, the following observations were identified:

- **DevOps capability concentration and density**: The segregation of people building software belonging to business IT areas and the people running software belonging to group technology caused tension and misalignment in the operating model domain's design. The technology operations teams were not embedded in the incumbent's DevOps adoption and therefore were not able to influence the operating model, which was primarily driven by the business IT areas having a dominant presence in the governing bodies. Also, as the business IT areas had built their own shadow IT DevOps solutions, they were very reluctant to move to common platforms, which resulted in solution interoperability challenges and the poor capturing of business IT requirements.

- **Strategic direction influence**: This was a one-to-many relationship on the leadership side reporting to the group COO, which shifted the balance of strategic influence and direction setting toward the IT business areas, which were also closer to the corporate strategy formation process. A conflict of interest came about as the most influential CIOs in the business IT areas favored their own interests and opposed the central group technology direction.

- **Decision-making distribution**: The business IT areas had full authority within their organizations and were not fully aligned, with the digital frontier CIOs having more decision-making freedom and influence, especially over group technology. In addition, group technology was being funded by the business IT areas, which also influenced the distribution of decision-making power. Therefore, decision-making was technically anchored to the most influential COOs and CIOs of the business IT areas.

- **Power polarity**: The situation involved balancing multipolarity and bipolarity among the several IT business areas that were, on the one hand, joining forces when in conflict with group technology but, on the other hand, were also acting unilaterally.

Bonus Information

Polarity in international relations refers to the way power is distributed within the international system. The main three types of polarity are *unipolarity*, one superpower; *bipolarity*, two superpowers; and *multipolarity*, several superpowers. Our current international system's polarity is characterized by multipolarity between the United States of America, BRICS, and the European Union.

Use case 2 – segregated business and technology

There was complete segregation between business and technology, with all technology units, including those concerned with the development and operations of business applications, being under the same organization. However, there was a dotted line connecting the business lines of the CIOs and COOs:

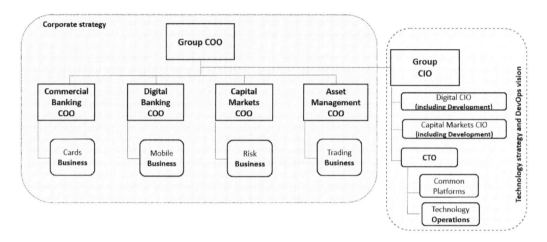

Figure 3.6 – Segregated business lines and technology

The following are the main observations regarding the four elements of focus:

- **DevOps capability concentration and density**: All the technological capabilities, including application development for the business areas, were concentrated under the group CIO, who owned the group's technological means of production. This situation resulted in a better jumping-off point for striving toward technological capabilities consolidation, as well as alignment with DevOps organizing principles and topologies. The structural segregation between business and technology was bridged by the reconciliation of the DevOps and business agility operating models, with business stakeholders being embedded in the SDLC and holding the product ownership role.

- **Strategic direction influence**: An initial strategic gap formed as the priorities of the corporate and technology strategies became misaligned when it came to the DevOps enterprise OKRs, which also impacted alignment with the DevOps vision. This was primarily driven by the group CIO. While the business units' influence over the business CIOs reporting to the group CIO and their control of the DevOps team's backlogs was maintained, the gaps were eventually bridged to a certain extent.

- **Decision-making distribution**: The decision-making process initially followed the path of the strategies, with the business COO focusing primarily on business line decisions and the group CIO driving the technological ones. This resulted in several decisions being misaligned in the DevOps capabilities evolution. A representative example is the public cloud provider's due diligence case. *Did anyone ask the business?* was a question that was raised repeatedly, highlighting the situation.

- **Power polarity**: This was the definition of a bipolar setup between business and technology. A broad coalition of the business areas was observed towards the group technology unit in cases of disagreement with the decisions and direction taken by group technology.

Use case 3 – consolidated business and technology domains segregated from the core technology

This use case is characterized by a heavy concentration of the business lines, where both the application and operations development teams were under them. They faced a "slim" group CTO area that was primarily offering infrastructure and common platform services:

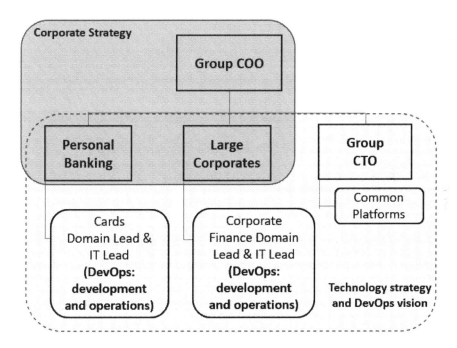

Figure 3.7 – Consolidated business and IT domains segregated from the core technology

The observations according to the four design elements we are focusing on are as follows:

- **DevOps capability concentration and density**: There was a very uneven concentration of DevOps capabilities, between the business lines and group technology, with development and operations fully embedded and autonomous under the business lines, owning their own DevOps solutions, and having full control of the DevOps budget. The group technology unit was struggling to create demand for its common platforms and was soon faced with internal competition due to public cloud capabilities being built into business IT areas.

- **Strategic direction influence**: The business and technology domain lines had full influence over the corporate and technology strategies as well as DevOps vision, with the group technology unit being perceived purely as a utility delivering on the business line demand.

- **Decision-making distribution**: The vast majority of important decisions were taken by the business and technology domains, with the core technology unit just being informed after the fact. However, there was a challenge in gaining collective agreement due to the large number of IT leads not being represented by a single person. The absence of a single IT lead representative led to decisions not being followed equally by all IT leads.

- **Polarity**: The most definitive characteristic was the unipolarity of the business and technology domains.

As we can see, organizational structures have a significant influence on your DevOps enterprise evolution and governance. This influence will become more profound if you combine your DevOps evolution with organizational changes, as well as evolution in your business agility model, which is a common approach that many incumbents follow.

Summary

In this chapter, we introduced the core pillars of the DevOps 360° operating model, which we will discuss in more detail in the coming chapters. We also defined the two main governing bodies of the evolution – the vision authority group and the design and advocacy group, while we also discussed the workstreams setup. We covered their responsibilities.

Then, we outlined the core DevOps enterprise stakeholders' domains that are of relevance to the evolution, along with their value propositions. The need for all these stakeholders to speak the same language was addressed and we proposed how to define a common DevOps evolution lexicon.

After that, we moved onto a critical dimension of the evolution, which is to understand the governing dynamics by identifying the power dynamics of the key stakeholders, as well as to capture the operating model differences within your organization, focusing on the organizationally aligned and organizationally autonomous teams. Finally, we discussed three different use cases based on three incumbents, proving that different organizational structures can have a variety of effects on a DevOps enterprise evolution.

The next chapter is dedicated to two core orchestrating bodies of the evolution, the enterprise architecture and the DevOps center of excellence, the roles of which we will discuss extensively.

4

Enterprise Architecture and the DevOps Center of Excellence

This chapter introduces two orchestrators of the DevOps evolution and is divided accordingly into two main parts. We start with **Enterprise Architecture** (**EA**), outlining its overall value proposition for the DevOps evolution, and afterward we discuss the three layers of domain criticality, as well as their importance in the DevOps evolution, using examples. Continuing, we define the main alternative choices for platform modernization-facing incumbents by providing the business case and examples for each choice. Afterward, we shift focus to the importance of reference architectures in accelerating the DevOps evolution and we discuss the most decisive and dominant of these in the financial services industry. Closing the first part, we highlight the importance of establishing an EA assembly. The second part starts by discussing the value proposition of the DevOps **Center of Excellence** (**CoE**) and outlines the four potential roles it can have. The client engagement role is discussed in more length and is accompanied by an example. The chapter continues by providing tips and alternatives on how to staff and fund the CoE. It moves on to outline four different DevOps CoE use cases derived from four different incumbents and closes by proposing the three major life cycle steps of a successful DevOps CoE.

In this chapter, we're going to cover the following main topics:

- Enterprise architecture
- DevOps Center of Excellence

Enterprise architecture

One of the main DevOps evolution orchestrators that incumbents use is EA. With the term EA, we refer to both a functional unit, as in a part of the organization dedicated to EA causes, but also a discipline, as in the frameworks and mechanisms supporting the required EA decisions and the direction that will both influence and enable the DevOps evolution.

What is the banking DevOps EA value proposition?

To some of you the answer is obvious, to some others maybe not. The EA value proposition is multidimensional and pivotal as it establishes some fundamental governance groundwork for the DevOps evolution, but also some frameworks to guide its direction and intelligence if you wish. The main responsibilities of EA, which are directly related to the DevOps evolution, are listed as follows:

- Identifying critical business domains and flow identification

- Defining the platform modernization strategy

- Establishing reference architectures

- Architecture assembly formation

- Business application and technological stack portfolio classification

The combination of these responsibilities and their corresponding outcomes provide some core elements of **intelligence** in a DevOps evolution, at relevance and in a multi-speed context. In the following sections, we will discuss all of the preceding responsibilities except the last one, to which we have dedicated *Chapter 10, Tactical and Organic Enterprise Portfolio Planning and Adoption*, combining this with service governance due to the close relation between them.

Defining the critical path of the banking portfolio

Your EA function will have neither the bandwidth nor the expertise to maintain its focus across your portfolio of business and technology platforms during the evolution. Bear in mind that an incumbent's average portfolio has more than 2,000 business applications. As we will see in *Chapter 10, Tactical and Organic Enterprise Portfolio Planning and Adoption*, normally such portfolios are split into certain categories based on their criticality to the business. EA will focus only on the most critical ones, sharing the responsibility with the business IT units to define which they are. As with EA, the key stakeholders of your broader DevOps evolution will be unable to maintain their focus across the whole portfolio. Focus must be deployed tactically and intelligently. In this section, we will focus on what incumbents often call the **portfolio's critical path**, defining this from a DevOps perspective.

Critical business domain/function

We define the incumbent's business operations and activities as critical domains or functions when their discontinuity is very probable to result in the disruption of services essential to the incumbent's revenue generation, the real economy, and the financial system's stability, and could trigger supervisory involvement. Remember that the sample of incumbents represented in this book is of systemically important banks.

> **Did You Know?**
> An incumbent has to report its liquidity risk numbers to its main regulator daily. Failure to deliver the updated numbers for three days in a row results in a regulatory investigation.

There are certain eligibility criteria with which to classify criticality across the incumbent's service portfolio and domains. The main ones are cited in the following list, together with examples:

- **Revenue generation**: For example, wealth management and loans
- **Impact on real economy and reputation**: Payments, savings, and deposits
- **Regulatory impact**: Group risk and liquidity reporting
- **Risk hedging and funding**: Profit and loss reporting
- **Market share**: Account opening and trading
- **Partner impact**: Open banking
- **Enterprise shared services**: Core technological infrastructure utilities (for example, a network)

The most critical (or **core**) domains that you typically find in an incumbent bank are outlined as follows:

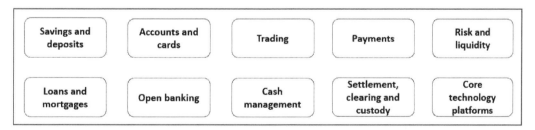

Figure 4.1 – Core business criticality domains example in banking

All incumbents, especially the systemically important ones, have their critical domains identified, as they are tightly connected to their business continuity, as well as the requirements of their regulatory and supervisory bodies.

Let me clarify something before we move on

It is important to clarify that with the term *criticality* in this book, we do not take the traditional approach focused on reliability and compliance, but also include the time to market, following the DevOps equilibrium we outlined in our DevOps definition. Innovating quickly with new mobile banking features is equally as important as ensuring the service's stability and adequate compliance adherence.

From critical business domains to critical path business flows

The business criticality domains that we outlined are on criticality level 1. Drilling one level down into criticality level 2, we have **cross-domain critical flows**. With flows, we define a sequence of (cross-) domain activities that contribute to the execution of business unit, customer, and regulatory **core-critical activities**. To explain this concept, we will use two examples.

Critical path of the trade life cycle flow

The following is an illustration of a sample critical path crossing the *trading, settlement, clearing and custody*, and *risks and liquidity* domains. The flow consists of different IT applications, each of which applies its own business logic to the flow and utilizes certain technological components.

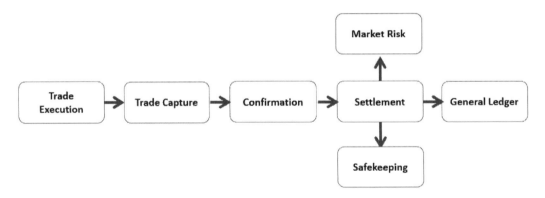

Figure 4.2 – Trade life cycle flow example

Failure in any step of the flow will result in an interruption to the trade life cycle and will result in a domino effect that, if severe, can spill across to other critical domains. The failure can be caused by a human mistake for which the IT applications do not have adequate *error-handling* capacities, or most often by a technology failure that can be as simple as latency on processing trade downstream, or something more severe, such as a network outage across the board.

Critical path of cross-border payments through mobile banking

A second example comes from a flow that crosses the *saving and deposits* and *payments* domains. As with the trade life cycle example, with payments, we also have several IT applications applying business logic and any interruption, small or fatal, will disrupt the flow.

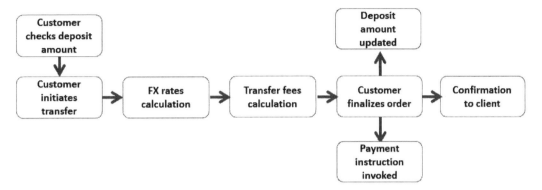

Figure 4.3 – Cross-border payment flow example

In both examples, a wide range of technological utilities is used by the IT applications, from servers to databases and from network to data transmission channels, which belong to the critical domain of core shared technology platforms.

From critical-path business flows to critical applications and services

Critical applications and services are the last level of criticality. Taking the example of the trade life cycle, the two most critical applications are those of trade execution and settlement, with the two most critical services as the following:

- **CS 1**: Equity trade deal capture service – trading execution system
- **CS 2**: Equity trade settlement service – settlement system

Why is defining these levels decisive for a DevOps evolution?

We intentionally drilled down into the criticality levels with examples as they are fundamental for the approach we take in this book. As we will see in later chapters, the criticality approach, apart from providing client, society, and regulatory DevOps centricity, will practically do the following:

- Support the DevOps evolution at relevance framework
- Define the tactical adoption candidates – that is, areas to front-run the evolution
- Define the scope of client engagements for the DevOps CoE

- Define candidates to front-run the **Site Reliability Engineering** (**SRE**) adoption (see *Chapter 13, Site Reliability Engineering in the FSI*)

- Define the portfolio prioritization for the compliance-as-code pilot areas (see *Chapter 8, 360° Regulatory Compliance as Code*)

- Visualize the interdependence across business domains when evolving DevOps at scale

Mastering the strategy of platform modernization

Incumbents are presently faced with what we call a strategic core **legacy dilemma**, while taking a tactical approach to platforms that are not necessarily classified as legacy but that do require modernization efforts to remain fit for purpose in the future.

> **True story and a tip**
>
> Once upon a time, we were discussing in a DevOps design authority how to deal with the legacy of our portfolio and whether it was indeed worth investing in DevOps engineering. Two interesting points arose during that discussion. First, we had to define the exact meaning of **legacy**. Was it only the applications written in Cobol and HPS, or also applications in C++, that we would decide to stop using as a technology? Second, who within our bank was actually holding the keys to the platform modernization strategy and could guide us? What if the mainframes were to stay for 20 more years and we had descoped them by mistake?

Your EA unit is the ideal place to anchor the creation of the master plan, undoubtedly in close collaboration with the business IT areas and core technology units. Obviously, one strategy will not fit every platform and budget, and skill set availability always has certain limitations. Nonetheless, there must be a strategic direction that will be followed at a minimum by the core strategic platforms. Typically, the strategic direction (which primarily concerns the core) offers three main choices for incumbents:

- **Total replacement of the legacy core** with modern platforms through *strategic one-off initiatives*. Most often the choices for this direction are sourced from vendors instead of self-built.

- **Gradual modernization**, keeping the legacy core but minimizing dependencies on business logic by reproducing it into modular microservices and decoupling the data dependencies through APIs. This approach is usually balanced between vendors and self-built solutions.

- **New greenfield core** based on cloud-native designs *from scratch*, architectural principles, and new modular business logic with gradual data migrations from the legacy core, which either partly stays or is decommissioned gradually. Most often, this results in the coexistence of self-built *greenfield* solutions alongside vendor-based *brownfield* ones.

Defining this strategic direction will strongly influence your DevOps evolution due to the domain and platform dependencies, but also guide you to be targeted when investing in new and long-lasting elements, especially regarding the engineering aspects. Examining the portfolio outside the core, you will discover several other business IT and core technology platforms with slightly more versatility regarding approaches to modernization. To shape their broader platform modernization strategy, banks have several options depending on their operating model, market concentration, risk appetite and profile, line-of-business demarcation, data strategy, platform criticality, and investment capital allocation.

Let us start by looking at the two less radical, safer approaches:

	Do nothing and sustain	Upgrade or incrementally improve
Business case elements	The platform is considered to be: • Fit for future purpose • Sustainable • Cost-effective • Low to no operational risk fragility	The platform is considered to be: • Made fit for future purpose via gradual improvements and/or upgrades • Sustainable • Cost-acceptable • Low operational risk fragility
Portfolio examples	1. CRMs, HR, and payroll systems 2. CI/CD pipelines 3. Non-client-facing applications and tools, used by small internal business teams 4. Very low criticality and stable non-mainframe applications with a release frequency of twice a year	5. Highly reputable vendor platforms, especially in the trading and group functions domains, with vendor lock-in and no intention or expertise to self-build (examples: Front Arena, Calypso, Murex, and SAP) 6. Self-built applications and platforms that are not part of the core or digital frontier and do not go through frequent code changes (examples: reference data and FX)

Table 4.1 – The "Do nothing and sustain" and "Upgrade or incrementally improve" approaches

Let's move on to some more radical approaches that are effort-, risk-, and capital-intense:

	Refactor and/or decouple	Full replacement, consolidation, or divestment
Business case elements	The platform is considered to be: • Not fit for future purpose • Unsustainable from maintenance, efficiency, and cost perspectives • Posing short- or long-term operational risk On decoupling, a full replacement is considered operationally risky or cannot be funded.	The platform is considered to be: • Unfit for future purpose • Unsustainable from the perspectives of operations, meeting business needs, and cost • Under pricy soon-to-expire vendor contracts • Unable to cope with innovation growth The platform will either be replaced or terminated.
Portfolio examples	1. Migration and replication from HPS and PL/SQL business logic to Java, primarily in back and middle office functions, such as accounting and reporting 2. New platforms; replacing legacy logic with new business logic; built-in microservices; eliminating data dependencies through APIs 3. Cloud-native transformations and business logic migration to a public cloud 4. Ecosystem refactoring for regulatory purposes	1. Core banking platforms, primarily replaced by well-reputed vendor solutions (example: Temenos) 2. Legacy country-specific platforms, whose business logic is recreated and consolidated under one global platform, both vendor and self-built 3. Lines of business being terminated, consolidated, or divested 4. Legacy data transmission channels and storage 5. Legacy observability, automation, and identity and access management tools

Table 4.2 – The "Refactor and/or decouple" and "Full replacement, consolidation, or divestment" approaches

"How are these approaches linked to the DevOps 360° enterprise evolution?" you might wonder. The answer is simple – you need to be forward-looking and targeted on your evolution, especially on the engineering aspects of it. You will not invest heavily in DevOps engineering for a platform that you only plan to sustain, or that will be decommissioned in a year. At the same time, you might find limited DevOps engineering scope in a vendor platform, of which you do not own the code base and you just upgrade; plus, in most scenarios, such vendor platforms provide out-of-the-box observability capabilities, for instance. You need to have a plan for how your portfolio's modernization is to evolve. Of course, you will never have perfect evolution data across your business, and your technological portfolio and plans will always be changing, but you will certainly have a fair picture of the direction you are to take, at least in your core domains.

Expect the Unexpected

Twice in my career, modernization plans have been changed and to some extent delayed, impacting the DevOps transformation. The first was due to a major organizational line-of-business change; the second was due to a restructuring of the firm's legal entity. Things happen!

The reference architecture proposition in banking DevOps

Reference architectures have in recent years been very relevant and foundational to DevOps evolutions. Scaling fast and accelerating on an enterprise level requires recipes for adoption to be available and reusable. For these reference architectures, we define solution architectures and designs, which are provided as ready-to-use templates that can be reproduced, and may solve architectural challenges that someone else within your organization or in the industry solved before you. They promote a common vocabulary (remember the DevOps lexicon?) and support simplicity and standardization in both the business technology domains and core technological platforms. In this section, we will outline some of the main reference architectures that we propose to incumbents to define based on the latest industry trends.

The extended value proposition of reference architectures on DevOps evolutions

We have already mentioned simplicity and standardization, but the extended value proposition of reference architectures for banking is much larger and multidimensional:

- Streamlining digital customer journeys within and outside the bank

- Interoperability efficiencies across the ecosystem

- Harmonious *plug 'n' play* accelerated portfolio modernization

- Reusability of DevOps engineering frameworks and solutions

- Compliance, reliability, and security built in by design

- Compliant hybrid multi-cloud solutions

- Shared service integration models across the DevOps ecosystem

- Market experimentation and speedy delivery of new products and services

As can be easily understood, all the preceding aspects can directly or indirectly accelerate the DevOps enterprise evolution. Let us now outline some of the reference architectures that we consider to be of great importance to the DevOps enterprise evolution journey of an incumbent bank.

From monolithic to distributed modular microservices

A hot industry trend is the modernization and re-factoring of tightly coupled (monolithic) applications and platforms via domain-driven design principles, toward distributed architectures based on independent business logic microservices, packaged and deployed as containers. This involves the utilization of infrastructure-as-code provisioning independent of CI/CD pipelines and observability perspectives, using APIs for data transmission and overall fundamental cloud-native capabilities.

Enterprise message buses and communication layers

A domain of high focus for incumbents and closely related to distributed architectures is the domain of real-time and asynchronous data processing. Striving to move away from tightly coupled messaging queues and scheduled batch jobs and toward enabling dynamic interoperability with legacy and modern data sources, decoupling data dependencies, and increasing operational resiliency and observability are often requirements of clients, lines of business, and regulators. Yes, indeed, several regulatory standards around real-time data processing and transparency, especially in the payments and trading domains, have been developed in recent years. Enterprise message buses and communication-layer technologies gain ground as part of platform modernization journeys, replacing old *transmission spaghetti* solutions.

Composable banking

The term *composable banking* is used in the industry to refer to the ability of composability enabled by banking platforms, which provides the opportunity to select and compose components in various combinations to satisfy specific requirements. Composability is different from modularity, especially in core banking platforms. While in core banking, modularity indicates the extension of business logic from the core to individual predefined components, composability indicates the ability of the business logic extension to dynamically remove or add components that external partners can integrate with. Think of modularity like pieces of a puzzle brought together, while composability is more like Lego bricks brought together. Composable banking can create opportunities for incumbents to expand fast in new markets, with new customized products and services, reducing the build and maintenance overhead and supporting clients to personalize their journeys and service consumption, while further integrating with the Fintech ecosystem. Composable banking reference architectures are considered to be the industry's future, especially for incumbents conducting regular M&A activities, as they provide patterns for *plug 'n' play* solutions to existing portfolios. Composable banking reference architectures are also applicable in cases where incumbents form new ventures by decomposing certain parts of their portfolios with the intention to recompose them under a separate legal entity, with its own independent business model.

Interoperating in one single DevOps technological ecosystem

As we will see later in the book, for various reasons, an incumbent will almost never be able to achieve perfect standardization and harmonization across its DevOps technological ecosystem. Some teams will keep utilizing their home-grown observability stacks, some others will not move to your common container platform and will keep conducting their own Docker image vulnerability scans, while others will keep their own CI/CD pipeline backbone but will migrate to the central open source scanning and code quality tools. When enabling interoperability across a hybrid technological ecosystem and balancing between home-grown and common core solutions, reference architectures can be proven silver bullets.

Greenfield banking

Greenfield is the new black in the industry without a doubt. Greenfield banking is gaining rapid momentum, mostly in the mobile banking, payments, and trading domains, and is seen by incumbents as a new business model that can support the independence of new digital services and products from legacy constraints, whether these are related to technology, data, processes, policies, or infrastructure. Through greenfield, banks can launch new products and services to various markets and regions more quickly, ensuring a full customer digital experience at a lower cost, while building the respective services and infrastructure under cloud-native principles from day one. However, building a greenfield bank is not as simple in reality as it sounds. The decoupling and demarcation of responsibilities from the legacy incumbent bank need to be carefully designed around five domains in particular:

- Data transmission, management, and synchronization
- Business logic integration to the core (if applicable)
- Dependencies on core infrastructure; landing zones
- Security policies
- Compliance

There are also scenarios for certain products and services where pure greenfield is not possible and a balance between green and brown is required. For all these reasons, reference architectures can provide predefined and proven designs to decode the greenfield landscape.

Public cloud adoption and migration

Most incumbents are well into their public cloud journey, or actually their multi-cloud journey, to be more precise. Business requirements, the plurality of public cloud solutions and capabilities, a strong focus on PaaS (over a traditional focus mostly on IaaS and SaaS), strategies to avoid *vendor lock-in*, and continuously evolving regulatory requirements can make the public (multi-) cloud adoption strategy an academic exercise. Reference architectures can support the optimization of the public cloud model choice and journey for candidates, as well as educate them in advance on the modernization journey and operating model changes that need to be undertaken to derive the most from the public cloud efficiencies. Reference architectures are everywhere in the public cloud journey, from industry-specific vendor patterns to proven solution designs, and from clarity on vendor due diligence to the practical adoption of certain PaaS capabilities such as analytics and machine learning. Moreover, the utilization of reference architectures can support the building of the public cloud business case and ensure alignment on the foundational capabilities that need to be established.

The most typical reference architectures found in the industry are as follows:

- Data center offloading through IaaS
- Hybrid cloud for resource-intense risk and liquidity calculation engines and models
- Mobile and online banking, as well as trading platform frontend migrations
- Big data and machine learning PaaS working on predictive customer analytics
- Enterprise message buses' and operational data storage's PaaS
- Greenfield digital banking and payment gateways
- Provisioning of CI/CD pipelines and observability tools

Going further in the EA value proposition

There are further domains where the DevOps evolution can be supported by EA:

- **Architecture design assessments and compliance**: Assess certain architectures based on pre-defined criteria and accordingly propose improvements
- **Cloud-native assessments**: Set the standards and conduct assessments on platforms' public cloud migration eligibility
- **New platform due diligence**: Supports the assessment of future fit for purpose
- **Incremental and iterative architectures**: Coach business IT and core technology teams on incremental, continuous, and iterative architectural evolution practices
- **Technology menu**: Defines the catalog of pre-approved technologies that the business IT and core technology teams can consume
- **DevOps adoption application portfolio classification**: Supports the portfolio classification based on non-functional parameters such as business criticality and impact

The EA assembly

On governing and collectively coordinating the EA work, we propose that you establish an EA assembly with members from your EA unit and solution design architects from your business IT areas and also from the core technology units. Their responsibilities can include the following:

- Alternative dispute resolution in case of architectural approach disagreements

- Architectural design reviews for common platforms strategic to the DevOps evolution solution

- Approval and maintenance of reference architectures

- Approval and maintenance of architectural standards and frameworks

- Portfolio modernization and classification decisions

As we discovered in the preceding section, the value proposition of EA for DevOps evolutions is solid, foundational, and multidimensional, while not so obvious. We will now move on and discover the value proposition of the DevOps CoE.

DevOps Center of Excellence

CoEs have become a mainstream industry approach in recent years to establish, enable, and orchestrate DevOps adoptions. A DevOps CoE is most often perceived and enabled as a function where rare DevOps experts are concentrated, aiming to enable organizational *DevOps excellence*. DevOps CoEs have various operating models without a standard shape but nonetheless with some commonalities around proven practices. This chapter discusses core aspects of DevOps CoEs, as well as proven practices, by comparing four different use cases from incumbent banks.

What is the value proposition for the CoE and its potential roles?

A DevOps enterprise evolution is a demanding endeavor. Legacy, culture, capability fragmentation, lack of expertise, leadership misalignment, multi-dependencies, and *"Trust me, I'm an engineer"* arguments will all raise barriers and can even generate adverse effects moving you toward further DevOps complexity instead of harmony. You must establish some functions that will keep the big picture together while orchestrating and facilitating the evolution, ensuring the deployment of DevOps expertise and excellence. In this section, we will discuss the various roles and respective value propositions of DevOps CoEs.

The DevOps enterprise evolution maestro

When defining your DevOps 360° operating model and adopting it at an enterprise level, your organization needs to get into almost perfect synchronization like a well-trained orchestra. Your various functions and stakeholders need to be orchestrated in order to achieve the most harmonized and synchronized *DevOps tune*. The DevOps CoE can act as the *maestro*, setting the rhythm and facilitating the journey toward DevOps alignment and harmony based on the definition of your new model. This orchestration involves the Head of the DevOps CoE coordinating the daily workstream operations, and the CoE members having strong representation in the DevOps design and advocacy group defining the future state, leading the prioritization of capability enablement across the DevOps technological ecosystem, and driving capability launches and adoption plans, but primarily getting everyone to align on a common vision through a broad coalition. Your DevOps CoE is the function that brings the pieces of the DevOps model together, while also bringing your people together and guiding them.

The DevOps CoE as the owner of the 360° operating model and DevOps governor

Imagine you have been through your evolution: you have created your brand-new DevOps 360° operating model and have started enabling its various pieces, while adopting it in parallel in certain areas. Your model will not stay steady, and you have to make sure that continuous evolution is applied to it. Your internal context and business strategy will evolve, your regulatory environment will probably tighten, digitalization will further disrupt your capabilities, new cloud services will become available, and your business units will become more aggressive. Obviously, you will have to evolve the model collectively as an enterprise and based on domain demarcation and expertise, but someone still needs to own the big picture. The DevOps CoE is the natural place for the complete model to be anchored and owned. Now, let me make sure that I am not misunderstood. Ultimately, the model will be owned by your COO, who is responsible for the operations of the organization, leads the business and technology lines and is the main counterpart of the regulator. Also, the several different parts comprising your model will be owned by the various DevOps stakeholders as appropriate. Now, you cannot expect your COO to ensure the model's continuous evolution and integrity, nor the vast number of stakeholders contributing to the model to self-coordinate on keeping the big picture together. As the CoE will also naturally own parts of it anyway, we propose the CoE also having the overall responsibility of ownership to ensure that the model's capability demarcation across stakeholders is clear and respected, that any major changes to it are centrally discussed and approved, and that there is a continuously evolving vision. The rest of the stakeholders will have accountability for the model sub-domains they own.

With the role of the internal **DevOps governor**, the CoE is by no means to play *DevOps police*, but to support the resolution of DevOps evolution disputes and provide model adherence guidance. For instance, some major vendor applications that your business IT teams use come with CI/CD and observability capabilities already embedded. The respective teams can raise a request to the DevOps CoE to get approval to utilize those capabilities, such as avoiding the central CI/CD pipeline, for example. Or a team might be uncertain about the difference between using AppDynamics or Prometheus for monitoring, with both being standard core offerings. The CoE should be able to guide that team to take the optimal decision.

The DevOps CoE as a (technological) capability provider

In this role, the DevOps CoE is responsible for providing certain technological and conceptual capabilities across the DevOps technological ecosystem that will support the DevOps evolution. They can span from technological features (CI/CD pipelines) to processes (open source scanning vulnerability remediation management) and from proven practices (backup and restoration of MongoDB) to policies (static code quality). As we will see in the coming chapters, the complete *DevOps capability anatomy* is quite complex and requires a strong mandate and domain expertise. Therefore, it is considered irrational and inadvisable to offload a large number of those capabilities to the CoE. Instead, we propose you strive toward domain-specific demarcation across your organization.

In industry adoptions, you will typically find DevOps CoEs primarily owning and offering the central and common technological and framework capabilities of CI/CD pipelines as a service. This is because they are perceived to be the core technological backbone of DevOps, as well as due to the incorrect perception that DevOps and CI/CD are the same thing. Let us not delve further into this fallacy as we have already outlined the DevOps definition used in this book. On top of CI/CD capabilities, we often find DevOps and cloud CoEs merged into one, offering further private cloud services and opening the path for the consumption of public cloud services. Whether or not a CoE is positioned to offer technological capabilities, it will have to be involved in keeping the DevOps technological ecosystem tightly together. In this chapter, we will not discuss this potential CoE role further, as we will get back to it later in the book in the chapter dedicated to the *DevOps technology ecosystem as a service*, where platform teams will be discussed in detail.

The DevOps CoE as a tactical adoption enablement partner

The last role that we typically observe in the industry is that of tactical adoption-enablement partners. Through this role, the DevOps CoE members are embedded in to either the business IT or technology utility areas and support their DevOps evolution capability enablement. The meaning of *tactical* in this context is that those areas are of high importance to the business and the benefits of their DevOps evolution can have a significant positive impact, which can potentially be maximized by other parts of the organization. You will often find these engagements in client-facing digital services domains, which are linked to revenue, competition, regulatory demand and reputation, or strategic DevOps technological utility areas, such as public cloud and core infrastructure services.

The engagement of the CoE's members in the tactical adoption areas is characterized by formal agreements and by becoming a fully integrated part of the daily operations and strategic direction of the team they support. It is advisable to combine the CoE services with 360° evolution packages in order to provide a more targeted, complete, and interrelated engineering and advisory approach. You should not engage with single IT applications, but with whole domains or critical flows.

Your main two offerings can be as follows:

- **Engineering services**: Hardcore hands-on DevOps engineering evolution
- **Advisory services**: Consulting, observing, coaching, deputing, and guiding

The resulting detailed service catalog could look like the following example:

1 **Evolution Engineering**

CI/CD migration & completeness
Containerization
IT controls automation
Public cloud migration
Observability
Infrastructure as code

2 **Evolution Advisory**

Operating model transition
Shift left practices
Coaching and shadowing
Value streams
Hiring
Controls adherence attestation

Figure 4.4 – CoE engineering and advisory services catalog example

Ideally, around the two pillars of your service offering you should build dedicated squads or pods of expertise from which you select people based on the objectives of your engagements. Note that a tactical engagement does not mean resource augmentation used to fill in skill gaps and getting consumed by business-as-usual activities, but scaled teams focusing on *hardcore* DevOps implementations that do not go after the *land-and-expand* tactic, but *evolve, hand over, and move on*.

Tactical adoptions are a golden opportunity for the CoE and the organization for the following reasons:

- They allow the collection of DevOps market insights into the DevOps evolution progress and state from both the business IT teams and infrastructure utilities.

- Hands-on support for the promotion of the DevOps 360° operating model and corresponding capability standardization, and feedback on improvements, applicability, and relevance.

- Cross-organization solutions can be implemented, creating success stories that can encourage others, allowing important alliances to be built and economies of scale to be achieved.

- Enabling a variety of career advancement paths and options for the CoE's people, which can support talent retention.

What are the eligibility criteria when determining which tactical engagements to go for? We partly covered this earlier in this chapter when discussing criticality, but we will discover more in *Chapter 10, Tactical and Organic Enterprise Portfolio Planning and Adoption*, later in the book.

An example of getting the most out of your service catalog

Good deals make good partners, hence it is important to establish a formal agreement, ensuring the right investment by the CoE, solid preparation of the client, and a mutual and transparent understanding of the objectives and benefits to be realized.

Engagement Name	Market and Credit Risk Flow DevOps Acceleration and Compliance
CoE Members	Three engineers: Michal, Alex, and Aurimas; two expert advisors: Tomasz and Mario
Objectives & Benefits	• Migration of home-grown CI/CDs to the central CI/CD pipeline: *Improve time to market and reduce maintenance overhead* • Microservices and containerization: *Platform modernization, data decoupling, and technical debt reduction* • Monitoring and logging standardization: *Enhance visibility and proactive capacity management* • SDLC controls completion and shift operations left: *Enhance compliance as coded coverage and improve reliability*
Funding	The **Fundamental Review of the Trading Book (FRTB)** program

Table 4.3 – Sample engagement template

In our hypothetical engagement called *Market and Credit Risk DevOps Acceleration and Compliance*, five CoE members were engaged. Aurimas, Michal, and Alex provided engineering services such as the migration of the shadow IT ELK instance to the common core cluster and the implementation of synthetic monitoring, the containerization of microservices, and the migration from Docker open source to an OpenShift central core. They also achieved the migration from the shadow IT Azure DevOps instance to the central one and made a shift toward a GitOps approach. In this scenario, from the central platforms mentioned, the DevOps CoE offered Azure DevOps and ELK as a service. So, this was a great win for the CoE as they increased their client coverage, promoted standardization in line with the new model, and passed direct feedback to the CoE's platform segment team on potential enhancements through their observations of the engagement.

In parallel, Tomasz and Mario observed the operating model of the client team and provided suggestions on proven practices around completing the implementation of the SDLC controls and shifting operations left, as well as how to register their control adoption process in the service registry mechanism and how to use concepts such as error budgets to balance innovation and reliability on the product backlogs. Such engagements provided both engineering solutions and advice, while increasing the utilization of common platforms and fulfilling DevOps evolution governance objectives. This is where the return on investment is maximized both from the perspective of tangible (such as standardization and new engineering capabilities) but also intangible (such as new ways of working and governance) results for the CoE, the client, and the broader DevOps evolution.

Staffing and funding the CoE

Excellence can only be built by excellent and empowered people who combine strong domain experience and expertise and a combination of soft and hard skills. Important considerations on staffing are as follows:

- Strategically move some of the very best of your organization's DevOps people to the CoE, either permanently or temporarily.

- Open up either for volunteers who might be interested in temporarily working for a function that has a broad organizational role, or people who might want a career change. This is a good way to maintain talent in your organization.

- Hire or incubate Π-shaped profiles. The CoE people must be fluent in the broad DevOps picture (horizontal) and have specialization in two domains (vertical).

- Hire software engineering profiles as well, not only DevOps engineering-oriented ones.

- Use a blend of internal and external hiring, so you mix organizational context insights with *how DevOps is done elsewhere* inspiration.

- Do not go the *manage services* way when scaling fast.

- Grant the CoE a *hiring wildcard* for periods when hiring freezes are imposed.

You need to continuously ensure that the CoE is funded, and its operations will not be disturbed by budgetary issues. The funding can be ideally addressed through four mechanisms:

- A **client pot** from multiple business IT and technology teams as part of the tactical adoption, with these teams contributing equally to fund the CoE from their improvement budgets.

- A **DevOps evolution pot** or a large compliance or digitalization program.

- **Your own CoE budget**, established through the annual maintenance budget cycles.

- **Pay as you use**: The clients pay for the services as per their consumption.

Four incumbent banks – four different use cases

There is no silver bullet for establishing a DevOps CoE but traditionally, incumbents have been pretty creative, following different approaches. In this section, we will look into four different use cases across a variety of DevOps CoE adoptions and will discuss what worked well and what didn't in each case. As we cannot exhaust all aspects of a CoE's operating model and topologies, we will focus on the following parameters that we consider the most important:

- DevOps operating model ownership

- Core CI/CD capabilities ownership

- Client engagement services
- Level of centralization
- Design motivating factor

Use case 1 – the three angles modus operandi CoE

The first use case is characterized by the following parameters:

- **DevOps operating model ownership**: DevOps CoE
- **Core CI/CD capabilities ownership**: DevOps CoE
- **Client engagement services**: Available and rotational
- **Level of centralization**: Highly centralized

Design motivating factor: The logic behind this decision was that a single unit should hold the keys to the DevOps operating model, support the flagship tactical areas of the organization by adopting the model in a sequence of waves, and offer the core CI/CD pipeline as a service. The aim of this is to ensure that the technological backbone of the adoption was close to the model and its future development would be closely influenced by the flagship adopters. The tactical adoption members of the CoE rotated between lines of business and were not dedicated to those lines of business. The CoE was located under the group technology unit, as the DevOps evolution was driven by the group's CIO:

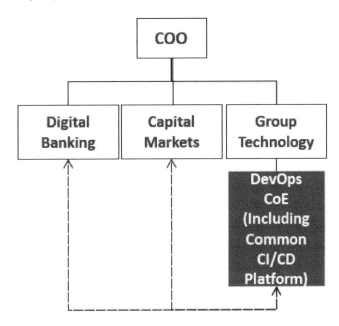

Figure 4.5 – The three-angles modus operandi CoE

The following table shows the pros and cons:

Pros	Cons
Standardization and simplification of DevOps practices across engagements.	The CoE could not scale outside the pre-defined client engagements.
Effective and tactical utilization of the CoE's resources.	The "DevOps gap" between those supported and not supported by the CoE widened.
Economies of scale through reusability.	The CoE could not capture all the business IT context-related feedback and specialties.
A single recognized owner and point of entry for the DevOps operating model.	High capability concentration and density occasionally resulted in CoE unilateralism.
Career mobility within the CoE.	The client engagement rotations had a mixed effect due to switching context and focus frequently, as well as leaving gaps behind.
DevOps model frameworks and CI/CD technology alignment.	Feeling of exclusion in the broader organization due to fixed CoE engagements.
The CoE's engagements dominated the backlog evolution (this is a positive, as those teams were the most advanced in the organization).	The CoE's engagements dominated the backlog CI/CD (this is a negative due to the feeling of exclusion for the rest of the organization and a lack of focus on their requirements).

Table 4.4 – Pros and cons of the three angles modus operandi CoE

Use case 2 – the model owner and tactical adoption enabler CoE

The parameters characterizing the second case are as follows:

- **DevOps operating model ownership**: DevOps CoE
- **Core CI/CD capabilities ownership**: Platform teams, outside the DevOps CoE
- **Client engagement services**: Available and specialized
- **Level of centralization**: Highly centralized

Design motivating factor: The logic behind this decision was that a single unit should hold the keys to the operating model and support the flagship tactical areas of the organization in adopting the model, while building business domain specialization. The latter was done with the intention of intensifying and accelerating the evolution in those areas and they eventually absorbed the CoE people. The CoE did not own any technological capabilities as the decision was made to bring the broader DevOps technological ecosystem under a single unit, called **Common Platforms**. The CoE was under the CIO's organization, based on the evolution's ownership:

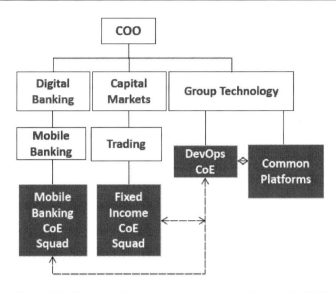

Figure 4.6 – The model owner and tactical adoption enabler CoE

The following table shows the pros and cons:

Pros	Cons
Standardization and simplification of DevOps practices across engagements.	The CoE could not scale outside the pre-defined client engagements.
Effective and tactical utilization of CoE resources focused on building the business IT area solutions.	The "DevOps gap" between those supported and not supported by the CoE widened.
Economies of scale through reusability.	Priorities and authority conflicts arose between the CoE and platform teams.
A single recognized owner and point of entry for the DevOps operating model.	The organization continuously and mistakenly thought that the CI/CD platform team was under the CoE, which resulted in communication and expectation complexity.
The CoE's engagements dominated the backlog model (*this is a positive, as those teams were the most advanced in the organization*).	The CoE's engagements dominated the backlog model (*this is a negative due to the rest of the organization feeling excluded and a lack of focus on their requirements*).
Cross-business IT areas experienced a certain degree of synergy driven by the CoE.	Due to their dedication to business IT areas, the CoE people lost the sense of belonging to the CoE.

Table 4.5 – Pros and cons of the model owner and tactical adoption CoE

Use case 3 – the enterprise CoE as part of a broader DevOps community of practice

The third use case we will discuss is quite a hybrid one. The parameters characterizing this use case are as follows:

- **DevOps operating model ownership**: Enterprise DevOps and business IT CoEs
- **Core CI/CD capabilities ownership**:
  - Enterprise DevOps CoE – group technology CI/CD
  - Business IT DevOps CoEs – own CI/CD pipelines
- **Client engagement services**: Not available
- **Level of centralization**: Highly decentralized

Motivating factor: Using a decentralized and hybrid setup, an enterprise CoE was created with ownership of the DevOps enterprise operating model and only the CI/CD used by the group technology engineering teams, without offering client engagement services. Each line of business had its own DevOps CoE responsible for local enterprise DevOps operating model adherence, but *with exceptions*, meaning they could follow their own path with exceptions granted by the enterprise CoE. The business IT DevOps CoEs handled their own internal client engagements, as well as owning the lines of business' common CI/CD pipelines. The reasoning was the existence of DevOps specializations per business domain and therefore focused domain expertise was required when adopting DevOps *locally*. All the CoEs together formed the DevOps **community of practice (CoP)**, with a mission to collectively align around the DevOps enterprise operating model's adoption and evolution:

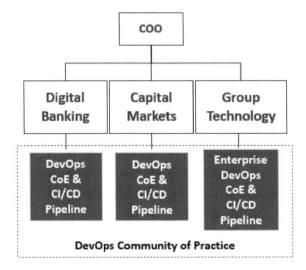

Figure 4.7 – The Enterprise CoE as part of a DevOps CoP

The following table shows the pros and cons:

Pros	Cons
Flexibility and focus on the lines of business, allowing them to evolve as required by the business context.	Cross-organizational standardization was made very complex.
A degree of sharing practices across the organization was achieved through the CoP.	Lack of transparency about the enterprise DevOps adoption "exceptions."
Economies of scale and cost management within business IT lines and group technology were achieved.	The CoP lost attention from its members in the long run, while unilateralism increased between the lines of business and the group technology.
The central ownership of the model was broadly recognized.	Lack of enablement teams in the group technology to support adoption.

Table 4.6 – The Enterprise CoE as part of a DevOps CoP pros and cons

Use case 4 – the CI/CD DevOps CoE

This is a simplistic use case and very much an example to avoid regarding setting up and operating DevOps CoEs. The parameters characterizing this use case are as follows:

- **DevOps operating model ownership**: Business IT areas
- **Core CI/CD capabilities ownership**: DevOps – common CI/CD pipeline
- **Client engagement services**: Not available
- **Level of centralization**: Ambiguous

Motivating factor: DevOps in this organization was simply perceived as the implementation of CI/CD pipelines and a team was established to centrally offer it as a service. It was only due to industry trends that it was given the *CoE* title.

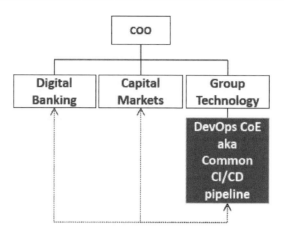

Figure 4.8 – The CI/CD DevOps CoE

You can probably guess that this type of CoE did not last long. It had no mandate on the DevOps adoption and was purely seen as a utility provider of a service that was already replicated in the lines of business. It achieved only limited standardization and simplification, with the CoE having almost zero visibility and involvement in the DevOps adoption taking place in the lines of business. Such CoEs are promptly either restructured into one of the preceding models or naturally or tactically terminated.

> **Which Approach Do I Propose?**
>
> It depends on your context, ambition, and capabilities, among other things. Going by experience only, I would choose a model between 1 and 2, as those are the ones I have seen delivering the most value and being decisive and sustainable in the long term.

The CoE's long-term ambitions

In the long run, as the evolution becomes organic and institutionalized, the CoE's importance, role, and necessity should be eliminated gradually, but in a controlled way.

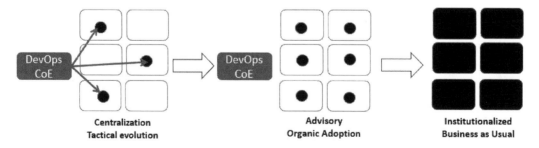

Figure 4.9 – The main phases of the CoE's life cycle toward scaled DevOps institutionalization

It is a paradox indeed, but the DevOps CoE and the broader organization have only truly delivered on their *DevOps promise* if one day, the CoE is not needed anymore, having enabled a DevOps institutionalized autonomy in the business IT teams. And the future of its people? No worries at all. They will be in high demand both internally and externally.

Summary

In this chapter, we introduced and discussed the value proposition of two very important functions/orchestrators of the DevOps evolution: the EA and the DevOps CoE. We highlighted the importance of the business domains, flows, and service criticalities for a DevOps evolution using two examples of trading and mobile payments. Later on, we discussed the four portfolio modernization options that incumbents have, along with providing the business case parameters and examples for each. We then deep-dived into the essence of reference architectures for the DevOps evolution, and we discussed six of them in further detail. Next, the establishment of an EA assembly was outlined, along with some further value proposition extension domains that EA as a function can support during the DevOps evolution.

The chapter continued by providing the DevOps evolution value proposition for the DevOps CoE, presented through four potential roles, each of which was discussed at length. Continuing, we focused on the tactical adoption enabler role and defined a sample service catalog, complemented by a CoE engagement example, demonstrating how the CoE can potentially add a combination of engineering and advisory value. Furthermore, we provided clarity and tips on the essential matters of staffing and funding the CoE in the form of advice from real lessons learned. Closing the chapter, we outlined and discussed the pros and cons of four different DevOps CoE real-world approaches taken by four different incumbent banks.

In the next chapter, we will learn about the fundamental aspects of defining the DevOps model's organizing principles through a proven practice and will examine how DevOps can be reconciled with business enterprise agility models in an agnostic way.

Business Enterprise Agility and DevOps Ways of Working Reconciliation

This chapter is related to the DevOps evolution **Ways of Working (WoW)** workstream and is divided into two main parts – the DevOps and business enterprise agility relation, reconciliation, and agnosticness as the first part and the design of the DevOps organizing principles in an agile context as the second part. We will start by providing a short overview of the relationship between DevOps and Agile, introducing the point that the two concepts can be reconciled agnostically. Then, we will discuss four agile models: basic agile, **Scaled Agile Framework (SAFe)**, Spotify, and value streams, all of which have been adopted by incumbents, while also providing an overview of their organizing structures. Moving on, we will discuss in depth the agile principles of autonomy and self-organization relating to an incumbent's DevOps context and outline the main reconciliation and agnosticness conceptual dimensions of DevOps and Agile.

In the second part of this chapter, we will outline a tested practice of how to design the organizing principles of DevOps evolution for agile teams while considering the element of relevance through an 11-step framework. We will use the Spotify model as the basis of business enterprise agility. As part of the 11-step framework, an array of guidelines, methods, and lessons learned, as well as points of consideration, will be presented.

In this chapter, we're going to cover the following main topics:

- The interrelation of Agile and DevOps
- Four examples of incumbents adopting business enterprise agility methods, focusing on basic agile, SAFe, the Spotify model, and value streams/clusters
- The paradox of autonomy and self-organization in Agile DevOps teams
- How DevOps can be agnostically reconciled with business enterprise agility

- A framework for designing DevOps organizing principles in an agnostic agile context

- At relevance elements that need to be taken into consideration

Business enterprise agility and DevOps reconciliation

Agile and DevOps are two concepts that have historically been interrelated in the industry, and this is no coincidence. Following this book's pattern of discussing real use cases of incumbents, in the first part of this chapter, we will look at four agility models adopted by four different incumbents. We will discover profound similarities in their expected outcomes and principles, and we will reveal their respective reconciliation dimensions and features regarding DevOps.

Why the interrelation of Agile and DevOps is natural and inevitable

To preserve space in this book, and for other obvious reasons, we will refrain from discussing in depth, both academically and theoretically, how Agile and DevOps are interrelated. I imagine this will be quite intuitive and familiar to you. The apparent interrelation and mutual inclusiveness of the two concepts is one of the reasons why it is a common phenomenon in the financial services industry to have them combined under *WoW evolutions*. It is indeed a universal truth that DevOps adoptions require agility fundamentals to be in place, and in order to achieve the objectives of Agile, DevOps capabilities need to be enabled. It is not only a matter of mutual success dependency but also a business case materialization objective, to increase the return on investment, by getting the most out of the two concepts in a given organization.

It is simple; you will not get the most out of a CI/CD pipeline (DevOps engineering) if your product teams do not plan and deliver their work incrementally (agility). Equally, you will not be able to measure progress based on working software (agility) if you do not have the means for automation and quality assurance (DevOps engineering) to deliver working software. With the same logic, you will not have cross-functional teams (agility) if you do not shift the operations people left in the **software development lifecycle**, also referred to as the **SDLC** (DevOps WoW). The examples can go on forever.

> **Proving a Point Early in This Chapter**
>
> Spend some time attempting to reconcile the principles of the Agile manifesto with the principles of DevOps one by one and relate them to real examples from your organization. You will discover that the principles of the two are 100% reconcilable, especially if you read between the lines in a couple of cases. They are also agnostic in the sense that each reconciled principle can be applied in any Agile and DevOps context. It is beautiful, isn't it?

But enough with the overarching (yet important in setting the scene) theoretical background. Let's get practical and down to the reality of this reconcilable relationship, starting with discussing the most well-established business enterprise agility models that incumbents adopt.

Four business enterprise agility methodologies

The term **business enterprise agility** has become very common in the industry and refers to the incumbent's ability to adapt rapidly to external environment changes, such as customer behavior, competitive rivalry, and new technological advancements, as mentioned in *Chapter 1, The Banking Context and DevOps Value Proposition*. Responding rapidly to events in the external environment requires agility in the internal business environment. For example, suppose there are French presidential elections taking place this coming Sunday and polls predict the victory of a candidate that global markets do not seem to favor. Therefore, you should be able to predict the volatility of Monday's markets and perhaps proactively handle the capacity of your trading systems, adjust the thresholds on your services' monitoring, double-check your auto-healing mechanism, conduct the markets opening operational readiness check earlier, and even execute a risk-hedging trading strategy on the business side. Being able to rapidly respond to either planned (such as elections) or unplanned (such as COVID-19) events through combining business and technological means is the core of business enterprise agility.

In this section, we will discuss four enterprise agility models through the lens of banking, inspired by how incumbents adopted them. Note that it is not in our scope to discuss every single detail of the models or compare them. The objective is to outline them and get a better understanding of the influence they can have on a DevOps evolution, as well as examining how DevOps can be agnostic to the business enterprise agility model.

Basic agility – the greenfield paradigm

This is the most basic Agile WoW setup and yet is a fundamental step in moving toward enterprise business agility in the long run. It is characterized more by *isolated agility* and not any methodology of scale based on domains, flows, or capabilities, as we will see in the other three models. Its main objective is to establish the fundamentals of agility with a focus on adopting Scrum and its ceremonies (backlog refinement and prioritization, sprint planning, and retrospectives), Kanban, or even **Scrumban** (combining elements of **Scrum** and **Kanban**). It also involves establishing agility-inspired roles, such as the product owners holding the product feature prioritization keys, the Scrum master ensuring that the agile teams have everything they need to deliver for a sprint, and the agile coach ensuring continuous evolution in the teams' agile WoW. This kind of setup is often observed both in business IT as well as infrastructure and technological utility teams, and we mostly find it in small new entrants to the industry or greenfield banks established by an incumbent parent. Some examples of the agile teams found in such a setup are as follows. Here, we are using a greenfield digital bank as an example:

- **Agile feature team**: Payments functionality in the mobile banking application's backend

- **Agile product team**: Temenos Banking-as-a-Service

- **(Agile) platform team**: Google Cloud Platform

The dependencies between the agile teams are mostly handled on a need-to-know basis by teams aligning individually or by simple portfolio planning mechanisms. In such setups, we observe relatively high autonomy and self-organization in the agile teams, characterized by a relative variation in WoW, organizing principles, topologies, and skill sets. Standardization and economies of scale are easier to achieve on the technological side due to their low complexity and lack of legacy.

Scaled business enterprise agility

Now, let's discuss scale by looking into business enterprise agility models that organize structures and principles. With the self-descriptive term **organizing structures and principles**, we refer to the structures and principles under which an incumbent is organized to adopt the respective model. It is important to clarify two things before we move on. Though most of the use case examples we will cover in this section come from business IT product areas, the models have also been applied to the infrastructure and technological utility areas within those incumbents' organizations, which is an important element from a DevOps evolution perspective. Another element of commonality across the three is that they use scaled portfolio planning mechanisms to synchronize their organizational structures.

SAFe – Scaled Agile Framework

The first of the scaled agile models we will look at is SAFe, which is widely adopted by several incumbents. To better relate it with the incumbent's content, we will use a customer account opening example from the digital banking domain.

What are the value streams?

Value streams are defined as the steps that an incumbent's teams need to follow to deliver an end-to-end solution (from concept to revenue) that continuously flows to the customer, in the form of either a product or a service. Normally, value streams are attributed to a specific business line, such as retail banking or capital markets, depending on the incumbent's business operating model. The fundamental usage of value streams is in identifying and understanding the sequence of steps that need to be executed and their chronological order, to add customer value, in addition to identifying bottlenecks and gaps in order to improve them. Do you remember the business-critical flow examples from *Chapter 4, Enterprise Architecture and the DevOps Center of Excellence*? It is the same concept, with the difference that in that chapter, it wasn't within our scope to cover end-to-end value streams, but only their critical path.

The anatomy of a value stream is based on three main elements:

- **Event trigger**: An important event that triggers the flow of value; for example, a customer fills in the online form to open a new deposit account

- **Steps**: The sequential activities that the incumbent needs to follow to successfully open the customer's new account

- **Value**: The final value that the customer receives (a new deposit account), upon successfully fulfilling the value stream's steps

What are the operational and development value streams?

In SAFe, value streams are primarily of two types, but there are also cases where the two are mixed:

- **Operational value streams**: The sequence of activities conducted and people who perform them, to deliver the final product or service to end clients. This final product is the one built by the development value streams:

  - A marketing specialist attracted the client through a targeted email, based on insights from the customer behavior insights analytics team.

  - A retail banking accounts officer reviewed the customer's application.

  - A compliance officer conducted the background checks.

  - Another retail banking accounts officer opened the deposit account.

- **Development value streams**: The sequence of activities that need to be conducted and the people who follow them to deliver a business solution by utilizing technological means:

  - The customer analytics application that was developed by the analytics IT agile team

  - The mobile banking application that was developed by the online banking agile team

  - The KYC application that was developed by the compliance IT agile team

The relationship between the two types of value streams is *one to many*, with several development value streams supporting an operational value stream (see *Figure 5.1*). The development value streams comprise agile teams, which are cross-functional and should contain all the necessary people and skills to ensure independent value delivery across the SDLC. The philosophy behind this approach is to enable the best possible autonomy level for each development value stream and eliminate dependencies at both the intra-value stream level and the operational value stream level:

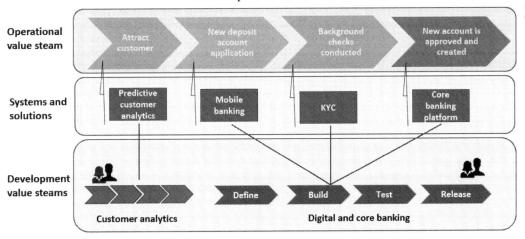

Figure 5.1 – Diagram of new deposits account opening value streams

Agile Release Trains (ARTs)

The concept of **Agile Release Trains (ARTs)** refers to a long-lasting and self-organized collection of Agile teams, which, along with other stakeholders, form a virtual organization that plans and delivers a particular operational value workstream together, aligned toward the same mission. ARTs also follow the objectives of cross-functionality, autonomy, and independence in delivering value. Depending on the size of the value stream and its products and services, the relationship of ARTs to it can be from *one to one* to *one (value stream) to many (ARTs)*.

Certain roles and topologies are applied to an ART. Let's take a look.

The roles are as follows:

- **Release train engineer**: A leadership role that facilitates the overall execution of the release train, including possible dependencies on other ARTs.

- **Product manager**: Responsible for the overall product and services roadmap.

- **ART architect**: Overlooking the entire ART's architectural matters.

- **Business owner**: A business stakeholder who holds the ultimate responsibility for the products and services delivered.

- **Agile teams**: They do the work.

The topologies are as follows:

- **Stream-aligned teams**: Organized around delivering direct end value to customers

- **Complicated subject teams**: Organized around subsystems that require deep expertise and specialization

- **Platform teams**: Organized around shared platform offerings to the agile teams

- **Enabling teams**: Organized around providing advancement support to the agile teams

Spotify model

The name of this model is borrowed from one of the world's largest audio streaming subscription service providers, Spotify. The Spotify model was first introduced to the industry in 2012 as a business and team agility model, inspired by how Spotify has organized and scaled its WoW to improve software development and product delivery agility. There are certain industry rumors on whether this is really the case, but they are not our concern. In this section, we will look at the core aspects of the model while using the risk business domain as an example.

What are the Spotify model's organizational structures?

The Spotify model consists of five main organizational and operational structures:

- Squads

- Tribes

- Chapters

- Guilds

- **Centers of excellence (CoEs)**

What is a squad?

A squad is an autonomous and self-organizing unit that is responsible for the design, implementation, launch, and operations of specific products and services within a certain business domain. They correspond to the agile team of SAFe. Taking the example of the business domain of risk, the following are possible squads:

- Squad 1: Market risk

- Squad 2: Credit risk

- Squad 3: Counterparty risk

- Squad 4: Liquidity risk

The roles and profiles that we will find in a squad vary per implementation and typically consist of software developers, operations engineers, DevOps engineers, **software development engineers in test (SDETs)**, cloud engineers, and architects. As with all models based on Scrum principles, each squad has a product owner (squad lead), Scrum master, and agile coach (usually shared across squads).

What is a tribe?

A tribe is a collection of squads that operate within the same business domain. For instance, the collection of squads that we provided as examples previously would all belong to a tribe called **group risk**, which is responsible for the incumbent's enterprise risk calculation and reporting activities. Typically, each tribe has two leadership profiles – a **tribe lead**, who is a senior director from the respective business line, and an **IT lead**, who is responsible for the technological aspects of the tribe. Another important role is played by the **tribe architect**, who overlooks the overall architectural evolution of the tribe and is usually linked closely to the tribe's representation in the DevOps evolution working groups. Tribes are formed not only around business domains but also around technological utilities, with concentrated DevOps capabilities platform teams being an example.

What is a chapter?

In the Spotify model, chapters are defined as the concertation of specific competencies in terms of people skills, knowledge, and expertise building. The typical chapters that you will find are as follows:

- Software development
- Operations engineering
- DevOps, referring to DevOps technological capabilities such as CI/CD
- Quality assurance engineering
- Cloud engineering

In essence, each squad consists of people from various chapters, and the versatility of their skills depends on the portfolio the squad supports and how it is to evolve in the future. Each chapter is led by a chapter lead, who is responsible for the HR and personal development matters of the chapter's members.

What is a guild?

Guilds represent informal structures across the chapters and squads of a single tribe or across tribes. The purpose of guilds is to share knowledge and best practices across several disciplines, as well as standardizing and achieving economies of scale. Typical guilds that you can find in industry adoptions are around streamlining and aligning the following:

- Operations, compliance, and quality assurance
- DevOps adoptions from a WoW and technological perspective
- Customer journey digitalization
- Public cloud capabilities and operating models

What are CoEs?

CoEs are staffed with scarce people/resources from various disciplines and domains and act as enablers that support a domain's advancements in the tribes. DevOps, enterprise architecture, quality assurance, and the cloud are common examples.

The following diagram shows the Spotify model's organizational structures and roles in terms of group risk and digital banking. In this example, the chapters that we covered previously have been depicted, along with how their members form cross-functional squads consisting of five profiles each. The two tribes are supported by the DevOps CoE in adopting the DevOps model and have formed a guild (joined two squads, one per tribe) to collectively pilot the new SDLC *compliance as code* framework:

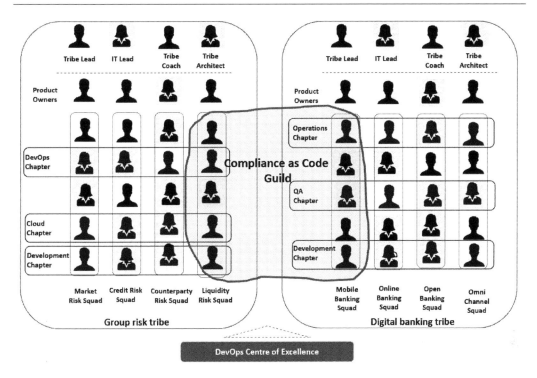

Figure 5.2 – Group risk and digital banking tribes representative example

Agile value streams or clusters

This model is not a formal industry framework or methodology but a construction of collective proven practices, which I have seen being labeled as either Agile value streams or clusters.

What are the organizational structures of Agile value streams or clusters?

The organizational structures of Agile value streams or clusters will remind you a little bit of SAFe in terms of the operational and development value streams approach and the Spotify model in terms of the business domains approach, while you will consider them identical from an autonomous and self-organizing Agile teams perspective.

What is a value stream or a cluster?

This is a collection of the needed capabilities, from a people, process, and technological perspective, to deliver end-to-end value for a particular business line. To explain this, we will use the example from the market's trade life cycle flow, which we saw in the previous chapter when discussing critical flows. The trade life cycle flow represents the end-to-end value that is created for the capital market clients, after the execution of sequential activities, which comprise various capabilities coming into play.

What is a sub-value stream or cluster?

This is a subset of a value stream or cluster that is independent, autonomous, and dedicated to a specific sub-business line of the value stream or cluster. For example, in the trade life cycle, we can have three major sub-value streams or clusters:

- **Trading front office**: Responsible for trading sales and execution
- **Trading back office**: Responsible for post-trade safekeeping and settlement
- **Trading middle office**: Responsible for trading risk and accounting calculations

What is a cross-sub-value stream or cluster?

These are temporary virtual structures where people across sub-value streams join forces for a certain period to deliver a large-scale program. This is normally either of a regulatory, internal restructuring, or scaled simplification nature. The following are examples from markets:

- FRTB and MiFID II regulatory programs
- Trading legal structure changes
- Consolidation and simplification of global assets trading activities

What are Agile teams?

Agile teams are autonomous and self-organized teams that belong to the sub-value streams or subclusters and are responsible for all the activities to design, build, deploy, and operate IT applications while utilizing cross-functional skills.

What are functional pods or tactical enablers?

These are highly specialized teams that support *on-demand* people allocation in the Agile teams for a certain period of time in a rotational mode. Rotational indicates movement from supporting one team to another. The pods consist mostly of people with expertise in advanced technologies that are rare across the DevOps technological and infrastructure ecosystem.

What are communities of practice?

Communities are where people across the value streams gather to share knowledge and experience on a particular domain. Examples include the DevOps **community of practice** (**CoP**; CI/CD proven practices), the quality assurance CoP (regression test proven practices), and the cloud CoP (application modernization best practices).

What are platform teams?

Platform teams also have an important role in value streams or clusters as they offer fundamental technological and infrastructure capabilities.

The following diagram shows the value stream or cluster organizing structures from the perspective of a representative incumbent, which focuses on the markets and core banking life cycles:

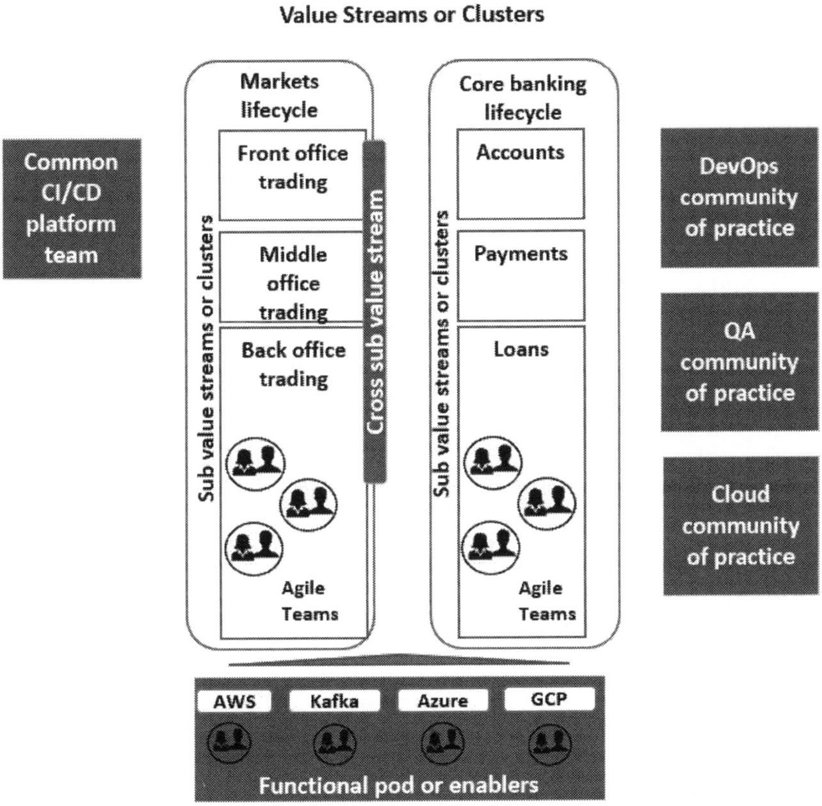

Figure 5.3 – Visual representation of the value streams or clusters organizing structure

What are the main roles of value streams or clusters?

At the value stream/cluster level and the sub-value stream/cluster level (that is, the value stream business lead and sub-value stream business lead), the following roles exist:

- **Business lead**: This is the business director, who has ultimate accountability for the products and services delivered by the value stream. This would be the global markets COO.

- **Tech lead**: This is the technology director, who has ultimate accountability for the technological aspects of the value stream. This would be the global markets CIO.

- **Agile coach**: This person overlooks the value stream's overall Agile journey.

- **Chief architects**: This person is responsible for the value stream's target portfolio architecture evolution, also in alignment with architectural dependencies from other value streams. Each of them is dedicated to a sub-value stream.

Business enterprise agility field guides and playbooks

A common tool that is used by incumbents to support their business enterprise agility evolution and adoption of the new WoW is what are commonly called **field guides** or **playbooks**. These are *manuals* on the steps to follow during the transition. The following are some common elements that you can find in those manuals:

- The value proposition of shifting to the new methodology

- The fundamental big shifts in agile practices between the old and new WoW

- Overview of the structures and ceremonies in the new setup

- Roles and responsibilities of the new organizational structures

- Guidelines on the enterprise portfolio planning mechanism

- Adoption steps and lessons learned from the areas that first piloted the transitions

This is an important artifact that must be reconciled with your DevOps evolution WoW organizing principles. Based on my experience, such agility field guides and playbooks usually lack a strong DevOps embodiment, which eventually results in inadequate designs and adoptions, characterized by concept reconciliation gaps in the long run, and often require the redesign of certain principles. In the next section, we will examine the dimensions that enable the DevOps and business enterprise agility model's **reconciliation agnosticness**.

DevOps and business enterprise agility agnosticness

So far, we have outlined and discussed the dominant business enterprise agility models that a representative sample of incumbents have either already adopted or are in the process of doing so.

There were three reasons why we outlined those models:

- To inspire you on potential approaches you can take

- To examine conceptual similarities across them that are related to the DevOps evolution

- To collect data so that you can make a point that DevOps and business enterprise agility models can be reconciled in an agnostic way

I hope you have got some inspiration! Before we look into the other two objectives, I would like to make an aside and discuss a *paradox* that the enterprise agility models we have discussed have in common that also has a broader influence on the DevOps evolution. This paradox is *autonomy and self-organization in an incumbent's context*.

Bringing clarity to the autonomy and self-organization paradox

Autonomy and self-organization can become ambiguous terms in your DevOps evolution, as on the one hand, they will be open to various interpretations that, in some cases, will be backed by personal motives of individuals and teams, while on the other hand require specific contextual characteristics that are probably absent from an incumbent's context. Therefore, it is of absolute importance to *DevOps decode* the two terms and come to a consensus about what those two principles imply for your DevOps context. Does, for instance, autonomy mean that our agile DevOps team can have their own priorities, bypassing the enterprise planning mechanisms, or does self-organization mean that they can bypass fundamental organizing principles and structure designs and therefore do it *their way*? To answer those questions, you need to provide convincing answers backed up by solid business justifications. Remember that you come from a hybrid setup of daily organizing principles and people could have developed certain habits that require persuasive and, in some cases, coercive means in order to change.

Decoding autonomy and self-organization in a DevOps context

A common objective in all business enterprise agility models is to enable autonomous and self-organizing agile teams, which should also be an objective for your DevOps WoW organizing principles. Let's attempt to decode those two terms in our DevOps context.

Understanding autonomy

Autonomy has ancient Greek roots as a term and means self-governed (αὐτόνομος; αὐτο meaning *self* and νόμος meaning *law*). Going by this definition, we can interpret that agile DevOps teams should have their own law and be self-governed in the way they operate. Now, self-governance also implies the absence of external interventions. But in a corporate environment of an incumbent, that is rarely the case (if at all). Top management business decisions, regulatory demand, and inevitable dependencies on other DevOps agile teams often jeopardize your ability to be self-governed. One way or another, in one shape or form, eventually, your agile DevOps teams will have to give up their right to autonomy. If you are being told you need to organize into squads; you need to prioritize compliance requirements above your backlog; you cannot have dedicated DevOps engineers in your squads; you cannot go directly to the public cloud, but need to wait for the landing zone to be ready; you cannot release daily because you have not yet been granted your license; and you cannot hire because you are under a hiring freeze; are you really autonomous? In an attempt to be self-governed, you will realize that you need to balance self-governance and central governance. *C'est la vie!*

Confusing autonomy with self-sufficiency

An anti-pattern that I have observed in several DevOps contexts is the mistaken conflation of autonomy with **self-sufficiency**. Self-sufficiency refers to an Agile DevOps team requiring little or no support and interaction with others. This mistaken interpretation is one of the main sources of DevOps complexity in organizations, especially in the domain of DevOps engineering, characterized by a proliferation of home-grown solutions, built under protectionism practices, and supporting self-sufficiency/empire-building motives. Under a self-sufficiency *modus operandi*, every team has its own CI/CD pipeline, observability tools, implementation of IT controls, means to verify access, and security policies – the list can go on. Self-sufficiency-driven implementations damage DevOps evolutions in the long run, bringing complexity, operational risk and cost, lack of compliance, and conflict of internal interests and priorities. Therefore, it is vital to make this distinction between autonomy and self-sufficiency clear to your agile DevOps teams.

Understanding self-organization

Self-organization is the ability of individuals to interact with each other to establish order without the need for external intervention. In our DevOps context, this means the agile DevOps teams establish an internal order to their daily *modus operandi* without constraints imposed on them by the broader organization. They can agree on how often they can release, how to monitor their services, who will be on call this weekend, and how many of the regression test cases will be automated and run in every build. But isn't this a paradox? How can we be self-organizing if, for instance, strict segregation of duties and identity and access management requirements are forced on our daily operations? If, for instance, Andrius, who is a developer, is only allowed to code and Paulius, who is an operations person, only does operations, your team is put into groups of self-organization boundaries, right?

The pragmatic conclusion

Please do not misperceive me, as my intention is not to make autonomy and self-organization seem impossible. Quite the opposite – especially for true agile DevOps teams of high maturity, essential elements of autonomy and self-organization elements can be observed. But still, my experience in the financial services industry taught me a lesson, through constant repetition: *Be pragmatic and do not fall into "buzzword" fallacies*. In a real banking context of a systemically important incumbent, agile DevOps teams cannot be fully autonomous and their ability to self-organize will be frequently compromised.

The most suitable phrase that summarizes this reality is *DevOps organizationally aligns autonomy through the ability to self-organize where applicable*. I appreciate it sounds paradoxical, but this is the reality. There are mechanisms through which teams can apply for greater autonomy and self-organization and gain the corresponding allowance, as we will see later in this book.

> **Self-Determination, Sovereignty, and Organized Hypocrisy**
>
> These three international relations terms always come to my mind when I hear about teams' autonomy and self-organization in DevOps. In international relations, self-determination refers to the legal right of people (referring to nations) to define their destiny in the international system through the creation of states. Sovereignty refers to the ability of a state to self-govern, after its self-determination, without any external intervention. Does this sound similar to the autonomy we described previously? We all know, however, that, in many cases, state sovereignty is compromised by other states (humanitarian intervention) or due to belonging to a global governance body (European Union). This fact of sovereignty, which is, in essence, fragile and compromised, is called **organized hypocrisy** in international relations. This is the paradox of being recognized as self-governed without being self-governed.

What are the reconciliation agnosticness dimensions?

The agnostic nature of business enterprise agility modes and DevOps can be observed across four major dimensions, with countless subdimensions that rise through the conduct of the actual reconciliation activity:

- General principles that underpin the concept, as we saw earlier in this chapter
- The expected outcomes that aim to be achieved by the concept's adoption
- Common organizing structures and mechanisms that are deployed in each team
- Specific DevOps implementation principles that can be applied in any agile team

Before we look into the outcomes, organizing structures, mechanisms, and implementation principles, let's define what agnostic means. In our DevOps context, agnostic means being able to reconcile different concepts (agile) and adapt to different contexts (incumbents) without significant alterations. In other words, a DevOps 360° operating model can and must be reconciled with the basic agile model, SAFe, the Spotify model, and the value streams model in different incumbents' contexts, without major alternations.

Reconcilable and agnostic desired outcomes

The following are outcomes that characterize both business enterprise agility and DevOps:

- Ensure consistency and reusability.
- Improve speed of delivery and time to market.
- Improve productivity and experience.
- Get close with the business partners.
- Improve customer outcomes and value.

- Focus on end-to-end value and flows instead of isolated products and services.

- Improve business performance and agility.

- Optimize delivery performance and operational efficiency, eliminating lead times.

Reconcilable and agnostic organizational structures and mechanisms

Both DevOps and business enterprise agility models recognize the importance of utilizing the following organizational structures and mechanisms:

- **Platform teams**: On achieving harmonized scale and respective economies, it is a necessity to have solid and reliable DevOps platforms that offer a wide range of DevOps engineering capabilities, products, and services.

- **Shared services**: Their importance in supporting operational efficiency and improving DevOps productivity is recognized.

- **DevOps CoEs, CoPs, and enablement teams**: The value of CoEs, CoPs, and enablement teams to support and facilitate the adoption in the DevOps agile teams is a commonality.

- **Value flows**: Mechanisms of end-to-end value delivery as well as end-to-end feedback loops have a special position in both concepts.

- **Organizational applicability**: Both concepts recognize the importance of being equally adopted across the organization both by business IT teams and also infrastructure and technological functions, as well as utility functions.

- **Software development methodology**: Scrum is at the heart of both concepts.

- **Enterprise portfolio planning**: This is a synchronization and alignment mechanism that is set up through the business enterprise agility models and is utilized by the DevOps evolution as part of DevOps enablement and adoption.

DevOps Lessons Learned on Organizing Structures

Once upon a time, there was an incumbent bank adopting the Spotify model with the ambition to have all the newly established tribes moving from shadow IT CI/CD pipelines to the central one. For this purpose, they decided to omit DevOps (also known as CI/CD engineering) chapters, under the belief that in the absence of dedicated CI/CD engineers, the squads would be forced to migrate to the central offering. I leave it to your imagination to guess how effective this approach was and what its impact was on the overall DevOps transformation.

Reconcilable and agnostic DevOps implementation principles in agile teams

Regardless of the business enterprise agility model that you go with, and even if you do not have just one, the deployment of DevOps principles in DevOps agile teams should and can be agnostic. This will help you avoid *DevOps disruptions*, in case your business enterprise agility model changes in the future, enabling a *DevOps lift-and-shift* approach if need be. Certain DevOps implementation principles can be adopted in any agile DevOps team, despite the enterprise agility model under which it operates:

- Shift operations left, operationally and organizationally.

- Embed DevOps engineers in the agile DevOps teams.

- Automate and optimize across the SDLC.

- Utilize technological common platforms and CoEs.

- Be measured upon commonly agreed DevOps performance measurements.

- Organize under segregation/separation of tasks and not duties.

- Build compliance and security by design across your portfolio.

- Adopt DevOps capabilities at relevance across your portfolio.

- Cater for multi-speeds across your portfolio.

- Offload any operational overhead to shared services.

- Enable DevOps skills cross-functionality across the SDLC.

- Continuously identify and implement DevOps improvements.

I am certain that the preceding dimensions provide clarity on the concepts that enable concept reconciliation while keeping a context-agnostic character. While it might sound simple, needless to say it requires effort, experience, creativity, and organization, along with a little bit of *reading between the concept's lines*, to achieve a practical high degree of reconciliation and agnosticness between Agile and DevOps.

Agile DevOps teams – organizing principles design

In the second part of this chapter, starting with this section, we will look at an approach to define the core of your DevOps 360 model WoW by examining organizing and, consequently, operating principles. This exercise is fundamental as it lays the foundation of how you will organize from a DevOps context perspective, which will sequentially be reconciled with your business enterprise agility model, comprising your complete Agile DevOps WoW model. In the upcoming sections, we will outline a proven approach to conduct this exercise in the form of steps. We will take a representative real-world example and use the Spotify model as the business enterprise agility model.

> **Tip**
>
> This exercise should be carried out behind closed doors to ensure minimal organizational disturbance, resistance, and uncertainty. Due to its influence on upcoming responsibility distribution, it can turn into a diplomatic and political matter, so it is advisable that, among the governing bodies of your evolution, you build an early coalition on the precise expected outcome and steer the exercise accordingly. You get my point, right? Before involving people within the governing bodies, you already know the potential outcomes of the exercise.

In the upcoming sections, we will outline and describe the steps to be followed, which, when conducting the exercise in real life, should be executed iteratively.

Step 1 – defining the core capabilities and actors

We propose four main groups to be part of this exercise:

- **DevOps 360° vision authority**: To resolve any potential disputes and make the ultimate decisions, as well as granting intermediate approvals

- **The DevOps 360° design and advocacy group and the DevOps CoE**: To orchestrate the primary and secondary actors and be the counterpart for the vision authority

- The DevOps WoW workstream (recall the workstreams we defined in *Chapter 3, The DevOps 360° Operating Model Pillars and Governance Model*), which will be subdivided into two main groups:

  - **Primary actors**: The people directly involved with building and running software. They are part of the business tribes – that is, Agile DevOps teams. This also includes software developers and application operations specialists, some of which should already be part of your DevOps 360° design and advocacy group.

  - **Secondary actors**: A selection of stakeholders from the broader DevOps ecosystem to whom the primary actors have a first-level dependency from a DevOps perspective. CI/CD tooling and core infrastructure teams, shared services, and CoEs can be on this list, which can grow to the extent you please. Some of those should also already be in the DevOps 360° design and advocacy group, as well as in the squad or satellite members of other workstreams.

Each actor should represent a DevOps capability, and it is proposed that you start outlining the capabilities before you appoint anyone. As a technology director told me once, "*Don't tell me who you need, but what you need them for.*" Needless to say, the appointed people must have deep and well-rounded DevOps experience, meaning that they can see the big picture while having the ability to deep dive into the details.

> **Tip**
>
> In choosing the actors, try to be as broad as possible in terms of state-of-the-art DevOps operating models, business lines, and technological foundation. Remember that your outcome will be enterprise applicable and that you must capture the best possible extent of contextual variations.

Step 2 – capturing the detailed business enterprise agility model

Ensure that you have captured and communicated both the big picture and the details of the chosen business enterprise agility model to those involved. Simply put, get them to read and understand the agile field guide/playbook. As we discussed earlier in this chapter, the business enterprise agility model has probably been developed in advance, so you need to tap into that and even propose amendments to it after completing the exercise.

Step 3 – capturing the detailed regulatory/compliance context

It is an absolute necessity that you do your regulatory homework and have a fair idea of which organizing principles model you wish to end up with, with those that were initially validated across the respective compliance and audit functions. The primary area of interest is identity and access management to production, including infrastructure, data, and business logic, as well as people roles from a separation/segregation of duties perspective. Also, any specific requirements on organizational structure, such as people having operations responsibilities, people being unable to report to a squad product owner, or that people accessing very restricted and confidential data should report to a product owner, need to be captured. In addition, get clarity on whether you are subject to hardcore separation/segregation of duties policies or whether flexible *just-in-time access* mechanisms on accessing production data, given valid business justifications, are considered adequate. The inability to conduct the compliance background check well in advance may lead to the outcome of the organizing principles exercise either not complying at all or only partially complying, with significant engineering efforts required. I warned you!

> **Reminder**
>
> If we ever meet, remind me to tell you the story of the 10 gaps that we identified in an incumbent's capabilities during the organizing principles adoption feasibility study.

Step 4 – capturing the current Agile DevOps teams' topologies

There are mainly two ways to evolve from the old WoW to the new one:

- Start with the current state of the art and evolve it to the future, gradually.

- Define the future desired state and work backward, again gradually.

I propose you start with the future desired state and work backward. It is always more refreshing, provides people with a new perspective, and makes them forget existing constraints and boundaries, allowing them to unleash their creativity on what an ideal future fit would look like. Then, once you have the ideal defined, you work backward through the steps required until you reach the current context. But to work backward, you need to have a fair idea of how your current topologies are shaped.

Having said this, you need to document in some way the current state for various reasons, including the principle of *do not attempt to change something if you do not know it well*. Capturing the context of your current organizing principles will serve various objectives, including the following:

- Ensure that your target organizing principles are not too challenging to be adopted.

- Your teams will be able to identify themselves and plan a gradual evolution.

- You can define options for your evolution journeys and transition playbooks, as not all teams will have the same destination. Remember that we evolve DevOps *at relevance and in a multi-speed incumbent*.

- Provides visibility on the enterprise effort ahead to complete the transition.

Let us have a look at the most frequent scenarios that can be seen in the context of an incumbent bank:

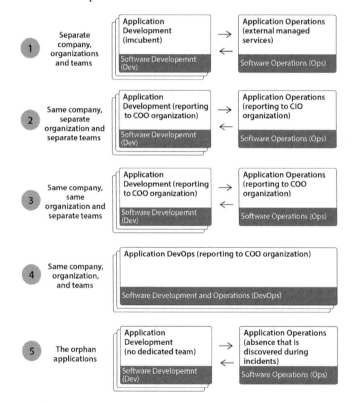

Figure 5.4 – The common models of the primary actors that you can find coexisting in an incumbent

Naturally, you can challenge me here and say, "*Spyridon, you have been saying from the beginning of this book that DevOps should be adopted at relevance. What is wrong with the five different models, if all five are relevant?*" The answer is that there is nothing wrong, so long as there is a strong business value proposition on why teams have chosen model one and not two. For instance, there is transparency and clarity on the decision's business line justification, but also the necessary means to prove its regulatory compliance, as well as ensuring the elimination of any doubt of operating model overcomplications due to "just because" arguments. Moreover, due to the impact of your enterprise agility model organizing structures, you will be forced to streamline, so in many cases, it is simply a matter of choosing between options A and B. Later in this section, we will prove that only two models, with small modifications, can fit any context, business justification, and value proposition.

The Organized Anarchy Paradox

In international relations, this term refers to the absence of a supreme authority to govern the international system of states. As mentioned in the example of the Leviathan (*Chapter 3, The DevOps 360° Operating Model Pillars and Governance Model*), the lack of a central government equals anarchy in some theories of international relations. But looking at our international system, states managed to get organized despite the absence of a universal government. This is called **organized anarchy**. Looking at the variation of DevOps organizing principles in the preceding diagram, the situation looks *anarchical*, though it is paradoxically organized to some extent.

Talking about grasping the current topologies and organizing principles, I can assume with high confidence that you do not have insights into how every single Agile team across your firm is currently organized and, at the same time, you do not have the percentage allocation for each of the various organizing principle models. I also assume that the five models presented previously are the dominant models in your organization, and you will certainly discover a sixth one along the way. I used to call this sixth model the *God knows what they do* one. On grasping the most accurate situation that currently characterizes your organization, I propose you use the representatives of the DevOps design and advocacy group, as well as your primary and secondary actors of the exercise, and then take the parts of the organization they represent as samples, having the outcome validated by the vision authority group.

Across the possible topologies and organizing principle models mentioned previously, we can usually identify some specific and rather typical characteristics:

- Fragmentation of organization structures, planning, and delivery mechanisms.

- A hybrid "waterfall and agile" working methodology.

- Ambiguity on separation/segregation of duties policies.

- Application operations and infrastructure teams are not an integral part of the SDLC.

- Development teams own a wide range of home-grown shadow IT solutions.
- Lack of clarity on SDLC processes and policy adherence requirements.
- Ambiguous utilization of common platforms, shared services, and functions.

Step 5 – getting the notation and templates defined

Provide the exercise's actors with some common templates and notation so that, on the one hand, you get to standardize the output, but also so that they use the same language. You can use any notation you feel comfortable with, which may be one that you have traditionally developed within your organization. In our example, I will use the notation I've been using for years as I do not wish to direct you toward any specific methodology and also because I have seen it working with my own eyes. When defining the notation, you should primarily focus on the following aspects:

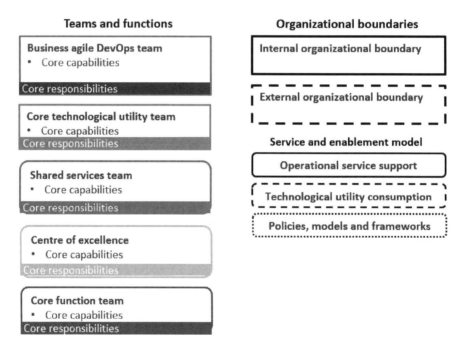

Figure 5.5 – Spyridon's topologies and organizing principles notation

Note that if you cannot fit all your exercise's actors into your notation, this means that you need to enrich either the notation or the list of people you appointed.

Step 6 – setting the approach and principles of the design

You need to clearly define the approach to conducting the exercise and set the guiding principles, especially to be able to steer the result if need be.

Approach 1 – starting to design the core Agile DevOps teams and then expanding

It is proposed that you start with the primary actor's organizing principles and gradually expand toward the broader DevOps ecosystem:

- **View 1 – Agile DevOps squad zoom-in**: Start with the organizing principles of the Agile DevOps teams.

- **View 2 – fundamental DevOps utilities and keeping the lights on**: Expand from the Agile DevOps teams to the most fundamental secondary actors to DevOps.

- **View 3 – expanded ecosystem**: Start broadening to the extent you please.

Approach 2 – taking the future technological landscape perspective first

Even though you need to cater to a hybrid technological landscape of business IT applications, spanning mainframe and public cloud platforms, it is advised that you start with the most modern part of your portfolio, in this case using the *shift right* principle of portfolio classification, as we will see in *Chapter 9, The DevOps Portfolio Classification and Governance*.

Approach 3 – splitting the actors based on the hybrid context and expertise

Ideally, set up a minimum of two groups working in isolation with a hybrid mix of DevOps backgrounds and experiences. Allocate people equally from the design and advocacy authority and the DevOps CoE between each group so that they can steer and coordinate, if need be, but also proactively inform the vision authority about any rising concerns.

Approach 4 – designing principles, guidelines, and considerations

Each group should come up with two models: a proposed one and an alternative one. In doing so, they should consider the following principles, guidelines, and considerations:

- Ignore historical organizational dynamics/structures that led to the current setup.

- Be forward-looking in terms of the capabilities of the DevOps evolution.

- Shift as many capabilities as you can to the left of the SDLC.

- Balance self-sufficiency with economies of scale and operational efficiency.

- Consider the full utilization of platforms, shared services, and functions.

- Cater to a hybrid technological portfolio in each squad.

- Consider access management and separation/segregation of duties principles.

- Business line context, proximity, and relevance are important.

- Make it flexible to evolve in the future and business enterprise agility agnostic.

Step 7 – conducting the actual design

This step is about doing the actual work. In our representative example, our groups were quite aligned and came up with identical proposed and alternative models. Let's see how they evolved with some interesting *at-relevance* elements arising.

View 1 – Agile DevOps squad zoom-in

The purpose of this view is to focus specifically on the Agile DevOps teams, which constitute the core of the exercise.

The proposed – dynamic/rotational model

The people that build and run software are perceived to be the same person, under the role of the *software developer*, in a *you build it, you run it modus operandi*, and are part of the same squad. Using the squad names from the *Spotify model* section of this chapter, according to this model, the market risk squad consists of developers that also conduct operations in a rotational mode. For instance, if the squad comprises five developers, one out of the five is responsible for performing operations every week with this person rotating. When not much is required from an operational perspective, the person contributes to operational improvements, which are part of the backlog. The value proposition for this model is that small- to medium-sized platforms and applications that are not exposed to external clients have low to moderate production support needs and do not contain **personally identifiable information (PII)**, so a dynamic separation of tasks model provides more flexibility, autonomy, and operational efficiencies.

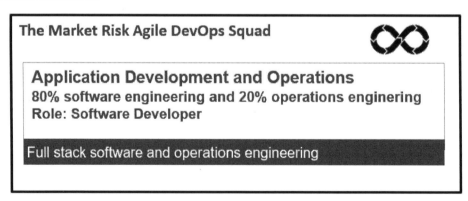

Figure 5.6 – The dynamic/rotational model – separation/segregation of tasks

The exercise's actor found a good number of platforms and applications potentially falling into that category, and some have already been operating under those organizing principles successfully.

The Story of an Angry Aurimas

While discussing the percentage split between development and operations, during the exercise, Tomasz, driven by proven practices, proposed a target of 80% capacity allocation to software development and 20% to operations. Aurimas reacted with *"Why should we allocate fixed boundaries to certain activities? This is micromanagement!"* He continued, *"Just tell me what the performance indicators are that I need to meet and let me organize my team myself!"* Both made strong points. Tomasz was setting the right ambition. Shifting operations left in the SDLC would enable us to spend a maximum of 20% of our agile team's capacity on operations. Aurimas was also right in avoiding the definition of capacity boundaries on how the allocation of people should be managed. Set the performance indicators and let the team self-organize to meet them.

The alternative – fixed model

A separation/segregation of duties is proposed between the people doing software development and those doing software operations. However, both roles are proposed to be part of the same squad, with the operations people shifted left in the SDLC. It is also proposed that you have the operations people's skills uplifted from an engineering perspective so that they can contribute to the actual product and service innovation backlog by approximately 50% initially. The goal is for this percentage to further increase through operational stability and improved efficiency:

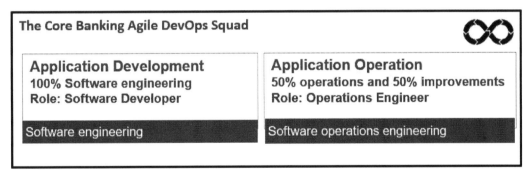

Figure 5.7 – Fixed roles model – separation/segregation of duties

The arguments, as with the proposed solution, were pointing again to the same elements of relevance, such as the platforms and the size of the teams, exposure of the platforms to external clients, large internal business segments, data confidentiality, and the critical need to have people dedicated to production inquires, with speed and proximity being crucial factors of customer satisfaction. There's also the fact that large platforms turn out to be more business-critical and have a higher focus from a regulatory perspective.

Defining the roles further to the core software development and operations

Once you're done with the core roles of this view, it is the right moment to drill down to the roles and profiles that a squad will need to be cross-functional. This will have an impact on the chapters that you will have to define. For instance, in both models of our representative example, people asked for DevOps, cloud, and test engineers to be embedded in each squad to facilitate the DevOps evolution from an engineering perspective. This request creates demand for the business enterprise agility model to cater to DevOps, cloud, and QA chapters, if they're not already in the plan.

Tip

Please do not make the mistake of thinking that in your Agile DevOps teams, you do not need dedicated DevOps engineering profiles, believing that developers will be enough to advance your DevOps engineering adoption. Especially in large setups, such as core banking, you need dedicated DevOps engineering people focusing on DevOps engineering solutions that developers can use. The absence of those profiles is one of the top reasons for DevOps evolutions slowing down.

View 2 – fundamental utilities and keeping the lights on

Having organized the Agile DevOps team, it is time to start including the teams that provide fundamental DevOps utilities and keep the lights on.

The proposed – dynamic/rotational model

An evolution toward *View 2* in the dominant model is shown in the following diagram:

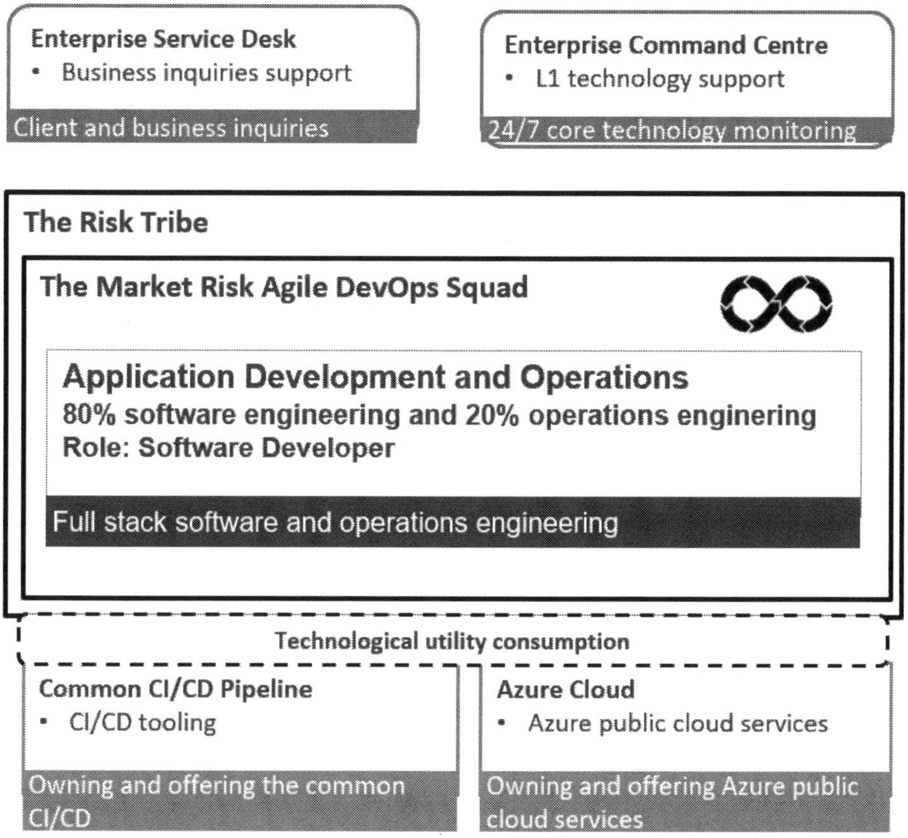

Figure 5.8 – View 2 of the dynamic model

As you can see, the technological utilities of common CI/CD pipelines and the Azure cloud have been added, where the squad is to consume the corresponding technologies and embed them into its SDLC. We have also added two shared services – the enterprise service desk (used for business support inquiries) and the enterprise command center (used for first-level technological support inquiries). Since we have smaller and more compact teams in this model, it has been decided that the squads in this model do not utilize those two shared services and have become self-sufficient both from a business and technical support perspective. This means that the market risk squad in our example will handle the full cycle support of the market risk portfolio from a business inquiry perspective as well as a first-line-of-operations perspective. However, it was proposed to leave the option open and let the team decide whether to utilize the shared services, upon agreement with the respective shared services teams.

The alternative – fixed roles

The approach that has been proposed for the alternative model looks slightly different, and this is where context, speed, and relevance again become important. For the teams falling under the alternative, it was proposed to utilize the common technological utilities as well as the shared services utilities. The latter has two consequences on the organizing principles – the core banking squad in our example will not be responsible for business support inquiries as this responsibility will move to the enterprise service desk. It will also not be the one performing first-level operations support, as this will move to the enterprise command center. However, both shared services, on top of ensuring the handover of responsibilities, will have to establish a feedback loop process toward the squad so that L1 business and technological inquiries can be fed back to the Agile DevOps squad for backlog improvement items. L2 support remains with the Agile DevOps squad.

What were the reasons behind those decisions? Let's take a look:

- Due to the scale of the core banking platform and its scale on the business nature of facing external and internal client, the business inquiries are of high load and have strict SLAs, which require business line knowledge specialization. Having a dedicated core banking business officers squad sitting at the enterprise service desk is more effective.

- The core banking platform backlog requires full undistracted capacity due to its richness but also the business line's aggressive time-to-market targets. Minimization of production support disturbance will increase DevOps productivity.

- As the operations people have shifted left in the SDLC, the ambition is to minimize the operations *noise* toward them so that they can focus on improving the platform through engineering work.

- The incumbent bank's internal data has proven that handing over L1 to the global enterprise center has minimized the requests that reach the development and operations team by 50% and supported the increase in the mean time to detect and recover.

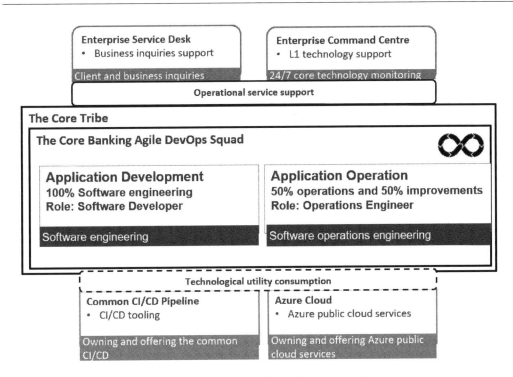

Figure 5.9 – View 2 of the fixed-roles model

A special situation: The markets trading floor flavor on dedicated support services

In both the rotational and fixed models, there is a subflavor when it comes to the utilization of shared services such as service desks and command centers, which is very much related to the nature and proximity of the business line, complemented by zero tolerance for latency and mean time to detect and recover. For example, across capital market areas on incumbents, I have seen a dedicated-to-market service desk, with people sitting next to the traders (literally), and dedicated reliability engineers also sitting next to the traders (literally), resolving inquiries such as `trade_ids` missing books, the trader blotter not loading, and trade amendment confirmation being processed. It happens I had both roles once upon a time supporting global rates interbank trading, and it was a super insightful experience.

The Story of an Angry Dan

It was a Friday and in the DevOps vision authority group, the outcome of our organizing principle's work was being presented. Do you remember in *Chapter 3, The DevOps 360° Operating Model Pillars and Governance Model* how I advised you to check these group members' temperatures individually? I did not before that meeting. When presenting the alternative model's part of offloading technical L1 to the enterprise command center, Dan got furious. "*This is not agile, it is not DevOps, and it violates self-organization.*" He continued, "*Who came up with this idea?*" I responded, "*Jan and Amit from your team did, arguing that it will help increase the team's productivity and minimize the MTTR.*" This topic dominated the meeting on that day, but I will get to the point. For particular areas of your organization, it makes sense to offload L1 support to shared services, even though it does not sound *agile*. It may sound like something from old-school ITIL v1 books and against DevOps principles, but when it comes to autonomy, it's worth compromising for operational efficiency and productivity gains.

View 3 – expanded ecosystem

From this point on, you should start expanding and stop when you believe that you have sufficiently covered the broader DevOps ecosystem of stakeholders. In our representative example, there was consensus that both models are to utilize the outcome of the DevOps and Enterprise Architecture CoE's work in terms of the DevOps 360° operating model and reference architectures, as well as following the policies and procedures of the enterprise service governance and IT risk controls functions. The following diagram shows the representation of the fixed roles model:

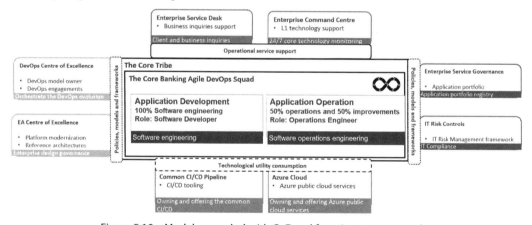

Figure 5.10 – Model expanded with CoE and function team examples

Final remarks on this step

Of course, this was just a representative yet pragmatic and practical example. Naturally, there are also other variations and subvariations of models that your context and ambitions might lead you to examine and adopt, while every model will inevitably have its advantages and disadvantages. However, some fundamental DevOps design principles and *at-relevance elements*, such as shifting operations left, considering business proximity, assessing the usage of managed services and CoEs, and considering compliance and client impact are common and agnostic. Also, it is important to make clear that even though in our example we focused on business Agile DevOps teams being the primary actor, the same exercise needs to be conducted on the technological utilities of your organization.

Step 8 – evaluating based on predefined criteria

Once you have the proposals, you need to evaluate them across some common parameters, which can take the form of a questionnaire. Those parameters should have already been defined as part of the exercise's homework. I advise you to ask the following questions:

- Do you see compliance gaps that can put your license to operate at risk?
- Do you see issues of adaptability if the business enterprise agility model changes?
- Do you foresee any severe constraints during the adoption by the tribes?
- Can you spot hardcoded elements that will be difficult to adjust?
- Do you foresee any conflict with other models adopted in the organization?
- Does it require shared utility capabilities that are currently not enabled?
- Does it require adjustments in the business enterprise agility model?

Step 9 – feasibility study and compliance foundation

This is the point when you need to open up consciously to the actors of the exercise and carefully and ask them to break the model, while also asking them to point out whether they see design gaps from the perspective of the part of the organization they represent. Ideally, you should also bring people from areas that currently operate under those models so that they can share their experience and provide solid arguments for potential concerns raised.

Mind the compliance part in the early days

Incumbents, especially systemically important ones, are under strict regulatory supervision. Two of the main areas of regulatory concern are as follows:

- **Separation/segregation of duties**: Referring to which role is responsible for what within the organization.
- **Identity and access management**: Based on the separation/segregation of duties policy, this specifies what access each role requires, focusing on read, write, and execute.

A typical and traditional *hardcoded* separation/segregation of duties and identity and access management example is as follows:

Role	Access
Developer	Non-production data
DevOps engineer	
Test engineer	
Operations	Production data
Application specialist	
Reliability engineer	

Table 5.1 – Family hierarchy and basic access principles

The primary concern relating to the separation/segregation of duties and identity and access management is the following parameters. As part of the Agile DevOps team organizing principles, you need to come up with the respective requirements on roles and access while highlighting the differences between the proposed and alternative models:

- **Production IT assets**: Servers, databases, messaging queues, and logs

- **Production data**: Any data stored and used in the production of IT assets

- **Business logic repos**: Functional code repositories

- **Operational logic repos**: Non-functional code repositories

- **Development and operational tools (also known as DevOps)**: CI/CD, ITSM, and observability

- **Test environments**

We will come back to this topic in *Chapter 8, 360° Regulatory Compliance as Code* where we will focus on compliance as code.

Step 10 – defining the basis for a job description

As you design the organizing principles and define the required roles, you need to start drafting the basis for the job descriptions, primarily for three reasons:

- Input for the incubation plan in terms of competencies, as we will see in *Chapter 13, Site Reliability Engineering in the FSI*

- Input for the DevOps WoW white paper on responsibilities

- The DevOps capability responsibility demarcation and direction based on the organizing principles need to be defined:

  - DevOps engineers are utilizing the common CI/CD pipelines to onboard the applications of the squad they support, through the migration of home-grown solutions where applicable.

- DevOps engineers build their own CI/CD solutions according to the squads' internal discretion, using the common CI/CD pipelines where applicable.

Step 11 – defining the DevOps WoW white paper

It might sound like an old-school practice, but it is not from a practical perspective: legalize your DevOps evolution operating constitution to specify who is accountable and responsible for what in terms of your daily *modus operandi*. Remember that you are coming from a proliferation of hybrid operating models situation in a condition of *organized anarchy*, where there might even be extreme variations of who is currently responsible for what. For instance, in your market domains, the development teams and not the operations teams might be responsible for deployments, while in transaction banking, the operations team is responsible for deployments, while in domains where responsibilities are *gray zones*, neither the development teams nor the operations team is responsible, and certain activities are conducted based on convenience.

When conducting the white paper exercise, please consider the following:

- It will eventually become a diplomatic game as some will have to give up autonomy, responsibility, and authority.
- Avoid any (at least) obvious favoritism toward particular teams.
- The purpose is not to put boundaries on the team's self-organization but to create clarity.
- It might trigger or be triggered by organizational changes.
- Nonproliferation agreements on duplicated solutions must be included.
- The broader DevOps ecosystem capability owners and providers should be included.
- It should be a binding agreement and part of your firm's broader operating model.
- Cater for flexibility and allow deviations from it on non-core responsibilities.
- It needs to be reconciled with your enterprise business agile field guide/playbook.

A Band Analogy for Responsibility Realignment

When conducting responsibilities realignment, make sure that people have the necessary skills and means to fulfill them. If not, create a skills uplift/incubation plan. Do not just reassign responsibilities in the form of baptism. Think of a band. Giving the drummer's responsibility to the vocalist and the guitarist's responsibility to the drummer just to refresh the band wouldn't be a good idea.

Summary

In this chapter, we discussed the foundation of the DevOps evolution's WoW, combining business enterprise agility and DevOps organizing principles in a way that proves the ability to reconcile the two concepts agnostically. We went through four examples of Agile adoptions by incumbents (basic Agile, SAFe, the Spotify model, and value streams/clusters), relating them to banking context adoption examples. By doing so, we discovered similarities in their organizational structures in terms of principles and objectives. We also discovered several similarities across four dimensions from a DevOps evolution perspective and explained how those similarities enable the concepts to be *agnostically reconciled*. We also mentioned the principles of autonomy and self-organization and provided arguments on why they cannot be perfectly achieved in an incumbent's DevOps context. Continuing, we provided an 11-step guide, based on a proven practice, on how to design the organizing principles of the Agile DevOps teams' evolution; we used the Spotify model as the business enterprise agility model. We also examined the core aspects of the exercise, such as actor and capability identification, the importance of the *state of the art* in organizing principles and compliance background work, the relevant elements that influence the designs, as well as what questions to ask during the model evaluation. We concluded that the outcome should be documented in a white paper and outlined considerations to make once the actual artifact has been defined.

In the next chapter, we officially enter the second part of this book on the *DevOps capabilities evolution and enablement*. In particular, we will look into what I call the DevOps *backbone* and discuss the importance of evolving, interoperating, and engineering your DevOps SDLC.

Part 3: Capability Engineering, Enablement, and Launch

This part will focus on how to design the new 360° operating model capabilities, focusing on primarily three domains: technology ecosystem, software development lifecycle, and compliance as code.

This part of the book comprises the following chapters:

- *Chapter 6, DevOps Software Development Life Cycle 360° Evolution and Engineering*
- *Chapter 7, The DevOps 360° Technological Ecosystem as a Service*
- *Chapter 8, 360° Regulatory Compliance as Code*

6

DevOps Software Development Life Cycle 360° Evolution and Engineering

In this chapter, we will focus on the DevOps **Software Development Life Cycle (SDLC)** 360° evolution and engineering. In the first part, we define the DevOps SDLC and position it at the core of the broader DevOps 360° operating model evolution and our DevOps definition. Then, we define the meanings of evolution and engineering in the DevOps SDLC context, and we outline the SDLC's multidimensional value proposition. The first part continues by examining the DevOps SDLC layers, the main four phases, frameworks, and capabilities, discussing their value propositions and anatomies. In the second part, we focus on outlining a proven practice for designing an evolved and engineered DevOps SDLC while engaging the broader DevOps domain stakeholder ecosystem through an eight-step guide. As part of the guide, we examine aspects such as the evolution tactic, portfolio classification and prioritization, the core elements of background work to be conducted, and the importance of templating to ensure a harmonized outcome and a common understanding. Then, we will describe the process of defining the DevOps SDLC catalog, providing an example, and follow the evolution of the catalog through its five phases, from defining its critical path to ensuring a broad coalition and getting sign-offs. The chapter closes by discussing the importance of DevOps SDLC *stakeholder views* and briefly cites an alternative approach.

In this chapter, we're going to cover the following main topics:

- The definition of the DevOps SDLC 360° evolution and engineering
- The DevOps SDLC 360° value proposition
- The DevOps SDLC 360° layers and anatomies in terms of phases, frameworks, and capabilities
- A proven eight-step practice for designing the DevOps SDLC 360°
- A sample DevOps SDLC 360° catalog

Defining the DevOps SDLC

With this chapter, we have officially entered the second phase of defining our DevOps 360° operating model, which is **capabilities evolution and enablement**. This chapter is dedicated to the heart of evolving and enabling the model – the DevOps 360° SDLC evolution and engineering. Before we continue, I would like to take you back to the DevOps definition that we specified for this book:

A set of practices, frameworks, and technologies that enable flows, continuity, and collaboration across the SDLC, toward materializing common objectives, while achieving an equilibrium of time to market, reliability, and compliance of services.

As you can see, the SDLC is at the heart of our definition. This is not a coincidence, as the SDLC is the main backbone through which the DevOps objectives and equilibrium of value delivery materialize. But let us define what we mean by *SDLC* in our book's context. We define the SDLC as the composition of processes, technologies, frameworks, capabilities, tools, mechanisms, and people that are involved in enabling the end-to-end product and/or services life cycle, from the ideation and planning phases to development and testing, and from staging to deployment, to operations and maintenance, and eventually sunsetting. In this book, as is obvious from our DevOps definition, we consider the concepts of a product and a service equal to the concept of software. I sincerely cannot think of any banking product or service that does not utilize software in order to be designed, built, launched, and used. Note that we take it for granted that you know more than the fundamentals of the SDLC and therefore we will become a little more sophisticated and take the SDLC to an advanced level, beyond the mainstream fundamentals. Keep reading to discover more.

What is DevOps SDLC 360° evolution and engineering?

Do you recall the element of 360° that we discussed in the first chapter and its importance in the DevOps evolution? Let me refresh your memory. 360° in our context indicates a complete and flawless rotation across DevOps capabilities. In the DevOps SDLC case, a 360° evolution and engineering indicates a complete and flawless rotation across the phases that comprise it, ensuring the following:

- Evolution in terms of gradual advancements across the SDLC
- The utilization of DevOps engineering means to improve flows and productivity across the SDLC

By ensuring gradual advancements and the utilization of engineering means to improve flows, the following four core qualities of 360° are also fulfilled:

- **Completeness**: The inclusion of the totality of capabilities
- **Continuity**: The assurance of infinity loops across capabilities
- **Reconcilability**: The ability of capabilities to co-exist through complementation
- **Interoperability**: The ability of capabilities to be seamlessly interconnected, engineered, and event driven

Why you need a DevOps SDLC

The reason you need a DevOps SDLC is that you need to define the ways you design, build, deploy, run, and monitor software in the future along with the corresponding capabilities you will have to enable, evolve, interoperate, and replace as your DevOps 360° operating model materializes. But going beyond that, the DevOps SDLC's value proposition is the definition of multidimensional, as follows:

- It provides a "journey map" to your teams on how to adopt the DevOps 360° operating model at relevance and how far they are from achieving that.

- The frameworks that result from it will support an acceleration of the DevOps evolution and adoption in your organization.

- It is often a regulatory requirement for systemically important incumbents.

- It will enable you to define your DevOps evolution OKRs.

- It will serve to define the *at-relevance and multi-speed adoption model*.

- It enables DevOps productivity and experience through value streams.

- It enables integration with your broader industry ecosystem and vendors.

- It can support your business partners to understand the end-to-end flows across the service and product delivery value stream.

- It will define the future people skills and technological utilities that you need to acquire.

Why is it important to understand the DevOps SDLC anatomy?

The breadth and depth of the DevOps SDLC can range from being rather simple to being of significant magnitude, and this naturally depends on how broad and deep your DevOps evolution aims to be. In this section, we will examine the breadth of the DevOps SDLC in the sense of the end-to-end perspective (continuous delivery), and its depth in terms of phases, frameworks, and capabilities that enable it.

The three-tier DevOps SDLC

In this book, we use a three-tier system to define the anatomy of the DevOps SDLC, having the philosophy that from a practical perspective is divided into continuity phases, which are in essence a collection of frameworks consecutively enabled through a combination of various capabilities. The three main levels are the following:

- **Level 1 – DevOps SDLC core phases**: The main continuity phases that comprise the highest level of the DevOps SDLC

- **Level 2 – DevOps SDLC frameworks**: The frameworks enabling the various SDLC phases

- **Level 3 – DevOps SDLC capabilities**: The collection of capabilities that enable the frameworks

The following diagram displays the three-tier system with examples:

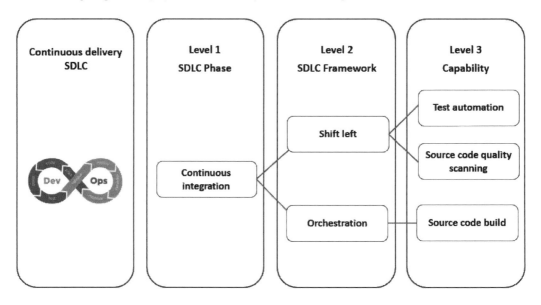

Figure 6.1 – The SDLC levels anatomy example

The coming three subsections will discuss the anatomy of each of the three levels.

What is the anatomy of the DevOps SDLC continuity phases?

The word *phases* might remind you of more *waterfall-ish* models, though by adding the word *continuity* I believe the term **DevOps SDLC continuity phases** sounds very legitimate and descriptive, defining the core phases that comprise the end-to-end DevOps SDLC. Now, personally, I do not fancy the term *end to end* as in my mind it indicates that there are *ends*, while in the essence of DevOps there is only continuity. So, I have decided in this book to replace the term **end to end** with **continuous delivery**. With the term *continuous delivery*, I consider the continuous delivery of value throughout the DevOps SDLC phases. If we view DevOps in an orthological way (and we do) and not in terms of the mainstream and traditional split between CI and CD, we realize that, for instance, executing your regression test suite during every build might be considered part of continuous integration, but it is also contributing to the continuous delivery of value. With the same thinking, ensuring in the early days of software design that your architecture can evolve incrementally is also part of the continuous delivery of value.

The Story behind the DevOps SDLC Phases Design

I have always found it interesting how people find it difficult to practically map the infinity symbol of DevOps to the SDLC and instead map it to CI/CD pipelines. I have also observed on several occasions that people not familiar with DevOps, coming from old-school waterfall methodologies, have difficulty shifting from a staging approach to a continuity one. Inspired by those situations, I took the liberty of gently manipulating the mainstream continuity phases in order to help my colleagues, but also to go little bit more broadly into what I believe a complete SDLC should look like in an advanced DevOps context.

Defining the continuity phases

Let us now define the continuity phases, which, as you will notice, all contribute to materializing our DevOps definition of delivering toward common objectives (customer value through working software) while maintaining an equilibrium between time to market, reliability, and compliance:

- **Continuous delivery**: The total output across the DevOps SDLC phases that delivers an end value to clients

- **Continuous design and development**: The incremental evolution of software design and increased DevOps experience through the flawless "as a service" consumption of capabilities

- **Continuous integration and testing**: The automated orchestration of the steps to produce functional, compliant, and reliable software that is considered operational and ready to be deployed

- **Continuous deployment and release**: The incremental and automated deployment and consecutive release of software that can be used by the end customer

- **Continuous monitoring and operations**: The assurance of proactive/preventive and undisruptive software operations, through the utilization of engineering means

- **Continuous planning and feedback**: The agile and incremental planning of gradual software advancements based on observations across the continuous delivery phases, new business requirements, and technological advancements

The following diagram shows the DevOps SDLC continuity phases and value equilibrium:

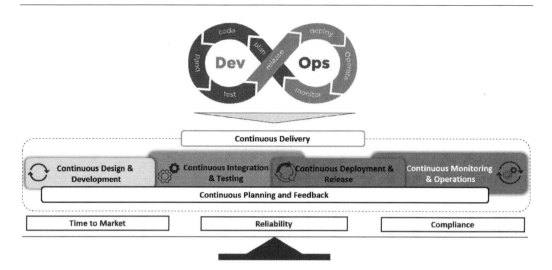

Figure 6.2 – The DevOps SDLC continuity phases and value equilibrium

I do hope that the DevOps SDLC phase definitions provide more clarity on my rationale behind them, without overcomplicating their essence and reality. In the coming subsection, we will double click on the phases and discover the role and importance of frameworks in materializing them.

What is the anatomy of a DevOps SDLC framework?

In this book, we define *DevOps SDLC framework as* a collection of capabilities, the orchestration of which contributes toward the materialization of the objectives of a single or multiple DevOps SDLC phases. A DevOps SDLC phase consists of multiple interoperable frameworks that on the one hand can be overlapping with each other and on the other hand can belong to more than one phase. The following diagram provides an example of the CI orchestration framework, which is mainly part of the continuous integration and testing phase but also shifts further left to the continuous design and development phases.

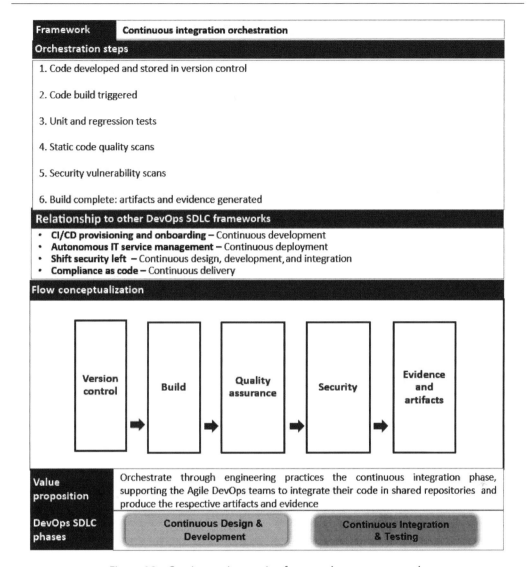

Figure 6.3 – Continuous integration framework anatomy example

There are numerous DevOps SDLC frameworks; your choice on which to use depends on your objectives, portfolio composition, and evolution approach, and on how broad and deep you wish to go. Despite the breadth and depth you wish to have, it is advisable that you define a framework catalog that you assess against the four qualities of 360° and is eventually mapped to the broader DevOps continuous delivery SDLC.

The SDLC's frameworks will be a proven key mechanism for standardizing, harmonizing, and scaling fast, especially if you are coming from a "free will – shadow IT" historical background. A common industry practice is to enable frameworks through engineering practices, which will eventually accelerate their cross-reconciliation and adoption across your portfolio.

> **Tip**
>
> Be mindful not to be super prescriptive with frameworks. It is not a matter of "the enterprise way or no way." The same outcome can be achieved by different approaches, in different contexts and at different speed levels. You do not know every single detailed context of a sub-situation and therefore your frameworks should be flexible, allowing adoption in different contexts and at relevance.

What is the anatomy of the DevOps SDLC capability?

We define *capability as* the facility that gives us the ability to do something in the DevOps SDLC. For instance, we would like to monitor our application, and a monitoring tool is a facility that provides us with the ability to do so. Capabilities are the foundation of the DevOps SDLC. Without them, neither frameworks nor phases can be materialized. Therefore, it is important for your DevOps evolution that you build a solid conceptual understanding of the pieces that comprise a "complete capability." As the following diagram reveals, a complete capability is quite rich in its composition of elements.

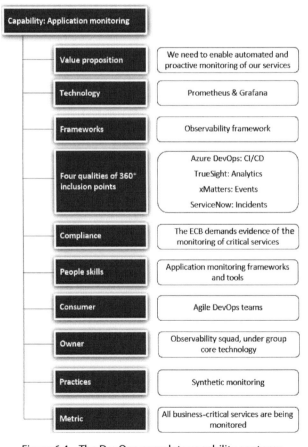

Figure 6.4 – The DevOps complete capability anatomy

Outlining and understanding the capability anatomy is of multidimensional necessity, which I believe is obvious upon looking into the anatomies of each of the parts of the SDLC, and can be decisive in ensuring a fundamental DevOps SDLC 360° evolution. When defining capabilities, you should keep in mind two major perspectives. Firstly, capabilities that evolve in isolation, break the continuous delivery flow, and should be repositioned. Secondly, a single capability can be part of several frameworks and several phases, and its value proposition should be repurposed accordingly.

Going deeper into the SDLC anatomy levels

The phases, corresponding frameworks, and their respective capabilities are at the core of the DevOps SDLC enablers. That said, there are several other DevOps SDLC elements, some of which I often see being overlooked and omitted in the industry or being equated with capabilities, while having "blurry" definitions and applicability. A list of those additional elements along with their definitions is as follows:

- **Standards**: A common and typical way of adopting a capability or framework in an organization. These are normally mandatory. Example: All source code repositories must be version controlled.

- **Methodology**: An already proven practice of adopting a capability or framework in the industry or within the organization. These are normally optional. Example: YAML templates are used to define deployment plans.

- **Policy**: An artifact that defines the organization's standards for protecting its IT assets. Example: The specific open source libraries that can be used by developers.

- **Control**: A mandatory checkpoint that validates adherence to a policy. Example: All code repositories are scanned against code quality standards.

- **Process**: A series of actions that are conducted in order to achieve a particular result. Example: The incident and problem management process steps that are to be followed in production incidents.

- **Guideline**: Practices and examples of how to adopt a framework or capability. Example: Prioritize the creation of automated regression test suites around the application's critical path.

So far, we have focused on outlining the foundation of theoretical concepts in this chapter. In the coming section and onward, we will focus on the practical perspective.

A proven practice for defining your DevOps SDLC

In this section, we will look into a proven approach for how, collectively across your broader DevOps ecosystem, you can define your new evolved and engineered DevOps 360° SDLC. This exercise should be considered part of the *DevOps speed, journeys, and experience workstream* that we outlined in *Chapter 3, The DevOps 360° Operating Model Pillars and Governance Model*.

Step 1 – define the actors and respective DevOps domains

The actors involved will look very similar to the setup of the DevOps organizing principles we saw in the previous chapter, with a major difference around scale this time. The following actors are the ones I propose you involve:

- **DevOps 360° vision authority**: To approve the final DevOps SDLC outcome
- **The DevOps 360° design and advocacy group and the DevOps CoE**: To orchestrate the actors and be the counterpart of the vision authority, as well as being the core team of the second iteration, as we will see in the coming sections

The DevOps speed, journeys, and experience workstream can be subdivided into two groups:

- **Primary actors**: The Agile DevOps teams or squads, depending on your business enterprise agility model.
- **Secondary actors**: The totality of stakeholders that we identified in *Chapter 3, The DevOps 360° Operating Model Pillars and Governance Model*, as part of the DevOps enterprise evolution ecosystem. *Totality* needs to be interpreted according to your context and ambitions.

The relationship between actors in this exercise is *demand* (I need), *supply* (I offer), and *hybrid* (I need and I offer):

- **Primary – Agile DevOps team**: I *need* a test automation framework.
- **Secondary – QA function**: I *offer* a test automation framework.
- **Hybrid (part of secondary) – IT risk and controls**: I *need* a controls SDLC framework, and I *offer* advice on interpreting the regulatory audit remarks.

While the role of the primary actors is straightforward, with them setting demands and being the end consumers of the SDLC, the role of secondary actors needs clarity to ensure effective execution of the exercise. As you probably remember, along with the DevOps domains' stakeholders, we have also outlined the DevOps **value proposition per domain**. This value proposition brings clarity to the role that each stakeholder involved is expected to play.

For instance, consider the following stakeholders and their roles:

- **Enterprise architecture**: Should support the portfolio classification mechanism
- **Cybersecurity**: Will focus on the security policies across the SDLC
- **Quality assurance**: Will cover the QA aspects of the SDLC

To ensure a balanced involvement on a *need-to-contribute* basis, it is advisable to split the stakeholders based on the iterations that we define later in the chapter.

Step 2 – define the evolution tactic in alignment and consensus with everyone

To bring people together from a diplomatic but also practical perspective, you need to ensure that you build on top of your current SDLC offering. Of course, not everything you currently offer and plan to offer in the short term will be absolutely fit for purpose in the new DevOps SDLC, but this is rather irrelevant at this point of the exercise.

The various DevOps stakeholders already have their evolution backlogs and some of them are already quite aligned to your vision because of "DevOps sense." They are also probably aligned with their first-level dependencies. You must neither disrupt nor freeze the work already in the making, but rather agree on how to bring everyone in alignment and achieve consensus on an evolution. You have succeeded in this activity if every single participant can see their part of the organization in the new DevOps SDLC and understand the value they bring to the big picture.

Perhaps your organization is not used to working collectively at this degree of enterprise scale, or maybe you tried in the past and the results were not as expected. Maybe you got together people representing different parts of your organization when you were to assess enterprise vendor tools or when defining your enterprise test strategy – and in both cases, despite the healthy disagreements, you managed to collaborate. This time you are to gather at a larger scale for a larger purpose, and in your collaboration model you should consider what worked and what did not work well last time.

> **Tip – Be Clear on Your Evolution Message**
>
> You are not to be radical, but to build on top of the great things that have already been implemented across your organization. You need to play it smart and build on top of the various success stories that already exist. Obviously, in certain cases you will have to be radical, but only after you have built a coalition on the fundamentals of the DevOps SDLC.

Step 3 – define the portfolio under scope

This is where we hit a major *at-relevance* element to do with your portfolio landscape. One DevOps SDLC cannot fit your entire portfolio across platforms and technologies and there are valid reasons for that:

- Technicalities, such as legacy technologies or vendor applications, will restrict you.
- You will have to adopt the DevOps SDLC tactically across your portfolio.
- Your modernization strategy dictates priorities.
- Different levels of speed driven by specific contexts will require different SDLC paths.

But how can you decide where to start from, as you need to use some parts of your portfolio as a basis around which to evolve the DevOps SDLC, and only afterward start incorporating the rest? A viable and pragmatic technique to use is your portfolio classification and strategic modernization direction. We will introduce this in this section for the purpose of supporting our current exercise and will return to look at it in depth later, having dedicated *Chapter 9, The DevOps Portfolio Classification and Governance*, to this purpose.

Building your portfolio rationale and tactic

Using rational and strategic thinking, you are naturally expected to start with the most modern parts of your portfolio, following the principles and motives that are listed here:

- You want to be forward looking, enabling a fit-for-future-purpose DevOps SDLC.

- The most advanced parts of your portfolio will offer more possibilities for an advanced DevOps SDLC, enabling you to explore your full potential.

- You want the people who will be part of the exercise to be energized by considering how to shape the future and not how to fix the past.

- It will be an acceptable approach to your regulator if backed up by modernization plans with 3-year horizons.

- You want to use the DevOps SDLC as a tool to define the modernization journeys for the parts of your portfolio that have not yet entered this phase.

- For certain legacy applications, the actual business needs around them might not require DevOps advancements to achieve the desired outcomes.

In our broader DevOps 360° context, when referring to the term **portfolio**, we include both the following categories:

- **Business applications**, such as core banking, mobile banking, and collateral management

- **DevOps technological platforms and tools**, such as CI/CD pipelines, private cloud, public cloud, events gateways, change management systems, and landing zones

This DevOps SDLC exercise is focused on the business applications as the main SDLC consumers, while the technological platforms are perceived as enablement utilities. This is a mainstream and pragmatic distinction used in the industry; keep it in mind as we will return to it in the coming chapters. Note that we also deliberately omit other core infrastructure and technology platforms such as network, storage, data centers, and workspace management as they are considered fundamental enterprise foundations by default.

Getting back to the business classification portfolio, we will use the following four categories, providing some brief definitions here, while reserving the details for *Chapter 9, The DevOps Portfolio Classification and Governance*:

- **Mainframes**: Business applications' built-in technologies such as the IBM Z series and SAP R/2, with Cobol and HPS being the programming languages

- **Decoupled legacy**: Non-mainframes with a three-tier architecture and strong data and business logic dependency on mainframes, and that are built on technologies that your organization has decided to stop investing in

- **Decoupled modernized (on-premises)**: Applications that are decoupled either fully or partially from the legacy business logic and data, are developed in languages such as Java and .NET, and are hosted on Linux or Windows machines

- **Cloud native (on premises or public cloud)**: Applications built in line with cloud-native principles, hosted either in your private cloud or on public cloud providers and/or utilizing PaaS public cloud utilities

The portfolio Shift Right approach

It is advisable that you start with the cloud-native, decoupled, and modernized parts of your portfolio. Then you can incorporate (maybe never fully, but partially) the mainframes and decoupled legacy parts of your portfolio. Normally, to incorporate the latter you are just required to remove parts (slimming down) of the SDLC and add only a couple of technological and architectural aspects specific to your legacy applications.

Step 4 – get the background work done

This activity requires some effort of background work in order to be conducted in a timely manner while avoiding confusion and delays.

Capture the as-is context of the various SDLC models and capabilities

Helping people to relate to the current context is important for them to be able to design the future, especially for those stakeholders not directly involved with your current SDLC. It is important that you utilize existing elements from several SDLCs that are probably already adopted in your organization, both to ensure an evolved approach (as opposed to radical) and to facilitate the *trace-back gap analysis*. Being able (at least at a high level) to capture the similarities and differences between the old and the new is important from the perspective of capability enablement and adoption. As with the organizing principles, the proposal is that you start with the future and then work backward.

Prepare the SDLC skeleton in advance

To help our participants out, we use a jump-start activity. Let's use the example of a puzzle to explain. When completing a puzzle, you use guidance, which is the picture on the box, and you put the pieces together to complete it. In our case, you will not give the complete picture, but you will give the basic fundamentals (a skeleton) and ask the participants to enrich, advance, and complete the puzzle seeing the DevOps SDLC from the perspective of their part of the organization. This is similar to you providing the DevOps SDLC core skeleton and asking the participants to add the muscles of their respective DevOps domain.

Conduct the regulatory background work

As we have also seen in the previous chapter, you need to be thorough when collecting and understanding your complete regulatory landscape, this time going way beyond separation/segregation of duties and identity and access management. Most probably you already have either a regulatory requirement or an open audit remark from your main regulator on IT risk management across your SDLC. You need to collect, consolidate, and understand them as part of your background work to ensure compliance in your SDLC, and should start planning in the early days to collect this evidence.

Align on definitions and interpretations

The lexicon that we proposed in *Chapter 3, The DevOps 360° Operating Model Pillars and Governance Model* is a fundamental tool for this exercise, as the nature of it will almost certainly end up being lost in translation with so many stakeholders from various domains and backgrounds involved. This is also a great opportunity to test the quality and coverage of the lexicon as you might have omitted certain terms, or your current definitions might not be contextually correct and will require amendments.

Understand the implications of the organizational structure and governing dynamics

As we saw in the last section of *Chapter 3, The DevOps 360° Operating Model Pillars and Governance Model* your organizational structure will have an influence on the success of the exercise and the future enablement and adaptation of its results. Ensure that you understand the governing dynamics in advance and conduct a psychological scan of the stakeholders appointed to support the design and enablement of the DevOps 360° SDLC.

Spend time getting the slow DevOps up to speed

Most often, the business areas that find the exercise more difficult are those with a modus operandi based on traditional software development practices and ITIL. You will have to spend more time with those stakeholders, maybe prepare extra visuals or run individual small workshops to better help them understand how they fit in the phases of continuity. It will be quite difficult for them to relate without support. The task of providing that support is something that your DevOps CoE can invest time in.

Step 5 – get your logistics in order

To harmonize outcomes and ensure a common understanding, templating is important.

The SDLC template

You will have to create a shared template for use by all relevant groups, as mentioned in the previous section. You will also have to provide some inputs in the form of a DevOps SDLC skeleton to jump-start the participants and help them better relate. This template is not for one-off usage; it will have a long-lasting value, as it is to be elevated to a core artifact of your SDLC and broader DevOps evolution, as we will see later. The following is an example of an evolved DevOps SDLC capture template:

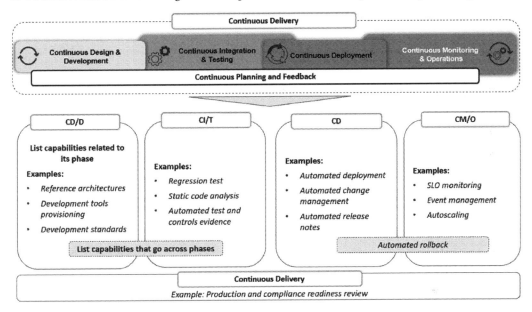

Figure 6.5 – Evolved DevOps SDLC capture template

Notation

Notation adds a strong level of sophistication to your SDLC and will be of high importance as it belongs to the enablers of the corresponding SDLC capabilities. The following figure shows some examples of DevOps SDLC notation:

Figure 6.6 – DevOps SDLC notation

Get an interactive and collaborative working setup

For efficient interactive collaboration, I propose you use tools such as Miro, WeBoard, and Stormboard (without the intention of advertising any in particular). The ability to collaborate interactively will be essential during the actual design.

Step 6 – first iteration and respective guidelines

Each DevOps domain team that you have identified will receive the template to be filled in individually within each domain in the first iteration. This is done to help teams unleash their own creativity and without being influenced by the entries of others. It is also a matter of tactics, as you want to see which DevOps domain teams will appoint the same capabilities, which will reveal the breadth of demand and consensus. Also, it is preferred in this first phase for teams to work individually to avoid conflicts and to maintain a good atmosphere, as some teams (depending on their input) might be perceived as entering foreign territory, especially with teams that are known for not having the best of relations due to historical events.

The following guidelines should be adhered to:

- Continuously reiterate throughout the SDLC phases, while shifting as many capabilities as possible to the left.

- Specify a value proposition per entry and link that to the DevOps evolution objectives.

- Start with the capabilities outline, then map them into the SDLC phases, then form the frameworks around them. Afterward, add standards, methodologies, and so on.

- Classify the capabilities into two categories:

  - **Critical path**: The bare-minimum capabilities of absolute importance across the SDLC and required to deliver value

  - **Advancements**: The additional capabilities to the critical-path capabilities, which advance the SDLC and enable the time to market-reliability-compliance equilibrium

- Highlight whether your entries are currently offered in the organization and provide a link to the corresponding portal, wiki, tool, and so on.

- Be technology agnostic and think of capabilities and not technologies. Remember that you have experience with various DevOps operating models and a proliferation of technological solutions, but specific technologies are not equally relatable to everyone. You also want to eliminate any feeling of *technological favoritism*. Therefore, it is not Jenkins: it is the build and orchestration capabilities of the SDLC.

- Make an initial assessment against the four core qualities of 360°.

- Use the lexicon, and if amendments are required, make a request with the DevOps CoE.

- Indicate which entries require business partners' involvement.

Indicate the Need for Business Partners' Involvement – The BDD Story

For every standard, practice, or methodology you wish to introduce, consider whether your business partners' and end users' involvement is required during the implementation. Once upon a time in one of the banks I used to work with, we came up with the idea of introducing **Behavioral-Driven Development** (**BDD**) through a new test automation framework in order to increase collaboration and improve test automation coverage. It all went as planned, up to the point that we had to teach the business users how to write test cases in Gherkin format. This did not fly in all areas due to a lack of time and desire in the business areas to learn the new method.

With the completion of this first iteration, the DevOps design and advocacy authority together with the DevOps CoE members will reconcile the input of all DevOps domains teams, do the necessary cleaning up and reshuffling, and prepare some clarification questions for the DevOps domain teams. Then the representatives of these two groups will meet the DevOps domains teams one by one and give a *handshake* indicating the input has been captured, clarified, and well understood. The outcome of this exercise will be the master DevOps SDLC 360° catalog, a representative sample of which we can see in the following figure:

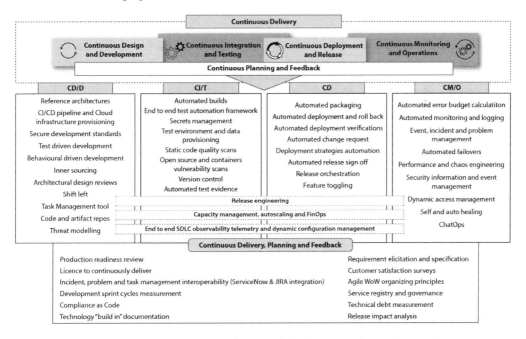

Figure 6.7 – DevOps SDLC catalog sample (indicative and not exhaustive)

Looking closely at the catalog, we see entries related to time to market (automation), reliability (release engineering), and compliance (compliance as code), along with some key mechanisms for monitoring the equilibrium such as the production readiness review and license to continuously deliver. Ensuring this balance, along with the respective mechanisms that help maintain it, is a vital element of your catalog.

Step 7 – second iteration – scenario-driven end-to-end value stream

The second iteration includes the actual design of the model based on real portfolio scenarios and value streams. This phase is where the DevOps design and advocacy group together with the DevOps CoE and selective Agile DevOps teams do most of the work. This is also the turning point for agnosticism in the model since from now on you have to be specific, at least for the capabilities that have already been enabled in your organization across the broader ecosystem of DevOps domain teams.

When conducting the second iteration, the selected members from the DevOps design and advocacy group and the DevOps CoE and Agile DevOps teams act like a full cross-functional squad that needs to design, build, deploy, and operate two applications from two different real banking business context scenarios based on the portfolio classification, categories three and four, which are the following:

- A decoupled modernized application
- A cloud-native application

In both scenarios, our group of people pretends to start from scratch designing those applications and considers the totality of capabilities defined in the first iteration using a value-stream practice while constantly validating the flow against the 360° qualities of completeness, continuity, reconcilability, and interoperability. I propose you follow four main phases in evolving toward the complete model. We will look at these in the following four subsections with the support of illustrations based on a small subset of the representative catalog entries.

> **The Big Reconciliation**
>
> In this phase, you are to hit a great reconciliation point and address one of the greatest industry debates. You are to reconcile DevOps, SRE, and ITIL capabilities that were most probably coming into structural and interpretational conflict up to now in your organization.

Phase 1 – DevOps SDLC critical path

Start with the slimmest version of your DevOps SDLC, which is that of the critical path, defining the bare-minimum capabilities of absolute necessity required across the SDLC to deliver value, as the following representative diagram indicates:

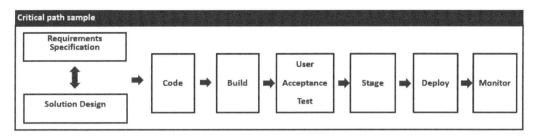

Figure 6.8 – Simple and representative SDLC critical path sample

The term **paths** has special importance from a DevOps evolution adoption perspective, as we will see in detail in *Chapter 10, Tactical and Organic Enterprise Portfolio Planning and Adoption.* While saving the details for *Chapter 10, Tactical and Organic Enterprise Portfolio Planning and Adoption,* I can mention that the word *critical* in *SDLC critical path* defines the importance of having that path adopted across your portfolio. On the other hand, a *cloud-native path* probably defines the path that cloud-native applications need to follow. Adoption at relevance!

Phase 2 – advanced DevOps SDLC and cloud-native path

Next is to advance the critical path with more capabilities. Here is where you start defining clear paths, which will also enable the adoption at relevance. In the following representative diagram (*Figure 6.9*), we have started defining two paths:

- **Advanced SDLC**, with further capabilities, applicable to modernized decoupling

- **Cloud-native path** with cloud-native capabilities, on top of the advanced SDLC for cloud-native applications

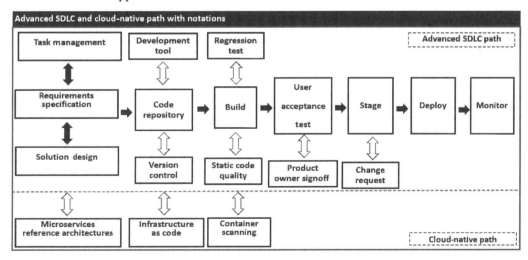

Figure 6.9 – Advanced SLDC and cloud-native path

From this phase on, it is visible how your portfolio classification plays a key role in the SDLC paths, not only defining the complete picture but also the application and DevOps journeys.

Phase 3 – further enrichment

In the first two phases, we focused primarily on capabilities. Phase 3 is where we start enriching by adding frameworks, policies, specific technologies, controls, and so on. Once we have conducted this phase, the model is almost there and must already fulfill the four elements of the 360° qualities in the sense that it is complete, continuous, reconciled, and interoperable.

So, in the following diagram (*Figure 6.10*), we indicate the following:

- There is a process around task management and a methodology around requirements specification that are both part of the agile field guide/playbook.

- There are guidelines around solution designs as part of architectural reviews.

- The execution of regression tests is one of the compliance controls.

- There is a policy that needs to be used when performing Docker container scanning.

- The standard monitoring tool offered by the central platform teams is Prometheus.

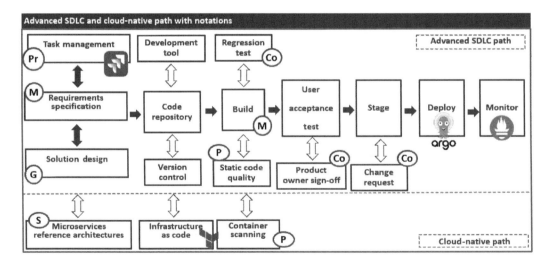

Figure 6.10 – Enriched advanced SDLC and cloud-native path

Phase 4 – value stream metrics

This phase is where you start measuring DevOps 360° SDLC speed. Value stream mapping enables you to define goals for the speed levels across several capabilities and frameworks of the DevOps 360° SDLC, as well as identifying gaps in the 360° qualities materialization, along with waste along the path of value creation. In the following diagram (*Figure 6.11*), we have added three value stream metrics along with the target values of maximum lead time tolerance. These metrics are regression test lead time to be no more than 3 minutes, change request approval lead time to be no more than 1 minute, and lastly, overall release velocity to be no more than 20 minutes. Obviously, these are efficiency ambition targets that should be adopted at relevance across your portfolio classification, as we will see in *Chapter 12, People Hiring, Incubation, and Mobility.*

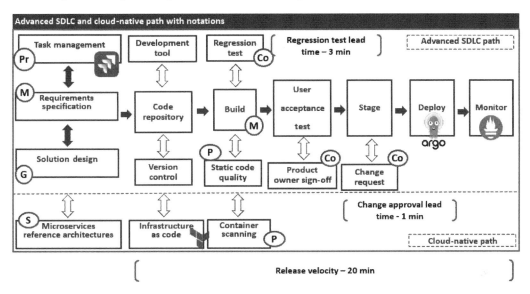

Figure 6.11 – Value stream enriched advanced SLDC and cloud-native path

The metrics that I propose you introduce to measure the performance of the SDLC's value stream are the following:

- **Lead times**: The time between the initiation and completion of a process (the technology provisioning step to the continuous integration step).

- **Release velocity**: The time from code commit to production release.

- **Development cycle time**: The time from a developer accepting a feature till the feature is implemented and merged into the master.

- **Wait time**: The time delay till an artifact is ready (solution design review, requirement specification, and offshore team to perform morning checks).

- **Mean time to detect**: The time required to detect an abnormality across the technological stack that disrupts the flow (build jobs taking ages to complete).

- **Mean time to repair**: The time required to repair the flow abnormality (provision new build agents).

- **Process time**: The time needed to complete the work. This excludes waiting time.

- **Percentage complete and accurate (quality metric)**: Helps to identify steps with poor quality. It represents the percentage of work that the next step can process without any rework.

Phase 5 – the big coalition

In this phase, you go back to the engaged DevOps domains teams, present the final outcome, and ask them to identify omissions and breaking points, as well as providing their sign-off and commitment to backing the new model. Congratulations! You have achieved something that, previously in your organization, would have been called *unthinkable*. You got the broader DevOps stakeholder ecosystem to collectively open up their backlogs, minds, and ambitions to a single forward-looking view. Game changing!

> **Mind Exercise**
>
> Go back to our DevOps definition and, word by word, try to reconcile it with the content of the first six chapters of the book. You will achieve a perfect reconciliation.

Step 8 – define the ownership demarcation

It is essential to do a demarcation of the DevOps 360° SDLC. This demarcation in essence is part of the broader ownership demarcation of the DevOps 360° operating model. The following table provides a sample demarcation based on the catalog that we presented earlier in the chapter:

Capability/Framework/Standard	Ownership Demarcation
Secure development standards	Cybersecurity
Shift-left standards	Quality assurance CoE
Public cloud infrastructure as a service	Public cloud platform team
Production readiness review	DevOps CoE
Task management	Agile WoW CoE
Reference architectures	Enterprise architecture
Deployment strategies	DevOps CoE

Table 6.1 – Example of DevOps 360° SDLC demarcation

The importance of different views

Different stakeholders have different interests and different DevOps expertise, which means that they will not derive the same messages by looking at the same view. In certain cases, you will have to help resolve the situation by providing different views that cover different perspectives in depth. Some good examples are the following:

- **Technical view**: Focused on the technical components enabling the capabilities and frameworks. Can support DevOps journeys across DevOps platforms.

- **Business view**: Focuses on visualizing the capabilities and frameworks value proposition to generate client and business value. Can support the understanding of where business or client involvement is crucial in the flow.

- **Regulatory view**: Focuses on the SDLC controls and how they meet the regulatory requirements. Will serve as evidence for the internal IT controls and audit teams as well as your external regulator.

> **Warning – Be Prepared for Mixed Feelings on the Final Outcome**
>
> The final outcome will be powerful without a doubt. The sight of the complete model will bring both feelings of fear, when people realize how much can be (and is being) done, but also at the same time excitement about what lies ahead.

The alternative method

Another approach that you can use is to have the DevOps design and advocacy authority together, with the DevOps CoE and a sample of Agile DevOps teams conducting the first iteration of the exercise up to the second phase of the second iteration, and then deliver that to the various DevOps domain teams for feedback. While that approach might sound faster, it includes two big risks. The first one is the risk of creating feelings of exclusion in the rest of the organization and making the exercise look like a *closed-group* matter. The second is that the DevOps design and advocacy authority, DevOps CoE, and Agile DevOps teams might not have enough insights and may omit certain capabilities that are in the process of being delivered by the broader ecosystem of DevOps domain teams.

What about the portfolio of mainframes and decoupled legacy components?

As you remember, we left two categories of the portfolio out of the scope of the exercise. Typically, incumbents will treat those legacy applications and platforms in their DevOps 360° SDLC evolution based on their portfolio modernization strategy. The following table summarizes the dominant approaches at a high level:

Modernization strategy	Approach to DevOps SDLC evolution
Mainframe to be decommissioned	Out of scope
Mainframe to stay	Focus on the reliability and compliance capabilities
Decoupled legacy to stay	Focus on critical path adoption
Decoupled to modernize	Adopt advanced SDLC on the new yet-to-be-built parts of the portfolio

Table 6.2 – DevOps SDLC adoption tactics for mainframes and decoupled legacy components

Defining the respective SDLC approaches based on your modernization strategy is critical from an at-relevance and multi-speed evolution perspective. Please make sure that you are pragmatic and forward looking and that your business counterparts are heavily involved.

Summary

Throughout this chapter, we touched on the heart of the DevOps 360° operating model. We highlighted the positioning of the DevOps 360° SDLC in our operating model and its relationship to the four elements that fulfill the *360°* quality of our model. Afterward, we considered the breadth and depth of the DevOps 360° SDLC value proposition and introduced its six continuity phases, as defined in this book. Then, we examined the anatomy of capabilities and frameworks by providing respective examples. We continued by outlining an eight-step approach to work collectively across your broader DevOps stakeholder ecosystem on defining the evolved and engineered DevOps 360° SDLC. On that journey, we went from DevOps domain stakeholder identification to defining the overall tactic to ensure alignment and a coalition, as well as proposing the scope from a portfolio perspective. We discussed the importance of setting clear guidelines, conducting background work thoroughly, and using appropriate templating and notation to harmonize outcomes. Continuing, we discussed an alternative two-iteration approach to design the new DevOps 360° SDLC, starting with isolated DevOps domain teams identifying capabilities, followed by capability consolidation toward a DevOps 360° SDLC catalog and value stream mapping based on real application portfolio scenarios.

In the next chapter, we will focus on the technological backbone that enables the new DevOps 360° SDLC and broader DevOps 360° operating model, looking at the key elements of the DevOps technological ecosystem from various perspectives, ranging from technological capabilities to platform service models.

7

The DevOps 360° Technological Ecosystem as a Service

In this chapter, we discuss the part of the DevOps 360° evolution that many in the industry find the most interesting to work with: the DevOps 360° technological ecosystem as a service. While interesting, the perception of this term, used by the technology and this book, is the source of most DevOps misconceptions. The chapter starts by discussing the value proposition of technology for the DevOps evolution, along with defining what is indicated by the term ecosystem and what the main counterparts of it are, in an incumbent's context. Continuing, we focus on bringing clarity to the biggest DevOps misunderstanding in the industry, that is, equalizing DevOps and technology, while we provide our view on the real interrelation of the two. Moving on, we touch upon two initiatives that characterize the current DevOps technology approaches of incumbents – one of engineering transformation and one of technology standardization. Continuing, in the heart of the chapter, we look at the DevOps platform teams, which are the main mechanism that incumbents use to enable DevOps capability engineering through technological utilities. We cover their value proposition, operating and service models, product and service catalogs, social contracts, and other important elements. The chapter closes by outlining the five core DevOps platform teams' domains from a representative sample of incumbents.

In this chapter, we're going to cover the following main topics:

- The definition of the DevOps 360° technological ecosystem value proposition
- The misunderstood relationship between DevOps and technology
- The six categories of technological ecosystem counterparts
- The focus of incumbents in engineering transformations and technology standardization in enabling DevOps capability engineering
- The DevOps platform teams in terms of operating and service models
- Examples of the five core DevOps platform teams' domains that incumbents focus on

The technology value proposition in the DevOps evolution

In the previous chapter, we discussed the importance of evolving and engineering the DevOps 360° SDLC while ensuring the fulfillment of the four 360° qualities. Without a doubt, the main mechanism to evolve and engineer your DevOps 360° SDLC is through technological means and advancements that enable capability engineering. What is the point in a cross-level test automation framework if you do not have the technological means to build it? Equally, what is the use of an open source library scanning policy if you do not have the necessary technological means to embed it? And how do you expect to improve your time to market without the necessary technological capabilities and automation across your SDLC? The role of technology is a fundamental necessity in materializing not only your DevOps 360° SDLC but also the broader DevOps 360° operating model, supporting your business to gain and maintain a competitive advantage. This multidimensional and foundational role of technology is becoming apparent also from a DevOps evolution enterprise **Objective and Key Results (OKRs)** (see *Chapter 2, The DevOps Multi-Speed Context, Vision, Objectives, and Change Nature*) perspective, as technology contributes to all of them and is not attributed to a specific one. Unfolding the rounded aspects of the technological value proposition for the DevOps evolution will be the focus of the upcoming sections of this chapter.

The DevOps 360° technological ecosystem as a service

The totality of technological enablers of your DevOps evolution is called the **DevOps technological ecosystem** in this book. And it is indeed, in my opinion, a spot-on term to use. We define an ecosystem as a geographic area where complex living organisms interact in a given landscape under certain conditions, working together toward enabling a cycle of life. A DevOps 360° technological ecosystem, therefore, consists of various technological teams in a certain organization that interact under the condition of the DevOps 360° evolution, enabling an infinite loop of technological capability engineering and consumption as a service. Before we move on and discover the core aspects of our technological ecosystem, let us first bust a *DevOps myth* to which we have also referred earlier in the book.

The misunderstood relationship between DevOps and technology

It is a widely known secret that the industry, to a large extent, has historically equalized DevOps with technology, and mostly with CI/CD pipelines and cloud capabilities, on several occasions, not even attempting to go further than those two, toward the broader technological ecosystem. The logic is simple: *I have a CI/CD pipeline, I do DevOps* or *We have a Kubernetes cluster, we do DevOps*. I have seen several *DevOps strategies* in my FSI DevOps career that were shaped with the main focus on the technological capabilities that enable DevOps. For all of us who have been part of DevOps adoptions at scale, we undoubtedly recognize the importance of technological enablement in DevOps. Though we also realize that while technology is the easiest (and most fun) of the DevOps enablers to be achieved, by itself it does not deliver the full DevOps potential. This *industrial* narrow dimension of the DevOps perception and the equalization of it with technology does more harm than good to DevOps evolutions. And even worse, this misconception has historically classified several DevOps adoptions as a failure, implying also that the concept itself is a fallacy. In many cases, that was simply because the implementation of an *advanced* CI/CD pipeline and the ability to spin up machines in the public cloud did not fundamentally transform the ability of certain organizations to deliver better value faster to end clients. I will get directly to the point now. Technology should not be equalized with DevOps in your organization, as it is *just* yet another enabler, like people skills, budgets, policies, culture, processes, WoWs, and your regulator are. At the end of the day, look at this book's outline. Technology occupies only one chapter out of the several that are equal parts of the DevOps 360° evolution.

Why incumbents combine an engineering transformation with their DevOps evolution

A very common approach that I have seen with every incumbent I have worked with is either combining or running in parallel the DevOps evolution with an engineering transformation. Those two often are further combined with a business enterprise agility transformation, as we saw in *Chapter 5, Business Enterprise Agility and DevOps Ways of Working Reconciliation*. An engineering transformation will typically involve several engineering-related initiatives that are applied across the incumbent's organization, including both the business' Agile DevOps teams as well as the technological and infrastructure utility ones. What do those engineering transformations include?

- A mindset and a cultural shift toward lean products and service offerings in an agile context

- Shifting toward the enablement of technological utilities as a service

- Engineering the uplift of people skills

- The replacement of human-manual service models with self-service automation

- A shift left of reliability engineering patterns

- A great focus on the tactical automation of repetitive tasks

- Enhanced modernization and interoperability across the ecosystem

- Supporting technology industrialization and democratization

- Formally embedding the technological and infrastructure utility teams in the business enterprise agility model

Uplifting your engineering skills, WoWs, and capabilities is vital in executing your DevOps 360° evolution. My personal experience says that it is indeed best to combine your business enterprise agility, DevOps, and engineering transformations into one change, but I need to warn you that, in combination with your business-as-usual and *unexpected* activities, it can be too much to handle in parallel as an organization. If you nevertheless manage, you will get the best return on investment and long-term, sustained change.

Why technology standardization is the new black for incumbents

Standardization and, in more realistic terms, *pragmatic standardization and where it makes sense* has become the *technological new black* in the industry and it is included in the DevOps evolution agenda of every single incumbent. If you remember, standardization and simplification are two of the core strategic objectives and DevOps OKRs that we defined in *Chapter 2, The DevOps Multi-Speed Context, Vision, Objectives, and Change Nature*. As we have repeated several times in this book, your organization is most probably coming from a technological solutions proliferation and duplication context, which, depending on the conditions and circumstances, is of a larger or smaller scale. There is no better space to look at materializing standardization than technology. The benefits can be numerous and its methods balance between coercive (cost cutting, technical debt, and regulatory demand) and operational efficiencies (maintenance overhead and interoperability gaps). The following are some of the main standardization benefits that your organization can achieve:

- Freeing up Agile DevOps teams' time by reducing the time spent on maintaining shadow IT
- Compliance out of the box in terms of the following:

  - Central teams take care of compliance adherence and evidence of the central platforms
  - Agile DevOps teams get the compliance policies and controls embedded into the tech

- Cost reduction in terms of licenses, servers, databases, and people
- Out-of-the-box full interoperability with the DevOps 360° technological ecosystem
- A clear governance mechanism through the central registration of technological solutions
- Common documentation built into the technology
- Inner sourcing opportunities
- Managing operational risk
- The ability to easily collect metrics across your portfolio
- Great solutions that have been built locally can be insourced and offered to the rest of the organization, minimizing the time and cost to innovate

> **True story – once upon a time on the trading floor**
>
> Once upon a time, I had a meeting with the markets CIO of an incumbent to discuss the DevOps vision for his organization. His office was on the trading floor and as I arrived a little bit early for the meeting, I was walking around. It is always entertaining to walk around a trading floor. The dynamic atmosphere and noise energize you. As I was walking, I noticed that the development teams were sitting quite close to the traders, grouped per asset class (equities, bonds, derivatives, and so on). All the development teams, who were sitting relatively close to each other, had big screens above their heads with any sort of DevOps technology you could imagine. Randomly, I came across an old colleague and I could not help asking (at the end of the day, it was for purely professional reasons, as I was to discuss the DevOps vision with their big boss), *Morten, why so much variation in technologies? Do you really need Prometheus, AppDynamics, Nagios, and Jaeger? And why are some on OpenShift and others on native Kubernetes?* He laughed and responded, *It depends. Some do have valid business justifications, like the .NET guys in FX trading that use Azure DevOps and Azure cloud services. But in most cases, every developer has taken their own decision. It is crazy, I know.*

Precautions and circumstances for standardization

Now, having outlined the potential benefits of standardization, I can already read your mind, *But Spyridon, standardization this and standardization that...Does standardization really pay off?* Let me clarify a couple of things, as the approach to standardization should be one of *standardization pragmatism*, per concept and context, while taking precautions, as the following sample cases describe:

- Let's take the example that you make use of Jenkins, the CI/CD orchestration standard. This doesn't mean that you will start building and deploying your applications the same way, nor that all the CI/CD steps and IT control thresholds are equally applicable to every Agile DevOps team.

- The degree of standardization will depend on the portfolio's technological foundation of each Agile DevOps team. For instance, the fact that you are to create a common static code quality check policy does not mean that Agile DevOps team B cannot amend that based on the programming language they use.

- Standardization, in certain cases, might not be worth it financially. You need to create your mathematical formula of *standardization due diligence*. Simply put, in some cases, it is not worth it, so skip it. Some technological setups are *too good and too big* to be killed. Advanced areas might currently have much better setups than your standard offerings. It is irrational to ask them to move to the standard offerings. As I used to say to the employees at one of the banks, *I have a Ferrari and you ask me to replace it with a Ford Focus.* (No offense to the Ford Focus, as it was my first, beloved car.)

- There will be vendor cases where you are technologically locked in, with low standardization possibilities.

- There are special cases, such as big data warehouses where the implementation of CI/CD pipelines should cater to specialties. For example, a mainstream pipeline for the purposes of big data implementations will not be sufficient.

- In many cases, standardization activities will never be prioritized in the Agile DevOps teams' backlogs by the product owners.

- You will face operational challenges as people will try to take advantage of standardization, not to migrate to standard offerings but to push to standard platform teams' technologies that those teams do not have the bandwidth and knowledge to operate.

- Your common DevOps platform teams might deliver with a delay, or not have the capacity to absorb the number of tenants.

- Do not *kill* local innovations, as they will be mostly linked to your business lines' specific context.

Standardization "clean cuts" is the most sustainable way

The most sustainable and pragmatic way toward standardization in my opinion is to define *clean-cut dates*. As in, providing a clear direction toward *pragmatic standardization* by giving an adaptation/planning period and then enforcing it for all new and modernized parts of your portfolio. For instance, from January 1, 2023, all newly built and modernized applications must use Azure DevOps as the CI/CD pipeline, OpenShift as their container platform, and provision infrastructure as code through a private cloud portal.

Standardization named "technology sustainability"

In identifying and registering duplicated solutions, a proven practice that I have seen is to have a specific and specialized team solely focused on that. The fanciest and most to-the-point naming of such a team I have heard is *technology sustainability*. There are plenty of license, code, binary, and IT asset scanning tools available out there that can reveal the level of duplicated solutions in your organization.

> **Countereffect of standardization**
>
> The tactic used to approach standardization is vital to its success. Be careful not to initiate a *technological arms race* across shadow IT, with Agile DevOps teams attempting to defend against standardization by growing their local setups to an extent that they are *too big, complex, and expensive to kill* anymore.

One last remark on standardization before we move on: your standardization tactic must be a very clear and targeted one, as you will have to include those activities in your enterprise portfolio planning, as we will see in *Chapter 10, Tactical and Organic Enterprise Portfolio Planning and Adoption*. Failure to provide a business justification and benefit realization plan will result in those activities not being prioritized. As we all know, technology standardization is mostly driven by the technology-oriented teams and functions of an incumbent bank. That being said, we also all know that it is the business partners of the incumbent who technically own the technological means of production, as they hold the funding for those. You need to be very convincing and/or creative to persuade them to do a *brave prioritization*, down-prioritizing new business features against migrating to the central ELK cluster. Last but not least, and quite needless to mention, it should be done *at relevance*.

The main DevOps technological ecosystem partners

We divide the main partners (organisms) of our DevOps 360° technological ecosystem into six main categories, with the Agile DevOps teams excluded, as we consider those to be consumers and not producers of technological utilities:

- **DevOps platforms**: Teams owning and offering utilities such as CI/CD pipelines, cloud services, test services, and so on

- **Technological utility services**: Teams offering utilities such as enterprise message buses, operational data storage, and tactical automation

- **Core infrastructure teams**: Responsible for mainframe platforms, network services, Linux and Windows platforms, middleware, and data centers

- **Shared services**: Include command and cyber security centers

- **End user services**: Workspace management, the IT help desk, and the virtual desktop belong in this category

- **Governance services**: Tools such as a **Configuration Management Database** (**CMDB**) and portfolio registry are included

In the rest of this chapter, we will focus on the DevOps platform teams, discussing them across a range of elements, characteristics, and approaches. It is important to clarify that we by no means downplay the importance of the rest of the technological partners, but we consider the DevOps platform teams as core first-level utility consumption partners to the Agile DevOps teams, as well as being at the core of the DevOps 360° SDLC and operating model, hence the focus.

The DevOps platform teams

Platform teams have, in recent years, become the mainstream way of enabling the DevOps 360° technological ecosystem and consequently support Agile DevOps teams in evolving their DevOps adoptions. We define platform teams as cross-functional teams that build frameworks, workflows, and technological utilities, enabling Agile DevOps teams to deliver end-to-end value to their clients through the utilization of technology. In this section, we attempt a rounded and broad deep dive into some of the core aspects of DevOps platform teams.

What is the value proposition of DevOps platform teams?

The DevOps platform teams' value proposition in our DevOps 360° operating model evolution is rather obvious, I believe, and as expected, is closely aligned with the objective of standardization, while its aspects are more multidimensional. Let us look into some of its core elements:

- **Economies of scale and maximization of operational and engineering efficiency**: The motto *you build it once and it gets consumed many times* is one of the objectives behind the establishment of DevOps platform teams. For instance, suppose you have a CI/CD pipeline platform team that builds the critical path of your CI/CD capabilities and workflow for cloud-native applications, piloting that for your asset management portfolio of business applications. The solution, upon success, can scale, creating operational and engineering efficiencies, while onboarding more business lines, without them having to build and maintain their own solutions.

- **Fulfill the comparative advantage theory**: With comparative advantage in economics, we define an agent's (DevOps platform team's) advantage over others (every single Agile DevOps team) in producing a product or a service, faster, at scale, and with a relatively lower cost. This advantage is generated through expertise concentration, full dedication to the product or service, and operational efficiencies generated by economies of scale. In simple words, the CI/CD platform team, by concentrating on CI/CD expertise and skills, being fully dedicated to the product, and creating the necessary means to scale it fast, is expected to be able to deliver faster and cheaper compared to the Agile DevOps teams.

- **Capture technological progress in relation to cost**: With technological progress, we refer to technological advancements through investment but also the increase in efficiency and output that those bring. By concentrating technological offerings in DevOps platform teams, both progress and cost become more transparent.

- **Operational data insights**: The utilization of the platforms offered by the DevOps platform teams can support operational data consolidation such as technology utilization, compliance, velocity, and lead times that can be used for multiple purposes.

- **SLDC adoption out of the box**: As the DevOps platform teams' utilities will be based on the DevOps 360° catalog, onboarding and utilization of those utilities will automatically imply the adoption of the SDLC for Agile DevOps means. That will also include the adoption of the fundamentals of fulfilling the *time-to-market-reliability-compliance* equilibrium.

- **Broad "state-of-the-art" visibility**: DevOps platform teams, as opposed to Agile DevOps teams or third-party vendors, have broad organizational visibility, which supports capturing the big DevOps picture and demand, and consequently translating that to utility offerings that can have a greater organizational impact.

- **Dedicated DevOps 360° technological ecosystem**: Bringing the dedicated DevOps platform teams close supports ensuring flawless, end-to-end DevOps value stream-based journeys, productivity, and experience, while fulfilling the four DevOps 360° qualities. In addition, the dedication of DevOps platform teams in specific technological domains will support excelling in those domains, establishing proven best-in-class practices, standards, frameworks, and methods.

Be aware of the "technology security dilemma"

Platform teams must be there to serve Agile DevOps teams while maintaining a balance of power and not dictating the technological vision. Observations of the latter will most probably result in Agile DevOps teams removing their consensus of support for DevOps platform teams, due to the effect of a security dilemma. In international relations, a security dilemma occurs when one state grows in military power, becoming a domination threat to other states. The latter then also invest in improving their military power, as well as building a coalition against the threat. I have seen this happen several times in Agile DevOps teams.

How does the DevOps platform team fit into the business enterprise agility model?

Before we deep dive into the technicalities of DevOps platform teams, let us first position them in the business enterprise agility context. Naturally, and as we saw in *Chapter 5, Business Enterprise Agility and DevOps Ways of Working Reconciliation*, you need to include DevOps platform teams in the enterprise business agility model of your organization and ensure that the respective organizing structures and principles also apply to them, along with the ability to be cross-functional in terms of skills, to achieve the best possible *DevOps organizationally aligned autonomy, through the ability to self-organize where applicable*. Two very good examples that I have seen in incumbents organizing DevOps platform teams under their business enterprise agility model are the following:

- **DevOps journey value stream**: Comprising the DevOps platform teams of the technological ecosystem, brought under the same organization and positioned in a sequence of steps based on the DevOps journey of the Agile DevOps teams.

- **DevOps engineering tribe/cluster/ecosystem**: Similarly, in this model, the DevOps platform teams are brought under the same organization, but this time are not organized as sequential value stream steps but as interrelated and integrated engineering capabilities.

I cannot stress enough the importance of embedding those teams in your enterprise agility model, as you need to achieve organizational cohesion and harmony, in the broader sense of WoWs, including your SDLC evolution and engineering, agility ceremonies, enterprise portfolio planning, and benefit realization. The embodiment is relatively intuitive, due to the agnostic reconciliation relationship of DevOps with business enterprise agility models. As we discussed in *Chapter 5, Business Enterprise Agility and DevOps Ways of Working Reconciliation* the key role of DevOps platform teams is recognized in every single business enterprise agility model, hence they all provide the necessary organizational structure means.

How does a proven operating model of DevOps platform teams look?

A fundamental aspect when designing DevOps platform teams is their operating model. By operating model, we refer to the way that the platform team is organized and operates on a day-to-day basis within its internal context, but also within its external context. Throughout my career, I have had the opportunity to experiment with various operating models. Through that experimentation, I am confident to say that I found what I call the **triangular model** (see *Figure 7.1*) to be the most effective operating model as I have literally never seen it not deliver and I have four examples of incumbents who are using it.

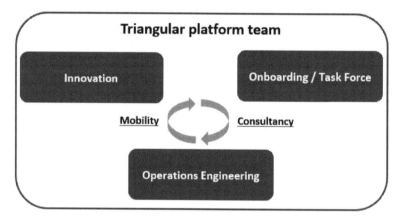

Figure 7.1 – Triangular platform team operating model

In the *triangular* operating model, depending on its size, scale, and clients, the team is either virtually or in person divided into three main parts, all belonging in essence to the same DevOps platform team. Each of the three parts has a special focus, while one complements the other. The naming of the three parts varies per adoption, though it is critical for the naming to be descriptive of the parts' responsibilities:

- **Innovation team**: Takes care of improving the platform from both a functional and also a non-functional perceptive and owns the improvements backlog. The backlog normally includes tasks such as the provisioning of tools and services, interoperability with the rest of the DevOps technological ecosystem, upgrades, tactical automation, and product built-in knowledge management systems.

- **Onboarding/task force team**: Do you recall the client engagement role of the DevOps CoE? This is very similar, if not identical, and in certain cases is a joint force between the DevOps platform and the DevOps CoE. This arm of the platform team either supports the onboarding of Agile DevOps teams to its platform, through starting from scratch or migration from another platform, conducts incubation and training, or acts as a task force supporting either cases of reliability issues or vast and critical business go-lives. This part of the DevOps platform is dedicated to the platform's client engagements and does not actually contribute to the platform's backlog but provides feedback for improvements based on the engagement observations. A very important role of this team is to work together with the Agile DevOps teams and other DevOps stakeholders on the DevOps journey, engineering, and productivity initiatives.

- **Operations engineering team**: This team has a dual role, and it is the *face* of the DevOps platform team towards the outside to the platform team world. Its first responsibility is to keep the platform's lights on in terms of incident management, monitoring, business continuity plans, and performing user request fulfillment. The second is to constantly conduct platform reliability improvements, as well as eliminating toil for the platform tenants, in collaboration with the platform innovation team, while gatekeeping the platform's operational readiness.

The people across the *triangular* operating model must be engineers at heart and in skills. Even the ones primarily focused on platform hygiene and request fulfillment should be engineers under incubation. Who, when ready, will move to more advanced engineering responsibilities within the team? Career mobility is also very much possible and advisable across the three teams. *Triangular* teams, you will typically notice, due to the key role their people have in the evolution, will be working very closely with the DevOps CoE and be core members of the DevOps 360° design and advocacy authorities.

How does a proven service support model of a DevOps platform team look?

The core part of a DevOps platform team's operating model is what is often called in the industry the service support model. By service support model, we refer to how the platform's utility consumers interact with the platform team for day-to-day matters – a core aspect of improving DevOps journeys, productivity, and experience. In this sub-section, we will look into the anatomy of such a service support model, through the lens of proven practice.

A strategy that I often see incumbents deploying to support the backbone of service support models is building their own custom-made portals, as a single point of entry across DevOps 360° technological ecosystem teams. Those portals have the nature of a *private cloud setup*, and you will often find them labeled *DevOps portal*, *Everything as Code*, or *Developer experience portal*.

Single point of entry and Level 0

The first layer of a *DevOps experience* portal is a user interface, often built in React or Angular, which displays the available options to the end user. These options can range from knowledge base articles to raising incidents for a specific platform, and from raising a new feature request to self-service through automation. The latter is the one that, in terms of support levels, I call **Level 0 (L0)**. L0 includes all the self-service capabilities, through chatbots, APIs, premade scripts, and templates, that DevOps platform teams have automated, eliminating manual interventions and lead times.

Service desk – Level 1

The next stage is what is often referred to in the industry as **Level 1 (L1)**. Typically, as part of this level, we find a service desk team that is responsible for the fulfillment of requests that has not yet moved to L0 through automation. This team normally covers the technological stack of more than one platform team or the totality of those. It is the ideal team to have new joiners of the platform teams embedded in supporting their incubation through exposure to clients and a wide range of technologies. Furthermore, this team is the perfect candidate for moving its positions to nearshore or offshore locations, combining savings and around-the-clock support. Principally, this team consists of engineers who, based on the client request observations and when time allows, can focus on improving the L0 capabilities.

Reliability engineering – Level 2

Moving on to the next level, which is typically called **Level 2 (L2)**, or reliability engineering in our context, this team is a very skilled and seasoned one and its primary responsibilities include the following:

- Emergency response to critical infrastructure incidents
- Catching the dispatched L1 tickets that cannot be resolved by the service desk
- Automation toward L0
- Proactive operational readiness and reliability engineering improvements

The reliability engineering team normally will be dedicated to a specific DevOps platform team as expertise and speed are vital to its operations. For instance, there can be a CI/CD reliability engineering team or a container platform reliability engineering team. It should should follow Google's SRE paradigm of 50% of its time invested in supporting the platform and 50% in improving the platform. Both the service desk and reliability engineering team belong to the *operations engineering* team that we discussed earlier as part of the operating model.

Innovation – Level 3

Last but not least comes **Level 3 (L3)**, which is in essence the innovation team that we discussed earlier in the operating model. L3 is mostly tasked with support that requires code/configuration changes in the platform or new interoperability capabilities, as well as with parsing requirements for new functionality to become available.

The following figure provides a visualization of the service support model, also providing some corresponding support examples per team:

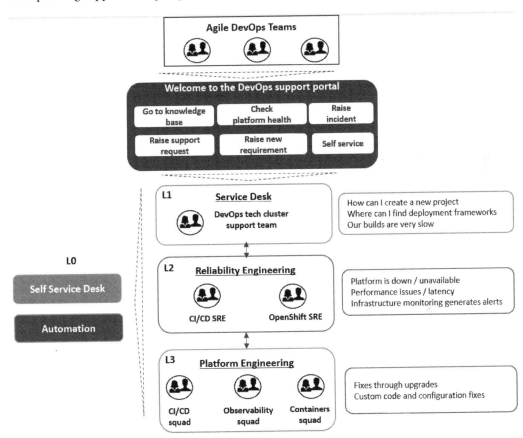

Figure 7.2 – Sample support model for the platform team

When it comes to platform onboarding for Agile DevOps teams, you should strive to provide that through a combination of **L0** (premade recipes/templates and interoperability APIs) and your *platform knowledge base* (*how-to* articles). The **L1** team should primarily handle any inquiries, with the support of **L2** and **L3**, depending on the support volumes and nature. Obviously, if you adopt the *triangular* operating model, and especially in tactical adoptions, there must be a dedicated team that is slightly detached from the *business-as-usual* service model, focusing exclusively on the flagship applications.

The DevOps platform product and service catalog

Obviously, each platform team's service model will very much depend on its product and service catalog. We define a product and service catalog as the complete and concrete list of products and services that a DevOps platform team offers to its consumers. Product and service catalog clarity directly indicates clarity to the value proposition and scope of the respective platform team and therefore tactical positioning in the broader DevOps 360° evolution. That tactical positioning serves a purpose from multiple perspectives: the Agile DevOps team's perspective on what utilities can be consumed centrally, the DevOps 360° technological ecosystem perspective on what the interoperability points and capability engineering demarcation are, as well as the broader DevOps 360° ecosystem on the DevOps 360° operating model enablement perspective. The following table provides an example of how a potential product and service catalog for a CI/CD platform could be formed.

Technology product	DevOps 360° SDLC capability engineering enablement	Platform team service
Azure DevOps	Task management Version control Code build Code deploy Test management	Platform maintenance and onboarding Standards, methodologies, and proven practices CI/CD control adoption Ecosystem interoperability Knowledge base Central compliance and adoption evidence collection
SonarQube	Static code analysis	
Artifactory	Build and deploy artifacts' storage	

Table 7.1 – Example of a CI/CD pipeline platform team's product and service catalog

From DevOps platforms' catalogs to enterprise technology menus

For many incumbents, the consolidation of all the technology catalogs across the DevOps 360° technological ecosystem forms what we often find called the **enterprise technology menu**. This consists of the totality of pre-approved and centrally offered *as a service* technologies that can be consumed when implementing the DevOps 360° SDLC.

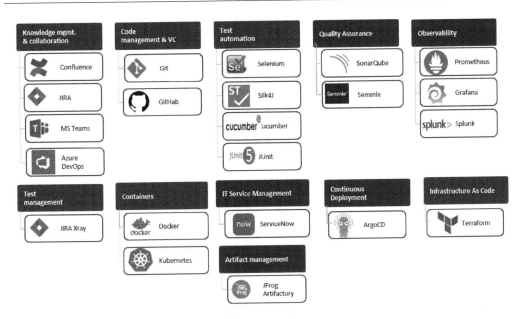

Figure 7.3 – Example technology menu

In my experience, enterprise technology menus are easier to define than implement. Firstly, moving to a standard technology is not always straightforward and often has several complications. For instance, if the Agile DevOps teams are obliged by the technology menu to shift to a new ETL tool, this most probably will not be just a lift-and-shift overnight exercise. It is highly likely that they will need to refactor their applications, investigate upstream and downstream data dependencies, redesign interfaces, and conduct thorough integration testing. And what about dependencies on external legacy platforms of partners and regulators that can only parse data in specific formats, through specific channels? In these cases, you will most probably end up with a significant period of parallel application runs (old and new running in parallel) or the move will never happen, either because of lack of time and money or high operational risk. Certainly, your organization, as we will see in more detail in *Chapter 10, Tactical and Organic Enterprise Portfolio Planning and Adoption* during the evolution, will face an adoption dilemma. *Are we happy to adopt the DevOps 360° SDLC using our own tools, or do we need to move to the standard ones?* The dilemma's scale obviously will depend on your DevOps context and strategic objectives and its real impact will become more apparent when you do the *evolution adoption mathematics*. But hold on to that thought, till we reach *Chapter 10, Tactical and Organic Enterprise Portfolio Planning and Adoption*.

To conclude, technology menus are without a doubt a solid approach to simplification and standardization, but in my opinion, only as long as they follow a pragmatic and tactical approach, as we discussed regarding *cut-offs*. And while *cut-offs* will not necessarily resolve your inherited DevOps complexity, they will most probably, as your modernization strategy progresses, make it more sustainable.

Why is the demarcation of responsibilities important for DevOps platforms?

As we saw in the previous chapter, the DevOps capability anatomy is rather complex. One of the main challenges I have seen in my career when it comes to DevOps platform teams is defining who is responsible for what in the platform, initially between the platform and its tenants, and afterward, across other stakeholders who have a role in a certain capability. Getting this demarcation clear through the platform enablement and onboarding process can save unnecessary waste and disagreements. Let us look into that through a practical example. Suppose that SonarQube is offered by the CI/CD platform team, and it is consumed by the Agile DevOps teams, while the DevOps CoE also comes into play as it owns the SDLC IT controls framework. A potential responsibility demarcation agreement could look like the following (*R* in the table stands for *Responsible*):

Activity/scenario	Agile DevOps team	CI/CD platform team	DevOps CoE
Tool ownership and offering		R	
Build plans onboarding	R		
Scans and remediation	R		
Control policy establishment			R
Tool operations and maintenance		R	
Integration with standard CI/CD		R	
Knowledge base		R	
Adherence evidence on the team's repository level	R		
Adherence evidence on the tool level		R	

Table 7.2 – Example of technological capability responsibility demarcation for static code quality scans

Remember that when more than one team is responsible, no one is in essence, as responsibility comes with clear liabilities and authority. Hence, agreeing on the fundamental single responsibility of enabling and consuming a capability has multiple purposes.

Why you need a "DevOps platform – tenant" social contract

Good bills make good DevOps partners. Therefore, *expectation clarity*, transparency, and alignment need to be established between the DevOps platform teams and their tenants, through a formal social contract. This is even more of a necessity as most probably, and due to historical reasons, there is an unconscious bias of your Agile DevOps teams toward the platform teams. The situation is even worse if trust is already lost on certain teams and heavy reputational restoration is required, especially if there is no change on the people side of those teams. Committing to responsibilty in writing will have a positive and binding impact. The following are the main areas where *social contract* transparency is required:

- Availability, performance, continuity, and the resilience targets of the platform

- New feature and vendor version upgrade velocity and cycle times

- Operating and service model agreements

- Ensuring the platform's *out-of-the-box* compliance

- The new capabilities prioritization process, product vision, and roadmap

- Platform interoperability with local home-grown solutions

It is inevitable that the nature of DevOps platform teams calls for focus in two directions in order to fulfill the social contract: to deliver and build the desirability of their products and services, while in parallel ensuring belief in their ability and credibility. But it's not only the DevOps platform teams that have liabilities from the social contract, but also their tenants. The fulfillment of the social contract by the DevOps platform teams will imply that the Agile DevOps teams will need to stop the proliferation of local home-grown solutions and support the common standard offerings.

> **Treaty on the non-proliferation of DevOps technologies**
>
> In international relations, the most well-known threat of non-proliferation is the one of nuclear weapons. The signing members (platforms and tenants) commit to stopping the spread of nuclear weapon technology (DevOps tech) and promote cooperation in the domain of nuclear energy. It is just remarkable how DevOps relates to international relations.

How can you enable DevOps journeys, productivity, and experience?

Very much related to the social contract is the term **developer experience** (**DX**), which in recent years has been used to describe the experience of a developer in accessing and using technology across the SDLC. In this book, given our non-developer-centric DevOps approach, but also looking at *experience* holistically, we will replace DX with DevOps journeys, productivity, and experience. A focus on DevOps journeys, productivity, and experience is essential to the success of DevOps platform teams. That is, to the extent that I would propose your platform teams have dedicated DevOps platform people, working together with the Agile DevOps teams on the cause of reducing friction, idle times, and bottlenecks across the flow of technological utility consumption. The possibilities are endless in this topic, with the following being some of the proven practices:

- Understand and visualize DevOps journeys across the entire DevOps 360° SDLC value stream.

- Set performance indicator benchmarks across the DevOps 360° SDLC phases and optimize against them.

- Identify and optimize lead times that slow productivity down and cause cognitive state switches.

- Automate the consumption and provisioning of IT assets through streamlined portals, also providing onboarding estimates to support effective planning

- Increase the interoperability of services across the ecosystem.

- Shift toward process and policy engineering with automated evidence generation.

- Improve self-service and utilize off-the-shelf public cloud capabilities.

- Document standards and methods in code repositories.

- Build and utilize scalable and reusable solutions through *templating and recipes*.

How technology consumption defines the organizing principles of Agile DevOps teams

Technological advancements and capability engineering positively impact DevOps journeys, productivity, and experience, and consequently, the organizing principles of the Agile DevOps teams that we discussed in *Chapter 5, Business Enterprise Agility and DevOps Ways of Working Reconciliation*. Where from and how Agile DevOps teams are consuming technology adds another element of *at relevance in a multispeed banking context* to your DevOps 360° evolution. Understanding those technological dynamics and how they shape the organizing principles of your ways of working and influence your platform modernization journeys is an important aspect of your evolution. Being able to proactively assess impact so you can plan a gradual evolution will be game-changing.

In the following figure, using the portfolio classification of this book, we illustrate the most dominant scenarios that we see rising when technological advancements and democratization take effect during the DevOps evolution.

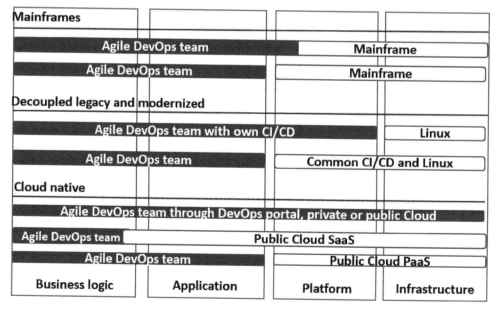

Figure 7.4 – Agile DevOps teams organizing principles illustration based on technology consumption

As is obvious, the influence of technology is profound in Agile DevOps teams' WoWs, as it defines and also impacts the levels of autonomy and responsibilities. This situation undoubtedly creates different speed levels, which we will come back to in *Chapter 10, Tactical and Organic Enterprise Portfolio Planning and Adoption.*

What to look for in DevOps technological utility due diligence

I would like to start this sub-section with a real story of mine that has a very deep meaning if you think about it carefully.

The cheeseburger story

Some years ago, we initiated a CI/CD pipeline standardization process in a bank. It was not dramatic at all, actually, in terms of variations, and we were all aligned in the chosen technologies, though everyone had separate processes. One of the differences we had was in artifacts management, with half the organization using one technology and the other half using another. Our group CTO asked for a comparison of the two to be conducted during one of the meetings. Then, one of the business CIOs spoke, *There is no reason to waste time. It is like comparing a cheeseburger from fast food A with a cheeseburger from fast food B.* I'll leave it up to your intuition to decode that ambiguous statement.

Sooner or later in your evolution, you will reach the stage of evaluation, due diligence, and comparison of various technologies. When you reach that stage, you need to make sure that you do not omit important aspects. What I have observed in several cases is that the functional requirements dominate the criteria of evaluation, with the non-functional being overlooked. In most cases though, it is the latter that proves to be a showstopper in the long run. In this sub-section, we will refrain from discussing functional requirements as they are heavily business context, technology, and capability dependent. Our focus will be on the often omitted non-functional qualities, as it is easier to use common and agnostic criteria for them. The following list is my favorite one from over the years.

Domains	Criteria
DevOps fit for purpose	Should fulfill the value propositions of the DevOps 360° SDLC catalog.
Required skills	The required skills are either available in the firm or can be acquired from the market.
Availability and performance	Ultra-available version is available and the performance test is passed.
Security	The security test profiling exercise across capabilities is passed.
Interoperability	Integration points to the rest of the DevOps technological ecosystem are provided.
Maintainability	Is of relatively low effort and new upgrades come frequently.
Adaptability	Can be adapted to different platforms.
Exit	Minimum technology and/or vendor lock-in.
Commercial support	Enterprise commercial version and vendor support are available.
Internal demand capture	Enterprise versus localized.
Customization	Can be configured and scripted.
Data accessibility and visualization	Can have access to data for observability purposes.
Service model	Provides self-service capabilities.
Compliance	Can support the IAM, SoD, data, policy engineering, and IT controls.

Table 7.3 – Non-functional/quality requirements technology assessment sample

Having thorough due diligence evidence is important not only for decision traceability purposes but also for future fit-for-purpose re-assessment purposes. Also note that this exercise is obviously not only applicable when deciding on new solutions but also during the consolidation of existing ones.

Why commercial versions gain momentum in the FSI

The preceding assessment can also provide answers to the *open source versus commercial version* dilemma, which in recent years has dominated incumbents' technological due diligence agenda. The overall observed tendency in the industry is to steer away from open source tools and toward enterprise and commercial versions. The main reasons are the following:

- DevOps platforms are mission-critical for running banks. Therefore, ultra-availability, continuity, and resiliency, along with vendor support, are required.

- Regulatory pressure on DevOps SDLC and platform audits, especially in a cloud-native context and particularly in the domains of security, compliance, and auditing.

- It's easier to attract employees that already have expertise in certain technologies, and also to incubate internal ones.

- Advanced interoperability capabilities.

- The product roadmap, especially in the case of GSI incumbents, can be influenced, along with the ability to exclusively customize products.

- Commercial product packages' bundling ability.

There is, as you can see, plenty of solid rationale behind this *commercial shift*. For all of you that have been part of a large DevOps transformation, you also know that community and open source technologies will not be sufficient when you start standardizing and institutionalizing at scale. Sooner or later, you will have to get into commercial discussions.

The industry's platforms versus direct cloud native dilemma

While DevOps platform teams still advance in the industry with many incumbents not yet harvesting their full potential, there is yet another DevOps dilemma that is rising on the horizon – one of DevOps platform teams versus direct cloud native. Direct cloud native in this context refers to establishing the necessary organizational, governance, and technological means in enabling Agile DevOps teams to consume DevOps technological utilities directly from cloud technology providers in a secure and compliant way, without the DevOps platform teams acting as an intermediary. This is a very interesting development that requires extensive preparations in ensuring sustainability and compliance and, moreover, in finding the right balance, with the DevOps platform teams serving the Agile DevOps teams who will stay on-premises.

How communities of practice strengthen DevOps platforms

We referred earlier in this book to the *strongly opinionated* developer. You know, that guy who walks around the office wearing an *I love Java T-shirt* (kidding). There are also strongly opinionated platform engineers in organizations. It is advisable to bring people with strong opinions together in communities of practice and get them to contribute the most to your technological ecosystem. To cover every single core DevOps platform team you must have some kind of connection to your DevOps CoE and the DevOps 360° design and advocacy authority. There are plenty of reasons for doing so:

- Providing the Agile DevOps teams with a sense of and ability to influence the DevOps platform roadmaps and backlogs, and actually allowing them to do so

- Giving the DevOps platform teams the ability to understand the business context of Agile DevOps teams

- Increasing awareness and incubation through training sessions and demos

- Enabling inner sourcing synergies

- Conducting joint demos and live sessions to promote each other's work

The main five strategic platforms incumbents focus on

Looking across incumbents, you will discover certain DevOps platform teams receive greater focus, and there are certain reasons for that: strategic positioning in the DevOps 360° SDLC, a strategic role in enabling the broader DevOps 360° operating model, high demand from Agile DevOps teams, and significant focus from a regulatory perspective. In this sub-section, we outline the most strategic DevOps platform teams we find in incumbents.

The ITSM platform

Perhaps it will come as a surprise to you that, often, we see ITSM platforms not being considered at the core of DevOps technologies. That is due to the dominance of the traditional ITIL interpretation of ITSM in the industry. In our book though, we approach ITSM from a process engineering and interoperability in the DevOps flow perspective. Moreover, we will examine it from a strong **site reliability engineering** (SRE) (more on this in *Chapter 13, Site Reliability Engineering in the FSI*) perspective, toward the enablement of autonomous operations. But let us save SRE for later and look at the following responsibilities of an ITSM DevOps platform team:

- Event, incident, and change management flow automation
- Simplification of the problem management procedures
- Configuration management database automation
- Automated calculation of availability for applications and services
- Automation of service onboarding to service catalog registries
- Automated release impact analysis, as part of release management
- Automation of production-readiness review assessments
- Tactical API automation and interoperability to the broader ecosystem
- Automation of service governance regulatory evidence

Through process engineering, those teams' mission is to increase the ITSM platform engineering capabilities and shift them left in the DevOps 360° SDLC. Also, our ambition was in one bank to gradually ensure that Agile DevOps teams will forget what the ITSM tool GUI looks like. In recent years, there have also been big developments in the reconciliation of ITSM platforms and processes with DevOps. Platforms such as ServiceNow have started offering DevOps module functionality and platforms such as BMC Remedy offer a rich API interoperability catalog. There's a lot to be done in this domain.

The CI/CD pipeline platform

The CI/CD pipeline platform team is the *king* of DevOps platforms, especially for organizations that have fallen into the misconception of equalizing CI/CD pipeline adoptions with DevOps adoptions. As is clearly described by its name, this team offers the core CI/CD capabilities required in enabling an evolved and engineered DevOps 360° SDLC. The offering of this platform team, I believe, is straightforward and, therefore, for the economy of your reading, I will refrain from mentioning code repositories and build tools. What I will focus on is an *at relevance in a multi-speed banking context* element that CI/CD platform teams have been observed as enabling in the reality of incumbents.

Do you recall the different paths that we mentioned in the previous chapter on the DevOps 360° SDLC? Think of your code and artifacts as a train wagon and those paths being railways. Depending on your programming language, platform technology, and portfolio classification, your code and artifacts can follow different paths, reaching different destinations where they are deployed. For many incumbents, different paths mean different or partially different CI/CD pipelines. The most dominant scenarios that I have identified in the industry are the following:

- **Mainframe CI/CD**: Dedicated to mainframe applications, the simplest of CI/CD versions
- **Decoupled CI/CD**: Dedicated to decoupled on-premises applications, covering mostly the CI/CD critical path
- **Cloud-native CI/CD**: Dedicated to cloud-native applications; very advanced and extending much further than the critical path
- **Mobile CI/CD**: Dedicated to the digital front tier of incumbent banks, which is mobile banking, especially in the case of greenfield initiatives; equally advanced as cloud-native CI/CD

Enterprise CI/CD versions gain momentum in incumbents' adoptions from a critical path perspective, with the Atlassian Stack, GitHub, GitLab, Azure DevOps, and CloudBees (Jenkins' enterprise version) being the dominant ones.

Naturally, the different pipelines have capability overlaps and to a certain extent utilize the same technologies, being extensions of the foundational critical path in essence.

The testing services platform

An often-overlooked platform, which lacks investment due to a struggle in understanding its value, complications in setting it up, as well as the cost of establishing it, is the testing services platform. All of us that have worked with DevOps realize the importance of testing services. In the absence of them, time to market and reliability aspects of software delivery can be jeopardized, SDLC implementation costs rise, regulatory evidence is hard to collect, and heavy manual interventions during testing increase the probability of defects. Now, I need to make clear one thing about the definitions. In this book, we do not refer to **Testing as a Service (TaaS)** as the practice of outsourcing testing-related activities to vendors or third-party companies in particular; we refer to the capabilities built by an incumbent in offering testing-related services and utilities to Agile DevOps teams.

Such a platform should focus on the following capabilities:

- Test management tools and test evidence generation

- Test automation frameworks, across test levels (regression, integration, performance, user acceptance, and so on) interoperated with the CI/CD pipeline

- Test environment provisioning both on-premises and also in the cloud in cooperation with DevOps platforms

- Develop disposable test and innovation/experimentation environments

- PaaS solutions for test data services (extract/generate – obfuscate – clone – load – clean)

Unfortunately, and primarily due to investment constraints, I have seen DevOps testing services platform teams either not being established in the first place, struggling to find their position in the organization, or having challenges in delivering on expectations. However, I strongly recommend you invest in them as they can prove to be game-changers.

The observability platform – telemetry

A domain where incumbents have invested in recent years is observability. Looking at an average representative example, we will find observability platform teams focus on delivering the following capabilities:

- **Open telemetry across the SDLC**: Through this capability, data is collected across the DevOps 360° technological ecosystem, serving multiple purposes, such as the following:

  - Technological capability adoption and utilization measurements

  - Operational efficiency metrics on velocity and lead times

  - Real-time audit and compliance evidence

  A quite innovative solution that is currently trending is the usage of real-time enterprise message busses, such as Kafka, to collect metrics across the DevOps 360° technological ecosystem, which are either streamed directly through visualization tools such as Grafana or are stored in operational data storage and sourced by reporting tools such as Power BI.

- **Application and infrastructure monitoring**: This service will primarily offer technological utilities and capability engineering, on application and infrastructure monitoring, from a complete *tiering* perspective. The following tiers are the mainstream ones in the industry, which we complement with examples:

  - **Tier 1** – Infrastructure: virtual machine CPU, memory, and network

  - **Tier 2** – Application processes and services: morning checks and starting engines

- **Tier 3** – Critical application-specific logic: client asset portfolio valuation
- **Tier 4** – Cross-application value stream data flows: clearing and payments straight through processing
- **Tier 5** – Business process and activity flows: approval of risk numbers
- **Tier 6** – Customer activity: account opening end-to-end value stream

There are plenty of solutions available for incumbents in this space with Prometheus, ITRS Geneos, AppDynamics, Elasticsearch, Jaeger, and cloud-native solutions (where applicable) being the dominant ones used by incumbents.

- **Application and infrastructure logging**: This service covers the logging of technological utilities, primarily covering the following four capabilities, and is of absolute focus to incumbent banks from a standardization and advancement perspective:

  - **Infrastructure logging**: Activity on virtual machines
  - **Operational logging**: Activity on the business logic layer of the application
  - **Security logging**: Security events on the infrastructure and operational layer
  - **Compliance and audit logging**: IT controls and data retention

  Splunk and Elasticsearch, as well as public cloud vendor-native solutions (where applicable) are the dominant solutions used in the industry.

On top of the technological utilities offered in the broader DevOps 360° technological ecosystem and to Agile DevOps teams, this platform team has a pivotal role from two relatively vital perspectives in the evolution:

- Providing dashboarding and visibility (often through the respective agile DevOps teams) to the business teams in order to increase the evolution's transparency
- Providing mechanisms for capturing the DevOps 360° evolution's technological but also broader adoption progress

As we will see in *Chapter 11, Benefit Measurement and Realization,* data is gold in measuring your evolution's progress and realizing benefits and this team is a core partner of that cause.

Private cloud platforms

In essence, and technically, this offering consists of custom-made portals that are used by Agile DevOps teams, but also the broader stakeholder's ecosystem, in materializing two main business cases:

- **Infrastructure as Code utility provisioning**: Various IT assets, from Linux and Windows servers to Oracle databases, and from Kafka instances to ELK clusters, including the necessary security policies, are provisioned automatically through premade templates, playbooks, and recipes (as code) that the private cloud platform team creates and maintains. The purpose is to eliminate lead times and the human effort of provisioning IT assets so software delivery can be sped up, as well as fulfilling standardization and out-of-the-box security and compliance aspects, along with enabling dynamic updates of IT asset utilization in the configuration management database and service governance tools. Terraform is the dominant technology currently deployed in *provisioning templating* solutions.

- **Container platforms**: These are used in order to host containerized applications, which, in this book, we include under the cloud-native portfolio classification category. Containerization is a method of building, deploying, and running applications in the form of containers, which are encapsulated with all the necessary dependencies of the application, such as libraries, binaries, and configuration files. Containerization is ideal for microservices and distributed architectures, following cloud-native principles, and can increase the speed and independency of delivering software. Container platforms provide an environment for applications to be built, deployed, and run, along with the corresponding deployment, orchestration, monitoring, security, and compliance mechanisms. Red Hat's OpenShift and Docker Enterprise Edition are the dominant choices of incumbents on container platforms.

Private cloud platforms technically serve as forms of IaaS and PaaS utilities that, in most cases, run on-premises (in a data center of the incumbent).

Public cloud platforms

Public cloud adoptions, in recent years, have gained momentum in the industry, from a software, platform, and infrastructure as a service perspective. With the path to the public cloud not being that straightforward due to legacy procedures, governance, security, and compliance requirements, incumbents have been establishing cloud platform teams to facilitate this journey. The focus of these teams in most cases is multidimensional:

- Deliver public cloud solutions, from an infrastructure, platform, and tooling perspective, across SDLC environments.

- Define the public cloud operating model along with the Agile DevOps teams and the core infrastructure teams, including capability demarcation, CloudOps, and FinOps.

- Ensure adherence to compliance requirements, through policy engineering controls and built-in by-design security baselines.

- Conduct public cloud due diligence exercises across various public cloud vendors.

- Hands-on support in the onboarding of tenants, either through lift and shift or application "cloud-native re-engineering."

- Definition of cloud-native standards and qualification assessments in cooperation with the enterprise architecture, core infrastructure, other DevOps platforms, and the DevOps CoE.

- In many cases, frontrunning of SRE standards implementation.

- Incubation and training of the agile DevOps teams.

Through my personal experience in working with incumbents, I have discovered two interesting findings when it comes to public cloud vendor choices and corresponding setups of public cloud teams. Firstly, their main focus from a diligence perspective is concentrated around the following dominant use cases and corresponding vendor choices. To make it clear, my intention is not to advertise any particular public cloud provider, and I appreciate that different incumbents make different choices. The following is, though, a very accurate, representative example of the industry's choices:

Use case	Vendor choice
Collaboration and office tools	Microsoft Azure
Data center offloading	Amazon Web Services
Scaled and rapid calculation engines	Microsoft Azure
Deployment of CI/CD pipelines	Microsoft Azure, Amazon Web Services, and Google Cloud Platform
Big data and machine learning	Google Cloud Platform
Composable banking	Amazon Web Services
Anti-money laundering and know your customer	Google Cloud Platform
Customer resource management and analytics	Amazon Web Services
Greenfield mobile banking	Amazon Web Services and Google Cloud Platform
Payments	Microsoft Azure and Amazon Web Services

Table 7.4 – Public cloud use cases and vendors in the FSI

As you can see from the preceding table, it looks quite balanced and confirms the multi-cloud approach of incumbents (my second observation), driven on the one hand by the business lines' use cases, and on the other hand by regulatory requirements around continuity and data retention across different geographical regions of the world.

Following the reality of the multi-cloud context, to ensure dedication and building expertise, incumbents are forming dedicated cloud vendor DevOps public cloud platform teams. In many organizational structure cases, they belong under the same public cloud center of excellence or the same public cloud community of practice. The scope of these teams is not only to achieve excellence in the adoption of a certain cloud provider's capabilities but also to ensure the highest possible degree of hybrid cloud *solution agnosticness* (compliance, security, orchestration, CI/CD, and observability), as well as enabling the pragmatic demarcation of the public cloud operating model's organizing principles and demarcation across the totality of the broader DevOps ecosystem of stakeholders.

Summary

In this chapter, we focused on the technological enablement of the DevOps 360° operating model. We outlined the inevitably strong value proposition of technology for the DevOps evolution, and we analyzed the term *technological ecosystem*, also outlining the six main organisms that comprise it. We continued by looking into arguments on busting the myth of equalizing DevOps with technology, concluding that technology is just another enabler of DevOps and not its whole essence. Afterward, we moved on to discuss two initiatives that currently dominate incumbents' DevOps technology agenda, which are engineering transformation and technology standardization. On the latter, apart from outlining its value proposition, we also discussed why it is important to take precautions. The DevOps platform teams dominated the core of this chapter and we discussed them across several dimensions. Starting by outlining their value proposition, we moved on to outlining proven operating and service models that incumbents have adopted, also discussing the importance of product and service catalogs. The latter we also connected with initiatives such as *technology menus*, which are presently gaining momentum in the industry. Continuing with talking about DevOps platform teams, we argued the importance of establishing responsibility demarcation, as well as a social contract between the platform and its tenants, highlighting their relationship to DevOps journeys, productivity, and experience. We closed the chapter by examining the five main domains of focus for incumbents when establishing DevOps platform teams.

In the next chapter, we will deep dive into the *dark* and misperceived world of DevOps compliance in banking.

8

360° Regulatory Compliance as Code

This chapter constitutes the third and last piece of the DevOps capabilities enablement and engineering part of the book and is dedicated to regulatory compliance. It starts with setting the regulatory compliance scene in the **Financial Services Industry (FSI)**, as well as discussing the four main categories of regulatory requirements that an incumbent bank can be subject to. The chapter continues with one of its core themes, which is the regulatory compliance value proposition for DevOps 360° evolution. That is presented through four real stories from my DevOps career in the FSI. Continuing, we enter the second main part of the chapter, which is focused on two core domains directly related to DevOps regulatory compliance, one of IT (or DevOps) controls and one of **Segregation/Separation of Duties (SoD)**. Starting with the DevOps controls, we examine their regulatory origin, along with their nature and relation to the DevOps SDLC capabilities. Continuing, we outline a pragmatic approach to define the controls, looking into aspects such as their anatomy and evidence tiering, along with feasibility and relevance assessments. We close the controls section by outlining important recommendations to consider when designing your framework. Moving on, we enter the last part of the chapter, which is dedicated to SoD. Through that, we provide the definition of SoD and its background and regulatory intention, accompanied by a traditional example. Furthermore, we deep dive into the two main distinctions that characterize and shape SoD policies, which are the ones of data and function. Following this, in an attempt to make the context more vivid, we use the Agile DevOps teams organizing principle models that we defined earlier in the book, outlining a pragmatic SoD approach. The chapter closes with a comprehensive outline of recommendations on how to manage the relationship with your regulator.

In this chapter, we're going to cover the following main topics:

- The overarching regulatory compliance scene for incumbent banks

- The regulatory compliance value proposition for DevOps, through four real industry stories

- A pragmatic approach toward designing DevOps controls

- A pragmatic approach toward an SoD policy

- Recommendations on how to approach the relationship with your regulators

Setting the regulatory compliance scene in the FSI

This chapter is dedicated to what you might call a *sensitive* and *misconceived* concept in relation to DevOps evolutions: the *notorious* regulatory compliance! As we mentioned in *Chapter 1, The Banking Context and DevOps Value Proposition* the main actor of this book is a systemically important bank of global scale. Our incumbent, due to its size, scale of operations, and importance in terms of global financial stability, is inevitably subject to significant regulatory demand. Especially following the global economic impact of the 2008 financial crisis (especially the collapse of Lehman Brothers), as well as the rapid technological advancements of the past decade, the regulatory demand has become tougher. This demand, as we also mentioned in *Chapter 1, The Banking Context and DevOps Value Proposition* is no longer predominantly focused on an incumbent's business operations, but it is equally applied to the ways that our incumbent designs, builds, deploys, and operates software, going across the SDLC. The regulatory puzzle can become even more complex for our incumbent, in cases of the global or regional systemic importance of its operations, which implies that it is subject to three layers of regulatory frameworks: local, regional, and global. To make the situation even more complex, our incumbent, in addition to being subject to external regulatory compliance demand, is also subject to internal compliance policies (banking secrecy and code of conduct). As you can understand from the context outlined so far, addressing regulatory compliance demand is literally a full-time job for an incumbent bank. It is not a coincidence that if you look into an incumbent's internal organizational structure, you will find several units dedicated to regulatory compliance causes, from group IT audit to business non-financial risk and controls, and from group data protection to anti-fraud and money laundering protection.

What are the regulatory compliance categories?

I am not entirely sure whether the following classification categories are formalized in the industry. But based on my own (quite extensive) experience, typically, regulatory compliance demand can be classified into four broad categories, with certain overlaps:

- **Enterprise wide**: These are requirements primarily delivered by the main regulator of the incumbent and include domains such as capital liquidity, business continuity, and anti-money laundering.

- **Business domain specific**: These are requirements that are business line focused, for instance, MiFID II and FRTB for capital markets and PSD 2 for payments and transaction banking.

- **Business/banking secrecy**: These are internal requirements defined by the incumbent's business and legal units, often in relation to responding to a broader regulation. An example of banking secrecy is who from the incumbent's employees can have access to specific data (for example, capital liquidity reporting) or to perform specific actions (for example, approving the market risk exposure numbers).

- **Technology operations and risk management**: These requirements are focused on the means that an incumbent is using to deliver and operate software and technological solutions, ensuring continuity and risk management.

As you can probably guess, you will rarely find a regulatory compliance requirement that one way or another does not have an impact on all four categories (regulatory spillover effect) and whose response will not require the involvement of technological assets. I mean, naturally, to ensure business continuity, you need technology continuity; to deliver on PSD 2, you need technological assets; and to restrict access to banking secrecy data, you need access management rights implemented in an application. As I have mentioned earlier in the book already, *technology is obviously becoming an integral part of the banking business.*

What can the impact of not being "compliant" be?

Different regulatory compliance requirements have different magnitudes and cause implications of different levels of severity if the incumbent fails to deliver on them. Running out of capital liquidity, for instance, can put the incumbent's ability to fulfill credit liabilities at risk. This can cause a broader economic domino effect. On the other hand, performing regression tests manually instead of automatically does not really have the same impact. Understanding a regulatory compliance requirement equals understanding its impact. So, let us look into what the main implications can be if an incumbent fails to satisfy regulatory demand:

- **The license to operate can be at risk**: I'm not sure whether a systemically important bank has ever lost its license due to a failure to comply with regulatory demand, but it is a possibility. This is also used as an argument by incumbents to ensure regulatory compliance work is focused on internally (I've just shared a secret of the business; don't tell anyone).

- **Monetary fines**: Fines can be applied in cases of failure to comply. They are either direct (special one-off items on the balance sheet) or warnings. The latter causes capital from the balance sheet to be reserved if the warning materializes.

- **Deadline extensions**: There is a saying in regulatory terms: *As long as you demonstrate satisfactory progress and transparency, deadline extensions can be granted.*

- **Reputational loss**: The image of the incumbent can be damaged in the broader industry and society. As an ex-CIO of mine used to say, *Let us not end up on the front page of the newspapers.*

- **Other initiatives are stopped**: Prolonging or delaying regulatory compliance work can have a significant and negative impact on other priorities and activities in progress. That is especially the case when compliance gets priority 0, as in, prioritized above everything.

- **People attrition**: When regulatory turbulence is there, it has been noticed that people start leaving the organization due to the uncertainty caused by the potential implications of failing to comply.

- **Supervision becomes tighter**: As expected, if discipline is not demonstrated, the pressure from the regulators will increase.
- **Threat to the overall financial stability**: Depending on the level and nature of regulatory non-compliance, the overall financial stability of the industry and society is put at risk.

The impact, in many cases, can obviously be a combination of the preceding implications, and as the regulatory compliance landscape has multiple sources and layers, the severity per business line can vary.

What is the compliance value proposition in relation to the DevOps 360° evolution?

As you would have expected, based on the nature of this book, we will focus on category four of regulatory compliance, with regard to technology operations and risk management. That does not mean that we will not touch on the other three categories at all, as it is inevitable due to the strong interaction and dependencies.

> **Before We Move on**
>
> Our focus in this chapter should be perceived as belonging to the responsibilities of the *compliance as code workstream* of the DevOps 360° enterprise evolution, which we defined in *Chapter 3, The DevOps 360° Operating Model Pillars and Governance Model*.

As with any other enabler of our DevOps 360° evolution, the value proposition of regulatory compliance goes two ways. As you already know or can guess, regulatory requirements influence the direction of the DevOps 360° evolution, while in parallel, the DevOps 360° evolution influences the response to the regulatory requirements. In detailing the value proposition in this chapter, I will follow a different approach than done in the previous ones. Instead of choosing a banking business domain or application and relating that to DevOps, I will recite to you four personal short stories.

> **A Personal Confession**
>
> These four stories made my DevOps career and all four were initiated by regulatory compliance, thus my passion for compliance.

Story 1 – the European Central Bank audit on technology operations

Once upon a time, in one of the banks I worked at, we were subject to a **European Central Bank** (**ECB**) audit. Part of the findings of the ECB report was: *significant manual interventions in the software development and quality assurance processes, which can cause human errors and software defects.* They were spot on, actually. The adoption of our CI/CD pipelines was in the early stages, the majority of deployments were manual, automated regression, integration, and user acceptance tests were very limited, and the lead time to provision a test environment with the necessary data was 1 month. In addition, there was a lack of harmony on how to automatically generate the change request evidence. As you can guess, we had to take action to comply, and we did with big collective success:

- All the business and highly critical applications were onboarded to the standard CI/CD pipeline.

- 70% of deployments across the portfolio became automated.

- A new cross-level test automation framework was created and adopted in the top 20 business-critical applications.

- The test environments and data provisioning lead times were taken down to 1 week.

- The necessary evidence for all change requests was populated (semi) automatically.

Did we just become compliant? No. We became faster and more technologically advanced. Keep this point in mind as we will come back to it.

Story 2 – the Markets in Financial Instruments Directive (MiFID II) ecosystem

MiFID II is a financial markets legislation instituted by the European Union in 2018 in an attempt to harmonize the financial services regulations across the European Union. Its main aim is to increase the investor protection of financial instruments (such as equities and bonds) through greater transparency of financial instruments information (asset type, price, performance, and so on). Part of this transparency includes what is called **transaction reporting obligation**, which is the main trigger for this story. Under the new regulation, the frequency of reporting transactions to the regulations dropped to no later than the close of the next working day. Without going into more unnecessary detail, back then, in one of the banks I worked at, our legacy infrastructure could not cope with that new frequency; it was as fragile as a drinking glass. We also had data completeness challenges. What did we do to make sure we could comply?

- Replaced legacy batch-oriented messaging queues with real-time event streaming APIs

- Improved our observability framework in terms of end-to-end transaction monitoring, data completeness, and reconciliation

- Delivered a new trade hub solution dedicated to regulatory transparency

- Improved the MiFID II ecosystem of application resiliency through engineered error-handling mechanisms

Did we just comply with MiFID II? No. We built solid technological capabilities and platform modernization patterns.

Story 3 – the Fundamental Review of the Trading Book (FRTB) platform modernization

FRTB is a global financial services legislation that defines the minimum regulatory capital requirements that apply to banking activities of trading financial instruments. One of its main focus areas is the domain of market liquidity risk. This is by introducing changes in how market risk is calculated, as well as introducing different portfolio stress test scenarios that banks need to be able to provide evidence of their ability to handle. These new introductions required the applications that handle market risk calculations to be able to cater to way more complex, frequent, fast, and large scenarios. As you could guess, our old-school market risk infrastructure and continuous delivery capabilities could not cope with the new requirements. Hence, we had to almost redo the entire market risk infrastructure to ensure compliance against FRTB, from both a functional and non-functional quality perspective. What did we do?

- Built from scratch two flagship cloud-native applications for market risk scenario incubation and stress testing. They were built on independent and containerized microservices and operational data storage.

- Implemented the latest state-of-the-art observability capabilities and onboarded the applications into advanced CI/CD pipelines, which could support 15-minute (commit to production) release velocity.

- Built a **site reliability engineering** (**SRE**) team dedicated to the operations and reliability aspects of the FRTB ecosystem.

- Improved the speed and quality of data deliveries of the upstream systems, delivering before the daily 07:00 a.m. cutoff, while reducing the time market risk managers were spending on manual corrections.

Did we just deliver for FRTB? No. We transformed legacy applications and infrastructure to cloud native, built the first-ever SRE team, and improved the experience of market risk managers.

Story 4 – the IT controls framework for the financial supervisory authority

In one of the banks I worked for, we had a revision inspection by the local financial services supervisory authority, where they assessed our risk management capacity in terms of software development and operations. In the inspection's follow-up report, it was stated that the IT risk management framework implemented in the SDLC did not provide adequate coverage of software quality, security, and reliability for a bank of our size. Therefore, we were given the task to advance it to higher standards. As expected, of course, we could not just refine the IT controls without impacting the SDLC's design, as the controls were to be implemented through the SDLC. Hence, we decided to take that as an opportunity to advance the entire SDLC, while advancing our IT controls. What did we achieve?

- We modernized the entire SDLC and divided it between legacy mainframes and modern/cloud-native applications and platforms, ensuring that we could enable at least two speeds.

- We totally revised the IT controls and redesigned them tactically across the new SDLC, following policy as code to speed the adoption up and remove manual interventions.

- We advanced our technological capabilities to be able to cater to the new policy as code controls, which are built in by design.

- We achieved a significant level of evidence-generation automation.

Did we just comply with regulatory demand? No. We modernized our SDLC, got together over 20 teams to collaborate on achieving that, and increased our policy as code and technological capabilities interoperability.

These were just four out of the many regulatory compliance-driven DevOps stories I have. I am certain that they were quite vivid in demonstrating the regulatory compliance value proposition for a DevOps 360° evolution. It is important that you realize this regulatory compliance value proposition in your organization, as it is also backed up by two fundamental assets of DevOps evolution success. As it is compliance, note the following:

- It has to be done, which means it (often) gets priority 0.

- It has to be funded, which means you can use the allocated budget to push the DevOps innovation boundaries.

As you could see in the preceding stories, regulatory compliance triggered us to explore new DevOps approaches, concepts, and technological capabilities and respond to regulatory demand through them. This is what we mean by *regulatory compliance as code* in this book: the ability to become compliant using DevOps concepts and technological and engineering means. Concluding this section, the value proposition of regulatory compliance in DevOps 360° evolution is of large magnitude. *Compliance work is a blessing and full of opportunities, if you are creative in your approach to it*, in my opinion.

What are the core DevOps-related regulatory compliance domains of the incumbent's focus?

In this section, we will get into the details of the core DevOps-related regulatory compliance domains that incumbents currently have a strong focus on. They are the DevOps controls and the SoD policy. In each of them, we will outline the background of their origin and the value proposition and present some practical suggestions derived from industry-proven practices.

> **Warning**
>
> The presented practices of the coming subsections have been agreed upon with the regulatory body of the respective incumbents. Do not take them for granted in your context without being aware of the contextual details of those representative incumbents and the relationship with their regulator. Nevertheless, you can perceive them as an indication of good quality and pragmatism.

The DevOps controls

You will find these controls named either SDLC or IT controls, but their scope is the same: *design and implement adequate controls across the SDLC to ensure reliability, security, and protection of IT assets*. In our book, we will use the term **DevOps controls** for obvious reasons. Let us start from the basics and define what a control is. The most mainstream, and accepted by regulators, definition of a control is *a policy or procedure that provides adequate assurance that the incumbent's technology assets are used as intended*. Do you find this definition vague? Welcome to the world of regulatory compliance in technology!

> **Be Careful!**
>
> The term *controls* has a negative connotation. The word implies that you want to control the actions of someone. Minimum viable adoption or adherence is a better term for positioning the controls in your DevOps evolution, as we will see in *Chapter 10, Tactical and Organic Enterprise Portfolio Planning and Adoption*.

Typically, the background of the DevOps controls does not originate from or is not attributed to specific legislation. The supervisory authorities mostly categorize them under IT risk management or technology operations frameworks. The lack of clear legislation makes the DevOps controls' clarity, depth, and strictness context dependent. Its context sensitiveness depends on mostly two parameters:

- The size of the financial services institution, which could be globally, regionally, or locally systemic, or not systemic at all. Without the intention to advertise or downplay any incumbent, you would expect HSBC to have stricter controls compared to DBS Bank and DBS Bank to have stricter controls compared to a small Greek bank.

- The main regulatory body responsible for supervising the financial services institution. I have personally worked in FSIs supervised by the ECB, the **European Banking Authority (EBA)**, the British **Financial Conduct Authority (FCA)**, and the four Nordic **financial supervisory authorities (FSAs)**. I can assure you that the more important the regulatory supervisor, the tougher the controls (I just revealed a business secret).

When explaining sensitivity, one must, for instance, expect the demand on IT controls of the ECB toward a globally systemically important incumbent to be greater than the respective demand of the Swedish FSA on an incumbent that is systemically important only from a Swedish economy perspective. This is natural, as the larger the potential economic disruption, the more precautions need to be taken as part of IT risk management. Having said this, in my experience of working with all of them, I have observed significant overlaps in their respective requirements, which is expected.

What are the domains and controls in focus?

The supervisors are quite targeted on the domains of focus when inspecting incumbents from an IT risk management and technology operations perspective. The main domains, along with proposed controls that can be adopted, are the following:

- **Service continuity and reliability**: Disaster recovery plans, evidence of full site failover testing, and evidence of SLA existence and adherence

- **Quality assurance**: Unit testing, test automation, production-like test environments, mandatory preproduction environments, test evidence, and test-level plans

- **Business signoff**: User acceptance test, traceability of requirements and test cases, and product owner change request signoff

- **Data integrity and protection**: Access management and permissions on business applications, IT assets, data and tools, SoD, and data classification

- **Service health visibility**: Monitoring of critical infrastructure services and events

- **Service logging**: Application, infrastructure, security, operational, and audit logging

- **Software development common practices**: Task management, solution architectural designs, static code analysis, non-functional requirements included in application design, secure code development practices, and application and service decommissioning

- **Security policies**: Container image scanning, application security scanning, secrets management, third-party dependency scans, open source library scans, artifact vulnerability scans, IaC security scans, and public cloud landing zone security baselines

- **SDLC automation**: Automated builds, automated change management, automated incident management, deployment automation, post-verification checks, and rollback automation

In addition to the previous mainstream categories, and as mentioned previously, the size of the incumbent bank and its regulatory body defines how much the preceding list is to grow in the depth and breadth of its coverage. Before moving on, I would like to clarify one thing. A pragmatic approach to designing and implementing DevOps controls must be inspired and enabled by balanced DevOps engineering capabilities. DevOps controls contribute to not only IT risk management but also fulfilling the equilibrium of *time to market-reliability-compliance*. While the latter two equilibrium elements can be associated with managing risk, the former is about speed. In other words, your controls should support your organization in moving faster, while proactively mitigating risks. It's a CD balance if you wish; controlled deployment while performing continuous deployment.

When should you think of controls in the DevOps evolution?

Do you recall *Chapter 6, DevOps Software Development Life Cycle 360° Evolution and Engineering* and the process we proposed in defining the DevOps 360° SDLC? And do you maybe recall *Phase 3 – further enrichment* as part of iteration 2? You will notice that that phase is when we started injecting the controls notation into the DevOps 360° SDLC. It is during the design of the DevOps 360° SDLC that I propose you need to either design from scratch or redesign the controls. In order to achieve that effectively, as part of your DevOps 360° SDLC background work, you need to make sure you understand the regulatory compliance demand from a control perspective. How much work this will be depends on your starting point of control adoption.

The DevOps control anatomy

We saw in *Chapter 6, DevOps Software Development Life Cycle 360° Evolution and Engineering* the DevOps capability anatomy; the DevOps control anatomy is of similar depth in order for it to fulfill the four elements of the 360° quality of DevOps, as well as to be classified as *complete and adequate* from a regulatory supervisor's perspective. The following figure demonstrates what we can with confidence call a DevOps control anatomy, using the regression test of the critical path of an application as an example:

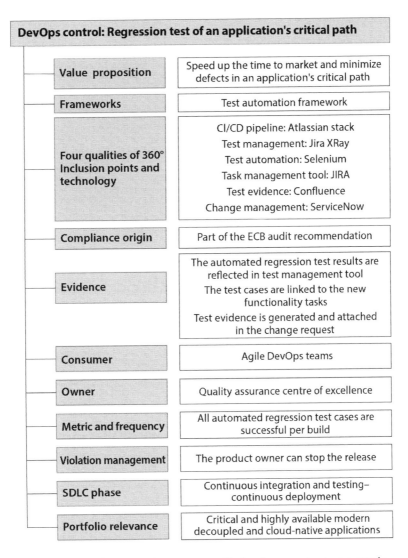

Figure 8.1 – DevOps control anatomy – critical path regression test example

I'm sure most of the anatomy elements will be quite intuitive to all of you. However, I would like to bring a couple of them into focus as they stand out in terms of importance:

- **Value proposition**: Controls are as much about speed as they are about risk. This must be boldly reflected in the value proposition. You should not implement a control only for compliance purposes, but to advance your DevOps evolution.

- **Compliance origin**: Be super specific on this one to ensure linkage, transparency, and traceability back to the regulatory requirement or recommendation you address.

- **Evidence**: If you cannot prove it, you are not doing it. It is vital to be clear on the evidence and ensure automation to bring the most harmonious outcome of the respective artifacts.

- **Owner**: Whoever owns the control on the one hand has accountability for it and on the other hand is the single point of contact for your regulator.

- **Metric and frequency**: How you measure the success or failure of the control's adoption needs to be clarified, as well as how frequently the control is triggered.

- **Violation management**: You need to be absolutely clear on what the consequences are if the control fails.

- **SDLC phase**: It is important to keep a good balance of controls and not overload certain DevOps 360° phases, while you shift most of them left in the SDLC.

- **Portfolio relevance**: Not all controls are equally applicable across your portfolio. In our example, only the critical and highly available decoupled and cloud-native applications will be faced with this control.

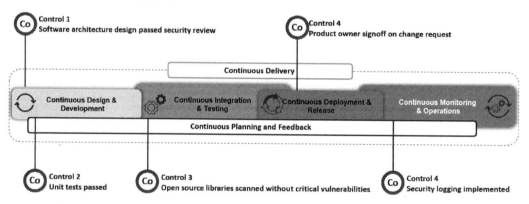

Figure 8.2 – Balancing DevOps controls across the DevOps 360° SDLC phase example

As was also mentioned in the DevOps capability anatomy, understanding the DevOps control anatomy is essential from multiple dimensions and is a key determinant that will lead both your adoption efforts as well as your regulatory talks.

What do control tree adoption and evidence look like?

The control adoption and evidence tree have three main levels. The following figure provides an example using the static code analysis control:

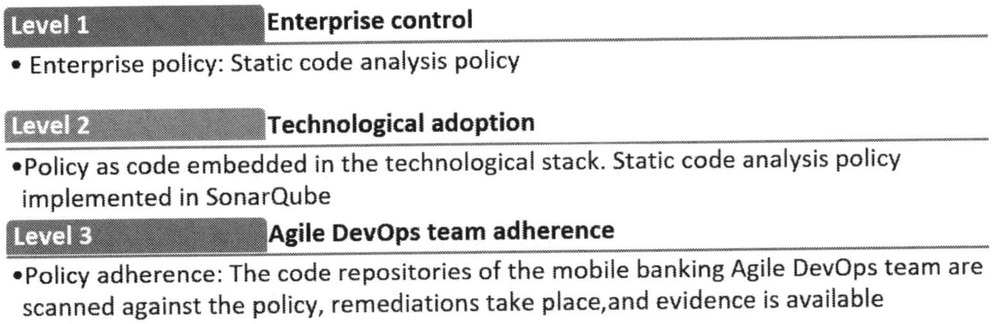

Level 1	Enterprise control

- Enterprise policy: Static code analysis policy

Level 2	Technological adoption

- Policy as code embedded in the technological stack. Static code analysis policy implemented in SonarQube

Level 3	Agile DevOps team adherence

- Policy adherence: The code repositories of the mobile banking Agile DevOps team are scanned against the policy, remediations take place, and evidence is available

Figure 8.3 – The IT controls enablement, adoption, and evidence tree for static code analysis

What are the important questions regarding your overall controls inventory?

Once you have conducted the design or revision of your DevOps controls process, the final outcome is your DevOps controls inventory. There are some key questions that you need to answer, looking at the inventory, which we have noted as follows:

- Do we need all the DevOps controls to demonstrate completeness and adequacy?

- Are all of them real controls, or are some operational efficiencies or capabilities?

- Have we exhausted the "shift left" approach and practices available in the SDLC possibilities?

- What is the priority of enabling and adopting? Is static code quality analysis more important than open source vulnerability scans?

- Are there any DevOps controls that we foresee challenges for in automating and therefore we need to descope to avoid introducing unnecessary slowdown in the time to market?

How to conduct a readiness, feasibility, and relevance assessment

Having looked at the totality of your DevOps controls inventory, you will need to conduct a readiness, feasibility, and relevance assessment for each control. Good questions include the following:

- Can it be enabled in the central and common technologies, using policy as code?

- Is it technology-/vendor-specific or agnostic?

- Can it be fully automated in the technology stack and be consumed as a service?

- Does it require a human signoff in order to be completed?

- Is it applicable across the portfolio of applications classification?

- Is it part of the critical path of the DevOps 360° SDLC?

- Can evidence be generated automatically?

- Does its violation constitute a justified reason to stop a release?

- Does it quickly generate false positives?

- Do we have full control of it, or do we depend on third parties?

- Are its input and output triggering events clear?

Top considerations to take when designing the controls

The following is my list of lessons learned from my collective experience over the years:

- You should enable a mechanism of periodical and random *trust but verify checks*. You will not be subject to regulatory assessments and revisions frequently and you do not know the relationship between your product owner and the respective agile DevOps teams. You need to establish your own means of monitoring good behaviors.

- Your aim should be to make the DevOps controls *invisible*. Your people should be adhering to control policies without realizing it. There are predominantly three principles to follow to achieve that invisibility:

  - Policy engineering

  - Controls embodiment across the DevOps technological ecosystem

  - Shift left from the application design phase

- Keep your vendors close as they will be a key part of implementing the DevOps controls in platforms where you do not own the source code. In certain cases, be prepared to face resistance. In one of the investment banks I worked at, when we asked a leading vendor in the market data domain to provide, together with the platform upgrades, evidence of vulnerability scans and code quality, the answer was, "*We do not do that, you have to trust us.*"

- Do not buy control frameworks off the shelf. You will realize that their language, concepts, and relevance to your context will make them difficult to adopt.

- Never, ever get a consulting firm to lead this work. Consulting firms should support you only with industry insights and conceptualization input.

- The people within your organization that will be part of the DevOps control framework work must be DevOps experts who can understand and interpret the regulatory language and ideally have done regulatory work before.

- Expect that the DevOps control institutionalization will be yet another barrier to the agile DevOps team's autonomy.

- Repeated and severe DevOps control violations should be complemented with sanctions. Internal audit remarks need to be opened, teams need to be prohibited from releasing frequently, and business engagement on changing the team's backlog priorities will be required.

- You will have to distinguish between what a DevOps control is, what DevOps efficiency is, and what is on the borderline. For instance, an automated rollback should be perceived more as a DevOps efficiency, not a DevOps control. The ability to roll back, though, can be perceived as a control. This is important on the one hand so you do not overload the controls inventory, plus it will take time for people to automate certain controls. Until the automation is in place, as long as the DevOps controls can be executed, even manually, you should receive the green light.

- There is DevOps control adoption and adherence to be mindful of. We will get back to this in *Chapter 10, Tactical and Organic Enterprise Portfolio Planning and Adoption,* and *Chapter 11, Benefit Measurement and Realization*:

  - **Adoption**: Use static code quality tools and scan your repositories.

  - **Adherence**: Conduct remediation on the findings.

- Collect the best possible degrees of baselines as it is important to track progress. You can call the progress tracking measurements **key control indicators** (**KCIs**) if you wish.

- Make them technology agnostic! Not all your teams will be using the same technologies and you will probably introduce new technologies in the future. Your DevOps controls should be as *lift and shift* as possible.

- Where automated implementation and evidence generation is not possible, consider descoping, simplifying, or merging the respective control. A control that slows down time to market is not fit for purpose. In addition, in terms of evidence, you should strive toward *evidence as code*.

- As with your DevOps capabilities, the controls should also be part of frameworks and consist of playbooks and recipes.

- Involve your business counterparts in defining the violation management procedures. This is not a task to take place unilaterally by the technology areas alone.

Separation/segregation of duties

This section touches upon perhaps the most *debatable and notorious* regulatory compliance topic in the domain of DevOps: the infamous separation or segregation of duties. I am absolutely certain that all of you that have worked in the FSI know what separation or segregation of duties means. For the ones that do not, here is a definition that is quite aligned with the regulatory wording:

A role-based limitation of performed duties and access to data in order to mitigate the risk of fraud, data manipulation, and system misuse, through a single person's control.

The definition has mainly two parts, which in our incumbent's case indicate the following:

- A person who develops (software developer) the functional code/business logic of a payment application should not be allowed to promote that code to production.

- The production data cannot be accessed by everyone but only by authorized people.

The main intent of separation/segregation of duties is to draw the line on who is allowed to do what in the SDLC and who is allowed to access what data. That line of duties intends to add an extra risk mitigation layer to prevent, for instance, scenarios such as the following:

- A developer promoting code to production that is not tested

- Sensitive production data being accessible by unauthorized people

- Fraud through business logic manipulation by a single person

- Prevention of manual errors

Making a parenthesis

SoD is also applied to the business lines of an incumbent, not only the technological side. Examples include the following:

- An equity trader can only execute a trade order. The settlement of it needs to be approved by a settlement officer manually or through automated **straight-through processing** (**STP**) validations.

- The daily market risk report that is sent to the regulator needs to be approved by designated chief market risk officers.

In simple words, separated duties indicate "four-eyes principle" assurance across the value stream.

What does a traditional SoD implementation in a DevOps context look like?

Incumbent banks, based on their systemic importance level and main supervisory mechanism, have taken slightly different approaches to SoD. There is, nevertheless, a typical *traditional approach*, as the following table presents:

Role	Data access	Duty performed
Software development	Non-production environments and data	• Can access and develop business logic • Can access and develop operational logic • Cannot deploy to production
Software operations	Non-production and production environments and data	• Can access but not develop business logic • Can access and develop operational logic • Can deploy to production

Table 8.1 – Roles of segregation/separation and basic access principles

So, as you can see in this example, the teams that develop and operate software are mainly divided into two profiles with two segregated/separated duties: building software versus operating software. Also, as you notice, there are two main determinants for this distinction: data and duty.

The data determinant

Access to data is one of the two main determinants that define the SoD policy. Data is primarily divided into non-production and production data in a DevOps context:

- **Non-production data**: This is data that is used in the lower to production (and preproduction in certain cases) environments, such as development, user acceptance, or integration, and is obfuscated. Obfuscation is the process of masking production data, so it is no longer recognizable. For instance, if Spyridon, with `client_id:005`, is a client of Bank Amazing, obfuscation will produce the results of Donald Duck (also known as Spyridon) with `client_id:999`. This way, Spyridon's data structure can be used for testing, but Spyridon and his sensitive information are not revealed.

- **Production data**: This is real client and bank data that exists in the production (and preproduction in certain cases) environments. Production data has mainly three subcategories that define who can access it in a DevOps context:

  - **Personally identifiable information** (PII): This is data that can identify an individual or a corporation. Name, birth date, ID or passport number, and client ID are examples. A complete list of what counts as PII would differ to some extent depending on the region of the world (there would be differences between the US, the European Union, and Australia, for example). PII has a strong relation to the **General Data Protection Regulation (GDPR)**, which incumbents also need to adhere to.

  - **Banking secrecy**: This is a form of data classification arising from the banking industry's context. As the name suggests, it refers to data that can reveal the secrets of the bank and can differ from bank to bank. Examples are liquidity or counterparty risk exposure numbers, general ledger and treasury numbers, or financial instrument orders to be executed once the market opens. What is protected by banking secrecy can reveal *secrets of the business*, which can be used for fraud and illegitimate competition.

  - **Open**: Data that everyone can access.

Data is gold and it is stored everywhere, such as in databases, tools, code repositories, and messaging queues. Therefore, data management is becoming a vital activity. Understanding the *where* and *what* is very important from an access management perspective, as in, how to manage people's access to data. In the SoD world, access management is an essential element that consists of four layers:

- **Layer 1**: Client or bank production and non-production data, as we described earlier.
- **Level 2 – assets**: The main distinction here is assets directly used by business applications, including the application layer (online banking frontend), and IT assets used indirectly (CI/CD pipeline code repositories and build plans or server security logs and Kafka topics).

- **Level 3 – duration**: Duration of access is mainly divided into permanent, meaning the respective data can be accessed by the allowed user at any time, and **just in time** (**JIT**), which is access granted for a certain period of time. On fulfilling a certain operation and after its conclusion, it is revoked.

- **Level 4 – permissions**: These are normally divided into the following:

  - **Ability to read**: Ability to view a list of payment transactions or reading code stored in a code repository or an automation script in a monitoring tool

  - **Ability to write/update/execute**: Ability to amend a transaction, change the payment data, write a function in a code repository, or amend the automation script in the monitoring tool

To make it a little bit more complex, access seen from the *who has access* perspective is divided into two categories. The first one is humans, like you and I, through our Active Directory accounts. The second one is what is called a **technical or service account**. These accounts are not attributed to an individual, but to the operations of a whole department. Such accounts are mainly used for operational efficiency, such as deployments of code to production. Nonetheless, they are not the most compliant mechanisms, as they do not leave a *trace* of who has performed the action, which is the deployment in our example.

The duty determinant

The second determinator is the one of duty, simply implying whose duty it is to perform a function. To simplify things, in our DevOps context, there are two main duties: building and running software. To better understand duty, it is important to first understand the term **business logic**, as it is a fundamental element of SoD. Business logic, in regulatory terms, is *functional code that supports the fulfillment of a business activity, through the execution of logic defined by its business users.* The following are examples.

Suppose you are an interest rate derivatives trader, and you want to "price/valuate" an **interest rate swap** (**IRS**) before you decide on whether to book the trade or not. You are to use a certain pricing curve available in the derivates trading application to do so. The code that software developers have developed for the pricing curve to become functional and provide you with the ability to price an IRS is called business logic.

In our example about equity trading that we used on several occasions earlier in the book, in order for an equity trade to be processed with STP from deal capture to settlement without the need for a settlement officer to assess the trade's data validity manually, there is business logic applied. The trade's XML fields are being validated automatically by the equity settlement application, based on predefined business logic rules and whether there is a valid `trade_date` value, `trade_nominal` value, `trade_book` value, and so on. Those business logic rules are implemented and expressed in programming functions, written by software developers. Naturally, if the trade XML fields are empty or contain invalid values, the *trade auto-settlement* process will fail, and a settlement officer will have to manually conduct checks.

In simple words, consider business logic as any functional piece of code that allows business units to run their business.

Now, there is also another type of logic used in SoD, and that is what is often called **operational logic**. Operational logic is code or scripts developed to enable operational efficiencies that do not directly enable a business activity. They can be as follows:

- Infrastructure auto-healing scripts
- Infrastructure as code provisioning scripts
- Application monitoring scripts
- Deployment playbooks

Having seen both types of logic, and also by simplifying the reality of banking operations a little bit, in an incumbent's SoD world, the people who write business logic meet either of the following:

- Cannot operate that logic in production
- Can operate it in production through certain organization, governance, and technological means

A pragmatic approach based on our Agile DevOps team's two models

Intentionally, I will not call the following approach a proven practice, as it might have been proven in a certain incumbent's context, but when addressing regulatory compliance, there are too many context-specific parameters to be considered. In outlining the approach, we will use as a basis the two models that we defined in *Chapter 5, Business Enterprise Agility and DevOps Ways of Working Reconciliation*: the dynamic/rotational model, which is closer to the segregation of tasks, and the fixed model, which is closer to the segregation of duties.

Refreshing our memory, the *modus operandi* of the dynamic/rotational model is close to *you build it, you run it*, corresponding more with the segregation of tasks or rotational duties.

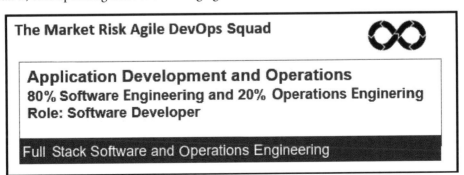

Figure 8.4 – The dynamic/rotational model – separation/segregation of tasks

On the other hand, the *modus operandi* of the alternative is *you build it, we run it*; the *build* under the software developer role and the *run* under the operations engineer role are clearly defined duties.

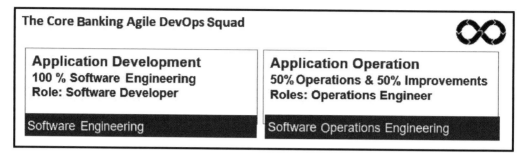

Figure 8.5 – Fixed roles model – separation/segregation of duties

The rotational model SoD approach

In this model, your SoD and corresponding access management mechanisms should allow the developers to rotate in the task/duty of deploying code to the production environment and running the application's operations. This means that during the rotation period, they will have access to production IT assets and data. The SoD policy will look similar to the following:

Role	Data Access	Duty Performed
Software developer	Non-production environments and data	• Can access (read & write) and develop business logic • Can access (read & write) and develop operational logic • Cannot deploy to production
Rotational developer supporting production	Non-production environments and data Production environments and data, using just in time	• Can access (read & write) and develop business logic • Can access (read & write) and develop operational logic • Can deploy to production

Table 8.2 – Rotational model sample SoD and IAM policy

What are the implications for the developer who will be rotating in supporting production?

- If needed for production support purposes, the developer will be granted *time-boxed* access to production through a JIT procedure. After completion of the needed task, the developer's access to production will be revoked.

- Under the four-eyes principle, the rotated-to-production developer will be the one deploying the release candidate to production, using special permissions in the CI/CD pipeline.

> **Note**
>
> Remember that the rotational setup is ideal for small applications, only used internally by the incumbent's business units, which require minimum production support and ideally do not contain PII data.

The fixed-model SoD approach

In this case, the situation is straightforward from the point of view of SoD and corresponding access management principles:

Role	Data Access	Function Performed
Software developer	Only non-production environments and data	• Can access (read & write) and develop business logic • Can access (read & write) and develop operational logic • Cannot deploy to production
Operations engineering	All environments and production data, using permanent access	• Can access (read) but not develop (write) business logic • Can access (read & write) and develop operational logic • Can deploy to production

Table 8.3 – Fixed-model sample SoD and IAM policy

The access rights of the software developers are identical to the rotational model. The differences are in the access of the operation engineers:

- No *write* access to code repositories that contain business logic. *Read* access is, however, allowed for incident and problem management purposes.
- The access to the production environments is permanent and not JIT.

> **Note**
>
> Remember that the fixed setup is ideal for large applications, used both internally by the incumbent's business units and external clients, which require dedicated production support and contain PII data.

SoD is a critical and sensitive matter and must be treated as such. The impact that it can have on your DevOps evolution, SDLC, WoW, organizing principles, adoption speed, employee satisfaction, and daily working efficiency is not to be downplayed.

> **Be Careful!**
>
> I have seen the preceding two setups working in certain contexts and upon enablement of strong organizational, governance, and technological influence, also with the necessary approvals and agreements with the respective regulators. Please do not take it for granted that they can be adopted in your context by default and ensure adequate compliance!

How to manage the relationship with your regulator

I am not sure whether most of you will agree with me on this statement, but your regulator should be perceived as one of the main stakeholders of your DevOps 360° evolution ecosystem (which we have come across in *Chapter 3, The DevOps 360° Operating Model Pillars and Governance Model*). How you handle this relationship will prove to be quite *strategic* in your DevOps evolution. While shaping your tactics, you should take two facts into consideration. Firstly, your regulator does not have the desire to punish you or make you fail. Quite the opposite, based on my experience, or as an ex-peer of mine used to say: "*It is just basic hygiene and good practices that they are asking for.*" At the end of the day, it is their job to protect society, the economy, and your bank. So, if they ask you to monitor your SLAs, prove your ability to fail over between data centers, and pass the penetration testing exercise, before you complain that they are asking for too much, consider why you are not already doing these necessary things. Secondly, most probably, your regulator will not be *DevOps advanced*. Normally, regulatory requirements come after industry concepts and technological advancements are launched in the market and adopted by incumbent banks. Therefore, your role will also be to educate them on DevOps WoW so they better understand your proposed approaches in order to address their requirements.

There are many areas to align with your regulator on, but here is a list of things that I believe are absolutely necessary to agree on, supported with some pieces of advice. I have divided this list into generic and *where relevant* items, as I wish to give special emphasis to the latter.

The general agreements are as follows:

- **Agree on regulatory bodies bandwagoning**: As a large incumbent of global operations, you will be subject to various supervisory authorities whose requirements might either overlap or conflict. Ensure you are in agreement with your regulators on who should be your main counterpart to ensure efficiency. The next agreement is another approach to respond to all your regulators.

- **Agree on the terminology and bare-minimum adequacy**: Different terms have different meanings for people; *complete* might mean one thing for you while meaning something else to your regulator. Agreeing on the meaning of fundamental terms is important to not misunderstand their requirements, as well as eliminating ambiguity. However, you should still try to take advantage of ambiguity. If a requirement or recommendation is not clear, do not go back for clarification as you risk overcomplicating the matter. Interpret it to your convenience and benefit (just told you yet another business secret). Also, it is important to agree on acceptable levels of adequacy, or as an ex-colleague of mine used to call it, **minimum viable compliance**. Is it, for instance, enough to automatically regression test only the critical path of an application, or do you need to cover all flows?

- **Is it a recommendation or requirement?** A trap that many fall into is differentiating between a regulatory requirement and a recommendation. The former is mandatory, with violations resulting in disciplinary action. The latter is as it states, just a recommendation, which is more of a good practice/piece of advice and not a hard requirement. Align on this aspect to avoid unnecessary extra work and urgency.

- **Agree on the evidence format and frequency**: Striving toward compliance, policy, and evidence "as code" is indeed the most effective way to address the regulatory demand and generate the respective evidence. But not all supervisory authorities are comfortable with reviewing GitHub repositories. Documentation is still one of the main means of regulatory evidence collection. While there is normally a grace period of up to 4 weeks to collect evidence, it is in your interest to do so more frequently, in certain cases triggered per code build, depending on the nature of the evidence.

- **The real deadlines**: We have all been in a situation of having *real* and *artificial* deadlines. Clarifying those can save time, stress, and money.

- **The SoD approach**: Obviously, there are many elements to agree upon in this domain. In my opinion, the two most important are as follows:

  - Whether or not the SoD is hardcoded

  - Whether the organizational, governance, and technological influence you plan to establish are sufficient to demonstrate compliance

The at relevance agreements are as follows:

- **Agree on the scope of the portfolio**: Here, you have to look at it from two perspectives:

  - **Application criticality**: How critical is the application for the incumbent, its regulator, clients, society, and the economy?

  - **Platform**: Mainframe, decoupled legacy, decoupled modernized, and cloud native

  Most probably, you will have in the (initial) scope the most critical applications that cover business-critical flows and will exist in your portfolio in the coming years.

- **Align your modernization strategy**: Should you spend time on an application that is to be decommissioned in 1 year? Normally, your regulator will allow you to descope applications that are to be decommissioned in 2 to 3 years. Nevertheless, they will ask you to frequently provide evidence of the decommissioning/modernization process and to add the potential replacements to your scope.

- **Agree on what a business application is and what a tool or an infrastructure asset is**: Typically, in an incumbent's context and portfolio, you will find five assets that come under regulatory consideration:

  - **Business applications**: These are applications used by internal business users or external clients. Mobile banking is one example.

  - **Business tools**: These are tools built by internal business users to support their daily work. Trade reconciliation business intelligence tools and trade pricing VBA scripts on Excel are examples.

  - **Operational tools**: These are tools that support the daily operations of your business. HR tools dominate this category.

  - **IT platforms and tools**: These are used by the technology teams to design, build, deliver, and operate software. Your CI/CD pipeline and observability tools belong here.

  - **IT infrastructure assets**: These are core infrastructure assets that support the SDLC, such as databases, servers, and ETL tools.

  You need to agree on which of the preceding assets are in scope and to what extent.

- **Exception process**: Last but not least, agree on what exactly the exception process is, what evidence is required for exceptions to be granted, and what the validity periods are.

As you can sense from the preceding, or as you will already know from experience, there is a lot you need to do with your regulator(s). Managing this relationship effectively can only have a positive impact on your DevOps 360° evolution.

> **Prevent a Dual Morality Standard on Addressing Regulatory Compliance Work**
>
> In international relations, a dual morality standard implies that certain rules and regulations are applied differently in state A than state B. This is not because of "relevance" criteria, but pure favoritism, due to state A, for instance, being a more powerful player in the international system's arena. Please do not treat the regulatory compliance pressure on your internal teams with favoritism.

Summary

In this chapter, we focused on maybe the toughest yet most important parts of the DevOps 360° operating model and evolution: regulatory compliance. We set the regulatory compliance scene for incumbents, also looking into the four main categories of regulatory requirements. In addition, we outlined the potential consequences an incumbent can be faced with when failing to address regulatory demand effectively. Afterward, we moved on to discussing the dedicated value proposition of regulatory compliance for DevOps, through the lenses of four real industry stories, which I had the pleasure to personally be a part of. In the second part of the chapter, we dived deep into the two main domains that have a direct influence on DevOps regulatory compliance, that of DevOps controls and the SoD. With the former, we explained its origin and outlined the core domains of regulatory focus, along with the proposed corresponding controls for addressing them. We furthermore looked into a pragmatic approach to design your DevOps controls framework. The focus was on presenting the detailed anatomy of a control, the three-level evidence mechanism, as well as some proven relevance and feasibility study questions. We closed the controls section by providing some top considerations, derived from real industry lessons learned. The last section was dedicated to the infamous SoD. Its background and regulatory motive were presented, along with an example of what it implies from a "traditional" approach perspective. We then zoomed into its two fundamental and determinant elements of distinction, data and duty, for which we provided detailed contextual parameters and examples. To relate SoD to real-world DevOps models, we used the two Agile DevOps team models we defined in the book: rotational and fixed. For those models, we defined some simple SoD and corresponding access management policy drafts, highlighting the similarities and differences between the two. The chapter closed with a real lesson learned and recommendations on how to handle the relationship with your regulator.

In the next chapter, we officially enter the third part of the book, which will focus on how to roll out, scale, and accelerate your DevOps 360° evolution. In particular, we will look at the fundamental aspect of *portfolio classification and service governance.*

Part 4:
Adopt, Scale, and Sustain

DevOps must be adopted at relevance. This chapter will discuss how to balance organic and tactical adoption and how to use techniques such as portfolio classification and service governance, as well as benefit measurement and realization.

This part of the book comprises the following chapters:

- *Chapter 9, The DevOps Portfolio Classification and Governance*
- *Chapter 10, Tactical and Organic Enterprise Portfolio Planning and Adoption*
- *Chapter 11, Benefit Measurement and Realization*
- *Chapter 12, People Hiring, Incubation, and Mobility*
- *Chapter 13, Site Reliability Engineering in the FSI*
- *Chapter 14, 360° Recap, Staying Relevant, and Final Remarks*

9

The DevOps Portfolio Classification and Governance

This chapter introduces us to the last part of the book, as well as to the third pillar of the DevOps 360° operating model: *rollout, accelerate, and scale*. In the coming sections, we will discover the aspects and importance of classifying, governing, and ensuring the readiness of your portfolio from a DevOps evolution perspective. The chapter starts by discussing the value proposition of portfolio classification for the DevOps 360° evolution. Moving on, we will look at the two dominant types of portfolio classifications that we can find in an incumbent bank context: one based on business and client impact criticality, and another based on a technological and architectural foundation. We will discuss both from a DevOps value proposition perspective, which will eventually lead to discussing the *DevOps speed formula*, as proposed in this book. Later in the chapter, we will introduce the concept of **license to continuously deliver** (LCD), which can be applied to a portfolio from a classification perspective and also from a DevOps adoption perspective. The anatomy of the LCD will be presented from eligibility criterion, license tiering, and governance model perspectives. We will dedicate the second part of the chapter to the portfolio registry, governance, and readiness mechanisms. We will cover their value proposition in relation to DevOps and, afterward, we will outline an example using a mobile banking application for reference. We will emphasize the DevOps attributes that can be assigned to a business application and provide guidance on its DevOps evolution journey requirements. The chapter will close with the framework of a production readiness assessment, examining its relationship with the DevOps evolution, while providing some examples for your inspiration.

In this chapter, we're going to cover the following main topics:

- The value proposition of portfolio classification for the DevOps evolution

- The two dominant DevOps portfolio classification mechanisms

- The DevOps speed formula

- The DevOps portfolio registry and governance mechanism

- The frameworks of LCD and production readiness review

What is the value proposition of portfolio classification in the DevOps 360° evolution?

As we have mentioned in several parts of this book, the DevOps evolution will not be equally applicable across our portfolio. *Relevance and speed* are two terms that underpin the foundation of this book, guiding us toward understanding the fundamental differences in situations and sub-situations that arise in an incumbent bank context. Those situations and sub-situations are tightly interrelated with the nature of the incumbent's portfolio of applications. Defining a mechanism for identifying relevance and speed criteria will add to the sophistication part of your evolution. In the first part of this chapter, we will uncover the aspects of portfolio classification in a DevOps context.

What do the terms portfolio and classification mean?

Let us start uncovering the terms by firstly defining them, starting with the term **portfolio**. In this book, with the term portfolio, we indicate the following:

- **Primary portfolio**: The business applications that are used by the incumbent's business units and end clients, which are delivered by the Agile DevOps teams. Examples include mobile banking, collateral management, online investments, and lending systems.

- **Secondary portfolio**: The core DevOps 360° technological ecosystem enablers (tools and platforms), which are used by the Agile DevOps teams on delivering the primary portfolio and consequently add business value. CI/CD pipelines, test automation frameworks, private cloud platforms, and more belong in this category.

The combination of the primary and secondary portfolios constitutes the totality of the DevOps portfolio. In this book, we will focus on the primary portfolio for several reasons:

- It is by nature subject to greater technological and business complexity.

- It constitutes one of the primary determinants of DevOps speed and relevance.

- It dictates to a significant extent the evolution of the secondary portfolio, being also its consumer and reason for existence.

- It is the one that adds direct end value to business users and external clients.

- It constitutes the main subject of regulatory compliance focus.

- It is the one that undergoes significant modernization work and is the core focus of the portfolio platform modernization strategy.

Moving on to our second key term of the chapter, which is **classification**, we define it as the grouping of the primary portfolio based on certain characteristics and parameters of similarity. In simple words, the main objective of portfolio classification is to group the business applications and launch your DevOps evolution to them accordingly, *at relevance in a multi-speed context*. That is, enable them to follow different DevOps evolution paths based on the groups they belong to, given their characteristics and parameters.

What is the difference between business applications and services?

Allow me to open a small parenthesis to clarify what we call a business application in an incumbent's context, as ambiguity can be caused by misunderstandings. The situation can get complex, especially if we are to distinguish between a business application and a business service. Therefore, in our book, we define the following:

- **Business application**: This is an information technology system that is used by business units and clients to conduct a sequence or variety of business activities.

- **Business service**: Activities that are enabled through a business application.

Let's visualize this using an example of mobile banking:

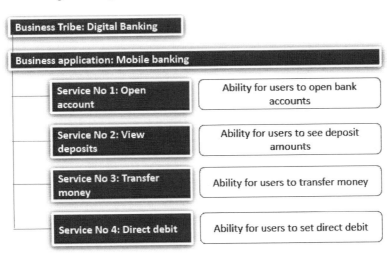

Figure 9.1 – Business application and services for mobile banking example

As we can see in the preceding diagram, the mobile banking business application contains four business services that provide users the ability to execute actions. In this book, we will focus on the business application level.

> **Note**
> Different incumbents and industries have different definitions of applications and services. The one we've provided, though, is considered to be a standard in the FSI and is accepted from a regulatory perspective.

How does a pragmatic classification of an incumbent's business application portfolio look?

Incumbents use various mechanisms to classify their business application portfolio. In this section, we will cover two different, yet dominant, classification types. The first one, which is accepted across the industry, is driven by the business application's criticality in terms of impact. Impact in this context is focused on business units, clients, and the supervisory authority in terms of service continuity and compliance. I have seen the second one adopted in advanced incumbents, and it is based on the technological and architectural foundation of a business application, strongly linked to its portfolio modernization strategy. In contexts where both classifications are applied, you will find them complementing each other.

What does a typical criticality classification look like?

This type of classification is driven by two aspects of criticality:

- **Business and client impact**: Considering the impact of the business application on the bank's business units and clients in the case of daily operations and activity disturbances. It also takes parameters such as revenue generation, client attraction, maintenance of competitive advantage, and overall reputation into consideration.

- **Regulatory impact**: This is based on how systemically important the business application is and whether disturbances to all or specific services can trigger domino effects in the FSI ecosystem and the broader real (local, regional, or global) economy.

As you can correctly guess, these two kinds of impact are interrelated and in a real incumbent's context, they are primarily measured against two parameters:

- Availability and resiliency levels of a business application
- Broader regulatory compliance coverage of a business application

> **Did You Know?**
>
> The primary criticality classification stakeholders in an incumbent bank are the business lines and the regulators. The technology teams can only advise and not classify business applications regarding criticality.

A quite representative classification based on business/client and regulatory impact is summarized in the following table:

Criticality level/ characteristics per impact category	Business and client impact (availability and resiliency driven)	Regulatory impact (regulatory compliance driven)	Availability and recoverability targets	Examples of business applications
Mission/ system critical	Significant disruption or total termination of vital business functions. Can result in broader economic ecosystem effects.	Results in license to operate risks and fines. Adherence to all the relevant regulatory compliance is a requirement.	Availability target: 99.9% **Mean time to restore (MTTR)** in case of natural disaster: 2 hours Restoration priority 1	Online and mobile banking Payments Regulatory and liquidity reporting Trading
Business critical	Considerable disruption to business functions. Could disrupt the society and economy.	Can result in fines. Adherence to all the relevant regulatory compliance is a requirement.	Availability target: 98% MTTR in case of natural disaster: 4 hours Restoration priority 2	Lending Market risk reporting Anti-money laundering and know your customer
Highly available	The impact on both the business functions and customers is noticeable but less severe.	Can result in fines. Adherence to certain regulatory compliance is a requirement.	Availability target: 97.5% MTTR in case of natural disaster: 8 hours Restoration priority 3	Safekeeping Invoicing
Standard	No impact on the end users and society and limited impact on internal business units.	Mostly descoped from the regulatory compliance work.	Availability target: 95% MTTR in case of natural disaster: 1 day Restoration priority 4	Business intelligence Data reconciliation Customer resource management

Table 9.1 – Business/client and regulatory impact criticality levels

The criticality classification based on business, client, and regulatory impact is considered a core mechanism for prioritizing the DevOps evolution adoption and regulatory work. The latter in particular is, in most cases, delivered in phases (waves) of criticality, as agreed with the regulators.

Beware the Reclassification toward Higher Criticality

Of course, during your evolution you will have to reclassify your portfolio, and there are ramifications if you do that. Licenses, doubling up the infrastructure cost, and on-call rotations are some of the elements you will have to add to the mathematical formula of the extra cost.

How does the criticality classification relate to the DevOps evolution relevance and speed?

Now you might be wondering how the criticality classification relates to the DevOps evolution. The higher the criticality, the more you need to invest in regulatory compliance adherence. This means that the DevOps controls for the top two criticality categories will be tougher than the latter two. If you also agree on a *waves adoption* approach with your regulator on your DevOps controls, then they will also have to be implemented first for these categories. Higher criticality also means you need to invest more in a business application's non-functional requirements, such as availability, resilience, performance, security, and scalability.

Higher criticality will most probably also mean that you need a dedicated operations engineering team (maybe an SRE team) for production support, indicating you will adopt the fixed roles Agile DevOps teams' organizing principles model. Moreover, higher criticality will mean that you need to be able to deploy fixes to production incidents with high velocity through advanced (speedy) CI/CD pipelines, but also have greater health visibility through advanced monitoring solutions. But also let us look at it from the lower two criticality category perspectives. For standard criticality applications, you will not have much to do from a regulatory compliance perspective and you do not need to stress the implementation of non-functional requirements. Moreover, your release velocity requirements will only depend on internal business demand, which means you have no market competition pressure.

Finally, the size of the applications puts them by default in the rotational mode of Agile DevOps teams organizing principles, which means you will not need a dedicated operations team.

Question

Have you already realized how the portfolio classification on the one hand reveals different speed levels and on the other hand provides the foundation of your DevOps at relevance evolution tactic? This is the beauty of adopting DevOps through sophistication.

Portfolio classification criticality and the DevOps speed formula

In this book, we are taking a broad perspective on criticality that does not focus only on availability and reliability. In our perception of criticality, we take into consideration a broad range of determinants that define it, as well as speed. Our argument is backed up by real DevOps adoptions and circumstances in the FSI. Those real examples make us realize that the more critical a business application is, the faster its release velocity is expected to be, the faster its ability to detect and recover from incidents has to be, and the greater focus on DevOps controls is required (remember that controls bring speed). This cannot be achieved without technological advancements, which in essence are triggered by the business unit's nature. It is technology and the business context and nature that in essence enable the means for release velocity, reliability, and compliance. With this logic, there are five determinants of criticality or speed, as outlined in the following formula:

Speed = criticality

(time to market + reliability + compliance + technology + business context)

Figure 9.2 – The DevOps speed formula

Let us elaborate on each determinant defining speed:

- *Time to market*: Critical factor for maintaining or creating competitive advantage in the market. It is critical that you can deliver new capabilities fast.

- *Reliability*: Application and service reliability is critical for maintaining or creating competitive advantage, demonstrating regulatory compliance, and increasing the Agile DevOps team's productivity. It is critical that either you are fast to prevent failure or when you fail, you fail fast, as in, you recover fast.

- *Compliance*: The faster you wish to move, the more you need to demonstrate adherence to certain controls in order to balance speed and IT risk management. It is a necessity to automate them so they do not slow you down. Therefore, the urge to move quickly makes you compliant and the other way around.

- *Technology*: Platform modernization and technological utility advancements enable you to move faster across the SDLC.

- *Business context*: Real-time, digital, and client-facing services that are also core sources of revenue and reputation demand a faster speed than non-real-time and internal services.

But apart from those preceding elaborations, please consider examples from your organizations. I am sure you will discover that the most critical parts of your portfolio are also the fastest at the same time, and this is everything but coincidence. Let us now go back to the traditional classification of criticality and enrich it based on our extended determinants of speed.

Criticality level/ characteristics per impact category	Business context	Time to market and release cycles	Business and client impact (availability and resiliency driven)	Regulatory impact (regulatory compliance adherence driven)	Technology modernization strategy
Mission/system critical	Real time and client facing	15 min on demand	Availability target: 99.9% MTTR in case of natural disaster: 2 hours Restoration priority 1	Strict adherence to all the relevant regulatory compliance requirements	Cloud-native incremental evolution
Highly available	Batch processing and non-client facing	Monthly	Availability target: 97.5% MTTR in case of natural disaster: 8 hours Restoration priority 3	Partial adherence to the regulatory compliance requirements	Mainframe – sustain with non-frequent enhancements

Table 9.2 – DevOps speeds criticality parameters

I will pause this topic here for now, as we will get back to it in the next chapter while discussing DevOps tactical adoption candidacy criteria.

What does a technological and architectural foundation classification look like?

We partly introduced this classification, if you remember, in *Chapter 6, DevOps Software Development Life Cycle 360° Evolution and Engineering* as part of defining the DevOps 360° SDLC. In this second classification category, it is not impact that is considered to be the determinant. It is the technological and architectural foundation of a business application. We will discover the details of this classification type by using a proven practice in the industry that is very pragmatic. The main four categories based on the technological and architectural foundation look like the following and are shaped around four main groups:

- **Mainframes**: Business applications built with technologies such as the IBM Z-Series and SAP R/2, with Cobol and HPS being the programming languages. The data is stored in databases such as ADABAS and DB2, with FTP files through batch processing being the dominant data transmission technology. Those applications are mainly large monolithic building blocks with a significant vendor dependency.

- **Decoupled legacy**: Non-mainframes that have a three-tier architecture with strong data and business logic dependency on mainframes. They are built on technologies that you have decided to stop using in your organization, such as PL/SQL and C++, IBM MQ, UC4 transmission channels, and MySQL databases.

- **Decoupled modernized (on-premises)**: There are applications that are decoupled from the legacy's business logic and data and built based on distributed architectures. They are usually developed in languages such as Java and .NET and are hosted on Linux or Windows machines. They might have undergone a microservices transformation and adopted basic cloud-native principles.

- **Cloud native (on-premises or public cloud)**: In this book, we classify independent microservices and containers-based applications that have undergone a cloud-native transformation or were built as such from the ground as **cloud-native**. The following two categories are included:

  - Applications hosted in your private cloud; IaC provisioned and/or hosted in your container platforms such as OpenShift or your internal Kubernetes instance

  - Applications hosted in public cloud providers and/or utilizing PaaS public cloud utilities

Business applications that fall into these four categories, to a smaller or larger extent, will undergo either a decommissioning, stagnation, evolution, or transformation journey, as we saw in *Chapter 4, Enterprise Architecture and the DevOps Center of Excellence*. This will depend on several circumstances (often unpredictable) and will influence their DevOps adoption over the course of your evolution.

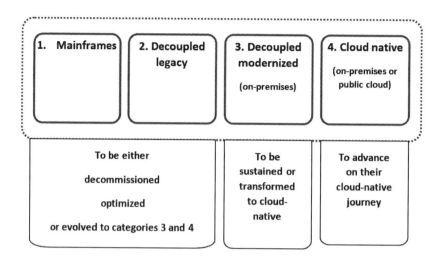

Figure 9.3 – Business portfolio classification based on a technological and architectural foundation

How does the technological and architectural classification relate to the DevOps evolution relevance and speed?

You will most probably find the business applications that you classify in category 4 to be the most DevOps advanced in your organization already. That is both a matter of necessity given their context (they need to move fast) and a matter of ability given their technological and architectural capabilities. For example, a cloud-native application provides a better foundation for the individual deployment of (micro)services within an application, the auto-scaling of those services, and independent monitoring. Moreover, and while it might be subject to increased DevOps controls, its technological foundation allows a great deal of control automation compared to a decoupled legacy application, for instance.

Furthermore, from a people perspective, you would expect to find talent that is willing to work with decoupled modernized and cloud-native applications. On the contrary, people with mainframe skills are not widely available in the industry, and you will find people working with decoupled legacy applications that wish to move internally toward the cloud-native portfolio. In addition, knowing that a mainframe application is on its decommissioning journey and is to be replaced with a cloud-native application, I doubt you will consider it in your DevOps evolution scope (maybe only from a reliability and operational perspective). The examples are countless, and you can keep going, considering that architecture and technology influence DevOps speed and relevance.

The linkage of your portfolio modernization strategy and DevOps evolution scope

Predicting the movement of business applications toward categories 3 and 4 is important. It is a task that many incumbents struggle with, though. Conflicting and changing priorities, unpredicted circumstances, difficulty to attract talent, and lack of know-how and funding make the prediction challenging and the future state of an application a moving target. Sometimes, actually, the situation becomes very complex, ending up with parallel runs on both the legacy and modernized applications, with uncertainty on whether the former will ever be totally unplugged. Things can really become paradoxical in this space. I have several personal stories, such as when we were building new interfaces to a legacy golden source instruments application, while at the same time working on decommissioning.

Nonetheless, you need to know (at least at a high level) the direction your portfolio is heading in order to target your DevOps evolution. And even if conducting this exercise on an enterprise level might be seen as an impossible mission, it is at least important that it is conducted on business lines, value streams, or at the tribe level. A sufficient time span to plan toward is 3 years, both by being pragmatic about what it takes, but also from a regulatory perspective.

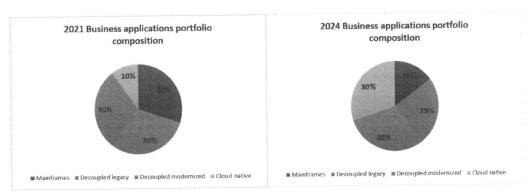

Figure 9.4 – Technological classification portfolio composition evolution sample

To conclude, it is needless to say your strategy will shift more business applications toward categories 3 and 4, which will automatically call for a revision of your DevOps evolution business case and increase the demand for DevOps SDLC capabilities engineering.

What about the classification of the secondary portfolio?

While we are primarily focused on business applications, your DevOps 360° technological ecosystem of platforms and tools needs to follow if not exactly the same pattern, at least a similar one. That should include both the criticality/speed-based classification as well as the architectural and technological classification. Imagine you have a disastrous scenario and your enterprise monitoring tool is classified as standard, which means it will be brought into life way later than your business applications. You will be blind to your production systems' health. A similar situation can occur if your enterprise strategic code and binary artifact repository tool are impacted. You simply cannot wait a whole day in order to start building and deploying code again. Equally, if you know that you are to replace your old messaging queues and private cloud, you will naturally not invest in their DevOps evolution.

The LCD

There are some frameworks and models that are used in the industry to complement portfolio classification. One of these is what incumbents call *license to continuously deliver*, *license to continuously deploy*, or *license to speed mode*. Such frameworks not only create transparency about what is expected so a business application can move with top speed but also push the organization's DevOps engineering innovation boundaries. Mechanisms such as *auto change request impact analysis validation* based on historical data, advanced application *self-healing* practices, and *zero-touch* deployment frameworks can rise out of LCD initiatives. Let me tell you a personal LCD story, which I have manipulated for deontological purposes.

> **The Network Outage Blessing**
>
> It was a cold winter day some years ago. In one of the banks I used to work at, the network engineering team was testing a new patch through a new deployment tool. Due to some incorrect configuration of the tool, the patch was applied directly and without testing to the production network instance instead of the test instance. That resulted in almost the entirety of the business application portfolio losing connectivity to the main data center, and therefore becoming unavailable. P1 incidents creation, restoration procedures, emergency calls, and communication inside and outside the firm were triggered in a situation that caused all our customer-facing services to become unavailable. We were simply out of business. Even Microsoft Teams was impacted. The group COO himself started receiving calls from our largest corporate clients, who could not trade on their portfolios. Long story short, after some hours of tremendous and collective effort across the organizations, our portfolio started to come back to life. The next morning, we all received an email from the group CIO stating that *Upon agreement with the group COO and group Risk Officer and with immediate effect, all intraday changes to production systems are forbidden and all changes can strictly happen only on Friday afternoon and outside business hours. The condition will persist till further notice and upon assurance that mitigating procedures have been established.* A direct bomb was set to the foundation of our DevOps evolution. Continuous delivery was dead. None of us, neither in IT nor on the business side, was prepared. Escalations, complaints, frustration, and anger across the organization piled up. We had to do something fast. A group of wise DevOps people gathered and proposed the creation of the concept of LCD. We spent a long afternoon and night, and the idea was ready to be presented to our group CIO. The rest is just a DevOps success story at scale! (Sweet DevOps memories.)

Let's go directly to the meat of the LCD concept, which is rather simple despite its complexity. The main elements that it comprises are as follows:

- A set of criteria/liabilities that assess the ability of a business application or platform to continuously deliver on demand without impacting its functional and non-functional requirements or risking creating a domino effect across the portfolio

- A mathematical formula that weights the aggregated results of the assessment and provides a rating classification based on a three-tier license

- A three-tier classification license based on the results of the mathematical formula mentioned in the preceding bullet point:

  - **Gold license**: Deployments on demand and intraday

  - **Silver**: Deployments daily but outside the business hours

  - **Bronze**: Deployments only on Fridays and outside the business hours

- A governance mechanism on how to govern and regulate the framework

The questionnaire of criteria and liabilities

This is basically a bundle of questions covering several aspects of continuous delivery readiness: from operational to organizational and from compliance to procedural. Some of the fundamental questions can be the following:

- Is the deployment and rollback mechanism automated?

- Is the application's failover mechanism automated and has it been tested successfully in the past 3 months?

- Is the application "P1 incident free" in the past 3 months?

- Does the application meet or exceed its SLA targets for the past 3 months?

- Are test management and automation evidence available?

- Are the application and its services monitored automatically?

- Is the application mission or business critical?

The licensing tiers

Based on the answers to these questions, considering the weighting of each and the aggregated results, a business application will fall within one of the three license types. The fundamental requirements for falling into each of the three license types are identical. Though as you would naturally expect, the more one moves toward the silver and gold licenses, the more the criteria become more related to plurality, as well as evidence of capability advancements and automation. The following example provides an overview of the three license types:

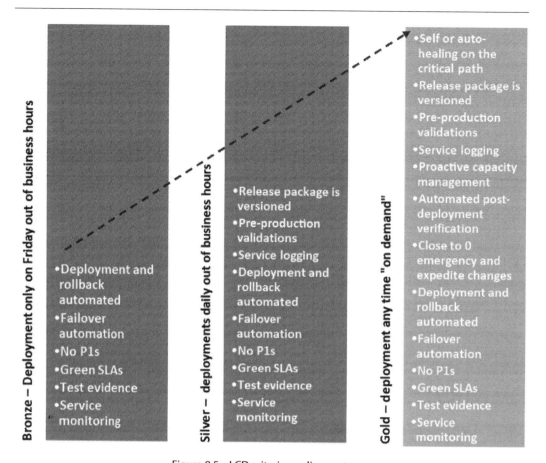

Figure 9.5 – LCD criteria per license type

The governance mechanism

The LCD framework needs to be complemented by a transparent and clear governance mechanism. The following should give you a fairly good idea of the important elements of the governance model:

	Tactical rollout (3 months)	Organic/scaled rollout
LCD framework ownership	Enterprise portfolio governance function	
License ownership and maintenance	Business application product owner	
Business areas in scope	Market trading and digital banking	All the rest
Assessment tool	LCD portal questionnaire and interviews	
Application assessment method	**Self-assessment and interview** 1. Application request sent and questionnaire filled out. 2. Results available. 3. Evidence evaluation. 4. Final interview and decision made.	**Self-assessment and spot interviews** **Gold:** Interview process to finalize license granted. **Silver:** License granted through self-assessment to all scoring it. Periodical spot checks take place. **Bronze:** License granted through self-assessment to all applying. Random spot checks take place.
Assessment result calculation	Criticality weighting is assigned to the various questions. The accumulation of points results in one of the three licenses: for example (0 to 40 points – **Bronze**, 41 to 80 – **Silver**, 81 and above – **Gold**).	
Request for a license upgrade revision by applicants	**On demand:** For the mission- and business-critical applications. **Quarterly:** For the highly available and standard applications.	
Inability to maintain status consequences	Lower quality observed in production - > Falls one tier. Inaccurate/manipulated input -> Automatically falls to **Bronze**.	

Table 9.3 – LCD governance sample for inspiration

Here are some important considerations for enabling the LCD framework:

- This type of work will cover several capability and readiness gaps across your portfolio, which might result in finger-pointing across stakeholders, such as *I can't deploy on demand because we don't have a self-service test data provisioning capability*. Manage that carefully as it might create a *toxic environment* for your DevOps evolution.

- A gold license should give its owners the ability to perform deployments during all change freeze periods, maybe including end-of-year processes, of course, depending on how gold or gold-plated you are, plus where you are positioned in the value chain.

- Due to the very large number of business applications to be assessed, a self-assessment signed by the service owner **Product Owner** (**PO**) is the only way to go. You will never have the time to go and check the evidence for everyone. You must, however, check the areas/teams that claim they deserve the gold license.

- Combine the evidence for the LCD with the evidence of the DevOps controls adoption, the evidence for the DevOps evolution adoption, and the evidence for the production readiness assessments, which we will discuss later. One evidence mechanism addresses them all.

Stop and Think

How many business applications in your organization do you think in their present DevOps state will deserve a gold license?

Licenses are becoming mainstream frameworks of assurance in the banking industry as more and more incumbents adopt these approaches. The second most in-focus domain after continuous delivery is the *license to public cloud*, ensuring that applications that are to run on the public cloud fulfill the necessary criteria.

Portfolio registry, governance, and readiness

A key and foundational parameter in your DevOps 360° evolution is to have a clear picture of which primary and secondary applications constitute the totality of your enterprise portfolio. Simply, which are the areas/teams of scope that need to adopt the evolution's outcome? Moreover, what are the attributes of those applications that are crucial from a DevOps evolution perspective? Are 2,000 business applications in scope? Are they all cloud native and client facing? Which of them have PII data stored in their databases? We label the exercise of collecting and registering all this information across your portfolio as *portfolio registry and governance*. In the first part of this section, we will focus on a good practice and a proposal on what to look for when registering your portfolio.

Question

Will it surprise you if I tell you that several organizations do not have a structured portfolio registry and governance mechanism? Simply, they do not have the total picture of applications running in their organization. As a client of mine once told me, "Every time we have P1 incidents with a domino effect, we discover new applications that are not registered."

Portfolio registry and governance

With the term **portfolio registry and governance**, we refer to two concepts. Firstly, we refer to a tool that is used in order to register your portfolio of applications. To give you an idea of the kind of tool we're referring to, without the intention to advertise, it is tools such as Clarity and ServiceNow. Secondly, we refer to a three-level tiering of information on the governing elements of your portfolio.

Registry

Every application of your portfolio should be officially registered in the portfolio registry for the following reasons:

- To understand your portfolio's size and composition
- To ensure a clear definition of an application's ownership, governance, and liabilities
- To define and agree on specific application attributes that will support you to evolve DevOps at relevance
- To collect evidence for regulatory purposes
- To provide a linkage of the application portfolio with its respective IT assets
- To be used as the basis for your portfolio modernization strategy

Governance level 1 – business domain, application, and services

The first level of governance is related to the business domain, expressed based on your business enterprise agility model (value stream or tribe), the respective business applications belonging to it, and the core critical services running on them (usually the top five for each application). That will look like the following representation for a mobile banking business application:

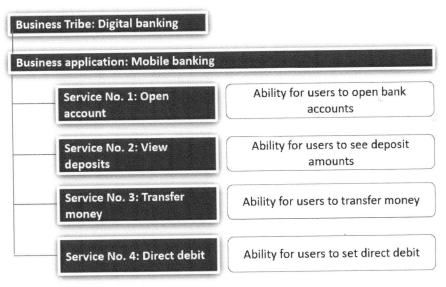

Figure 9.6 – Level 1 portfolio registry and governance for mobile banking application and services

The outcome will be decisive from an enterprise portfolio planning perspective of the DevOps 360° evolution, as we will see in the next chapter.

Governance level 2 – IT assets allocated to business applications

The second level provides the allocation and transparency of IT assets to the respective application and has a direct link to your **configuration management database (CMDB)**. Building on top of our example, we get a view like the following:

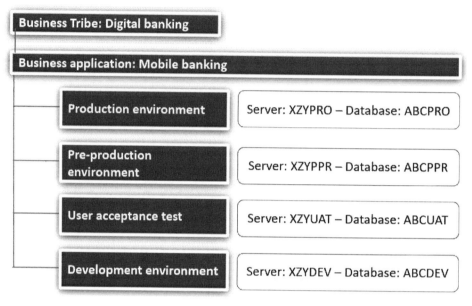

Figure 9.7 – Level 2 portfolio registry for mobile banking IT assets allocation

The information provided at this level can, from a regulatory evidence perspective, support operational matters, technical debt identification, capacity management in your data center, and cost reallocation or optimization.

Governance level 3 – DevOps attributes allocated to business applications

The data registered at this level is of dual importance. Firstly, you agree on which attributes per business application are important to your DevOps evolution, which supports your planning and actual adoption. Secondly, you agree on the value that is assigned to each attribute, as in, what target each business application is expected to reach. The following is an illustration for your inspiration based on the attributes I consider to be fundamental from a DevOps perspective:

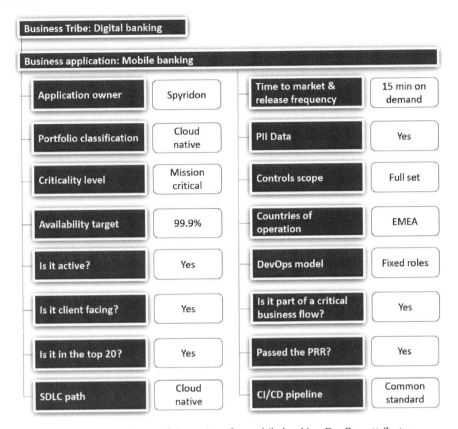

Figure 9.8 – Level 3 portfolio registry for mobile banking DevOps attributes

The attributes registry per business application should be seen as a combination of a social contract, expectation setting, and single-person accountability appointment. Selectively from our example, as Spyridon, I know that I own the mobile banking application and I am responsible for ensuring that, together with the Agile DevOps team, we reach the 99.9% availability target. We need to adopt the full set of DevOps controls using the DevOps SDLC cloud-native path and strive for on-demand release velocity.

From providing your DevOps evolution state-of-the-art to collecting evidence for regulatory purposes, as well as setting the DevOps evolution ambition per application, DevOps attribute clarity is necessary. Ideally, attributes are bundled under single frameworks or mechanisms, one of which we will discover in the coming section.

The production readiness review

Often also called **operational or onboarding readiness review (ORR)**, or **launch readiness assessment (LRA)**, the **production readiness review (PRR)** is a proven mechanism to ensure business application governance, onboarding, and readiness. As we will also see in *Chapter 13, Site Reliability Engineering in the FSI* the PRR is considered to be one of the main mechanisms that Google uses when deploying the concept of SRE across its portfolio. A PRR cannot go wrong (if properly executed), and I propose that you embed it as a solid framework at the heart of your DevOps 360° evolution.

What is the value proposition of a PRR for the DevOps 360° evolution?

As the name suggests, a PRR ensures that a business application and its corresponding services are *production ready*, as in, they can be operated safely in a production environment meeting both the expected functional and non-functional requirements. A PRR is applicable not only to business applications but also to technological platforms and tools and spans the DevOps SDLC phases and corresponding capabilities that enable them.

But what are the main elements of value that a PRR brings to the DevOps evolution?

- Establishes a common and early understanding among stakeholders (Agile DevOps teams, product owners, and utility areas) on the eligibility criteria for a business application to be classified as *production ready*. You can call it *shift right* in the sense that it outlines what *ideal in production* must look like, and then you can work it out backward from achieving that.

- Creates assurance, upon successful completion, that the business application will meet the functional and quality requirements in production.

- Supports the generation of readiness evidence that can be multipurpose: LCD, regulatory compliance, internal value chain of business applications, onboarding tenants to common platforms, third-party vendors, and partnering financial service institutions' contracts.

- Highlights capability engineering gaps both from an enablement perspective and an adoption perspective in the DevOps SDLC.

- Eliminates ownership doubts of the production readiness criteria across the stakeholders of a product's life cycle.

- Holds a single person accountable for the service quality, and this is the product owner, who technically owns the product, its prioritization process, and its budget.

What are the proposed domains and questions on a PRR?

PRRs can look different from organization to organization within the FSI, but also across industries. Nonetheless, there are some fundamentally common questions that are used in PRRs, despite the industry and internal context. As PRRs span the DevOps SDLC and include the full product life cycle, you would expect their respective questions and criteria to be broad and balance the *time to market – reliability – compliance* equilibrium of DevOps. Let us take a closer look at an example of what we propose you should be looking for when assessing the production readiness of your portfolio.

Core operational aspects
Have SLAs been defined and agreed upon with all the relevant stakeholders?
Has any potential knowledge handover to an operations team or third party been conducted?
Have the access rights and permissions been agreed upon among the relevant stakeholders and implemented in the identity intelligence system?
Has the operating support model been agreed upon with all the stakeholders?
Is the deployment and rollback procedure executed through a CI/CD pipeline?
Security aspects
Has the firm's passwords and secrets policy been implemented?
Are the code base, artifacts, and infrastructure free from critical security vulnerabilities?
Has the application passed the "secure design" assessment as part of its software architectural review?
Data aspects
Does the application contain PII or banking secrecy data? If yes, have the necessary access management and obfuscation rules been applied?
Monitoring and logging aspects
Has application and services monitoring been implemented for the critical services as a minimum requirement?
Has security events logging been implemented?
Quality assurance
Has the application been tested for each build and, ideally, automatically?
Are the automated test cases, artifacts, and data stored and versioned in code repositories?
Is test evidence across test levels available?
If the application is client facing, has a penetration test been performed?
Is static code analysis executed per build?
Reliability and continuity
Has a disaster recovery plan been created and tested successfully?
Have the data backup and restoration procedures been tested?
Have the non-functional requirements been documented and tested?

Table 9.4 – Example PRR questionnaire

I will stop here, as the list could be never-ending, depending on your SDLC's breadth and depth. Let us now look at some important parameters in the anatomy of the PRR. The following table presents the bare minimum fields that, in my opinion, you would wish to capture:

Domain	Question	Origin	Responsible	Accountable	Evidence
Continuity	Has a disaster recovery plan been created and tested successfully?	Regulatory compliance requirement DevOps 360° SDLC requirement	Agile DevOps teams	Product owner	**Test requirements and recovery document (TRRD)** Disaster recovery test results

Table 9.5 – PRR criteria fields sample

As you can guess, your DevOps 360° SDLC and controls are the foundation of the PRR:

- DevOps controls = regulatory compliance fulfillment
- DevOps 360° SDLC = SDLC advancement fulfillment

Both will ensure sufficient enablement of the *time to market – reliability – compliance* equilibrium. Ideally, each item of the PRR needs to be interrelated and traced back in your DevOps 360° SDLC and control capabilities. If you have designed your DevOps controls pragmatically and engineered them in the SDLC capabilities, you will find a perfect match. The following table provides a couple more examples of this interrelation:

PRR domain	DevOps evolution capability	DevOps controls domain
Access rights	SoD and IAM model	Access integrity and protection
Test evidence	Test automation	Quality assurance
Monitoring	Observability	Service health visibility

Table 9.6 – Interrelation of PRR domain, DevOps evolution capabilities, and DevOps controls domains˙

Frequency and fraud prevention

The PRR is a living and not a one-off framework. Obviously, it will be first used when an application or platform goes live, but moving forward it needs to be kept updated, ideally per new release, especially if changes to it are introduced. This process also fits very well with your DevOps controls regulatory evidence. As we mentioned earlier, with the DevOps controls being part of its foundation, you will have handy evidence at any planned or unplanned supervisory visit. The applications that are already in production prior to the framework's enablement will be obliged to run it retrospectively. To conclude,

I need to warn you about one thing. I think I have previously talked about the *friendly relationship* of the PO and the Agile DevOps team. Friends intentionally or unintentionally can overlook things, so while it is important to trust them, you should also verify the evidence. Periodic spot checks on change requests, primarily focused on your most critical parts of the portfolio, is a common practice that incumbents use.

Making Sure We Do Not Confuse the LCD and PRR

The LCD ensures that you can deploy and fail/recover fast, while not jeopardizing the functional and non-functional aspects of your application and its surroundings. The PRR ensures that either you can *go live* in production in the first place or your production is sustainably ready to be operated. For instance, the LCD asks you to be able to fail over automatically and automatically regression test your application's critical path so you can be fast. The PRR demands that you have the ability to fail over, even if not automatically, and that you execute regression tests, even if not automatically, so you can be operational.

Summary

In this chapter, we focused on fundamental and foundational elements of the DevOps evolution. We discussed the value proposition of the DevOps portfolio classification, registry, governance, and readiness. Initially, we focused on the core definitions of classification, and we deep-dived into the main classifications that incumbents use. For both classifications, we provided a proposed tiering using concrete examples. That led us to combine those classifications and enrich them toward defining the *DevOps speed* formula of this book. We continued with a short real-life story and saw how that inspired the creation of a complementary framework to portfolio classification: the LCD. We looked into some important criteria and provided a detailed governance model for inspiration, along with some points for consideration. We dedicated the second part of the chapter to the portfolio registry, governance, and readiness mechanisms. After initially providing the value proposition for DevOps, we used the mobile banking application as an example and examined its registering and governance aspects from a three-level perspective. We closed the chapter by providing an overview of the undoubted value that a production readiness assessment can provide in the DevOps evolution. We complemented that with some example questions, and we proposed the bare minimum parameters to be captured per question. Emphasis was put on how the DevOps SDLC and controls are the basis of the PRR through complementary reconciliation.

In the next chapter, we will focus on the mechanisms that will enable you to balance DevOps tactical and organic enterprise portfolio planning and adoption during your evolution.

10

Tactical and Organic Enterprise Portfolio Planning and Adoption

This chapter introduces us to the last part of the book, as well as to the third pillar of the DevOps 360° operating model: *rollout, accelerate, and scale*. The chapter will start with an outline of the enterprise portfolio planning and adoption value proposition, which is indeed rich and multidimensional. We will continue by highlighting the importance of balancing your enterprise portfolio planning and adoption between what we will call *tactical* and *organic* approaches. Afterward, we will deep-dive into the tactical approach, and we will discuss its value proposition and its four main aspects. Starting by outlining the predominant tactical strategic domains for incumbents, we will complement those domains with important considerations. We will enrich these considerations with a list of differentiations you can use to ensure that the tactical adoption candidates cover your wide organizational DevOps context. Concluding the tactical adoption, we will provide an *all-hands-on-deck* example.

In the second part of the chapter, we will focus on the practicalities of the enterprise portfolio planning and adoption, starting by outlining the core elements of the proposed mechanism, which we will also visualize. Emphasis will be put on distinguishing between the DevOps 360° enablement and adoption **objectives and key results** (**OKRs**) via two examples. We will continue by providing considerations derived from real lessons learned by adopting such mechanisms at scale. The chapter will close by introducing the DevOps minimum viable adoption concept, outlining its decisive importance and linkage to the DevOps equilibrium principles.

In this chapter, we're going to cover the following main topics:

- The value proposition of the enterprise portfolio planning and adoption mechanism
- The difference between a tactical and organic DevOps evolution
- The main elements of the tactical DevOps evolution

- Practicalities and important considerations of the enterprise portfolio planning mechanism

- The DevOps minimum viable adoption concept and framework

What is the value proposition of enterprise portfolio planning and adoption in the DevOps 360° evolution?

So far in this book, we have repeatedly mentioned that the DevOps 360° evolution needs to be performed *at relevance in a multi-speed context*. In this chapter, we will enrich this principle by adding an element of DevOps *collective intentionality*. We will include this element through the phrase of *enterprise alignment and consensus*, which we first introduced in *Chapter 6, DevOps Software Development Life Cycle 360° Evolution and Engineering*. By *alignment*, we mean the creation of the enterprise mechanism of planning the adoption, while by *consensus*, we mean certain agreements that need to be made and support the planning and adoption mechanism. Our evolution's guiding principle will consequently be reshaped to:

A DevOps 360° evolution at relevance in a multi-speed context, characterized by enterprise alignment and consensus.

I think our guiding principle looks more complete now, and you should not expect further changes to it till the end of the book.

> **Small parenthesis**
>
> I also like the term **synchronization** when referring to the enterprise level, but it is not a very realistic concept. With variations in your DevOps maturity, models, business context, technological capabilities, and speed, it is likely that you will never achieve synchronization on an enterprise level, although it will be possible to extend an ecosystem, value stream, or tribe level through the adoption of fundamental capabilities, as we will see later in the chapter.

At this point, you might wonder, "Haven't we been evolving DevOps in alignment already?" We have the vision and design authorities with representatives across the organization holding the DevOps enterprise OKRs, the DevOps CoE planning engagements across the organization, and the Agile DevOps teams and utility area representatives defining the DevOps SDLC and journeys. We evolve DevOps in alignment already, but with two caveats. So far in the book, we have engaged with only a subset of the organization's broader DevOps 360° stakeholders. We have also mainly focused on the *why* and *what* of the evolution, but not the *how, when,* and *whom*. As in, we have defined enterprise DevOps OKRs and created governance bodies and workstreams in designing the approaches toward fulfilling those OKRs through the establishment of respective initiatives. But now is the time to define how to materialize the enterprise OKRs and initiatives, by when (in terms of timelines) and by who (in terms of responsibility), all while ensuring we are not just engaging with a sample of the organization, but reaching every corner of it. We are aligning everyone toward, on the one hand, the **future desired DevOps state** and, on the other hand, how and by when to reach it.

> **Tip – spend some time refreshing your memory**
>
> At this point, I propose you go back to *Chapters 2* and *3*. In *Chapter 2, The DevOps Multi-Speed Context, Vision, Objectives, and Change Nature* please refresh your memory on the strategic objectives and enterprise DevOps OKRs. In *Chapter 3, The DevOps 360° Operating Model Pillars and Governance Model* please revise the workstreams that we have created, the scope of which is to define initiatives on materializing the enterprise DevOps OKRs.

As with any element of the DevOps 360° operating model, the value proposition of the enterprise planning and adoption is multidimensional and concerned with the following objectives:

- Align on an enterprise level on the governance mechanism of planning and adopting the DevOps 360° operating model by providing clarity on the parts of the DevOps 360° operating model that are to be enabled and adopted, as well as agreeing on the governing process and practicalities.

- Align on the *when*, as in, when the standard CI/CD pipeline should be ready and when the agile DevOps teams need to/can get onboarded.

- Align on the *who*, as in, who owns the initiative of enabling the standard CI/CD pipeline and who is adopting it, as well as who can support both the enablement and onboarding (see the *DevOps CoE* section in *Chapter 4, Enterprise Architecture and the DevOps Center of Excellence*).

- Build awareness and acceptance of the vital milestones of the DevOps evolution. For instance, create a consensus that by the end of 2023, your organization should have approval from your main regulator on the DevOps controls adoption.

- Understand how long it will take for the various teams to reach the evolution's milestones through their estimates on adopting the DevOps initiatives' outcomes.

- Plan the funding mechanism for enablement and adoption.

- Enable a common benefit realization process, anchored to the periodical planning and adoption revisions.

- Create transparency on the DevOps work of your various teams and enable a sense of collectivism and alignment across backlogs. Putting it in a romantic way, we do this together, working on helping each other to advance.

Jean-Jacques Rousseau and the "DevOps society"

Jean-Jacques Rousseau was a Swiss political philosopher who lived during the 18th century and significantly influenced the development of the Enlightenment across Europe. One of his main beliefs about modern society and humanity was that once humans give up their innate independence and become part of society, they become corrupted. In our *enterprise DevOps society*, the effect in most cases is the opposite, in my opinion. Getting your teams together during planning and adopting results in them being less *corrupted* during the DevOps evolution. This is because they need to act collectively, while also being measured collectively, which means, for instance, that they will more easily give up on their shadow IT solutions and collaborate on providing regulatory evidence, while working more closely overall, under *DevOps solidarity*, by feeling part of something bigger. This is not, of course, always the case (just to make sure I am not perceived as being naïve).

Why you should balance a tactical and an organic approach

Before moving into the mechanism and practicalities of enterprise planning and adoption, I would like to go back again to the concept of **speed**. (I am sorry, and I cannot help it, speeds are everywhere.) Two terms and corresponding approaches that I repeatedly use in my career, while balancing them effectively, are the **tactical planning and adoption** approach and the **organic planning and adoption** approach. The following are the definitions in our DevOps evolution context:

- **Tactical approach**: Going by the Oxford dictionary, the term **tactical** indicates "carefully and methodologically executed actions with the ambition to gain a specific advantage." In our context, suppose that the vision for the mobile banking application is to transform it toward the greenfield banking state-of-the-art to allow it to move at its own rapid speed. This is in order to gain advantages internally by eliminating dependencies, but also externally, by beating the competition. To achieve that, a careful, methodological, and tactical transition plan is required. The transition needs to be planned and executed carefully across DevOps aspects, involving several stakeholders who will have to dedicate time to the cause within strict timelines. You will probably conduct an architectural and technological transformation of the mobile banking application to eliminate data and infrastructure dependencies, as well as ensuring it can run in multiple public cloud providers. Your EA function and core infrastructure teams will be involved, providing reference architectures and autonomy over the enterprise public cloud landing zone. Perhaps you will also get the DevOps CoE engaged in speeding up the cloud-native path SDLC adoption and improving the release velocity, while you might also engage a dedicated SRE team to focus on reliability engineering. In addition, I assume you will focus heavily on zero-trust security, engaging your cyber security teams. Compliance as code will also have a strong focus and will possibly require the involvement of your IT risk management framework function. Coordinating and funding the targeted actions of all these stakeholders toward the mobile banking application requires a tactical approach. You cannot just rely on people finding the time and resources to get it done. Mobile banking is one of the several business applications or platforms that are candidates for tactical adoption. I like to call them **DevOps portfolio flagships**.

- **Organic approach**: My definition for this is derived from the Greek word *οργανικός*, which in English translates to *organic*. When it is translated, though, it loses much of its original meaning. The original Greek definition of *οργανικός* is the totality of elements a living organism consists of, which grow at their own pace over time toward collectively supporting the living organism's operations. The Greek interpretation also indicates growing from within, without external intervention. In our DevOps context, the living organism is the organization's teams, which grow their DevOps capabilities at their own pace, eventually contributing to the realization of the DevOps 360° operating model. That growth for the majority of teams also happens with restricted external support, due to either insufficient monetary, technological, and people capital, or dedication of that capital to other causes (see the tactical approach). Let's suppose that the mobile banking application, along with five other business applications, due to certain characteristics, will follow a tactical approach to the DevOps evolution, with full focus across stakeholders and specific deadlines. None of the other business applications and platforms in the organization (except those six) will have that dedicated focus and support, they might lack capital investment, and they will have more relaxed milestones to meet. They will also predominantly have to rely on their own competencies during the evolution without expecting significant external support. Those "rest of the organization, but not the tactical" areas are to consequently grow organically in their DevOps journey.

> **To avoid confusion**
>
> Limited external support for organic growth does not mean *you are left alone in your DevOps destiny*. The necessary means must be enabled to support the organic adoption, but that will primarily be in the form of artifacts, solution recipes, frameworks, patterns, and methodologies, and not hands-on support. The big difference from an organizational focus perspective is that tactical involvement is characterized by *We are dedicated to your cause and will provide hands-on support*, while organic is *Please find the solution in the GitHub repos of the CI/CD platform team and use the service desk if you have questions*.

The tactical adoption value proposition

The tactical and organic approach distinction automatically creates two major DevOps speeds in your organization, which is natural and sensible. The tactical approach areas that have the full focus of the DevOps stakeholders and the necessary capital secured will inevitably start earlier with the DevOps evolution, and move faster through it.

But what is the value of investing extra effort and early focus on tactical adoption?

- You need flagship applications and platforms to work toward the evolution's outcome first, on the one hand because their situation and circumstances require them to do so (for instance, market competitive advantage and reputation), and on the other hand because you need big success stories in the early phases of your evolution, or because you have allocated budget dedicated to those flagships in the evolution's business case, which you have reserved in your balance sheet and need to spend within certain timeframes.

- You do not have unlimited people and budget. This requires you to invest your monetary and people capital tactically. You cannot have the DevOps CoE focusing on SDLC engineering for 100 applications in parallel when your EA function cannot support the same 100 applications on defining business-critical flows. At the same time, I doubt you can go out there and hire hundreds of new people. (I already told you that most organizations are under cost pressure, and in *Chapter 12, People Hiring, Incubation, and Mobility* I will also discuss how they struggle with talent attraction as well.)

- Your regulators will primarily focus on certain flagship applications and platforms. Keep them busy with those while giving the organic ones the time to prepare to board the evolution train.

- You want to pilot your advanced DevOps concepts in applications and platforms where there is a certain long-term existence and a significant business and technological innovation space.

- Most probably, the tactical adoption areas are already ahead of the DevOps curve compared to the rest of your organization, which means that the ground is more prepared to receive the DevOps evolution seed. This will also help you to prove the new DevOps operating model and create solution recipes, frameworks, and patterns for the rest of the organization to adopt more quickly and with a forward-looking outlook.

- You need to make sure you get the flagships *done* as quickly as you can because unforeseen situations might jeopardize your efforts. Potential circumstances, such as changing market and economic conditions, a potential regulatory fine, stricter regulatory requirements, potential legal entity restructuring, a significant M&A activity, or severe and horizontal cost-cutting, have a high probability of either slowing down your evolution or even causing its absolute termination.

- Those areas consist of strategic technological utilities that the rest of the organization will need to use to adopt the evolution's outcome. For instance, the standard CI/CD pipeline, the public cloud capabilities, and data engineering and analytics should be considered part of your evolution's flagships.

As we mentioned in the previous chapter in the *DevOps speed* formula, technology is a key element of speed. Hence, it is not only business applications that must belong to the tactical approach, but also core DevOps platforms that enable capabilities that are fundamental to the DevOps evolution and belong to the DevOps 360° technological ecosystem.

> **Did you know?**
>
> Across the enterprise DevOps evolutions I have been part of in my career, the organic adoption officially started 6 to 12 months after the tactical adoption.

What are the predominant tactical strategic domains?

Having read this book so far, I believe you can guess what the determinants of choosing tactical adoption candidates are. It's about speed (criticality and impact) obviously, expressed using the formula we presented in the previous chapter, but also business context, time to market, reliability, compliance, and technology. But this time, the thinking is more strategic and goes beyond isolated business applications and platforms. Scale, not only speed, is important when choosing tactical adoption candidates. The main strategic domains that combine scale and speed in tactical adoption are the following, complemented by real industry examples. Note that the last entry in the following table adds a rather rare but important domain, which is one of *absolute critical necessity*.

Strategic domain	Examples
High-speed business domains and applications	Mobile and online banking, core banking, trading, asset management, and payments
End-to-end business-critical value streams and flows (either within or across business domains)	Trading life cycle, open banking ecosystem, know your customer, and customer account life cycle
Regulatory compliance ecosystems	FRTB, MiFID, Basel, PSD 2, group risk, capital and liquidity reporting warehouses, and monthly and year-end reporting
Strategic technological capabilities	Standard CI/CD, public cloud platforms, developer self-service portals, and big data engineering platforms
"Burning platforms"	Areas that have severe reliability issues and/or accumulation of unfulfilled regulatory demand

Table 10.1 – Strategic domains and examples of primary candidates for tactical adoption

Typically, you will find the tactical adoption portfolio to be balanced across the preceding strategic domains. And if you look closely at certain cases, you will also identify applications and platforms that are not necessarily fulfilling the criteria of the top speeds of the criticality portfolio. There are two main reasons for that. Firstly, in certain contexts, it is challenging to slice a business-critical flow or value stream with precision. Therefore, and inevitably, applications will belong to that flow or value stream that are not required to move at top speed. Secondly, there are *troublemaker* business applications and platforms that create direct reliability issues for the tactical adoption candidates. You take those in the scope with the ambition to fix them through the tactical adoption's means and capital (another secret of the industry revealed).

Some important considerations when choosing the tactical adoption candidates are listed as follows:

- Go for magnitude. The larger the ecosystem, value stream, or critical business flow, the more positive noise it will make in terms of benefits and evolution dynamics.

- Take advantage as much as you can of the regulatory compliance work to ensure full focus through prioritization, people allocation, elimination of budget constraints, and positive regulatory pressure.

- Ensure that not all the tactical candidates are the best in the DevOps class. Their further advancements will create a large gap in DevOps maturity between them and the rest of the organization, risking making the DevOps operating model too advanced for others to adopt.

- Cover a broad range of parameters and characteristics in the tactical adoption portfolio. If you only focus, for instance, on mission-critical cloud-native applications, you will struggle to create solution recipes and patterns for highly available decoupled legacy applications, and most probably you will forget about the mainframes. In other words, you need a balanced portfolio in your tactical adoption, which can be representative of most of the contexts across your organization. The following differentiation parameters can help you to make your tactical adoption portfolio versatile:

Differentiator	Degree edge 1	Degree edge 2
DevOps WoW principles	Rotational	Fixed
Availability	99.9%	95%
Time to market	On demand	Weekly
Release size	Incremental	Bulk
Platform	Cloud native	Mainframe
Hosted	Public cloud	On-premises
People skills	Cross-functional advanced	Skills gaps
Client facing	No	Yes
Regulatory impact	High	Low
Future life cycle	To continuously evolve	To incrementally advance
Service nature	Shared service	Business area dedicated
Programming language	Java	HPS
Vendor dependent	No	Yes
CI/CD onboarded	Yes	No
Passed PRR	No	Yes
Architecture	Distributed	Monolithic
Data transmission	Real time	Batch

Compliance gaps	Several	Limited
PII data	Yes	No
Market and advantage	Regional and new	Global and existing
In production	No	Yes

Table 10.2 – Tactical adoption portfolio differentiation parameters

Of course, you should not use all the differentiators of the preceding table to identify candidates but to define a subset that you consider relevant to your context and ambitions. As you can see, the last differentiator is underlined, and this is intentional in order to highlight emphasis. It is an absolute must to include business applications and platforms that are already in production, as well as those that are not yet. Or, even better, business applications and platforms that you have just started designing without having written a single line of code. There are significant differences between the two categories, and you want to take full advantage of that. Starting from a blank page with zero technical debt and legacy is the best way to unleash DevOps innovation and create game-changing patterns, especially in the domains of greenfield and composable banking. We will discuss "early versus late" further in *Chapter 13, Site Reliability Engineering in the FSI* when we discuss SRE.

All hands on deck

I like the phrase *all hands on deck* a lot, and I find it very relevant to DevOps tactical adoption. In our tactical adoption context, all hands on deck refers to dedicated determination across several DevOps ecosystem stakeholders to the success of the tactical adoption areas. Remember, two of the main motives behind the tactical adoptions are as follows:

- Get certain parts of the portfolio to move faster: top speed.
- Define, design, prove, conceptualize, and scale the DevOps 360° operating model and in particular its DevOps 360° SDLC capability engineering and evolution part.

Let's focus on the second point. The tactical adoption areas can be the first ones to adopt a multi-cloud strategy, the first ones to adopt GitOps flows through the standard CI/CD pipelines, or even the first ones to adopt the advanced compliance as code DevOps controls. To do so, they will need dedicated support from various DevOps stakeholder teams, but also a *demand/supply and feedback loops* mechanism. Do you remember the guilds and communities for practice we mentioned in *Chapter 5, Business Enterprise Agility and DevOps Ways of Working Reconciliation*? Something similar to that can be enabled within the tactical portfolio and its external support areas. On the other hand, tactical adoption is a golden opportunity for several DevOps ecosystem stakeholders to have a *playground* and pilot the parts of the DevOps 360° operating model that they are responsible for, while getting valuable insights into the organization's context, demands, and needs. The overall setup creates the operational environment and means for advanced DevOps collaboration opportunities, as well as promoting people mobility. As we have also seen in the DevOps CoE engagements, ideally, the external utility support areas move either temporarily or virtually in the agile DevOps teams that are part of the tactical adoption and become an integral part of them over the course of the evolution. That will enable them to better serve organic adoption in the long run, having built strong know-how, success stories, and contextual awareness.

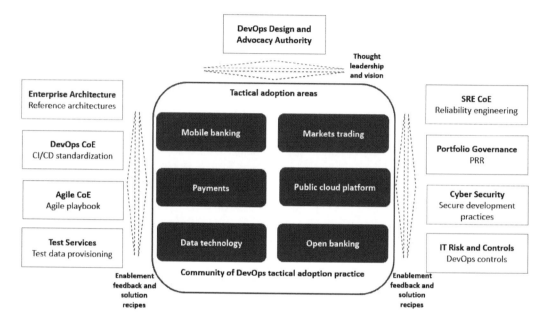

Figure 10.1 – The tactical adoption all-hands-on-deck ecosystem

The preceding diagram provides a visual overview of the tactical adoption ecosystem, which consists of three main actors in our example:

- The tactical adoption candidates that lead the evolution and move at their own fast speed, having communities of practice on creating tactical adoption synergies

- The DevOps 360° operating model capabilities owners, who support the enablement and adoption of the model, receive feedback from the adoption and create solution recipes, frameworks, and patterns that can support the organic adoption

- The DevOps design and advocacy authority, which provides expertise through leadership and aligns the tactical adoption teams with the overall vision of the evolution

At this point, we will close the tactical adoption section with the belief that you have got some valuable insights and ideas. The coming section will focus on the enterprise portfolio planning and adoption mechanism, touching also on the organic side of the evolution.

The enterprise portfolio planning mechanism

Different organizations, depending on their size of operations, organizational operating model, structure, and enterprise business agility model, follow different enterprise portfolio planning and adoption mechanisms. You will find cases where there are annual and quarterly enterprise-wide business reviews across a whole organization, and you will also find monthly priority planning dedicated to each business line or value stream, or even monthly or quarterly program increments for organizations that have adopted **Scaled Agility Framework (SAFe)**. Irrespective of your enterprise planning and adoption mechanism, you will have to fit the DevOps 360° evolution into it. You'll also need to agree on how you will balance your tactical and organic adoptions. Naturally, you must not create a dedicated mechanism only for the DevOps evolution, as you do much more than just DevOps in your organization.

What a pragmatic mechanism can look like

Some common patterns are applied to enterprise planning and adoption that I have observed being repeated in my career across various contexts. Of course, different organizations follow different practices, but we also need to remember that *imitation*, as we discussed in *Chapter 2, The DevOps Multi-Speed Context, Vision, Objectives, and Change Nature* among incumbent banks is also a dominant industry practice. Let us have a close look at some pragmatic mechanisms, which we will summarize through a holistic visualization at the end of the section.

The bank's strategic objectives

These objectives typically have a 3- to 5-year scope and are revised annually. As we also discussed in *Chapter 2, The DevOps Multi-Speed Context, Vision, Objectives, and Change Nature* the strategic objectives are initially shaped as corporate themes, which are then translated into technological themes. A transparency and reconciliation mechanism between the two is established and the progress is tracked on a quarterly basis.

The DevOps enterprise evolution 360° OKRs

These are defined by the DevOps 360° vision authority and are linked to the strategic objectives. Typically, they have a 3-year scope and are quarterly reviewed in terms of relevance to the DevOps evolution and benefit realization.

The DevOps enterprise 360° evolution workstreams

There is a workstream defined for every enterprise DevOps OKR on shaping and designing the initiatives that need to run in order to materialize it. The collection of the initiatives' outcomes across workstreams will eventually be the final DevOps 360° operating model. The workstreams are virtual constructions that should not last for more than 3 to 6 months. Once the initiatives are defined, they are institutionalized and become *business as usual*, represented in the enablement and adoption teams' specific OKRs, with the workstreams being dissolved.

The DevOps 360° enablement and adoption teams' specific OKRs

Once the initiatives are defined, there are two paths to institutionalization and materialization: organizational enablement and the agile DevOps team's adoption, in the form of epics and user stories.

Organizational enablement refers to activities that need to be conducted to enable the respective DevOps 360° operating model capabilities at the enterprise level, such as the following:

- DevOps SDLC and controls definition and built-in implementation on the DevOps technological ecosystem

- New dynamic and rotational identity and access management system to cater to the rotational model DevOps **Ways of Working (WoW)** organizing principles model

- A formal portfolio modernization mechanism

- Public cloud capabilities through the establishment of a new team

As you can see, these are simple capabilities that you need to enable on an enterprise level.

Organizational adoption refers to the activities that need to be performed at the agile DevOps team level when adopting the enabled organizational capabilities and the new DevOps 360° operating model. For example, and using the examples from organizational enablement, the agile DevOps teams in the payments value stream should do the following:

- Implement the new DevOps SDLC cloud-native path and corresponding controls.

- Onboard their applications running based on the rotational model to the new identity and access management system.

- Conduct their forward-looking platform modernization plan.

- Give up their current shadow IT public cloud implementation and utilize the cloud services of the new public cloud platform team.

Both organizational enablement and adoption are expressed in the form of DevOps team-specific evolution OKRs (over the course of 3 months to 3 years), which are further expressed in the form of overarching epics and user stories. The accumulation of those epics and their respective estimates is the data that shows how long it will take for the evolution to be adopted. Also, it will reveal what is possible and what is not possible in terms of your organization's capacity, conditions, and circumstances. Let's look at a couple of examples to explain how we get from a bank-wide strategic objective to an agile DevOps team-specific DevOps OKR expressed in epics and user stories. In the following two examples, we will see some representative examples of how an online banking agile DevOps team could potentially break down the enterprise DevOps OKRs of *compliance* and *operational efficiency* into team-specific DevOps OKRs of *DevOps controls* and *adoption of the fixed roles DevOps WoW organizing principles model*.

Here's the compliance adoption breakdown example:

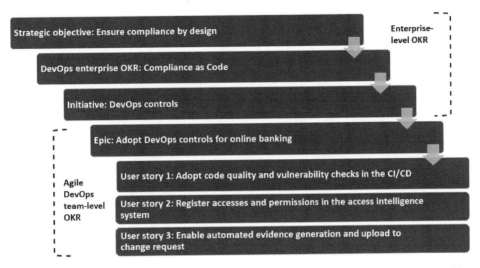

Figure 10.2 – Adoption breakdown for the example of compliance

Here's the DevOps models WoW:

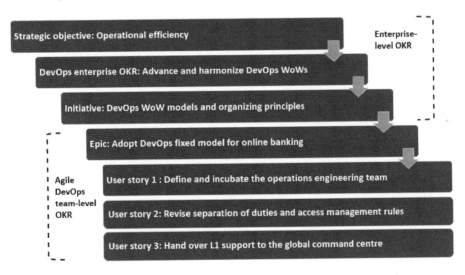

Figure 10.3 – Adoption breakdown for the example of DevOps models

As you would expect, situations, circumstances, conditions, speeds, and relevance will make different agile DevOps teams translate the enterprise OKRs differently. How can they nevertheless potentially be aligned toward common objectives? We will see in the last section of this chapter.

The following diagram illustrates an overview of the enterprise portfolio planning mechanism:

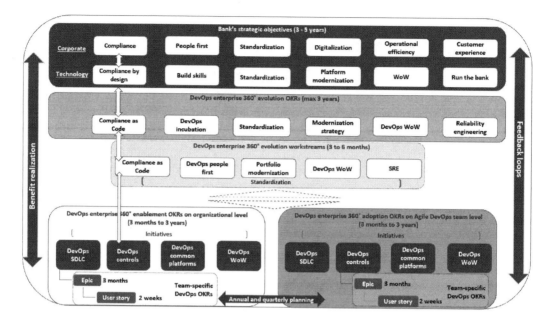

Figure 10.4 – Enterprise portfolio planning mechanism overview

What are the very important considerations when designing and enabling the mechanism?

The enterprise portfolio planning and adoption mechanism might sound straightforward, but it is quite the opposite when applied in reality, especially in cases where organizations are not used to planning and executing collectively. The following are my recommendations of considerations and decisions that you need to make in order to smoothen the process.

Define who is part of the mechanism

An anti-pattern that I have seen repeated is making the mechanism applicable only to the business lines and respective agile DevOps teams while excluding utility and technological functions. It is a must that you involve the broader DevOps 360° stakeholders' ecosystems, or at least the ones who own parts of the DevOps 360 operating model.

Agree on the estimate's measurement

Most probably, you are coming from a mixed context on making estimates. Some parts of your organization are used to estimate based on points in the user story, some estimate on days, some are based on weekly Scrum team capacity, and others do not estimate at all. Agreeing on a new way of providing estimates is vital in order to be able to get harmonized input when certain initiatives are planned to be enabled and adopted across your portfolio. Also, agree on who is responsible for providing estimates as part of the planning process. Please do not make the teams that are responsible for the initiatives enablement also responsible for providing adoption estimates on behalf of the agile DevOps teams. They do not know the context and state-of-the-art of each agile DevOps team out there. The responsibility should be ideally placed with the **product owner** (**PO**) of each agile DevOps team. In some cases, it is not even the PO as some things are of a purely technical nature. Though holding the PO responsible is what I advise you to do.

The Revolut example

I need to tell you this story. Once upon a time, we were participating in a program increment session, and our engineers provided rough estimates on several platform modernization tasks. Some of the POs thought the estimates were too much. One said, "*What do you mean 2 weeks, do you think it takes 2 weeks to do this at Revolut?*" The engineer replied, "*I have never worked for Revolut to be able to know how long things take there. But I can guess that Revolut can move faster than us.*" Be realistic about what you are asking people to deliver and by when and also leave the estimates for the subject matter experts.

Find the right balance between enterprise and business-line-specific planning

Typically, planning has two levels. The first level is what you wish to achieve as an enterprise from a corporate strategy perspective. The second level is what each business line wants to achieve internally. Different business lines have different market competitive advantages, client portfolios, countries of operations, and regulatory requirements and contribute differently to the revenue of the enterprise. The same logic applies to the DevOps technological ecosystem. Naturally, the teams that are part of enabling the DevOps journeys, experience, and productivity will also need to synchronize within their own ecosystem. Allowing for a minimum of two levels of planning while ensuring limited deviations will prove vital.

Define the DevOps initiative's acceptable definition of done (DoD)

Let me explain this one using the dominant example in DevOps adoptions: the adoption of CI/CD pipelines. Do you remember that we come from a context of various CI/CD pipelines across agile DevOps teams, with only a subset of them using the standard offering? Considering this CI/CD pipeline contextual element example, two questions arise that you need to answer:

- Is it sufficient to implement the new DevOps SDLC's capabilities and controls in our own CI/CD pipelines?

- Do we need to shift to the standard common CI/CD pipeline?

You will get those questions, plus similar ones, several times, so be prepared to answer with honesty, logic, rationality, and clarity.

Do not tell people exactly how to implement their team-specific DevOps OKRs

Each initiative needs to have a value proposition and a scope of work: the DevOps SDLC to implement the SDLC capabilities, the DevOps controls to implement the regulatory compliance controls, and so on. You need to provide a scope and expected outcome to the agile DevOps teams, but do not tell them exactly what to do. Provide the solution recipes, frameworks, and patterns where applicable, but allow them to take it from there. You do not know their context and the current state of the DevOps art in detail, plus you need to give to them the best level of autonomy and allow creativity and innovation. Just tell them what they need to achieve and when, and let them work on it. In cases where the scope of an initiative is not clear yet, which means that it is not possible for the teams to create specific DevOps OKRs, allow them either to descope that initiative until clarity is created or to use their intuition, expertise, and experience and act based on the value proposition.

Do not set priority zero initiatives

A common anti-pattern I have seen is setting priority zero for certain initiatives, primarily the initiatives concerned with regulatory compliance. Priority zero indicates that something needs to happen before everything else and *de jure* ("by law" in Latin). Avoid that practice as you do not have insight into the situation, condition, and circumstances of each agile DevOps team. You might ask them to prioritize DevOps controls while their production environment is on fire. Naturally, they will focus on reliability matters in the next sprint. Or you might ask them to focus on DevOps controls when they need to focus on GDPR as they will get a fine if they do not close the respective gaps soon.

Do not become prescriptive on the backlog allocation per agile DevOps team

Agile DevOps teams, as well as the DevOps evolution items, will have to work on delivering new features, hygiene tasks, compliance tasks, and so on. Therefore, their backlogs will have to cater to more than the DevOps evolution. How they balance their backlog should be up to their respective POs. Avoid prescribing that the priorities of each sprint should, for instance, be split like the following:

- **Innovation**: New features and improvements 60% of the time
- **Reliability**: Non-functional requirements 20% of the time
- **Compliance**: 20% of the time

Allow the teams to self-organize to the best level of allowance by just informing them what they need to achieve, as we will outline in the following section.

> **The behind-the-scenes DevOps wonder**
>
> Once upon a time in one of the banks I used to work for, our business counterparts were amazed at how we could balance innovation with reliability and compliance, while the POs were primarily prioritizing innovation in terms of new features. That was because we were playing the priorities and estimates smartly, delivering new features while advancing our DevOps capabilities. We were also quite focused on reliability and compliance with the DoD of epics and user stories.

The tactic of DevOps minimum viable adoption

Not all your teams by default will follow the same DevOps evolution journey and reach the same adoption level at the same time. They have different starting points, capabilities, ambitions, contexts, and the like. Nonetheless, you need to somehow get them to align on certain *DevOps evolution commonalities*, defining the key evolution milestones that they all need to meet. To define and group those commonalities, I like to use the term *DevOps minimum viable adoption*. With this term, in this book we define the common DevOps adoption milestones that all the teams need to reach, no matter their situation, context, conditions, circumstances, or starting point. The concept is twofold and links very well to the **production readiness review** (**PRR**) framework that we discussed in the previous chapter. In my relatively extensive experience with DevOps adoption across the financial services industry, *DevOps minimum viable adoption* is the most pragmatic and sustainable mechanism that you can follow as part of your organic DevOps adoption. Here are some practicalities around it.

Go by the DevOps equilibrium parameters and set objectives

This is a pragmatic way to make clear to all the teams what is expected from them in terms of the following three DevOps equilibrium parameters, complemented by associated KPIs. What is expected is not only to be expressed qualitatively and quantitatively per parameter, but it also needs to be made clear that the three must be balanced. What is the value if your time to market is close to the speed of light, but if your production environment is crumbling and you have 10 open audit remarks? Setting targets and balance as in the following example is solid and pragmatic:

- **Time to market**: On demand, with 15 minutes release velocity
- **Reliability**: 99% availability, while ensuring low latency
- **Compliance**: Adherence to the DevOps controls based on portfolio classification

If you remember, these are attributes in the portfolio registry mechanism that we discussed in the previous chapter. The portfolio registration process also sets the parameters targets' clarity. Having set the parameters, then it is up to the respective teams to judge which DevOps evolution direction they need to take in order to fulfill them and prioritize their DevOps adoption accordingly.

DevOps controls as the foundation of the evolution

To refresh your memory, DevOps controls are risk management, compliance, and speed. They are almost identical to the equilibrium parameters, and that is intentional. The logic is that you become compliant while getting faster and more reliable. What I propose you do, which is the practice I also follow, is to define a set of controls that are applicable to any speed/criticality and technology and architectural classification and make them mandatory across your portfolio. They need to be prioritized by your teams from the start in order to first meet the three equilibrium parameters, and afterward, build on top of them and plan their evolution from there. As long as your teams have met the DevOps controls foundation you set and are also meeting the three equilibrium parameters, you can consider them as *done* from an evolution perspective. What other DevOps advancements they do is not related to enterprise planning and adoption and so is not your business anymore. That is, of course, unless production data on the equilibrium parameters gives you different indications. Some teams might even decide to exceed their targets. If they have the capacity, capability, and PO support, let them do it. Having said that, you need, as mentioned earlier in the chapter, to make some brave decisions, especially in the domain of standardization and simplification. As in, are your teams *done* if they fulfill the equilibrium parameters while using none of the standard offerings and having only partially adopted the DevOps SDLC? You decide.

Shape it as a formal framework

The DevOps minimum viable adoption concept should be defined and launched as a formal framework, and its ownership ideally should be placed with the DevOps CoE (or with whoever owns the DevOps 360° operating model). The DevOps **minimum viable adoption** framework should also have a direct and transparent link with the PRR framework. The PRR is decisive and will eventually be the only source of truth on how your teams evolve with the DevOps adoption. A satisfactory PRR will also, to a large extent, indicate a satisfactory DevOps evolution state and progress. The following is a representation for your inspiration:

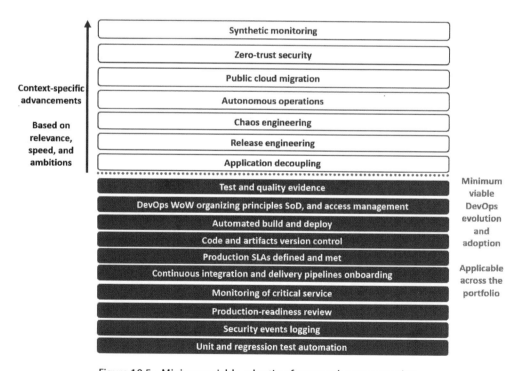

Figure 10.5 – Minimum viable adoption framework representation

As you can see, the capabilities under the minimum viable adoption line are quite fundamental to DevOps. But when we cross the red line and move toward context-specific advancements, the capabilities become more sophisticated.

Where to start on the DevOps minimum viable adoption

How to prioritize the minimum viable adoption capabilities is up to each agile DevOps team, on both the business applications and platforms portfolio, and depends on conditions such as the following:

- **Burning priorities and return on investment**: Is it reliability or time to market that we need to focus on in our circumstances, and will it give us the best value?

- **Priority agreements with the regulator**: Is production hygiene or quality assurance the top priority?

- **Available capacity**: After the prioritization of new functionality, what is the bandwidth left per sprint?

- **Available means**: We do not have cloud engineers at the moment and need to hire in order to focus on the cloud-native journey.

- **Capability readiness**: We don't have our own **security information and event management (SIEM)** solution, and it is not worth building one as the central common platform offering will be ready in 3 months. Let's stick with automated security logging then.

The element of DevOps minimum viable adoption is fundamental to your evolution but not as straightforward as it looks at first sight. There is further depth to it that can complicate the DevOps evolution for the agile DevOps teams. There's more on this in the next chapter.

> **What about the part of the tactical adoption areas?**
>
> I almost forgot about them. The DevOps minimum viable adoption is not really applicable to them. They push the DevOps innovation boundaries because on the one hand, they are your flagships, and on the other hand, you use them to pilot new concepts. Therefore, they need to be constantly advancing and be at the DevOps evolution and innovation edge.

Summary

In this chapter, we focused on the enterprise portfolio planning and adoption mechanism of the DevOps 360° evolution. Initially, we explained its vital value proposition for the evolution, and afterward, we argued why your adoption should be divided between a tactical and an organic approach. On the tactical side, we discussed its arguments, highlighting its strategic importance in the organic evolution. Moving on, we looked into the main strategic domains that organizations focus on when appointing candidates for the tactical adoption, the parameters of differentiation between the tactical and organic adoption candidates, and what the concept of *all hands on deck* implies for the tactical adoption. Afterward, we moved on to presenting a practical approach for the enterprise portfolio planning and adoption mechanism, focusing on the organizational enablement and adoption of the DevOps OKRs. We also provided two examples to explain the connection between strategic objectives and team OKRs. Continuing, we outlined some important points to consider when designing and executing the mechanism derived from various examples from the industry. Closing the chapter, we focused on the important concept of *DevOps minimum viable adoption*. We explained its DevOps controls origin, relation to the PRR framework, applicability, and importance for the DevOps 360° evolution and complemented it with an example.

In the next chapter, we will focus on the mechanism of benefit measurement and realization. We will look into the approaches of validating whether your evolution's business case materializes or not.

11
Benefit Measurement and Realization

This chapter introduces us to a rather complex phase of our DevOps 360° operating model – that of benefit measurement and realization. We will start by outlining the value proposition of measuring and realizing benefits during the DevOps 360° evolution and will highlight the importance of continuity and materializing the DevOps equilibrium while doing so. Continuing, we will highlight the important distinction between a **key performance target** (**KPT**) and a metric. These are two terms that the industry often confuses. Moving on, we will also bring clarity on how to assess whether a KPT or a metric provides either *proof of success* or an *indicator of success* when measuring or realizing it. Afterward, we will stress the importance of capturing the needs of your DevOps 360° stakeholder ecosystem on what to measure, also outlining a small exercise you can conduct to capture them. Later in the chapter, we will become quite *sophisticated*, discussing a three-tier approach to KPTs and metrics based on the DevOps principles of minimum viable adoption, viable adherence, and efficiency. We will complement that approach with an example. We will also provide a proven proposal for primary KPTs and metrics, along with some important recommendations. Coming to an agreement on the mathematical formulas and risk appetite thresholds of your KPTs and metrics is very important, and we will provide insights into this topic. The last part of the chapter will introduce us to the importance of *data dashboards*, providing some examples. We will close the chapter by citing insightful considerations that you can consult during your benefit measurement and realization process, along with a collection of KPTs and metrics *to avoid* that we have nonetheless seen certain incumbents attempting to adopt.

In this chapter, we're going to cover the following main topics:

- The value proposition of benefit measurement and realization
- The difference between key performance targets and metrics
- A pragmatic three-tier approach to DevOps KPTs and metrics

- A proposal for primary DevOps KPTs and metrics

- DevOps KPTs and metric mathematics, risk appetite, and "dashboarding"

- Important considerations when measuring and realizing benefits

What is the value proposition of benefit measurement and realization for DevOps?

If you cannot prove something, you are not doing it, people say. Adding further to that phrase, *if you cannot measure something, you cannot realize it and therefore cannot prove it.*

Most probably, your organization is not used to conducting benefit measurement and realization collectively on the enterprise level. This situation is underlined by the absence of fundamental organizational, process, governance, and technological means to achieve this measurement and realization. In addition, most definitely your DevOps evolution data is spread across various sources, in different formats, with different update ratios, and, last but not least, it will to a large extent be *corrupted*, in the sense that on the one hand, it does not tell the absolute truth on where you stand. On the other hand, it is probably available only in isolation and does not capture the entire SDLC. These characteristics – *various sources, corruption*, and *isolation* – create further challenges to baselining your organization before the evolution formally begins, which complicates measuring your progress compared to your starting point.

> **Did You Know?**
>
> Most incumbents I have come across predominantly rely on data stored in ITSM tools in order to keep track of their DevOps evolution. Incident, change request, and SLA numbers are the most commonly used data out there. Don't get fooled, though. It is not because it is the most important data to capture, but because it is often the only enterprise dataset available of decent quality.

In my experience, undertaking benefit measurement and realization of a DevOps evolution is regarded as the most complicated challenge by incumbents in the financial services industry (especially the return of investment to the capital allocation aspect). I came across this challenging benefit measurement and realization situation several times when I was directly employed by banks, but also currently while consulting for banks. What, how, and when does it make sense to measure? Who is interested in which measurement? What should we look for on the enterprise level and on the individual team level? Who is accountable and where is the data stored? These are the questions dominating the DevOps benefit measurement and realization agenda across incumbents. In this chapter, I will provide some pragmatic and practical approaches and recommendations on benefit measurement and realization that you can adopt in your DevOps 360° evolution.

Inevitably, you will have to anchor this process to a formally well-established mechanism. There will be several potential outcomes of your DevOps 360° evolution:

- Track the progress of evolution on the levels of both the enterprise and lines of business, as well as individual teams.

- Support decision-making, justify priorities, be able to steer the evolution accordingly, and provide clarity on how the DevOps objectives will be measured.

- Provide sufficient time to technological utility areas to ensure the availability of the required data.

- Calculate the return on investment in your DevOps business case.

- Create momentum and visibility to positively influence the evolution's dynamics.

- Collect evidence for your regulator and partners, along with showcasing your advancements to the industry and clients.

- Support the adoption at relevance in a multi-speed context, as not all targets and metrics will be equally applicable across your portfolio

> **Benefit Realization and Technology Standardization**
>
> A commonly enabled benefit realization process using data collected by common DevOps platforms can be a motivating factor for the agile DevOps teams to give up their own shadow IT solutions. Play that card wisely together with the DevOps controls one.

Deviating from the mainstream of DevOps benefits

In this book, our ambition is to take a rather sophisticated approach to DevOps, and this is also applied to benefit measurement and realization. Hence, where applicable and sensible, we present creative and innovative approaches compared to the mainstream ones that you will have observed in the industry. One deviation we will pursue in this chapter is to avoid labeling the overarching outcomes of benefit realization as **key performance indicators** (**KPIs**). This is because the word *indicator*, being sufficiently self-descriptive, only *indicates* and might not necessarily tell the truth of a situation. We are instead going to call them **key performance targets** (**KPTs**), meaning targets that not only indicate, but can also provide reasonable assurance.

A second deviation we will pursue is to go beyond the following four mainstream metrics used in the industry:

- Deployment frequency

- Change rate failure

- Mean time to recover

- Lead time for changes

We will not refrain totally from this, as you will see later in the chapter, but we will take a different stance on them. Indeed, these four metrics provide some fundamental data for assessing your evolution. I do not disagree with that. In my mind, nevertheless, these four metrics mostly focus on continuous deployment and operations. And that is just a subset of our DevOps 360° SDLC. They do not provide a 360° picture across a DevOps evolution.

Interestingly enough, I have not come across any bank that does not use (only) these four metrics to measure the benefits of its DevOps evolution. It is not a coincidence and while I know the reasons, I prefer not to distract you with unnecessary information.

What is the difference between a KPT and a metric?

Before we move on, let us build a common understanding of two fundamental terms of benefit measurement and realization. An important differentiation that often confuses people in the industry is between KPIs (KPTs in our book) and metrics. The difference is rather simple. Think about a KPT being a target for what you wish to achieve. Let us say that for availability, the target is 99% uptime. By contrast, think about metrics as being ways to measure how you perform on reaching that target. Let us say you are getting close to zero failures per release, which means that you are getting close to achieving 99% uptime or have already achieved it. The following table provides a comparative overview between the fundamental aspects of KPTs and metrics:

KPT	Metric
Focused on enterprise DevOps OKRs	Focused on team-specific DevOps OKRs
High-level target perspective	Low-level progress perspective
More harmonious across the portfolio	More at relevance per business application
Used for DevOps enterprise evolution decision making	Used for DevOps local evolution decision-making

Table 11.1 – KPT and metric major differences

As you can see from the entries of the preceding table, understanding the difference between a KPT and a metric is important across several dimensions in the DevOps 360° evolution. How to potentially reconcile the two is something we will see later in the chapter.

What is the difference between an indicator and a proof?

KPTs and metrics can be divided into two broad categories on the *quality* and interpretation of data they provide and consecutively the degree of realization. These categories are as follows:

- **Proof of success**: This is data that provides assurance on a measurement. For example:

  - SLA of 95% uptime: You have the means to verify with certainty that the application was available 95% of the time.

  - 100% change request automation: Again, you have the means to verify with certainty that the automated change management process has been implemented.

  - CI velocity of 5 minutes: Once more, you have the means to verify with certainty that CI steps are executed within 5 minutes.

  The nature of these measurements, backed up by your organizational means, provides sufficient assurance of progress and realization.

- **Indicator of success**: This data provides just indications and not assurance of realization. Therefore, it comes with the condition of *relative materialization certainty or uncertainty*. For example:

  - The number of incidents has reduced per change. This suggests that changes create fewer incidents, but what if they create more severe ones, even if there are fewer of them? Let's assume that in the past quarter in application A, we had 10 incidents as a result of changes. Out of those, 5 incidents were classified as P1 (priority) and the other 5 as P4 (priority 4). A quarter later, we have 7 incidents as a result of changes, so the total number has fallen by 3. Success! But all of these 7 incidents were P1. Has the application's reliability therefore improved? Most probably not.

  - You have a portfolio of 50 applications that process banking transactions, of which 10 have successfully passed the production readiness review. At the end of the following quarter, this number has increased to 20. But are you certain that the initial 10 have maintained the eligibility criteria quality since then, and that in the additional 10 apps, the claim that *there is sufficient knowledge on how to operate the service in production* holds true?

You get my point, right? Indications do not provide assurance. It is up to you to define your *DevOps benefit of doubt/indication* threshold when agreeing on your KPTs and metrics.

The importance of capturing the collective interest

The benefit measurement and realization phase is a fundamental part of the DevOps 360° operating model, and requires strong alignment and consensus across your broader DevOps stakeholder ecosystem. It is important that all major stakeholders have the opportunity to express their opinion about what to measure to realize the benefits of the evolution. Their backgrounds, expertise, and positions in the organization allow them to see your DevOps world from different perspectives. The core actors I propose should be included in this exercise are the main governing bodies of the evolution that we discussed in *Chapter 3, The DevOps 360° Operating Model Pillars and Governance Model*, plus the DevOps CoE. Therefore, you should engage the DevOps 360° vision authority, the design and advocacy authority, and the DevOps CoE. The exercise is pretty straightforward and intuitive. Ask them to use the statement *As a (title and profession) I am interested in measuring (this). The value proposition is (this)*. The statement and measurement must be mapped to the eight DevOps enterprise OKRs. During the course of the exercise, the DevOps lexicon needs to be consulted to ensure that the same DevOps language is reflected in the proposed measurements.

The following illustration provides a very realistic example of output per stakeholder:

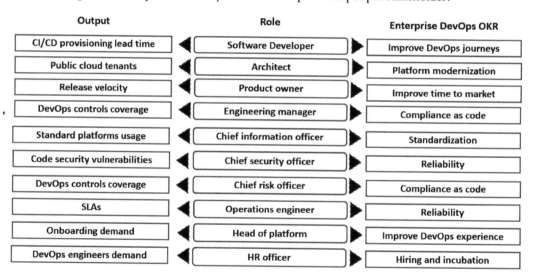

Figure 11.1 – Example desired metrics and linkage to enterprise DevOps OKRs

The outcome will most probably surprise in five ways:

- Several answers will be identical and overlap stakeholders.

- How broad the coverage will be across several aspects of your evolution.

- The answers will balance adoption, adherence, efficiency, and performance indicators, mixing KPTs with metrics.

- Some answers will be *proofs* of success and others *indications* of success.

- Some participants will really struggle to provide *non-mainstream inputs*.

A pragmatic three-tier approach to DevOps KPTs and metrics

In this book, we introduce the approach of *adoption, adherence, and efficiency/performance measurements* to measure and realize the adoption using KPTs and metrics. This approach is inspired by the DevOps equilibrium of *time to market-reliability-compliance* and uses the DevOps minimum viable adoption concept that we introduced in the previous chapter as a foundation. Let us look into the details:

- **Minimum viable adoption KPTs**: As we saw in the previous chapter, the elements of minimum viable adoption will be common across your portfolio and have the DevOps controls as their foundation. To refresh your memory, they can include the adoption of the standard CI/CD pipeline, monitoring of critical services, and automated regression testing for a business application's critical path. The KPTs (primarily) and metrics belonging to the first level, therefore, will be capturing the enterprise adoption of the controls/capabilities that belong to the DevOps minimum viable adoption framework.

- **Viable adherence KPTs or metrics**: Refers to the adherence of DevOps controls/capabilities to specific policies and thresholds around adoption. The logic behind this level is that you might adopt (as part of the MVA) an open source license security scanning tool when you move to the standard CI/CD pipeline and configure it so the scanning is triggered by your builds. Having done that, your code repositories will be scanned based on a list of pre-approved licenses and you will be presented with the results accordingly, highlighting any vulnerabilities found. Now, the action of remediating the vulnerabilities found is called *viable adherence*. If you do not perform the necessary remediations, you have only adopted the capability/control and have not adhered to its respective policy, and you will be subject to violation management procedures.

- **Efficiency/performance metrics (velocities)**: Being purely quantitative, these are insights into your actual performance and progress mostly in terms of velocities across your SDLC. Using our example, you might consider three types of velocity: release velocity, CI velocity (with or without open source scanning enabled), and remediation of security vulnerabilities velocity.

The following illustration provides an example based on our open source vulnerability scanning DevOps control/capability:

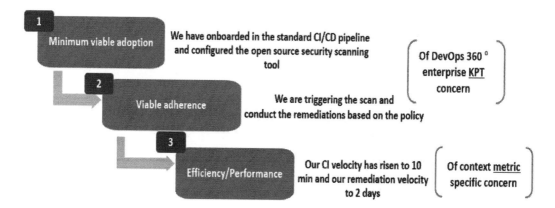

Figure 11.2 – The three-tier approach to KPT and metrics

The tiers, as you can see, break down the minimum viable adoption and create a distinction between KPTs and metrics. Note that the distinction between KPTs and metrics is not that clear across all DevOps controls and capabilities. In certain KPTs, for instance, such as the ones related to the people hiring and incubation, the viable adherence or velocity level can be omitted based on its nature and your requirements. In our example, the enterprise KPT is to have all teams adopting the open source security scanning technology and adhering to the prescribed open source license policies. How much this adoption and adherence could potentially affect the release velocity of the teams and the *time to market* and *compliance* equilibrium is up to the agile DevOps team to figure out. That is, unless the agile DevOps team belongs to the tactical adoption group. In those cases, there will be certain patterns and intelligence mechanisms to support the aforementioned equilibrium.

A proven proposal for DevOps KPTs and metrics

When I started writing this chapter, I was not intending to provide a proposal for what KPTs and metrics to adopt. I was under the belief that I do not know your DevOps context and desired outcomes and therefore it wouldn't be helpful. Also, I had no desire to provide you with the basics you would have repeatedly read elsewhere. Halfway through this chapter, I've changed my mind. The main reasons for changing my mind are on the one hand because I believe I have a model that is agnostic, and on the other hand because it is my wish to share as much knowledge as possible with you. The following is my basic foundation proposal for the KPTs and metrics you should consider adopting as part of measuring and realizing your DevOps evolution:

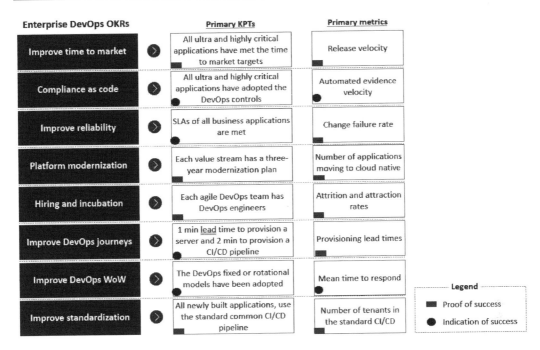

Figure 11.3 – Proposal for the top KPTs and metrics to adopt

There are a few points for consideration:

- Create the transparency link between enterprise DevOps OKRs, KPTs, and metrics.

- Define clearly which KPTs and metrics are *proofs of success* and which are *indicators of success*. You will have to prepare your data interpretation tactics accordingly.

- Be as quantitative and practical as possible.

- Go as broad as you can across the DevOps 360° SDLC.

Ensure fulfillment of the four qualities of DevOps 360° and the DevOps equilibrium

Measuring KPTs and metrics in isolation does not necessarily give you the true picture and definitely not the complete picture. DevOps is about continuity – measuring isolated targets and metrics simply violates the essence of DevOps. It is therefore key that your KPTs and metrics are all part of the same flow, materializing into the DevOps equilibrium. Imagine for instance that *time to market* is the primary (and maybe the only) KPT with which you measure application A. Maybe you have achieved a 5-minute release velocity, but your production SLA is scoring 75% uptime compared to the required 95% and your code repositories look deep red in terms of open source security vulnerabilities. Are you really succeeding with your DevOps evolution? The mechanism of DevOps equilibrium needs to come into play here, as in, you release fast enough while meeting the reliability targets and maintaining compliance. Primary outcomes must not be used in isolation to justify the means of achieving your teams' priorities (paraphrasing Machiavelli's quote from the Prince, *the end justifies the means*). Downplaying quality assurance KPTs and DevOps controls on security or oversimplifying your SLA's mathematical formula will not work for long. Your clients, business partners, regulators, and downstream systems will notice. On top of ensuring the DevOps equilibrium, you must also fulfill the four qualities of 360° degrees: **completeness**, **continuity**, **interoperability**, and **reconcilability** when looking at the totality of your KPTs and metrics.

Some Advice and a Kind Request

Advice: Go back to *Chapter 2, The DevOps Multi-Speed Context, Vision, Objectives, and Change Nature*, where we defined the key results per enterprise DevOps OKR. If you employ them and reshape them to your context, you will have more than 20 potential KPTs you can adopt.

Kind request: Do not attempt to measure individual developer productivity. It is just wrong and toxic. I know of an incumbent that proposed introducing such a mechanism. It was perceived as micromanagement and triggered HR involvement. It did not materialize eventually. How many lines of code a developer wrote and what the cycle time was on an individual user story tell you literally nothing about how productive a developer is. If you wish to measure *developer productivity*, focus on the whole agile DevOps cross-functional team.

You need to agree on the mathematics and risk appetite

Let me start this section by reciting a real story of mine. Once upon a time, I was brought in by an incumbent to advise them on their DevOps operating model. One of the elements they wanted me to provide input on was the challenge of having the various teams adhere harmoniously to the defined DevOps metrics. I was confident I knew exactly what was going wrong. I asked for the set of DevOps metrics and the mathematical formulas behind them, as well as the defined criticality thresholds. I was told (not to my surprise) that there were no commonly agreed mathematical formulas and thresholds. After interviewing a couple of teams, I realized that the main issue was exactly that: the agile DevOps teams were never instructed or consulted on which parameters were included in the metrics' mathematical equations. Equally, they were never told what the upper policy thresholds were on the quality assurance and security-related metrics.

Some TKPRs and metrics that I consider a must when *"doing the mathematics"* and defining criticality thresholds are the following:

- **Service level agreements (SLAs)**: Is it just pure availability uptime and downtime you wish to measure? Or should parameters such as latency and performance be included? Should any scheduled/maintenance downtime impact on the SLA be considered, or only unforeseen downtime? The same applies to error budgets if you have adopted that mechanism.

- **Mean time to recover**: Should it only include the time required to switch between data centers in case of a disaster and get the servers up and running again? Or should it also include the time required for the totality of microservices running on those machines to be operational again?

- **Mean time to detect**: Is it the time required for a monitoring tool to detect the abnormality, the end user, or an operations engineer? Is the raising of an alert by the monitoring tool and the auto-creation of an incident enough to provide detection time assurance, or does it require a human to log in to an application or server and witness the abnormality themselves?

- **Any type of velocities**: What are the parameters that are included in the release velocity equation? For instance, is it every single step in the SDLC from commit to production? Do lead times that are caused by external parties count as a real impact in your release velocity mathematical formula, or not?

- **Any vulnerabilities**: Do your repositories and release artifacts need to be absolutely *security-vulnerability free*? Or is remediating only the top critical ones considered sufficient to fulfill the respective KPT?

- **Quality assurance code coverage**: What is included in test automation code coverage? Is it only unit tests, or also regression tests? And if regression tests are included, is it sufficient to cover only the critical path of a business application or do you need to cover every single piece of functionality?

- **Operational level agreements (OLAs)**: Is it enough that data across systems are delivered on time, whether synchronously or asynchronously, real-time or batch, or is data completeness and reconciliation included in the equation? As in, if data from the upstream systems is delivered on time but is incomplete, is the OLA fulfilled or breached? And if the latter happens, does it also have an impact on the SLAs?

The preceding list is not complete, but I am confident that it provides some good inspiration for the KPTs and metrics you need, and helps you to bring clarity to how you calculate them.

Dashboarding is gold

Data is gold, and being able to gather and visualize it is game-changing in terms of measuring and realizing benefits – especially if this data is real time, credible, and connects the DevOps equilibrium continuity dots across your KPTs and metrics. As we saw earlier in the chapter, different stakeholders are interested in different KPTs and metrics represented in the form of data. Your DevOps evolution truth will be in the accumulation and aggregation of the data that your stakeholders are collectively interested in. Data can be represented in various views. In this section, we will outline the main four views that I find very valuable and insightful. But before that, I will give you a tip.

Present Data in Every Single Circumstance

I have been always supportive of making data available to various stakeholders in every single circumstance and on every occasion. Therefore, my teams always had live dashboards that delivered metrics to our business stakeholders, who were actually using them in their meetings with regulators as well (smart move). And I was always bringing my Grafana dashboards when meeting our CIO (to show off) and when giving presentations to different teams (to inspire). A good real-time metrics dashboard is way more insightful than the best PowerPoint presentation you have ever seen.

Good quality dashboards, especially where data is available in a raw format and can be manipulated (not in the bad sense of the term) as well as consolidated, can provide various views of your DevOps state from different angles, perspectives, and points of interest. My top favorite ones are as follows:

- **SDLC velocities**: I also like to call this one **SDLC observability**. It covers the collection of velocity points of interest and metrics across the SDLC. Examples are technology provisioning times, average epic cycle times, CI velocity, CD velocity, and release frequency.

- **End-to-end flows or ecosystems**: I also like to call this **flow integrity and completeness**. It covers (literally and technically) the end-to-end views of business applications' flows or value streams for data delivery and system availability. System uptime/downtime, data flow status tracking, data flow completeness in terms of delivery and data reconciliation, domino effect tracking in case of incidents, and SLAs and OLAs are all included in these views. A great use case is for front-to-back visibility of the health of the broader DevOps 360° technological ecosystem.

- **CI/CD events flow**: This covers metrics such as feature branch lifespan, commit frequency, numbers of open and reviewed PRs, static code analysis results, security scan vulnerabilities, test automation failures, build status, and so on.

- **Production operations**: This covers metrics such as incident events and impact on SLAs and error budgets, deployment/rollback status, post-deployment verifications, change success rates, and mean time to detect and recover from incidents, as well as change-request lead times and logging events.

As you rightly guessed, the combined data of the preceding dashboards can be used for what you could call **DevOps controls** or **PRR** dashboards and serve as evidence. Adopting dashboards from an early phase of the evolution is vital. Honesty and transparency are rewarded – but be prepared to answer questions if things do not look green.

Advice

As part of your evolution, prioritize the establishment of your DevOps KPTs and metrics *observability* (many call it "telemetry") framework. Utilize real-time data event streaming across technologies and create predefined dashboard templates that your stream can use out of the box and that you can build on top of.

Some very important considerations

There are many aspects to consider when establishing the measurement and realization mechanism. On top of the ones we already mentioned in this chapter, I would like to add the following.

The importance of various perceptions

Always remember the difference between *numbers-based reality versus perceptions-based reality*. Numbers will not always tell you the truth, and on some occasions, perceptions can be more accurate than numbers. Perceptions originate from two sources: firstly, the outside world, where you have your end users, partners, and regulator, and secondly, the inside world, where your organization's people involved in the DevOps evolution are. After many years in DevOps evolutions, I tend to believe that *corridor whispers* should be trusted primarily, with production numbers in second place. Looking at the former, those random chit-chats next to the coffee machine in most cases provide the most vivid picture of how well your evolution is moving and materializing. Embrace and trust those talks! I have heard the phrase *"trust me, it is worse than it looks"* so many times.

Do not go for absolute numbers when defining targets

When defining KPTs, avoid absolute numbers. Your ambition to meet absolute numbers is a pure fallacy when we speak of *enterprise scale*. It is only a matter of time before you fail to meet them (unless you manage to *cook/manipulate* them – seen that…). Therefore, you should not consider 100% availability uptime, zero P1 incidents, zero vulnerabilities, or zero failure rate per change. And even if you still decide to consider them and in the miraculous scenario that you manage to achieve those numbers in the early days, it will only be during an application's early lifetime, or even before that when you are in *technical go-live* mode. Once the application grows in terms of services deployed, together with your clients, volumes, and market coverage, your absolute KPTs will come under immense pressure. You also risk investing significant capital and people without having a true necessity, such as building ultra-resilient systems. Google claims that 99.99% availability is sufficient, so what is it that makes your applications so special that they require 100%?

On the monetarization of your DevOps business case

On the money side, to capture how your DevOps business case is helping materialize cost savings, you should include two types of cost:

- **Direct balance sheet cost**: DevOps efficiencies that resulted in savings from the operating expenses of your bank.

- **Opportunity cost**: This is what could have been achieved if the cost was not removed from the balance sheet, but instead deployed as capital back in the DevOps evolution. Consider it in terms of moving money from one pocket to the other. This type of cost is one that organizations often ignore, due to urgent needs to improve their cost/capital ratio and become more competitive in the market, as well as to satisfy their shareholders. Think twice before you write something off on the balance sheet and try to turn parts of your savings into *capital employed*.

Do not directly link people's bonuses to DevOps performance targets (if possible)

Ensure that the measurements are not linked directly to the bonus schema of certain individuals in managerial positions. They will inevitably be linked directly or indirectly in a corporate environment, but at least make sure that they are not in conflict. For instance, consider two peers: one leads a software development team and another leads an operations team. In this context, there must not be time to market and reliability measurements that conflict with each other (trust me, been there). You will create a conflict of interest and tensions behind the scenes that will only have a negative impact on the evolution. Link the measurement of individuals to flows. Each individual then has their own dedicated domain, and they all get rewarded if the flow succeeds in its totality.

Pilot the benefit measurements and realization in the tactical adoption first

Things will not work as expected from the beginning of the benefit measurements and realization. Take advantage of the tactical adoption areas to pilot the KPTs and metrics and test their sufficiency, validity, and sustainability. This is done to make sure that when the organic adoption formally starts, you will not dive into benefit measurement and realization uncertainty.

Link to the enterprise portfolio planning, classification, and governance

Naturally, when you conduct the enterprise portfolio planning, your DevOps OKR enablement and adoption teams need clarity on what targets to work toward and to be provided with support on which metrics to use to measure progress toward those targets. You will also have to touch on the portfolio classification mechanism to provide clarity on the targets based on speed, technological, and architectural parameters of each business application and platform. Last but not least, you must utilize the DevOps attributes in the portfolio registry to keep track of the KPTs and metrics on the tribe/value stream level, as well as on the business application and platform level.

Your business partners are key stakeholders in this

As we also mentioned in the previous chapter, it is your lines of business that have the first say on what your targets are. Next in line are your regulatory supervisors. The technology teams are responsible for consulting them on how certain targets can be measured, providing the technological means and data to do so, and where necessary, arguing against it. This is the part where you really need to have your business partners not only involved, but to a large extent driving the agenda. Consider also that targets are directly linked to monetary investments, and it is your business partners who eventually hold the DevOps evolution budget keys.

For each KPT and metric, it is vital to check "readiness"

Ask this question to you on every KPT and metric you set: *Do we have the necessary means to measure it?* What if a capability is not yet enabled? What if a capability is not yet interoperable? And even if it is enabled and interoperable, what if the available data is corrupted? Or what if you do not have access to the data at all? Or maybe the data is scattered across shadow IT solutions? Does it really make sense to go for that metric? In addition, can you survive by using empirical data in certain cases where real data is not available? All these questions have to be carefully considered when assessing readiness.

> **An Interesting Observation**
>
> I have not come across a single DevOps evolution where all the required data to measure and realize the benefits was available and of decent quality.

The funniest of the DevOps KPTs and metrics

I would like to close this chapter with a humorous attitude. DevOps (especially enterprise) is big fun, and several funny stories can arise during the course of an enterprise evolution! I am certain we all agree on that. One of the DevOps domains that I have enjoyed working on the most myself, and that is also a great source of observing "irrationalities," is the measurement and benefit realization domain. Throughout my career, I have come across several KPTs and metrics, some of which were very irrational (to say the least) and funny, based on my belief and understanding of DevOps. The following are the craziest ones that I would like to promote as anti-patterns to avoid!

Just to make sure, before we move on to outline these scenarios, note that they have been edited for ethical reasons, but at the same time do not deviate much from the reality I have encountered across multiple incumbents. Enjoy!

The 30% of developers onboarded in the standard CI/CD pipeline target

The problem was not only that there was no rationale about why 30% and not 35% or 36% of developers. When setting numerical targets, there must be solid arguments as to why you ended up with those specific numbers. It was also that there was no rationale on which areas those developers should be from, for instance, the top speed domains. Even worse, no one in the organization (not even HR) had clear visibility on how many people were labeled as developers in the HR systems and how many were developers in reality in the organization. Please bear with me; we are talking about individual developers, not agile DevOps team members. The result was something like, "one developer here and one developer there has been onboarded."

The magic CI/CD pipeline 15-minute release velocity target (just because)

First of all, no one could answer why 15 minutes and not 14 minutes. But leave that aside. Based on this target, if you were to use the standard CI/CD pipeline (not the one mentioned in the previous story, a different one), your release velocity was to automatically go down to 15 minutes. All the while, the standard CI/CD pipeline had no integration with the ITSM tool to raise and approve change requests automatically; all the testing phases but unit testing were done manually over a period of 2 weeks; test data provisioning took 1 week; the control evidence was collected manually; and there was only a deployment framework available for .NET applications.

The zero open source code vulnerabilities target (again, just because)

In one of the banks, there was the good ambition to *never end up on the front page of the newspapers* (that was the saying in the office). But they took it too far. They got an open source library vulnerability scan tool and onboarded every single code repository in it (even deprecated ones). The KPT was *vulnerability-free code.* When the teams started scanning the repositories, most of them had critical vulnerabilities of all levels (from low to major), some from false positives and some from real vulnerabilities. To become *vulnerability free* according to the developers, they had to stop delivering new features for months and just do remediations. (They were asked to provide that estimate on the actual effort required to meet the "vulnerability-free code" target.)

The 100% availability excluding external impact (just to be on the safe side)

True story. At one of the banks I've worked at, there was a target of 100% uptime availability, with the remark that "*downtime by events that are external to the application is not to be included in the calculation formula.*"

The 100% of IT people trained in the incident management process target

Literally everyone in IT (even if it's not relevant to the daily work and job functions of certain people) had to attend a 30-minute session where the incident process was presented to them by some incident managers. This was part of the DevOps incubation targets. Half of those present were doing other things during the session instead of listening to it (and I was checking them, implying that I was also not paying attention).

All secrets need to be stored in (absent) secret management vaults

To begin with, it was never made clear what should be included in *secrets*. Also, no one clarified which applications this was applicable to (the mainframe guys were asking). Even worse, the Agile DevOps teams were requested to report progress on onboarding to a respective central capability, that was not even available to them. That central secret management tool POC is still to be finalized, I guess. And then, once done (if successful), procurement needs to be involved, then we need to find the money and sign the contract.

The progressive regression test coverage up to 75% target (once you reach it, you can stop)

Not 74%, not 76%. 75% precisely! The target here was that all the business applications should gradually, within 3 years, grow their regression test coverage to 75%, following this progression scheme; 25% to 50% to 75%. Then, after meeting this target, they could rest. Three years of gradual test automation improvements was too much, don't you think?

The elimination of 1,000,000 hours of idle time target

My absolute favorite, and I am serious. This was a hybrid KPT/metric (a high-profile one, actually) in the context of one incumbent. So, what happened here? They managed to collect 12 months' data of all the technical requests raised by developers, focusing on the requesters' *wait/lead times* till the requests were resolved. They added up all the wait/lead times and that resulted in more than 1,000,000 hours a year of *developers not being able to do their work* (lost developer productivity, it was called formally). Then the target was to automate all these requests and 1) *reduce an operating cost of the organization*, which was 1,000,000 hours multiplied by rate/per hour of an internal employee, and 2) *give back to developers 1,000,000 hours of their lives*, as if developers were going home to play with their kids till their technical requests were fulfilled and once they were fulfilled, they were coming back to the office to work. The biggest problem (among other practical ones) behind this KPT/metric was the faulty assumption that developers were sitting idle doing nothing while waiting for their requests to be fulfilled. Obviously, in reality they were shifting focus to other tasks not related to their pending requests. (Don't ask… I have already got a headache while writing this paragraph and I did not even cover 10% of the real story).

I honestly have many more than those, but allow me to keep some for myself.

> **Kind Request**
>
> Please share with me if you have come across similar targets to the preceding ones. I will not tell anyone, I promise!

Summary

In this chapter, we focused on the benefit measurement and realization phase of the DevOps 360° operating model. Initially, we explained its vital value proposition for the DevOps 360° evolution, also outlining the importance of fulfilling the DevOps equilibrium and 360° qualities during the process. We next provided arguments on why the mainstream way of measuring and realizing benefits is not sufficient and why a more *sophisticated* approach is required. Inspired by the industry's misunderstandings and misconceptions, we moved on to providing clarity on the difference between a KPT and a metric, as well as the difference between a *proof of success* and an *indicator of success*. Focus was put on the importance of engaging the broad DevOps stakeholder ecosystem to elicit their desire around *what to measure* by also supplementing it with a practice that *always works*. We then moved to the core of the chapter, presenting a three-tier approach to KPTs and metrics, using the concept of DevOps minimum viable adoption as a basis. The elements of *viable adherence* and *efficiencies* were added on top, supported by an example. We complemented that approach with a proposal for the top primary KPTs and metrics you should use, while highlighting the importance of linking them to the enterprise DevOps OKRs. A common phenomenon and struggle in the industry was then discussed, concerning the *mathematics and risk appetite* while setting KPTs and metrics, with some examples. Under the belief that *data is gold*, we dedicated a section to *dashboarding*, providing some examples of dashboards that can be decisive in your evolution. As mentioned in the introduction, benefit measurement and realization is a rather complex endeavor, so to support you, we cited some very important considerations for you to think about. We closed the chapter in *funny mode*, outlining some irrational KPTs and metrics that we have come across over the years while working on FSI DevOps evolutions.

The next chapter is dedicated to the most valuable asset in any DevOps 360° evolution: the people.

12

People Hiring, Incubation, and Mobility

This chapter is dedicated to your most valuable asset in the DevOps 360° evolution: the people. The chapter will start by briefly outlining the value proposition of people in the DevOps 360° evolution. We will continue by highlighting the importance of creating Π-shaped DevOps professionals during the evolution, as well as the need to be forward-looking by ensuring that our DevOps-related professions will be fit for future purposes. Afterward, we will move into the domain of hiring for our DevOps 360° evolution and we will outline what we consider to be the most important elements of our hiring strategies. In that section, we will give complementary tips and recommendations regarding the value of 360° interviews and precautions on using external parties to scale. The second part of the chapter will be dedicated to the topic of people incubation. We will examine the importance of incubation for both leaders and *people on the ground*, why you should be conducting your incubation in a targeted and relevant manner, and how absences in or limitations on your incubation means can severely jeopardize your evolution. This chapter will close by providing the value proposition of people mobility for DevOps while providing 360° evolution considerations derived from real mobility cases.

In this chapter, we're going to cover the following topics:

- The value proposition of people in the DevOps 360° evolution
- DevOps Π-shaped profiles
- Strategic considerations in DevOps hiring
- DevOps incubation recommendations
- Practical DevOps mobility cases and precautions

The value proposition of people in the DevOps 360° evolution

We have smoothly reached the last, though definitely not the least, important part of the DevOps 360° operating model. In this chapter, we will focus on the most valuable asset within your DevOps 360° evolution. This refers to people. In contrast with the preceding chapters, in this one, we will not give a lengthy value proposition. It is a rather obvious one, in accordance with a Greek saying, "*τα εύκολος εννοούμενα παραλείπονται.*" In English, this means "*What is obvious can be deliberately omitted.*" Therefore, I will briefly summarize the value proposition of people in the DevOps 360° evolution in one sentence, and we will move on to the essence of the chapter:

People: the most valuable and challenging-to-acquire asset that will enable your DevOps 360° operating model.

In this chapter, we will focus on three important elements concerning people:

- **Hiring**: The process of bringing new people and skills into your organization

- **Incubation**: The process of uplifting your personnel's DevOps skills

- **Mobility**: The process of mobilizing people across the various DevOps 360° enablement and adoption domains

In the coming sections, we will go a little bit broader than the mainstream job descriptions, one-to-one meetings, and proposals to have all your people certified in **Google Cloud Platform** (**GCP**) as an example. Our focus will be on some decisive recommendations and perspectives on how to approach DevOps hiring, incubation, and mobility. In this chapter, you should not expect to find complex concepts and terms. We will be plain and concise about the context. You can actually perceive this chapter as a small *DevOps people pocket guide* of tips and recommendations.

Just to make sure (on people and culture)

In this chapter, we are following a lighter approach compared to other chapters, not because the people side is to be downplayed (unfortunately, it often is in reality) but because I consider people (and consequently, culture) a very context- and case-sensitive element of your DevOps adoption. This context and case sensitivity makes the people aspect of DevOps not very applicable to being addressed using proven practices, frameworks, and patterns. It requires more sophisticated and delicate means that heavily rely on specific use cases.

Question: did you notice that this is the first time in the book that I have mentioned the word *culture*? Culture in my opinion is not only heavily context-sensitive but also *intangible* and of historic organizational roots that require deep awareness of its evolution. In my opinion, only when someone is within a situation (and I am not working in your organization) can they provide advice on how cultural matters pertain to DevOps. Therefore, I'll leave it totally up to you on how to handle it, because you are the one who knows your organization. As I respond to every single new manager who hires me, when I am asked "*What do you plan to do with the people?*" – firstly, I get to know and understand them.

The importance of creating Π-shaped profiles

Before starting to structure your hiring, incubation, and mobility tactics, you need to define what DevOps profiles and professions you wish to create as an organization. Your focus should not just be on the engineering roles, but also on architects, process governance, and regulatory governance profiles – basically, the ones that directly and indirectly will have a stake in the DevOps 360° operating model. Are you going for a certain number of generalists and a certain number of specialists?

When defining the DevOps profiles and professions, there are some important questions that you need to answer collectively. Do you want your people to be able to *get the big DevOps* picture, while also being able to *deep-dive* into certain areas? Is full stack engineering the way to go? Or might that create *DevOps Swiss army knives* with a lack of deep expertise and people knowing *everything and nothing at the same time*? And if you decide to balance the breadth and depth of DevOps, how broad and how deep should you go?

I have come across these dilemmas in several DevOps evolution contexts in my career. And in all cases, there was a certain approach that was ideal and could fit every context (of course, upon tactical incubation). That approach is what is called in the industry the creation of *Π*-shaped profiles and professions. But what is a *Π*-shaped profile or profession? *Π* is a letter in the Greek alphabet (too much Greek in this book!). It is the equivalent of the letter *P* in the English alphabet. What is of interest in our DevOps case with regard to the Greek letter *Π* is not to do with linguistics but its shape. Take a close look at it. You will notice that it consists of a horizontal line with two vertical lines beneath. In our DevOps profiles context, the horizontal line symbolizes the breadth of DevOps knowledge, and the two vertical lines are the depth of the two domains of DevOps expertise. In simple words, a DevOps *Π*-shaped profile or profession characterizes a DevOps professional or practitioner that has broad DevOps knowledge and subject matter expertise in two DevOps domains. The following figure provides a representation:

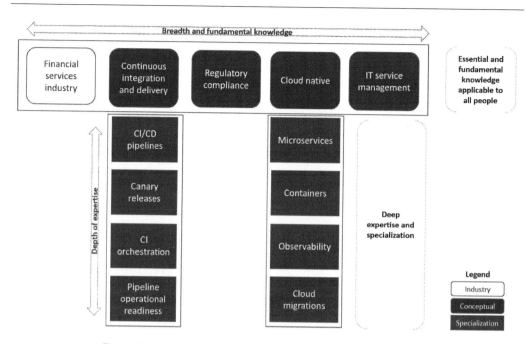

Figure 12.1 – Examples of Π-shaped profiles for a DevOps engineer

But what are the benefits we have seen in organizations of creating *Π*-shaped profiles?

- We ensure that people have broad DevOps awareness and therefore can connect the dots of the big picture, consequently understanding how they are to contribute to it. To some extent, they are actually able to grasp the complete DevOps 360° operating model.

- We build expertise in people. Not only do we move away from generalists, but we also enable people with primary (leading) and secondary (shadowing) expertise. This primary and secondary expertise enables us to ensure contingency and mobility.

- We moved away from the fallacy of *full stack engineering*. *DevOps Swiss army knives* do not work. You need specialization – in other words, *to demonstrate that you know your DevOps stuff in depth*, as in, to demonstrate DevOps expertise.

- We provide career paths to people and also a broad variety of *DevOps tastes* in their daily work, eliminating *DevOps single-domain fatigue*.

- It allows us to slice the responsibilities across the DevOps 360° technological ecosystem more dynamically, building cross-team complementary skills.

- We employ *four-eyes* principal peer reviews and senior/junior peering in truly cross-functional teams.

Is FSI knowledge a requirement of a DevOps Π profile in the industry?

It used to be high up in job descriptions, but in recent years, it has simply become a nice thing to have. The *talent war* in the market does not allow such luxurious requirements. It's preferable that you know Azure DevOps and resource management templates rather than cross-border payment flows. Nevertheless, FSI knowledge is a strong asset when pursuing opportunities in organizations.

Comparing Π-shaped profiles to other profiles

I will keep this short while adding a couple of extra arguments on why Π-shaped is the most sustainable way to go. Typically, DevOps professionals and practitioners fall into one of the following categories. In each of them, I have cited some disadvantages that I have observed in my career:

Shape	I-shaped	T-shaped	Π-shaped
Characteristic	Only specialization	Broad knowledge and a single specialization	Broad knowledge and several specializations
Drawback	Lacks broad knowledge and therefore struggles to get the big DevOps picture	Only one area of specialization and therefore limited mobility and fatigue	Too many areas of specialization, turning into a Swiss army knife

Table 12.1 – The disadvantages of different shapes for DevOps practitioners and professionals

Advice

Please get people with deep and broad DevOps expertise to design the Π-shaped profiles, not any random PMO or HR person.

The importance of predicting role evolution

You must be forward-looking with your hiring, incubation, and mobility tactics. The world is moving fast with new technologies emerging and evolving in the blink of an eye. The situation does generate business opportunities, but also requires adaptability for these opportunities to be pursuable. Certain DevOps roles and professions might advance, stagnate, or be eliminated in the years to come. Do you need to hire skills that you might not need in 2 years? Being able to predict (or follow) the future developments of DevOps professions is decisive. Using your current DevOps roles and professions as a baseline, you need to ensure that your current hiring and incubation actions will make your organization fit for future purposes. Perfect data you will not have, but you will definitely have a good number of intelligent technologies that can predict how your DevOps-related professions may evolve in the future. The following figure provides a representative example:

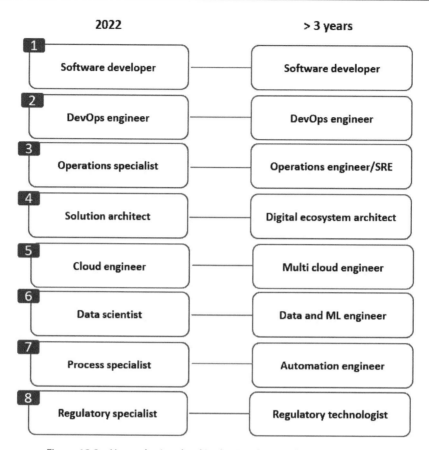

Figure 12.2 – How roles involved in the DevOps evolution can develop

Strategic considerations in DevOps hiring

In this section, we will outline some tips and recommendations derived from real use cases to consider as part of your hiring strategy or tactics.

Starting by defining your hiring strategy

I am certain that you do not have either the quantity or quality of people that you need to enable and adopt your new DevOps 360° operating model. Even if you think you do, as we mentioned in an earlier chapter of this book, it will be to the advantage of your DevOps 360° evolution to bring in some new blood that can disrupt your current DevOps status quo. Usually, organizations define certain hiring strategies to back up their DevOps endeavors. These hiring strategies can range from purely simple to rather complex. The parameters of the following table are the ones that I consider the most important as part of defining your DevOps hiring strategy:

Parameter	Considerations
Location	**Home countries**: Focus on highly experienced, specialized, former chief or senior people, where proximity to business teams is very important. **Nearshoring**: Focus on less experienced, specialized, and people where proximity to business teams is not important. **Offshoring**: Focus on the scale in terms of numbers without the need for high specialization and experience. **Note**: Avoid nearshoring lockup. Circumstances in developing or newly developed countries change rapidly and might force you to exit those locations.
Skill priorities (example)	**Necessity**: Java and .NET developers and DevOps engineers. **Tactical**: Cloud engineers and automation engineers. **On-demand**: Site reliability engineers. **Stop hiring**: Process governance analysts.
Internal domain priorities	You are not only competing in the market with other companies, but also competing internally. You may agree on who has priority internally, even though it might be perceived as discrimination. It is irrational, for instance, to hire DevOps engineers in non-critical domains, when you might have a scarcity of DevOps engineers on the tactical adoption teams.
Areas excluded from a hiring freeze	Hiring freezes are typical in organizations, especially in periods of cost cuts. Some of your areas, such as the DevOps CoE and the tactical adoption domains, need to have a hiring freeze "bypass card."
Mass consulting conversion process	This is when you have hired large numbers of consultants from a certain consulting firm, and eventually, you wish to convert them to full-time employees. You need to agree on which teams get conversion priority.
Dynamic salaries, rates, and trade-offs	Apart from defining what salaries and rates you are willing to pay in certain locations, you will also need to employ location trade-off tactics. Scenarios such as: "a DevOps engineer in location A gives us two DevOps engineers in location B. However, location B has more market competition than location A." You will phase through this repeatedly.

Table 12.2 – An overview of a sample hiring tactic

Did you know?

European incumbent banks prefer countries such as Poland, Lithuania, Bulgaria, Romania, and the Czech Republic to establish nearshoring DevOps capabilities teams. I have worked with Polish and Lithuanian teams and the engineers there are great. Trust me.

Introducing 360° interviews

360° in the *DevOps hiring* context indicates interviews being conducted by a sufficient cycle of relevant stakeholders, assessing both the broad and conceptual as well as technical and specialized DevOps knowledge of the candidates. This practice will give both you and the candidate a more spherical view and I highly recommend it. Where applicable, if you are hiring a business application-focused team, get them to also talk to the team's product owner so that they also get a good feeling and insight into the business domain they will be working with. Note that the 360° rounds do not all have to be formal interviews. Some can be *coffee talks*. In *coffee talks*, you are not really assessing the candidate, but you get a better feeling of who the person is, and the person gets a better feeling of who you are.

> **Two tips**
>
> Test their technical skills as the first thing in the interview process by conducting real-time, rather than *home-based*, assessments.
>
> Wherever possible, be flexible about the specific technologies you require. A senior DevOps professional who does not have Azure experience but does have GCP experience, with a good mentality, the desire to learn, and some support, can learn (beyond) the Azure fundamentals in 3 months. Seniority is usually accompanied by agnosticism. Take advantage of that while you look for the perfect job description match, as in "the unicorn employee."

In one of the banks I used to work at, in the engineering organization, we had CI/CD, private cloud, and public cloud teams. We got candidates to meet people from all three teams. That was, on the one hand, for us to get a spherical view of the candidate's technical awareness, but also for the candidate to be exposed to our broader DevOps technological ecosystem.

> **A practical perspective of 360°**
>
> A very practical perspective of 360° interviews is in cases where a candidate is proven through the interviews not to fit the requirements of the hiring team but is more suitable for the requirements of a *sister team*. Having both teams as part of the interview enables you to efficiently swap the person for a different position if they are interested. I've done that many times.

On using third parties to scale fast

You will face difficulties in scaling fast in your DevOps hiring. This will naturally make you consider going to consulting firms asking for support. In my experience, going to a large consulting firm and asking about 50 SREs in one go will not work. Either they will not have them at all, they will have a limited number, or they will even send you random CVs to review just to keep you warm, wasting your time. The most sustainable way to use consulting firms is to go to small but very DevOps-specialized consulting firms. They will probably not be able to provide you with a scale of 50 SREs, but they will be able to provide you with 4 to 5 very seasoned SREs. With those, you will be able to make a much bigger difference in your evolution. Another alternative, and a quite sustainable way to do it, is to use *incubation camps*. These are basically recruitment companies that train or incubate young university students and prepare them for the industry. You can go to them with your job descriptions and requirements, and they will do the incubation job for you. Afterward, they will share the profiles and you decide whether you wish to move on. You can also use these incubation camps to incubate your own people. Either way, incubation camps can be a golden opportunity for navigating through extremely challenging market conditions effectively.

> **Last tip**
>
> Have your procurement and talent acquisition people establish a fast-track process for onboarding consulting firms that are not on your *pre-approved* list. There are some small DevOps boutiques out there with tremendously skilled people that most probably are not part of your procurement's *approved list of vendors*. Put some pressure on them (procurement and talent acquisition) if they tell you, *"But we need to go through a lengthy process to get them approved. Is it really necessary to use them?"*. Losing out on good people for bureaucratic reasons is unwise.

DevOps incubation recommendations

In this section, I will open with a few political economy theories. Political economy is a sub-domain of international relations and can be easily related to DevOps.

> **Technological progress and human capital**
>
> Technology and human capital have a strictly interlinked relationship. The means through which the former is deployed in an organization can create a significant competitive advantage and is heavily dependent on the availability of the latter. For instance, let us suppose that two different organizations are building a GCP public cloud platform team. It is expected that the organization that is more advanced in terms of GCP knowledge and skills is likely to build a higher-quality GCP platform more quickly than the one that is less knowledgeable and skilled. Through the GCP example, we can safely and with certainty conclude that technology is directly proportional to the DevOps capability growth pace of an organization. Therefore, the organization's people must have experience and expertise with certain technologies to accelerate this DevOps growth. Ideally, that expertise and knowledge of technologies must not only come with education or practical experience but with a combination of the two. In conclusion, incubation will be proven a core accelerator in your DevOps evolution. The accumulation of sufficient technologically literate human capital will enable the full exploitation of your technological means and capabilities.

In our context, with the term *incubation*, we refer to the process of supporting your people to grow in the domain of DevOps throughout the DevOps 360° evolution. Mainly, incubation will have two aspects for your DevOps 360° evolution. The first one is that you need to ensure that your organization has the necessary skills to enable and adopt the new DevOps 360° operating model. The second is that the *DevOps job market* is getting extremely competitive. With the demand for DevOps professionals exceeding the supply, not only do organizations have difficulty attracting people but they also need to pay more. As you know from the fundamental principle of macroeconomics, low supply and high demand drives prices (as in, salaries) very high. Therefore, incubation in several cases becomes the only sustainable way to acquire the skills required by your DevOps 360° operating model. *If you cannot buy it, you need to build it yourself.* Let us now look into some tips and recommendations on incubation that I have collected through my experience with it.

Focusing equally on leaders and people on the ground

Let's start with a clarification. The phrase *people on the ground* is not entirely figurative. I use it to indicate *ground* as the solid foundation of your organization.

Throughout my DevOps career, I have made two classifications when it comes to people incubation: **direct** and **indirect**. The direct one is that organizations mostly focus on the *people on the ground*, not their leaders. The indirect one is that leaders in middle management positions in most cases become one of the most severe execution bottlenecks – on the one hand because they are not *DevOps literate*, so basically, they don't *get it*, and on the other hand, because their role is quite challenging in nature. It's challenging in the sense that they are the ones in between executive leadership and the people on the ground. Having said all this, I urge you to prioritize the DevOps incubation of your people in leadership positions. Just buying books for them (the most typical way I have seen) to read before going to bed or during vacation is not enough.

> ### Look for the "dark knights"
> I am borrowing this expression from an old peer of mine. He used to call the *DevOps incompetent* leaders *dark knights*. That is because, in an attempt to hide their DevOps ignorance or general ignorance, they were intentionally slowing down adoption to the disadvantage of the rest of us and the broader organization.

The most effective incubation for leaders in my opinion is *shadowing* by DevOps experts. Those people can act as advisors and indirectly incubate leaders through that advice.

Being targeted and driven by real work

All of us in managerial positions have had that employee who insisted on having DevOps training (*baking cookies with DevOps practices, for instance*) that was obviously irrelevant to what your team and the broader organization were focusing on. You will also have heard the story of a sister team attending SAFe training while your organization is already in the process of adopting the Spotify model. Or you'll have seen LinkedIn posts of your organization's DevOps engineers who are new to the public cloud getting Azure fundamentals certifications while your organization's public cloud strategic direction is AWS. Lastly, we've all had that peer who approved any random single training to keep their people happy and make the annual performance review look good. All these examples in my opinion are *incubation irrationalities*. Borrowing a phrase from an ex-line manager of mine, "*What is the value of training if you cannot use what you learned?*". When addressing this *incubation irrationality*, you should focus on three areas:

- Start saying *no* to random training certification requests.

- Base the people's incubation plan on the core of your DevOps 360° SDLC and technological ecosystem (there are more than enough already there).

- Create the ground for *real incubation* – through real work. Do not just send people to AWS training if you have started your AWS journey. *Learning by doing and getting educated while doing* is what you should strive for. If you do not provide this incubation through *real work* opportunities, employees will eventually find them in the building next door. And you will have paid for the training as well.

> **Personal confession**
>
> I myself have come into conflict with people in my teams several times when I did not approve training and certificates that I did not consider valuable to what we were doing in the organization. Training takes money and time away from daily work and therefore, you have to be conscious of where this time and money are invested. Balance what is best for the individual and the organization.

Utilizing your organization's graduates

Every single organization out there has at least an annual intake of fresh, smart graduates, thirsty for knowledge and full of ambition. I know because I was one of them back in the day and have incubated several in my teams over the years. While the era of graduates photocopying is in the past, there are still occasions when graduates are not given enough space and proper attention. Those guys can learn faster than you think and their young revolutionary minds can disrupt your DevOps status quo. Instead of giving them small tasks, pair them up with seniors and throw them in the *DevOps deep end* as early as possible. It's better to invest your money and time there than in questionable training and external consultants. Ensure that you also rotate them across business areas and technologies so they gain a broader DevOps perspective.

Incubating at relevance – eliminating the incubation red tape

Do you remember the *incident management* training mandatory KPT from the previous chapter? For some reason, organizations tend to train or incubate people using red tape and not relevance (you thought we would talk about relevance in this chapter, right?). I have repeatedly seen cross-organization horizontal training applied to everyone unnecessarily. Yes, I understand that some mandatory training is a regulatory requirement, as is the "*how to handle a client at a local branch*" training that I have done about five times in my career, even though I have never worked at a branch. Without overexplaining, *incubation or training* red tape is just a *box-ticking* exercise. People who do not see the relevance of an incubation initiative have already checked out before entering the incubation room. *DevOps productivity* is not just the fast provisioning of infrastructure. It also pertains to the time not wasted on irrelevant training. Your DevOps incubation plan should therefore be shaped by relevance.

To close, I wish to mention another ineffective incubation strategy I have seen failing repeatedly in incumbent contexts – the *notorious* in-house incubation schools. See, we live in 2022, so if a DevOps engineer wishes to learn Python, they will do it through online resources either during work or over the weekend. Bundling 70 engineers into a room to teach them Python with their colleagues as the teachers makes for a good post for LinkedIn that says "*Hey! Today, 70 of our company's engineers gathered to learn Python.*" But it's also lost *DevOps productivity*.

Stop the DevOps baptism – it's just wrong!

Let me just be bold here and include myself in the example so that I am not perceived as finger-pointing. The fact that someone attended GCP training and changed their job title from infrastructure engineer to cloud engineer does not make that person a GCP cloud engineer. Maybe they're a GCP cloud engineer *in the very early making*. I hold an MBA degree and learned tons while pursuing it. The degree itself, though, does not make me competent enough to become the CEO of an incumbent bank. Please take precautions around the coincidental (through re-organization) or the intentional (due to personal motives) baptism of people. It simply creates the wrong impression of their actual personal skills, which consequently creates the wrong impression of your border DevOps capabilities and capacity.

The inability to incubate will severely jeopardize evolution

A little bit of a personal story to cover this one – long story short, in one of the banks I used to work at, we designed the new DevOps SDLC while, of course, keeping the organization updated on our progress. Once our group was close to finalizing the *ready-to-be-discussed with management* version, we decided to open up a little bit to teams that were not involved in an attempt to collect feedback. As we had various DevOps maturity levels across the organization, we wanted to cover a maturity context as broadly as possible. I was considered to be one of the most senior DevOps people in our group and to possess good interpersonal skills, so we decided that I was to meet the more junior DevOps people. Lower maturity would have required me to spend more time explaining things, be patient, provide simple examples, and so on. Therefore, I went, I met that low DevOps maturity team, I presented the new SDLC, and the feedback was indeed very positive; the team liked it very much. "*Very ambitious, but it looks good,*" they said. Then I asked, "*Do you think that there is anything on the practical side of things that would make it difficult for you to adopt the new SDLC?*" Their chief architect said, "*You know we have a lower DevOps maturity; many of our applications do not even use CI/CD pipelines. We will need training and incubation for certain concepts and technologies.*" I told him to send to me a list of areas that they wanted incubation for based on the new DevOps SDLC. I got an email after 2 days with literally 21 (I honestly remember the number by heart) DevOps concepts and technologies that they required incubation for. That was too much and we were (for undisclosed reasons) not able to cover all of that using the central incubation mechanism. They basically had to learn DevOps from square one and, to some extent, had to do that themselves. Without going into much more detail, I volunteered to act as *DevOps advisor* to them over the course of the evolution and therefore had the chance to observe their progress firsthand. Things moved extremely slowly in that area and, eventually, the gap between them and the more advanced teams of the organization narrowed.

Practical DevOps mobility cases and precautions

The mobility of people is an important mechanism that I consider part of incubation and part of the tactical adoption approach. In simple terms, the concept of mobility enables people from different parts of the organization to change teams and positions either virtually (see the DevOps CoE engagements) or permanently (by full moves to new teams). Mobility as with our DevOps evolution adoption is divided into two main approaches – organic, when people self-seek new opportunities within the organization, and tactical, when people are intentionally moved from one part of the organization to another.

DevOps mobility is a concept that I have experienced in several forms, and while it can involve practical difficulties to implement, it has paid off in the following applicable cases:

- **As a retention mechanism**: People who wish to have a job change can find this change within your organization and don't have to look elsewhere.

- **As an incubation mechanism**: Promotes the organic growth of DevOps practices and free incubation with knowledge and experience *spillover*.

- **As an enabler and a contextual awareness mechanism**: Central utility areas such as the DevOps 360° technological ecosystem and the DevOps CoE, through tactical adoptions, engagement, and having their people virtually embedded in other areas, gain DevOps contextual and organizational awareness, and can therefore better serve the organization.

- **As a career growth mechanism**: Supports people advancing their careers within the same organization by moving to different areas – particularly applicable in large organizations.

Minding the mobility gap

The are some particular concerns and precautions to take concerning mobility:

- Moving people around in times of understaffing and cost-cutting can be impossible.

- Positions that require specific business knowledge are more difficult to fulfill through mobility.

- The higher the level of standardization, the greater the chance that mobility will succeed.

- Mobility within the same ecosystem, value stream, or tribe is easier to achieve.

- There is a form of mobility that is labeled **fixed rotation** where people move around areas and spend a certain amount of time in each area. Technological utilities are a great candidate domain for this, though some people struggle with changing context frequently.

- Emotional attachments and historical reasoning can prevent tactical mobility.

- It can be used by some teams as a mechanism for *getting rid of people*.

In conclusion, I have heard several stories from organizations that have not managed to get mobility to work effectively. My experience is different and I advise you to attempt something similar.

Summary

In this chapter, we reached the biggest milestone of the book. We covered the last (but definitely not the least important) part of the DevOps 360° operating model's third pillar. The chapter started by outlining the obvious people value proposition for the DevOps 360° evolution. We continued by making a case for why you should aim to enable DevOps *Π*-shaped professionals, along with why you should be able to predict how DevOps-related professions are to evolve in the future and start to plan accordingly. Afterward, we touched on some key elements of consideration for your hiring strategy. We also provided some tips on the value of 360° interviews and using third-party providers. We then moved on to discussing several dimensions of incubation. Starting with the urge to focus on leaders as much as *people on the ground*, we moved on to the importance of being targeted with how your people are being incubated, focusing on relevance but also creating real daily work opportunities. Finishing up the incubation part, we provided a real-life story about how the inability to incubate effectively can jeopardize the DevOps evolution. We closed the chapter by referring to the value that the mobility of people can bring to your evolution, while also highlighting several precautions to consider.

You should perceive the next chapter as a *bonus or special focus chapter*. In it, we will discuss my *favorite DevOps topic*, which is **site reliability engineering** (**SRE**).

13

Site Reliability Engineering in the FSI

This chapter introduces us to the world of **site reliability engineering** (**SRE**) and is divided into three main parts: academic/conceptual, practical, and real-world use cases. As with every chapter, we will start by outlining its value proposition in the DevOps 360° evolution, after we first define SRE based on Google's paradigm and publications, also outlining the SRE definition view of our book. We will then move forward by discussing the *DevOps versus SRE* dilemma that dominates the industry, looking into the similarities and differences between the two concepts. Afterward, we will detail the SRE value proposition by looking into its respective *tenets*, which is a fundamental aspect of adopting SRE. Continuing, we will introduce an array of proven practices and mechanisms that support SRE adoption *at relevance*. They will focus on engagement and adoption models, people, as well as reconciliation with concepts such as the **IT Infrastructure Library** (**ITIL**). The last part of the chapter will discuss some real-world examples of incumbents that have adopted the concept of SRE. We will discuss the respective operating models, motivating factors, as well as what is positive and what is not so positive.

In this chapter, we're going to cover the following main topics:

- The value proposition of SRE for the DevOps 360° evolution
- The DevOps versus SRE dilemma
- The fundamental SRE tenets
- Practical and proven practices for adopting SRE
- Different incumbent use cases for adopting various SRE operating models

What is the value proposition of SRE for the DevOps 360° evolution?

We will start this chapter with a small conceptual overview of what SRE is, before looking into its value proposition for the DevOps 360° evolution. SRE is a concept conceived by Google, sometime around 2003, when the first Google SRE team was formed. During the summer of 2016, the first official Google publication, under the title *Site Reliability Engineering: How Google Runs Production Systems*, officially introduced SRE into the world of DevOps. Since then, several financial services institutions (including ones that I have worked for/with) have started to embrace the concept – some of them by understanding its practical value and finding success with it, with others admiring its "coolness" and creating more LinkedIn posts and job titles than finding any real success.

How does Google define SRE?

According to posts on Google Blogs, SRE is a broad concept and open to various interpretations. Ben Treynor, VP of Engineering at Google and founder of SRE, defines the concept as *what happens when a software engineer is tasked with designing an operations team* or *what happens when you handle operations as a software problem*. Another, metaphorical definition that can be found in Google's publications is *SRE is what happens when you change the tires of a racing car while it is going at 100 miles per hour*. A third definition describes SRE as *prescriptive ways of measuring and achieving reliability through engineering and operations work*. I personally prefer to go through its acronym and explain the terms from *right to left*:

SRE – S: Site, R: Reliability, E: Engineering

The utilization of engineering means ensuring the reliable operations of a site.

To provide a little bit more clarity, *means* can be any technology, practice, process, people's skills, and so on that relates to engineering.

> **Short parenthesis – we will consider "S" to mean "service" from now on**
>
> The letter **S** in SRE stands for the word **site** in Google's context, and this makes sense. Think of google.com as being a site. In our book, the **S** in SRE will stand for the word **service**. That refers to a business application offering a service to the incumbent's clients or a DevOps platform offering a service to the incumbent's Agile DevOps teams.

From the preceding definitions, one can safely derive two main elements of SRE. Firstly, SRE is concerned with embedding software engineering practices in building and operating reliable services. Secondly, SRE lacks a universal definition. Do you remember which other concept in this book lacks a universal definition? You remember correctly – DevOps, of course!

> **Food for thought**
>
> I wonder why those great concepts lack a universal definition. Is it maybe on purpose, as pragmatic DevOps and SRE should be based on *what you want to make out of them*?

As you can rightly guess, and most probably have already observed within your organizations, the absence of SRE definition consistency reveals two aspects of it that are similar to DevOps. Firstly, it reveals the broadness and versatility of SRE as a concept. Secondly, it reveals how it is a source of misinterpretation in the FSI through misconceptions. The latter is also considered one of the main challenges in how organizations approach its adoption.

To ensure that we speak the same *SRE language* in this book, we will go with the way I find suitable to explain SRE. Therefore, in the coming sections, when I refer to SRE, you will know that I am referring to *the utilization of engineering means to ensure the reliable operations of a service*, which are practices we will see later in the chapter.

> **My favorite definition of SRE**
>
> *SRE is the purest distillation of DevOps!* This is a spot-on definition in my opinion, and I think most of you that have implemented SRE successfully and pragmatically would agree. Nonetheless, it is not a very practical one to use in a corporate context.

What is the concrete and pragmatic value proposition of SRE to the DevOps 360° evolution?

We will take an unconventional approach in this chapter compared to the previous ones in defining the value proposition. Indeed, we will be allocating almost half of this chapter's content to circulating the SRE value proposition for the DevOps 360° evolution, going through several elements of SRE. And we will start that circulation by providing our view on a dominant dilemma, not only in the financial services industry but broadly across industries.

What is the notorious "DevOps versus SRE" dilemma?

In order to agree, firstly, that SRE has a value proposition to the DevOps 360° evolution, we need to provide clarity on the relationship between the two concepts. The *DevOps versus SRE* dilemma in the industry is about whether organizations should adopt DevOps or SRE. It is an *either/or* in simple words, under the belief that the two concepts are conflictual. Going directly to the point, as I do not wish to spend time providing examples of nonsense dilemmas, SRE and DevOps are not conflictual concepts, as many in the financial services industry perceive them, or want them (in order to promote personal agendas) to be. In my book (literally and figuratively), SRE and DevOps are two complementary concepts. In essence and reality, in the way I have used and reconciled both, SRE is an effective way to scale and accelerate a DevOps evolution. I personally see SRE as part of DevOps and not as a concept to be adopted in parallel. There is the Google statement *class SRE implements*

DevOps. That statement, in my opinion, is the most targeted and clear way to state the relationship between the two. In other words, SRE can be interpreted, perceived, and applied as an extension of DevOps principles and practices through greater emphasis on the reliability aspects of a service. And now you will tell me, "But mate, that statement is not really practical. Especially when addressing people who have limited exposure to both DevOps and SRE. There must be a more tangible/practical way to explain the relationship."

I created the following table years ago in my attempt to explain to people what can be perceived to be the commonalities and specific focus areas between DevOps and SRE. My ambition was to capture the common principles and objectives of the two while emphasizing the reliability and operations focus of the latter. It worked well!

DevOps	SRE
Commonalities	
Embracing change and risk	
Breaking the organizational silos	
Automation	
Technology utilization	
Visibility and visualization	
Release velocity and engineering	
Gradual service changes	
Fail fast and learn	
Shift operations and quality left in the SDLC	
Specific Focus	
Production operations are part of it	Production operations are at the center of it
The focus is on releasing "fast"	The focus is on releasing "reliably"
Focus on functional requirements	Focus on non-functional requirements

Table 13.1 – DevOps and SRE mainstream commonalities and specific focus

Before you shoot me

I deeply acknowledge that the special focus areas in certain cases are not that distinct if the concepts are reconciled correctly. Although, in an average incumbent's context, as we saw earlier in the book, where DevOps is equalized with speed and CI/CD pipelines while focusing on developers and omitting operations, the preceding special focus distinction is spot on to get *SRE discussions* going.

There is an apparent, undoubted, and significant conceptual overlap, as well as an overlap of objectives, between the two concepts, as you can see. The main difference, if we go by the *traditional and mainstream distinction*, is that DevOps focuses more on speed and software development, while SRE focuses on reliability and operations. We do not, however, espouse that *traditional and mainstream distinction* in this book. Nevertheless, it is unfortunately deeply rooted in the financial services industry's perspective of SRE, and you might have to use it when explaining the relationship of DevOps and SRE to people. In our book, both DevOps and SRE complement each other in enabling the *DevOps equilibrium*. How do they do it in reality? There is no one solution and it depends on the reconciliation model you follow.

Closing this section, I am convinced through practical experience and not only academic theory that there is no *either-or dilemma* in the DevOps to SRE relationship. It is clearly a relationship of *co-existence and mutual inclusiveness* that very much depends on your business case and operating model in how it will be shaped.

> **Do you remember the DevOps lexicon?**
> SRE will bring new concepts and terminology to your evolution. You will need to enrich your DevOps lexicon with those.

Expressing the practical value proposition as "tenets"

In practically explaining the SRE value proposition to DevOps, I would like to introduce the term *SRE tenets*. Google defines *SRE tenets* as the basic set of responsibilities that SRE teams adhere to when tasked with supporting a service. At Google, adherence to SRE tenets is mandatory for every single SRE team. You can also perceive the collection of tenets as the SRE part of the DevOps WoW *white paper* that we referred to in *Chapter 5, Business Enterprise Agility and DevOps Ways of Working Reconciliation*. The basic SRE tenets that Google defines are the following, always concerning the reliability improvements of a service:

- Availability
- Performance
- Effectiveness
- Emergency response
- Monitoring

The preceding tenets are a core foundation of what an SRE team should be tasked with: monitoring the health of a service, improving its availability, and so on. Nevertheless, SRE as a concept goes much deeper than those five tenets. In addition, in a corporate environment of an incumbent, it is an impossible mission to promote a new concept such as SRE in such a simplistic way. You will hear arguments such as *we already monitor our service, we have an emergency response in place, and we call it "on call," and more*. Here comes the point. An inability to make clear to people what's in it for them and their service with SRE will make it impossible to get *buy-in*. Considering this parameter, but also four other factors, I deliberately adjusted the tenets the first time I implemented SRE at scale, mixing them with SRE practices. Otherwise, there would have been zero chance of getting buy-in. It actually worked and then that *adjustment* became my *repeated pattern*. Before we move on to the details of the *adjusted tenets*, let us look at the totality of factors that made me take that approach.

The four factors on top of *what's in it for me* are the following:

- SRE is *what you make of it*. Therefore, you shape the tenets to fit your context and ambition.

- You will have to reconcile SRE with ITIL, which you most probably started adopting many years before SRE. Therefore, you have to make SRE relevant to ITIL.

- You will have to reconcile SRE with DevOps, which again, you most probably started implementing earlier. Therefore, you have to make SRE relevant to DevOps.

- Do you remember the policy that is called segregation/separation of duties that we discussed in *Chapter 8, 360° Regulatory Compliance as Code*? You will have to make sure that it is not violated, to make the SRE duties clear.

At the end of the day, in the first pages of Google's first SRE book, *Site Reliability Engineering: How Google Runs Production Systems*, the authors state that their intention for the book is not to tell people *how to do it*, but to *inspire them in how to do it* (kind of the motto of this book also). Therefore, a huge *thank you* (and I honestly mean it) to Google for the inspiration.

The SRE balance – 50%-50%

Before we move on to the tenets, I wish to open an important parenthesis and introduce you to an SRE concept that underpins the tenets – the concept of *SRE balance*. SRE is a software engineering-oriented concept with a strong operational focus. This equilibrium between software engineering and operations work is materialized through the concept of *50%-50%*. *50%-50%* aims to ensure that site reliability engineers spend 50% of their time on improving a service's reliability through engineering work, with the other 50% invested in a service's operational activity. When it is observed that more than 50% of the time has been spent of service operations, the elimination of the excess amount must be achieved through engineering improvements, with the time being prioritized in the team's backlog. Ideally, and when your SRE team as well as the service they support is mature enough, you should strive to move the pendulum toward engineering – 20% of time spent on operations and 80% of time spent on engineering must be your target.

What are the fundamental "tenets"?

As I mentioned earlier in the chapter, *SRE is what you make of it*. Defining the *SRE tenets* is, in my experience, the first step in defining what you want to get out of SRE in your organization. The logic is simple, right? Defining what the SRE teams will be responsible for also defines what you want to achieve with SRE and, consequently, what the *SRE value proposition* is for your DevOps 360° operating model and evolution. In this section, we will look into what I propose the *bare minimum SRE tenets* can be, as I have seen them being implemented and paying off in various SRE adoptions across incumbents.

> **Important note: SRE is a production-focused function, keeping the "lights on"!**
>
> In the following tenets, I will deliberately avoid making special mention of the responsibility of SRE in operating the production environment of a business service or platform. SRE is an operations-oriented function, as we mentioned, and therefore operating production environments are taken for granted as a responsibility. Therefore, in the following tenets, there is no need to make explicit reference to responsibilities such as emergency response, incident management, postmortems, deployments, and continuity management.

SRE tenet 1 – maintain the balance of the DevOps equilibrium

To refresh your memory, the DevOps equilibrium as we have defined it in this book balances *time to market – reliability – compliance* across the SDLC and toward the final value added through software delivery for end clients. Let me make a clarification before I get misunderstood. It is not only a site reliability engineer's job to maintain that equilibrium. It is the responsibility of the entire cross-functional agile DevOps team and its product owner. However, there must be someone accountable and someone responsible for the equilibrium's maintenance. I'm sure you know from personal experience that where everyone is accountable and responsible, no one really is. To my mind, the accountability for maintaining the DevOps equilibrium should be with the product owner of the agile DevOps team, while the responsibility should be with the ones that *gatekeep* that production environment. That will be the SRE team (where one exists). As we will see later in the chapter, you must not – and technically you will not – adopt SRE across your portfolio.

There are several mechanisms that you can deploy in maintaining this equilibrium. The master mechanism, however, is the **production readiness review** (**PRR**) that we first introduced in *Chapter 9, The DevOps Portfolio Classification and Governance*, of the book. In pragmatic and sustainable SRE adoption, it is the SRE team that is responsible for the PRR mechanism. Obviously, the SRE team does not have ownership of all the items included in the PRR but is responsible for conducting it. That responsibility, as you might expect, comes with *relative* authority. As in, an SRE team, upon evidence that a product or a service is not *production-ready* (breaches parts of the PRR), upon agreement with the product owner, can stop the release or launch.

> **But that never happens in reality, Spyridon**
>
> It depends. If you have a healthy relationship with the development teams and you have gained the *blind trust* of your business partners through results, you can exercise your right to block product launches and releases.

Another fundamental SRE mechanism that is used to balance the time to market and reliability equilibrium and is normally included in the PRR is what in Google terms is called the *error budget*. The *error budget's* core objective is to address a *structural DevOps conflict* between operations, concerned with service stability and development as well as time to market. The core objective is to balance the concepts of release velocity and **service-level objective** (**SLO**). To explain that balance, I like the *car metaphor* SRE definition that we mentioned earlier. Suppose that service A is a car. The SLO of the car is that its speed should be constant at 100 miles/hour. The release velocity of the car represents the objective of changing the tires of the car, on demand, without impacting its speed. If in the attempt to change the tires the speed is reduced to 80 miles/hour, then its SLO is breached. If, on the other hand, the risk of changing tires (release velocity) is not considered as breaching its SLO, then its release velocity is jeopardized. Therefore, one of the core objectives of SRE is to maximize both the SLO and the release velocity, while maintaining the equilibrium between them.

The *error budget* in its simplest format is calculated as 100% availability minus the target SLO of a service. So, for example, if the defined SLO of a service is 99% availability, the error budget is 1%.

The error budget technically represents the amount of time that a service can fail, without contractual implications, and is complemented by corresponding policies that serve as *protocols* for balancing the equilibrium.

Typically, an error budget has a tolerance zone, and this is because it might be breached only slightly, or a breach might be caused by factors external to the specific business application. So, in our example, if we exceed 1% only by 0.5% (the tolerance percentage), there will be no real contractual consequences in an incumbent's context. But if we exceed the 0.5% tolerance zone, reliability enhancements will need to be prioritized compared to new features, till the error budget gets back within the target numbers.

SRE tenet 2 – service observability

The second very important SRE tenet is the one of service observability. In this context with service observability, we define a set of practices that support the collection, processing, and visualization of production data that represents the health status of a business application, a service, or a platform. Under service observability, we include both service monitoring and also logging.

> **Did you notice?**
> We called this tenet *service observability* and not purely *observability*. You will understand why when we reach the release engineering tenet later in the chapter.

The usage of such a set of practices is for several, critical to the SRE function, purposes:

- Production environment visibility
- Proactive incident management
- Problem management
- Error budget tracking
- Capacity management
- Input for the PRR
- Regulatory evidence

SRE uses some specific measurements that are embedded in service observability frameworks. These are the following:

- **Service-level agreements (SLAs)**: These are *contractual agreements* made between product owners and SRE teams on the desired availability uptime of a service.

- **Service-level objectives (SLOs)**: The measure that the SRE team uses for fulfilling SLA targets.

- **Service-level indicators (SLIs)**: Specific and directly measurable indicators of a service's health, such as CPU usage on production machines, connection to stock exchange latency on price feeds, or Kafka topics' data completeness.

Other metrics that are often used in an SRE context are the following:

- **Mean time to detect (MTTD)**: Indicating the acceptable, according to the SLA, lead time till a production incident, for instance, is discovered

- **Mean time to react (MTTR)**: Indicating the acceptable, according to the SLA, lead time till a site reliability engineer or the system itself (autonomous operations) reacts to initiate its restoration

- **Mean time to recover (MTTR)**: Indicating the acceptable, according to the SLA, lead time till the service is recovered

Of course, as well as the preceding metrics, we also need to include the error budget mechanism that we discussed earlier, in the previous section.

> **Service observability alone is "epidermic" reliability**
>
> A common anti-pattern that I have seen in the context of incumbents is to perceive the implementation of automated and real-time monitoring by itself as a proactive reliability improvement mechanism. The fact that you caught an alert fast and managed to prevent an incident is a preventive reliability approach. Finding the actual root cause and fixing it using engineering practices is a proactive approach.

SRE tenet 3 – elimination of "toil"

Delivering and running software inevitably requires manual interventions across the SDLC. Those manual interventions, especially if they are repeatable and automatable, in SRE terms are called **toil**. The elimination of toil through engineering means across the SDLC is a core tenet of SRE. There are three sayings in Google that I find very applicable in defining the SRE's relationship with toil: *invent more and toil less*, *automate this year's jobs away*, and *automate ourselves out of a job*. Toil comes in various shapes and forms, and despite the fact that SRE is an operations-oriented function, toil elimination must be targeted across the SDLC. The following are some examples where, typically, toil is observed across the SDLC:

- A lack of event-driven CI orchestration

- A lack of auto-failover capabilities built into the business application or platform by design

- A lack of automated generation of PRR evidence

- A lack of automated raising and closure of incidents and change requests

- A lack of autoscaling

- A lack of automated SLIs

- A lack of test automation

- A lack of automated change request impact analysis

The benefits of automating toil are massive, from increasing DevOps productivity to faster restoration of services, and overall SDLC operational efficiencies to minimizing the cost of operating a production environment.

> **The QA framework SRE – an SRE shift-left paradigm**
>
> In one of the banks I worked at, we had a QA framework site reliability engineer only taking care of advancing our test automation framework as well as the solutions of developer disposal test environments and data.

Addressing toil tactically is vital to also maintaining the DevOps equilibrium and the SRE balance. The more manual interventions across the SDLC, the more likelihood there is of defects and incidents, which can lead to reliability jeopardization and release velocity slowdowns. That, consequently, can make site reliability engineers spend more than 50% of their time on operations-related tasks, which will violate the 50%-50% SRE balance. Even more so, the accumulation of toil, adds to the long-term technical debt of a business application or DevOps platform, which can result in constant production *firefighting*.

Your ambition in addressing toil must be to *shift left* as much as possible across the SDLC while going as close as possible toward a sufficient degree of autonomous production operations and level 0 (self-service) request fulfillment for your clients.

> **The fallacy of NoOps in SRE**
>
> NoOps is a *buzzword* (in my opinion) that has made an appearance in the industry in recent years and has been associated with DevOps and SRE. Pretty self-descriptive by its acronym, **NoOps** stands for **no operations**, indicating that the level of autonomy of services through automation, engineering, and intelligence has to reach 100% – a pure fallacy looking at the context of an incumbent bank, even in *state-of-the-art* cloud-native applications. It is a sufficient level of *autonomous operations* you should strive for, not *NoOps*.

Important considerations for toil

Automating everything or automating without a tactical plan does not make sense (in certain cases, it is not practically and technically possible, actually) from various perspectives:

- Scaled automation can cause a domino effect in cases of scaled incidents.

- Some tasks need to remain manual because either they are needed for the incubation of new people, the automation ROI is not worth it, or your business partners or regulator require you to conduct them manually.

- You need to align on the mathematical formula of measuring the toil impact and ROI.

- Fix toil by using proper shift-left engineering practices and not simple scripts that restart servers when they are down.

- When toil cases are discovered during incidents, firstly conduct the root cause analysis, and afterward, consider your toil elimination options.

- Do not directly link toil elimination to reducing the number of people in your organization.

> **Automate everything! (Please don't)**
>
> Automate everything is yet another famous buzzword in the corridors of incumbents. Do you remember the *1,000,000 hours of lead time saved* KPT from *Chapter 11, Benefit Measurement and Realization*? The same thinking is behind the ambition/fallacy of *automating everything*. Automate "tactically" and "smart" is the right ambition.

SRE tenet 4 – release engineering

With the term release engineering, we define the SRE tenet that is concerned with the design and implementation of efficiencies and improvements across the SDLC, releasing high-quality software in a fast and reliable manner. In my book (literally and figuratively), and based on my experience with SRE in the FSI, release engineering must cover the following aspects across the SDLC from ideation to first launch, living production, and eventually sun setting:

- *Built-in* by design reliability engineering practices for how a service is designed, built, deployed, and operated

- Entire *SDLC observability* in terms of lead times and velocities

- Engineering implementation of DevOps controls across the SDLC, fulfilling the DevOps equilibrium

- Deployment strategies (technical release, canary, blue/green, and so on)

- Business application and platform modernization

- Automation of PRRs

- Optimization toward *autonomous operations*

- Shift left and by design non-functional/quality aspects of the SDLC

- Technological interoperability

As you can observe, the release engineering tenet covers several aspects of the rest of the SRE tenets and, in my opinion, must be the backbone of your *SRE tenets*.

SRE tenet 5 – reliability engineering framework

The last of the SRE tenets (as we define them in this book) is the *reliability engineering framework*. One core aspect and guiding principle of adopting SRE that I have not yet mentioned is the one of being *prescriptive*. Indeed, there is another definition of SRE, which states *SRE is prescriptive engineered ways of ensuring the reliability of a service*. Prescriptive, in our context, simply implies that the practices site reliability engineers use in fulfilling the tenets must be shaped in the form of *prescriptive frameworks* and enforced across SRE teams. But what are the benefits of being prescriptive?

- Faster scaling by creating reusable and scalable solution recipes.

- The cost of adopting SRE practices is reduced.

- Standardization and simplification are achieved in the portfolio that SRE is engaged with.

- Technical debt can be reduced.

- The mobility of site reliability engineers across SRE teams becomes more effective.

- The structural conflict between SRE, DevOps, and ITIL is addressed in harmony.

- The incubation of junior SREs.

- Evidence for regulatory compliance purposes.

The mechanism that I prefer using in achieving this SRE guiding principle of being prescriptive is the *reliability engineering framework*. It is an inner source framework that is built and maintained by SRE teams and simply comprises a set of prescriptive ways of applying SRE practices across business applications and platforms. The following are some practices that I have seen defined in a reliability engineering framework:

Reliability engineering framework elements
Automated monitoring of error budgets
Backup and restoration procedures
Reliability assessment on system design
Chaos engineering recipes
Microservice observability framework
IT service management automation
Deployment plans and strategies
Technological solutions' interoperability
Automated failover and restoration procedures
Event-triggered evidence generation
Launch coordination engineering practices

Table 13.2 – Example of elements in a reliability engineering framework

One of the areas around the reliability engineering framework that SRE puts a focus on is the simplification and standardization of the technological means that enable the framework's practices. It is in the SRE philosophy that the greater the scale to achieve, the greater the need for technology standardization.

A comprehensive and complete reliability framework should be perceived as a complete SRE adoption guide for the teams that wish to embark on an SRE journey. I have personally found them, in my career, to be excellent tools to promote and accelerate SRE adoption. Although, I have to admit that they are demanding frameworks to design, implement, adopt, and maintain.

Wrapping the tenets up

The following figure provides a summary of the potential responsibilities of an SRE team based on our SRE tenet definitions. As stated in the figure, the more your SRE setup matures over time, the more the *SRE balance* should be positively influenced, with more time available for engineering innovation rather than operations tasks:

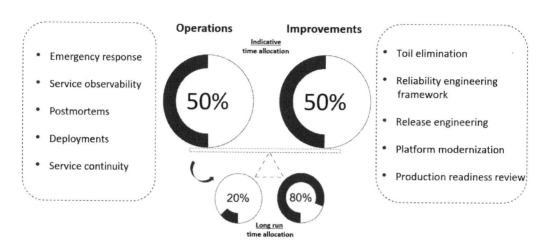

Figure 13.1 – Sample of the SRE tenets balance

I strongly recommend that you place absolute top priority when starting your SRE journey on clearly identifying the SRE tenets as one of your foundational steps. An inability to do so will generate several challenges on your way, from defining the white paper of responsibilities and demarcating them with other teams to securing funding, and planning the SRE incubation of people to achieving *SRE recognition and acceptance* within your organization.

> **Did you notice?**
> We did not mention any business inquiry support tasks as part of the tenets. That was intentional and you will discover why in the third part of the chapter.

Concluding this section, the SRE value proposition for the DevOps 360° evolution and operating model is that SRE adoption can provide the necessary governance and procedural, capability, and organizational means for embedding reliability engineering practices and ways of working across your DevOps 360° SDLC and *at relevance*. Whether SRE is relevant to every part of your business applications and platforms portfolio and what the relevance eligibility mechanism can be will be examined in the next section.

What are the foundational elements of SRE adoption "at relevance"?

In this section, we will investigate some of the fundamental aspects of how to design an SRE relevance mechanism that can support you in being tactical and pragmatic in your approach.

SRE eligibility

One of the most well-known *SRE mottos* of Google is *not all areas require SRE involvement*. That is an absolute truth, which makes us conclude that you should adopt SRE *at relevance in a multi-speed banking concept*, as with DevOps. But what are the criteria of relevance that you should consider? As you might guess, they do not differ much from the relevance criteria that define *DevOps speed*, which I cite here to refresh your memory:

Speed = criticality

(time to market + reliability + compliance + technology + business context)

Figure 13.2 – The DevOps speed formula

In the SRE context, the application of the speed formula is a little bit more focused/complex compared to broader DevOps adoption. This is due to two key determinants in our DevOps speed equation, as well as one enabler and one parameter, which are the most crucial in adopting SRE-specific practices, compared to other DevOps practices. The two key determinants are the ones of reliability and technology:

- Reliability in the sense that SRE is primarily concerned with service reliability aspects with this becoming the dominant equation determinant. The tougher the reliability requirements, the more need there is for site reliability engineers. Talking from experience, only the absolutely ultra-critical parts of an incumbent's portfolio really require SRE engagement. Those are either flagship applications, widely shared enterprise DevOps platforms, or core infrastructure components.

- Technology in the sense of how appealing and adaptable to SRE practices the technological stack of a business application or platform is. Appealing in terms of *attracting people* to work with these technologies and adaptable in terms of providing the ability to implement modern SRE practices (see a mainframe compared to a cloud-native setup).

And now, we come to our enabler, which is *the people*. There is an expression in the industry that goes *SRE does not scale*. That expression refers to the challenge of finding on the market the necessary SRE people and skills in terms of quality and quantity. In simple words, it is more likely not to find people that have *SRE know-how*, the mentality, and the desire to focus on reliability engineering practices compared, for instance, to people with experience in and desire to work with the software development of CI/CD pipelines. And you will also face challenges convincing internal people to move from software development roles to reliability engineering roles. Some find operations a downgrade of their CV, while others are scared of the idea that they will be tasked with the reliability engineering of your portfolio flagships. Last but not least, a key parameter to consider when deciding on your SRE eligibility is scale. In my experience with SRE, the greater the scale of a business application or platform, the greater the *SRE need* is and the greater the ROI. Scale, in our case, can be the variety and size of infrastructure assets, the number of developers, the number of dependencies on other business applications, the number of deployments per day, and so on. That is why I always advise taking the ecosystem and value stream approach in an SRE adoption.

In summary, reliability targets and technological aspects of a business application or platform, as well as the availability of people skills and the setup's scale, are the key determinants in my opinion in defining where SRE is *pragmatically eligible and where not*.

A true story about the importance of technology

I am certain any ex-site reliability engineers of mine that read this book will vividly remember this one. In one of the SRE teams we worked in, we had only cloud-native technologies in our portfolio of responsibility. Due to an internal reorganization, I inherited some legacy applications. We had to make sure they operated smoothly till they were decommissioned, at some point in the future. When we took them over, we realized that their technical debt was massive. Literally, none of the cloud-native site responsibility engineers wanted to work with those legacy applications. Several warned me that if we did not get rid of the legacy applications, they would leave the team. The team's climate was damaged, but we eventually worked around it with contractors. Lesson learned: if your technological stack is not *SRE-appealing* or is not in the modernization process to become *SRE-appealing*, it is not *SRE-eligible*.

Tactical versus organic SRE adoption

As we mentioned, not all areas are SRE-eligible and the demand for site reliability engineers is always higher than the supply. The latter is one of the reasons why many in the industry claim that *SRE does not scale*. The concept can scale perfectly in reality. It is the people that support its scaling that there will never be enough of in your organization. Let me explain by using the distinction between the tactical and organic approaches that we discussed in *Chapter 10, Tactical and Organic Enterprise Portfolio Planning and Adoption*, while adjusting them a little bit to a pragmatic SRE context. Therefore, in an SRE context, we have the following:

- **Tactical SRE adoption** will not be characterized by only an *all-hands-on-deck* approach (as we described in *Chapter 10, Tactical and Organic Enterprise Portfolio Planning and Adoption*), but also by the number of pairs of *hands available*, which will indicate the presence of site reliability engineers that are permanently placed and are dedicated to those areas, as well as *exclusive* site reliability engineer hiring rights for tactical adoption areas. Due to the scarcity of site reliability engineers, tactical adoption areas should be shaped in ecosystems or value streams, which will allow teams to share site reliability engineers (rotations or scaled operations), enabling an environment for *SRE economies of scale*.

- **SRE organic adoption** refers to any other area that will not have dedicated site reliability engineers, will probably struggle to incubate its available people, and also is not *SRE-eligible*. Nonetheless, those areas can, to the best possible and relevant extent, adopt parts of the reliability engineering framework where viable and applicable.

Storytelling – the tactical SRE eligibility assessment

In one bank I worked at, we built (our CIO was aware) a very solid SRE setup behind the scenes, both technologically and organizationally. It simply worked great. Once we started opening up about our practices and successes, many more teams wanted to follow our path and get help from us. They started pinging us to ask for support, inviting us to give presentations, buying and reading the Google SRE publications, and creating their own SRE visions and job descriptions while requesting a budget to hire site reliability engineers. And there was the real problem. We neither had the available budget to hire site reliability engineers for all teams, nor were we able to find them in the market, or we would have followed that "anarchical approach." We clearly needed a tactic for how to scale SRE. Our CIO came to me and asked me to create a mechanism that people could use to assess their portfolio and discover whether they had a real business case and were eligible for SRE support. The idea was to have them assessed, collect the results, and see what the actual need was so we could create a tactical scaling plan. It is important to mention that the top-10 ultra-critical services of the bank (plus our setup in capital markets) were by default in scope. It was the rest of the business applications and platforms portfolio we had to assess in an aligned and transparent way. I went ahead and created that eligibility criteria assessment based on the lessons we learned doing SRE for 2 years in my area. It was a self-assessment based on questions across a service's SDLC and its questions had different *reliability importance weight points*. The accumulated points of all the questions flagged your area as *SRE-eligible or not*. Not to our surprise, not many areas passed the eligibility zone. And again, not to our surprise, we could already – before seeing the results – predict which areas passed. There are two messages that I wish to pass through this story. One, you need a structured way to assess *SRE eligibility*, and two, the areas within your organization that are SRE-eligible are easy to spot.

The engagement model mechanism

The eligibility classification results, as well as the broader SRE operating model that your organization wishes to deploy, define another very important aspect of deploying SRE – what, in Google's terms, is called the **engagement model**. Being self-descriptive, the SRE engagement model defines the *business case* of site reliability engineers being engaged with a particular service. The engagement model is equally applicable in centralized, hybrid, and decentralized SRE operating models, which we will discuss in the last part of this chapter. What is the value of an engagement model?

- It ensures that engagements are value driven through clarity in the scope and outcomes.

- It enables effective tactical scaling.

- It defines the depth level of the engagement with a particular service in terms of tenets.

- It defines the required skills that a site reliability engineer should possess.

Site reliability engineers and the Π-shaped profiles

Do you remember the *Π*-shaped DevOps professionals of the previous chapter? I also advise you to enable *Π*-shaped site reliability engineers.

With my SRE experience, I have slightly amended Google's engagement model, the same as I have done with the *tenets*, so I can fit it into the different contexts of various incumbents. The three different engagement models I use are the following. I need to clarify, as is visible in the following table, that SRE engagements can combine both hands-on implementations as well as advisory:

	Early engagement	Late engagement	Full engagement	Advisory
SDLC phase of the service	Ideation or early design	Either first "go live" or already in production	Ideation or early design to sunsetting	Any SDLC phase
Objective	Establish the fundamental practices of reliability engineering from day 0	Assess production readiness Support with the gradual deployment of the service in production Address severe instability Operate the service in production	Ensure service reliability across its life cycle	Provide consultation on adopting the reliability engineering framework
Ownership level	Limited: Set up the fundamentals and move on to another service	Limited: Release or resolve the reliability issues and move on to another service	Full ownership of the service across its life cycle	No ownership

Table 13.3 – SRE engagement model parameters

Adapting and visualizing the SRE engagement models in our DevOps 360° SDLC, we get the following figure:

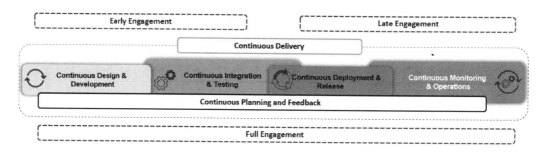

Figure 13.3 – SRE engagement models visualized in the DevOps 360° SDLC

Another important element of the *engagement model* framework, in addition to *who* across the portfolio will get SRE support, is also to define the *extent and duration* of the support. It is needless to mention that despite the engagement level, the SRE practices deployed must be based on the reliability engineering framework.

Reconciling SRE and ITIL

The second major *SRE debate/dilemma* (after the one between SRE and DevOps) is the one concerning the relationship between SRE and the ITIL. The conceptual interrelation of the two is quite significant, with Google claiming that SRE is their flavor of implementing IT service management. A big challenge that incumbents traditionally face is how to reconcile SRE and ITIL in a pragmatic way. For reasons derived from misconceptions, and a lack of practical experience with SRE, arguments such as *we are not Google*, and protectionism over ITIL implementations, incumbents seem to struggle with both the theoretical and practical reconciliation of the two concepts.

> **The ITIL obsession of incumbents**
>
> For the vast majority of incumbents, their ITIL implementation is considered to be their *IT gem* that needs to be protected against external invaders such as DevOps and SRE. I have not come across a single incumbent that is not obsessed with ITIL, even though several do not admit it. *"We are not an ITIL house,"* I was told once by an incumbent I was advising. Though when I got access to their IT operations model, it was ITIL v3, *pure copy-paste*. Back to the point. This obsession with ITIL, in my opinion, is derived from three sources. Firstly, it is easy to label an organization *ITIL done*, while with DevOps and SRE, you can never be done. Secondly, adopting ITIL requires less mental capital (*two available brain cells*, an old colleague of mine used to say), compared to DevOps and SRE. Thirdly and lastly, the core ITIL processes are the backbone of regulatory inspections of the IT operations procedures of incumbents.

I will not provide further information on ITIL as it is not in the scope of the section. What I wish to focus on is giving you a taste of how you can approach the reconciliation of the two concepts. The recipe I invented over the years, which has worked with a 100% success rate, is based on the following distinction/argument:

- **ITIL offers** process definition, design, and governance around IT service management, such as change management.

- **SRE offers** the means of engineering those IT service management processes across the SDLC phases and embedding *left*, such as raising CI/CD event-driven change requests.

Conceptually (and to a large extent, practically), this is it. Honestly, each and every ITIL process can be engineered using SRE practices. Of course, this requires in-depth knowledge of both concepts and the respective experience in implementing them. Now, how can you prove the successful reconciliation of the two? Mainly in three ways:

- The first one is to design the two concepts' reconciliation mechanism. The following figure provides a solid example of how SRE and ITIL concepts are fully reconciled. I acknowledge its oversimplification, but it is important to keep it simple:

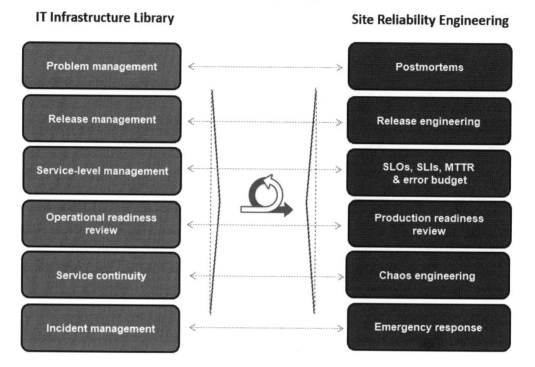

Figure 13.4 – Example of SRE and ITIL reconciliation

- The second is to visually and practically shift the reconciled outcome left in the DevOps 360° SDLC, so your people can also see its reconciliation with your broader DevOps capabilities.

- The third is to prove it practically through your SRE adoption, by collecting evidence on how you have been *ITIL compliant* in an engineered and efficient way. Automated raising and closure of incidents and change requests, automated service failover, automated service monitoring, automated IT asset reflection in the CMDB, and postmortem reports will be sufficient.

> **Not to be misperceived**
>
> ITIL is a good framework to set ITSM process governance for large incumbents (I doubt any neobank is using it). But it must not be a showstopper in your DevOps and SRE adoption. With good intentions, knowledge, experience, and creativity, DevOps, SRE, and ITIL can be reconciled under one DevOps 360° SDLC beautifully.

The most dominant SRE professions

As the SRE concept has been gaining momentum in the financial services industry, more and more professions and job titles around it have been created by different incumbents. Four are the most dominant and in this section, we will present them. Before looking into those, it is necessary to refer to the core mechanism behind defining these professions. It is your SRE operating model (as we will also see in the next section) that should be the foundation of what SRE professions and respective skills you require. Now, let us look at them:

- **Service reliability engineer**: This profile will primarily be associated with Agile DevOps teams who develop and operate business applications, either used by internal business units or external clients.

- **Client reliability engineer** (**CRE**): Client reliability engineering, according to Google, is a discipline in which the main objective is to create trust in the reliability of services between Google and its clients, combining engineering and advisory acumen. The customer reliability engineer is a profile that, in an incumbent's context, can be found as follows:

  - Fully embedded with an agile DevOps product team dedicated to the non-functional/quality requirements of the product

  - As a member of an SRE CoE, supporting service reliability engineers and developers of tactical adoption areas

  - In a DevOps platform team, working on eliciting the agile DevOps teams' requirements and supporting their onboarding to the platform

- **Platform reliability engineer**: This profile is primarily associated with core platforms that are part of the DevOps 360° technological ecosystem, tasked with their daily operations and reliability improvement matters. Depending on the platform, you will find platoform reliability engineers have corresponding designations – AWS reliability engineer, Azure DevOps reliability engineer, or ServiceNow reliability engineer.

- **Platform recovery engineer**: This profile will primarily be associated with the core foundation infrastructure and be tasked with minimizing the MTTD, MTT Respond, and MTT Recover in the case of major, disastrous events in the firm's data centers. In most cases, you will find those reliability engineers sitting in enterprise command centers and control rooms, surrounded by health check monitors.

Figure 13.5 – Overview of the SRE roles on the technological stack

The tenets among the four profiles are the same and when operations in their respective areas do not require attention, they might join forces on broader reliability improvement initiatives, engineering transformations, or maintaining the reliability engineering framework. But how do organizations deploy the various reliability engineering professions, based on their SRE operating model, while also utilizing the engagement model mechanism? We will look into how various incumbents approach SRE in the coming section.

Did you know?

The most common method that incumbents use to incubate their people to become SREs is what I call either a **baptism** or **knighthood ceremony**. I have seen it in the context of every single incumbent, literally. People who build monitoring solutions instead of performing manual morning checks or people who write scripts to automate manual processes instead of performing them manually are just repurposed from *operations or IT analysts* to site reliability engineers. The site reliability engineer title, in my opinion, needs to be earned with decisive reliability engineering work that has shifted left in the SDLC. And while I appreciate that *SRE is what you make of it*, there are still patterns and anti-patterns in the making.

What are the dominant SRE operating models in the financial services industry?

Throughout my DevOps career, I've had the real pleasure of either directly working with various SRE operating models and setups or indirectly being exposed to them through consultation. I have to admit that incumbents and, in general, the financial services industry have been extremely creative in how to approach the SRE operating model. In certain cases, with success, creating strong *financial services industry SRE patterns*, and in some other cases, not so successfully creating strong *financial services industry SRE anti-patterns*.

There are, of course, several ways that an SRE operating model can be deployed in the context of a given incumbent. In this section, we will discuss some of the most dominant SRE operating models that I have discovered in the financial services industry, outlining their context and motivating factors, as well as their pros and cons.

> **Clarifying the term "SRE operating model"**
>
> I am certain that, throughout the book, you will become familiar with what I mean when I use the term operating model. I nevertheless want to make sure. With an *SRE operating model*, we define the WoWs and organizing principles that the various teams subject to the SRE adoption operate upon and interact with.

Use case 1 – the SRE task force model

In this model, the SRE team was a central one and was acting as a task force to support business applications or platforms that had severe reliability issues. The following table summarizes its characteristics.

SRE operating model ownership	SRE task force
Engagement model	Late – solve reliability issues and move on
	Rotational
SRE service ownership	None
Level of centralization	Highly centralized

Table 13.4 – The SRE task force operating model parameters overview

Modus operandi: In this model, the site reliability engineers centrally belonged to a team called the **SRE task force**. They were deployed either as squads or individually in certain agile DevOps business teams (tribes and squads in that context) or common DevOps platforms that were experiencing significant reliability issues. The guiding principles of the setup were *join – stabilize – handover – move on*. The *reliability engineering framework* was owned by the SRE task force organization and was mandatory for engagements.

Here are the motivating factors:

- The organization wanted to avoid a massive and uncontrolled "SRE baptism." Only people belonging to the task force who had proven their skills and went through special interviews could carry the "SRE title."

- The skills' scarcity in the market could not allow for massive hirings of site reliability engineers and the organization wanted to tactically use the available ones by centrally and tactically controlling their embodiment to certain client engagements.

- The incumbent wanted to promote SRE primarily as a philosophy and a way of working and secondarily as an engineering practice. Having SREs only in a central team, in timeboxed rotational engagements, passed the message that SRE is a culture that should be embraced and adopted organically in the organization.

- There were certain areas with severe reliability issues and closely supervised by the incumbent's regulator. For budgeting and "political" reasons though, those areas were not allowed to hire. The "SRE Task Force" was a convenient alternative both to support those areas and also to prove the concept.

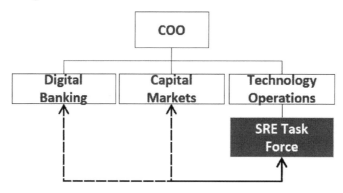

Figure 13.6 – The SRE task force topology

The following table shows you the SRE task force operating model pros and cons:

Pros	Cons
"Baptism" was avoided. The organization knew that those who were called site reliability engineers had the necessary qualifications.	The SRE task force, after a certain number of engagements, could not scale anymore.
The SRE people were not misused and were placed tactically in certain areas, delivering decisive work.	Exiting certain engagements became challenging due to the absence of people to hand knowledge over.
The rotations across various areas provided extensive organizational awareness to the SRE task force team.	The rest of the organization, due to the absence of hands-on support, struggled to implement more than the basics of the reliability framework.
There was a single area owning the "reliability framework," which was enriched through task force engagements.	The engagement rotations had a mixed effect on the site reliability engineers. Switching context and needing to constantly be onboarded to new setups create frustration.

Internal career mobility for the site reliability engineers was promoted through the rotations.	In certain engagements, site reliability engineers ended up performing more than 50% of the operations work, which resulted in frustration, especially in periods of significant "on-call" involvement due to constant firefighting.
A certain level of standardization of reliability practices was achieved in the task force engagements.	In several cases, it was challenging for the SRE team to influence the agile DevOps team's backlog on prioritizing reliability matters over new functionality.
	Onboarding of the site reliability engineers in terms of domains and technological stack knowledge as well as access rights management prolonged the start of the engagements.
	A lack of certain technical skills of the site reliability engineers did not make them a good fit for certain engagements.
	With all SREs in engagements, it was challenging to focus on keeping the reliability model updated.
	Several disagreements over the responsibility "white paper" arose, for instance, who was performing the deployments or who was responsible for L1 (emergency response).

Table 13.5 – SRE task force operating model pros and cons

If you want to know what happened to the SRE task force, "rotation fatigue" kicked in and resulted in the site reliability engineers being absorbed by the areas they were supporting.

Use case 2 – the "triangular" SRE CoE and tactical hiring

In this model, the SRE CoE team is a central one but is acting in a triangular operating model, as the following diagram displays:

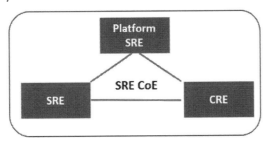

Figure 13.7 – The three parts of the triangular SRE CoE

The following table summarizes its characteristics:

SRE operating model ownership	SRE CoE and tactical SRE areas
Engagement model	Early, late, and full rotational and fixed
Service ownership	Full ownership of certain parts
Level of centralization	Hybrid

Table 13.6 – The "triangular" SRE CoEoperating model and tactical hiring parameters

Modus operandi: The modus operandi of this is simple despite its complexity. The SRE CoE consisted of three major teams, with several sub-teams:

- **The platform SRE teams:** This part of the SRE CoE owned several SRE technologies and tools that were used by SRE teams. These included observability tools, part of the CI/CD pipelines, and several cloud-native technologies.

- **The business applications SRE team:** This part of the SRE CoE was responsible for the reliability aspects of business applications that were part of the tactical adoption eligibility, having full ownership of them, with its members embedded in the agile DevOps teams. Those applications were not chosen by coincidence and were part of an "SRE ecosystem" that supported dedicated business value streams.

- **The CRE team:** This sub-team was acting as a combination of advisors and a task force, supporting different areas with reliability engineering aspects.

The three teams together were responsible for maintaining the "reliability engineering framework."

Now, in parallel, the agile DevOps teams that were not part of the business applications that the SRE team (the second SRE CoE team) was engaged with had the budget and approval to hire site reliability engineers. They were still part of the "tactical adoption eligibility."

Here are the motivating factors:

- The ambition was to create a complete SRE ecosystem that would include both platforms and business applications, with the ambition to fully implement SRE in a prescriptive way across them.

- To ensure that the complete set of tactical adoption areas could either be supported directly by the SRE CoE or indirectly also through the ability to hire their own site reliability engineers.

- To create a fully cross-functional SRE CoE where a potential site reliability engineer could be incubated but also existing site reliability engineers could have different career paths.

- To enable a sufficient level of technological self-sufficiency for the teams engaged with the SRE CoE so they could move at top speed. Also, to have the site reliability engineers support the modernization strategy of those areas to eliminate dependency on legacy applications and platforms.

You can see the topologies in the following figure:

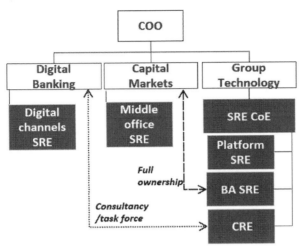

Figure 13.8 – The triangular SRE CoE and tactical topology

To get an overview of what worked well and what didn't work so well in this case, see the following table:

Pros	Cons
The SRE CoE through dedicated focus delivered decisive work.	Due to its portfolio versatility and hybrid setup, leading the CoE was perceived as "empire building" by certain parts of the organization. That generated cooperation resistance in certain areas.
The visibility across various areas provided extensive organizational awareness to the SRE CoE team.	Running the daily operations of the CoE and aligning the three teams over priorities and communication was quite a complex task.
There was a single area owning the "reliability framework," which was kept updated. Scaled reliability engineering recipes were also added.	At a certain point, the CoE struggled with capacity due to parallel runs (old and modernized setups).
Internal career mobility for the SREs was promoted through the rotations across the three teams.	Only a few of the CoE people had a software development background and it was challenging to improve reliability through business logic changes.
There was a very high level of standardization of reliability engineering across business applications and platforms.	In several cases, it was challenging for the SRE team to influence the agile DevOps team's backlog on prioritizing reliability matters over new functionality.
Due to the magnitude of decisive deliveries, a "high desirability" SRE momentum was created.	In time, there were conflicts of interest between the platform SRE and business application SRE teams on the platform's priorities and deliveries.

The platform modernization of the SRE CoE-engaged areas moved fast, eliminating dependencies on legacy platforms and applications.	Operational confusion rose among the business application site reliability engineers as, functionality-wise, they were referring to the agile product team PO and, HR-wise, to the SRE CoE team leads.
The SRE-owned platforms and tools were ultra-reliable; they were piloted in flagship business applications and direct feedback was captured.	It took time to assemble and make effective the CoE team as it was a combination of external hiring, internal incubation, and moves.
The tactical areas that did not have direct SRE involvement could advance through their own hiring and the CRE interaction.	

Table 13.7 – Triangular SRE CoE operating model pros and cons

Do you wonder what happened to the SRE CoE? It is still there but with some changes. Due to budget constraints, it has stopped hiring and therefore did not scale much further. It has lost some people to the tactical agile DevOps teams, who actually became software developers there. Due to enterprise technology standardization and consolidation initiatives, the platform SRE team moved out.

> **How should SREs approach business support inquiry work?**
>
> In my experience, your site reliability engineers should not be conducting business production support work. As in, they should not be contacted by the end users of a business application in order to resolve questions of a purely business nature. There are three main three reasons for that. Firstly, SREs are by nature "technical people" and thus enjoy purely technical work. Secondly, you will struggle to find SREs with domain-specific business knowledge or you will find it difficult to get them interested. Thirdly, you need to distract them (the same as with developers) as little as possible from their engineering work. In domains where you adopt SRE, offload the business support work to a service desk, exactly as we proposed in *Chapter 7, The DevOps 360° Technological Ecosystem as a Service*, when discussing platform team service models.

Use case 3 – business applications and platform SRE

In this model, the site reliability engineers were embedded in the business application areas and the core common DevOps and infrastructure teams. There was no central SRE team and, as you can imagine, no commonly agreed upon SRE operating model and reliability engineering framework. The following table provides a summary of the parameters:

SRE operating model ownership	Non-existent
Engagement model	Each team could specify its own
Service ownership	Full for either the business application or platform
Level of centralization	Hybrid

Table: 13.8 – The business applications and platform SRE operating model parameters

Modus operandi: In this model, two approaches were balanced. The first approach was around SREs embedded in the business application areas. That embodiment was not planned tactically, and it was more based on the desire and ability of certain business applications' agile DevOps teams. The second approach was more coordinated and tactical, where platform reliability engineers were tactically embedded in the core platform and infrastructure teams.

Here are the motivating factors:

- The organization was simply facing more reliability issues in its core platforms and infrastructure. That was revealed by production incidents and problematic management of data. Therefore, the reliability focus and budget were invested in that area.

- There was an objection to having a central SRE team as the intention was that the various agile DevOps teams should take full responsibility for their reliability aspects. Also, under the motto "SRE cannot scale," there was a strong internal belief that a central team would become a bottleneck.

- Management wanted to avoid any sense of discrimination in the business application areas in case they were left out of tactical SRE hiring.

- The SRE adoption did not have an enterprise focus and therefore there was no funding allocated to SRE hiring and incubation for the business applications. The platform teams nevertheless had funding allocated under the "infrastructure and platform stabilization" program.

The following figure displays the organizational topologies of use case 3:

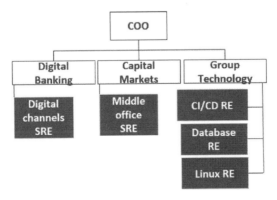

Figure 13.9 – Business application and platform SRE topology

This operating model's positive and negative results can be found in the following table:

Pros	Cons
The platform reliability engineering teams on the platforms made decisive reliability improvements that hugely benefited the broader organization.	Due to a lack of funding and coordination, the site reliability engineers hired in the business applications teams could not do decisive reliability work. Incubation through "baptism" was also observed.
Mobility, sharing of reliability engineering practices, and standardization were performed in the platform teams.	There was a significant variation in the SRE operating model and practices among the business application's site reliability engineers but also among the platform ones.
The cloud-first central capabilities' delivery was accelerated.	A lack of a single source of reliability engineering practices for business applications.
The platform onboarding and service support procedures were improved dramatically and the agile DevOps teams were brought closer to influencing the platform's backlogs.	
It was the first time that the platform teams conducted an enterprise capacity planning exercise.	

Table 13.9 – Business application and platform SRE operating model pros and cons

Are you wondering what happened? The platform team site reliability engineers are still there currently focusing on advancing the public cloud journey of the organization and DevOps platform portfolio interoperability. Some of the business' agile DevOps teams have replicated some of the platform reliability solutions in their areas with success.

Use case 4 – "baptized" and/or "random" SRE enablement

I am certain you were expecting this one to come up as I have mentioned the terms in various sections of the chapter already. This model was not coordinated by any central change management activity and was planned and executed on an individual area level, either on business applications or platforms. You can find the parameters of this unorthodox use case in the following table:

SRE operating model ownership	Non-existent
Engagement model	Each team could specify its own
Service ownership	Hybrid in either the business applications or platform areas
Level of centralization	Decentralized

Table 13.10 – The "baptized" and "random" SRE parameters

Modus operandi overview:

- **Baptism**: The new SRE modus operandi was almost exactly the same for "traditional L1 support" ITIL-based IT operations conducted by people with either absent or limited engineering skills. The major difference was that the title of those people changed and they attended some sort of training as part of an "incubation plan." In most cases, the development teams kept full authority across all aspects of the SDLC, including backlog prioritization, deployments, L2 support, and so on. The newly branded site reliability engineers were primarily doing business inquiry support, restarting servers, working on monitoring solutions, and automating manual tasks where they had the skills, being pushed by the development teams on the extreme "right" of the SDLC involvement.

- **Random**: This simply characterizes organizations where literally every team is free to adopt SRE in its own way, without any alignment.

Motivating factors: Misconceptions, no belief in the real value of the concept, a lack of funding and transformation means, and a desire to rapidly make posts on "SRE successes" on LinkedIn. Doing it for real takes time and effort, you see.

Such SRE adoptions end up being more of a fallacy rather than a real investment and making a positive impact. In my experience, they do not last for long, as they do not deliver on their promises.

> **Important note**
>
> Especially in large and global presence incumbents, several of the processing SRE operating models can be found within the context of a single incumbent. There is literally nothing wrong with that approach (except for use case 4), as long as they are reconciled with the enterprise DevOps operating model and do not come into direct daily operational conflict.

Summary

In this chapter, we technically finished the walk-through of the main elements of our DevOps 360° operating model. Our focus has been on SRE, the value proposition of which we examined both from the lenses of its relationship with DevOps and also through its fundamental tenets. For the former, we concluded with the argument that it is a relationship of mutual inclusiveness and not conflict. For the latter, we discussed the importance of concepts such as the "SRE balance," "error budgets," "reliability engineering frameworks," as well as "reliability engineering," on the one hand with regard to accelerating the DevOps 360° evolution, as well as defining the responsibilities of your SRE teams. Later in the chapter, we did a deep-dive into some very important proven practices on how to adopt SRE at relevance. Our focus was on adoption and engagement models, eligibility criteria, reconciliation with concepts such as ITIL, as well as the potential SRE roles you can shape and deploy. The last part of the chapter was focused on discussing real use cases from approaches that various incumbents have taken when adopting SRE. We covered the respective motivating factors behind each use case and the core aspects of the various operating models, and we also examined the positive and negative results that those incumbents observed.

The next chapter is the last one in this book. In it, we will have a recap of the most important points of all the book's chapters and will also provide some final advice for consideration.

14
360° Recap, Staying Relevant, and Final Remarks

We have reached the end of this book. In this chapter, we will go over all the parts of the DevOps 360° operating model that we have seen throughout this book. We will highlight the most important concepts, frameworks, and aspects of each phase that we consider key takeaways from this book. Following that, we will provide an extra set of final remarks that various incumbents discovered during their DevOps evolutions so that you can learn from the *mistakes* of others.

In this chapter, we're going to cover the following main topics:

- Recapping the DevOps 360° operating model phases
- Final remarks

Recapping the DevOps 360° operating model phases

Throughout this book, as we unfolded the core phases and aspects of the DevOps 360° operating model, we covered several DevOps terms, concepts, frameworks, and practices. This book and its flow were structured based on a triangular model:

- Each chapter consisted of a small "DevOps pocket guide" for the domain and phases of the DevOps 360° operating model that it was representing.
- The sequence and flow of this book's chapters took you through a potential array of steps for designing your model.
- All the chapters represented a relatively complete DevOps 360° operating model.

We covered quite a lot in this book, so you may not be able to remember everything. You may have also been a little bit puzzled about what knowledge to retain from each chapter. In this section, we will go back to the beginning of this book and reflect on it. This will help you refresh your memory regarding the most important aspects of the DevOps 360° operating model.

Context and DevOps value proposition

In *Chapter 1, The Banking Context and DevOps Value Proposition* we started by introducing the main actor of this book: the incumbent bank. That was not only to introduce you smoothly to this book but to also highlight that *who you are* as an organization can significantly influence your DevOps adoption. We also stressed the importance of examining and understanding your internal and external context and how they work together from a DevOps perspective. After, we defined the DevOps value proposition for banking, starting with outlining the definition of DevOps that we would use throughout this book. The value proposition we detailed went word by word through our definition, providing examples of DevOps practices that support its materialization, while using a mobile banking application as an example.

Then, we introduced two of the major themes of this book that underpin its philosophy and approach: *relevance* and *360°*. I strongly recommend that you also use these as guiding principles in your DevOps evolution. Regarding the former, we discovered how situations and circumstances vary across the context of an incumbent by using examples of equity trading and settlement. Try to find similar examples in your context so that you can use them as foundations for your *at relevance* mechanism. Regarding the latter, we outlined the four qualities of 360° with examples – that is, completeness, continuity, reconcilability, and interoperability. Please keep these in mind throughout your DevOps evolution. The concepts of relevance and 360° were continuously used throughout this book.

"Multi-speed," vision, objectives, and change elements

Chapter 2, The DevOps Multi-Speed Context, Vision, Objectives, and Change Nature was very rich in terms of content due to its importance in setting the foundation for the DevOps 360° operating model. Initially, we defined the concept of *multi-speed* in banking, which, together with the concepts of *at relevance* and *360°*, constitutes the foundation of this book. Examples were provided on how speeds are constructed *naturally* but also *intentionally* and we stressed the importance of understanding this. Understanding how different speeds are shaped in your organization will help you apply *sophistication* to your evolution.

Then, we highlighted the decisive need to understand your internal DevOps *state-of-art* concept and outlined a representative picture of it as a collection of several incumbents. In particular, we explained the multi-layer nature of your DevOps *state-of-art* context and the need to capture it. Please invest heavily in understanding where you stand in the early days of your evolution.

The most important part of this chapter was defining the DevOps vision and objectives. We started by highlighting the role of the corporate and technology strategies while providing a representative example of where incumbents place their focus when shaping them. The need to reconcile the two strategies was highlighted as a fundamental element of defining your DevOps enterprise OKRs.

We focused on the DevOps enterprise OKRs and provided some concrete examples that you can use in your evolution. For each, we investigated the main objectives, key results, linkage to the corporate and technology strategies, as well as motivating factors. The consolidation of all those OKRs and their materialization led us to define the overarching object of a 360° DevOps operating model.

Finally, we focused on the need to decide on the nature and extent of your DevOps adoption, concluding that *evolution* is the most suitable and sustainable path. Please do not boil the ocean by being unnecessarily radical!

The 360° DevOps operating model skeleton and governance

We opened *Chapter 3, The DevOps 360° Operating Model Pillars and Governance Model* by providing a visualization of the core pillars and phases of the 360° DevOps operating model so that you could *foresee* what was to follow in this book, all while grasping the *big conceptual picture*. As we moved on, our main focus was to provide recommendations around the governance bodies that you could consider establishing during your evolution to steer its direction. The *DevOps 360° vision authority* and the *DevOps 360° design and advocacy group* were mentioned as the leading governing bodies. Then, we looked at the broader DevOps stakeholder matrix, where we outlined a plethora of stakeholders that you could potentially involve while stating the DevOps value proposition for each. References were also made to the DevOps workstreams you could establish by designing the outcome of each of the DevOps enterprise OKRs.

Finally, we focused on the necessity to understand the dynamics of the DevOps 360° evolution and its stakeholders, who have a significant influence on that evolution. In an attempt to make the dynamics more *vivid*, we presented and discussed three use cases from different incumbents, whose organizational structure had an impact on their evolution.

Enterprise architecture and the DevOps center of excellence

Chapter 4, Enterprise Architecture and the DevOps Center of Excellence focused on two vital orchestrators of the DevOps 360° evolution, which we also perceive as part of the main governing bodies: the enterprise architecture and the DevOps **Center of Excellence (CoE)**.

We looked at the multidimensional value proposition of the enterprise architecture and focused on three main domains. We discovered the importance of defining your portfolio's critical path in terms of domains, flows, applications, and services. That, as we saw later in this book, provides the foundation for the tactical part of the evolution. After, we examined the four major platform modernization strategies that an EA function can help form. We complemented this by covering their business case drivers and providing real financial services industry examples. The last domain that we discussed from an enterprise architecture perspective was reference architectures, where we outlined their importance for DevOps acceleration and standardization while citing the most important reference architectures that incumbents adopt.

From a DevOps CoE perspective, we examined its value proposition through the potential roles it can have in your evolution. We looked at it from the angles of the evolution's *maestro*, the *DevOps 360° operating model owner*, the technological capability provider, as well as the tactical enablement partner. We concluded that, as with DevOps as a concept, the way you set up your DevOps CoE is characterized by "what you make out of it" and it will be shaped according to your ambitions. To create some inspiration, we provided four use cases from four different incumbents that approached their DevOps CoE establishment in different ways.

Business enterprise agility and DevOps ways of working

Chapter 5, Business Enterprise Agility and DevOps Ways of Working Reconciliation introduced us to the world of business enterprise agility. We started by discussing how it can be reconciled with DevOps, concluding that both concepts need each other to deliver the maximum return on investment. After this, we discussed the four dominant enterprise agility models in the financial services industry and examined them from a DevOps perspective. We concluded with two main observations that I am certain you can relate to. The first one is that DevOps can be adopted agnostically in any enterprise agility model, while the second is that all enterprise agility models share *similarities* in how they deploy certain DevOps concepts. I urge you to invest your time and effort heavily in ensuring the agnosticism of these two concepts.

After that, using the Spotify model as a basis, we provided an 11-step proven practice on how to define the DevOps ways of working and organizing principles for your Agile DevOps teams. By doing so, we examined important elements of relevance that you should consider since *one WoW* cannot fit all. The proven practices were based on certain templates that you can adopt in your organization.

DevOps SDLC 360° evolution and engineering

Chapter 6, DevOps Software Development Life Cycle 360° Evolution and Engineering was dedicated to the heart of the DevOps 360° operating model. To start this chapter, we discussed the importance of considering the four qualities of 360° when designing an evolved SDLC, along with ensuring the DevOps equilibrium is fulfilled. Then, we provided you with some inspiration about the potential SDLC phases, which you can use as a foundation to design your evolved SDLC. In particular, we focused on the importance of frameworks and the capabilities that belong to their various phases. Carefully designing these fully is an important proposal we made. In supporting you, we provided a proven eight-step guide that you can use either *by the book* or adjust to your own needs. You should be extra conscious about designing your DevOps 360° SDLC paths based on relevance and speed. Not all of your portfolio has to follow the same path and that should be reflected in your *DevOps paths* designs and DevOps capability catalog. In addition, from the SDLC early design phase, you should set the target for the velocities that you expect to meet via its adoption. This move is foundational for the next phases of the DevOps 360° operating model and how they benefit measurement and realization.

The DevOps 360° technological ecosystem as a service

In *Chapter 7, The DevOps 360° Technological Ecosystem as a Service* we focused on the part of the DevOps 360° operating model that most people find more interesting to work with: technology. We started by looking at the high importance of bringing clarity to the misunderstood relationship between technology and DevOps. Technology is a DevOps enabler, not DevOps itself, and this is something you need to clarify within your organization. After this, we provided a detailed picture of why you should pursue technology standardization during your DevOps 360° evolution, while also taking precautions and carefully assessing your circumstances. Using standardization *clean cuts* is the most viable approach that we proposed for your consideration. Then, we discussed the value proposition of platform teams while looking into proven operating and service models that you can consult when designing yours. Remember to put extra focus on defining the platform team and agile DevOps team's *white paper and social contract* to ensure clarity of expectations from both sides. The DevOps journeys, experience, and productivity should be another area to focus on, along with assessing their impact on the ways of working applied by the agile DevOps teams. In case you decide to pursue the approach of platform teams across your DevOps 360° technological ecosystem, we highlighted some platform team domains, along with their corresponding services, that you can consider enabling.

360° regulatory compliance as code

Chapter 8, 360° Regulatory Compliance as Code was dedicated to the *notorious* regulatory compliance domain of DevOps. Understanding the regulatory landscape that influences your DevOps 360° evolution helps with your evolution's fundamental activities, along with conducting a preliminary impact assessment in case you do not manage to fully comply with regulatory requirements. Our advice is to take full advantage of these requirements to accelerate your DevOps 360° evolution. For inspiration, you can go back and look at the four stories that we provided. Primarily, my advice is to focus from a regulatory compliance perspective on the DevOps controls and segregation/separation of duties domains. Understanding the full anatomy of the former and embedding them using engineering means across your SDLC should increase your speed while ensuring compliance and improving reliability. You can consult the array of controls we proposed and adopt them based on their relevance to your context. We also provided very rich considerations that you can benefit from when designing and implementing the controls. Regarding segregation/separation of duties, you must focus on two determinants: data and duties. **Separation of Duties (SoD)** must be applied with relevance to your context. We saw how that can happen regarding the rotational and fixed-model ways of working. Having dynamic and robust identity and access management capabilities, as well as strong logging capabilities, will be fundamental to proving SoD compliance. Discuss these with your regulator to avoid a *hardcoded SoD*, meaning implementing SoD as an impenetrable wall between development and operations. Remember that this must happen early in your evolution to bring clarity to your relationship with your regulators in terms of scope, decisions, and expectations. To define the topics of this discussion, you can consult the list we provided.

The DevOps portfolio classification and governance

Chapter 10, Tactical and Organic Enterprise Portfolio Planning and Adoption was the core of the *at-relevance* principle. We highlighted the strong importance of classifying your portfolio and noted that not all of your applications will go through the same DevOps journey. Two classification types that you can consider using are **criticality and impact** and **technology and architecture**. Combining the two will give you an even more well-rounded and dynamic *at-relevance* mechanism. You can consult the examples we provided regarding whether DevOps becomes relevant or not based on the classification of each business application or platform. Remember to include the DevOps platforms in the process. To help you define the DevOps speeds to complement the portfolio's relevance, we provided a speed formula based on five variables that you can play around with and shape the formula according to your context and ambitions. Speed comes with responsibility, and you should *trust but verify*, along with providing direction. You can get inspiration on how to launch the concept from the sample governance model we provided. Later in this chapter, we discussed the portfolio governance aspects, and we stressed the importance of performing a tiered portfolio registry based on the **business domain**, **applications**, **services**, **IT assets**, and **DevOps attributes**. These are the DevOps attributes you must use as part of defining relevance and speeds. The core mechanism that we proposed you use during the portfolio registry, also alongside your evolution, is the production readiness review. You can consult our example and build on top of it. To relate the license to continuously deliver and the production readiness review, you can look at the distinction we made at the end of this chapter. One of the most important elements of this chapter to remember is the concept of DevOps minimum viable adherence. If you manage to effectively launch the minimum viable adherence concept, you will achieve a decisive victory in your evolution by aligning your whole organization with the adoption of fundamental DevOps capabilities.

Benefit measurement and realization

Chapter 11, Benefit Measurement and Realization introduced us to the traditionally challenging domain of benefit measurement and realization. We provided arguments on why you should try to think more broadly than the mainstream DevOps indicators and metrics. In addition, we talked about why you should aim to define *targets*, instead of *indicators*, considering the difference between a *proof of success* and an *indicator of success*. Distinguishing between targets and metrics will be very beneficial. Remember that the former is what you wish to achieve via the target, while the latter defines how you measure progress toward achieving that target. We strongly recommend engaging the broad array of stakeholders in your DevOps ecosystem to help define the target and metrics; you can use the small exercise we proposed to help with this. To bring more sophistication to this measurement, you can consider using the *minimum viable adoption – minimum viable adherence – efficiency* three-tier system. Come back to this chapter and look at the example we provided for guidance. For your reference, we provided some practical KPTs and metrics that you can borrow with pride. Finally, when doing the math for calculating your KPTs and metrics, remember that data is gold and its visualization helps you demonstrate progress. Once again, read through the further recommendations we provided to avoid pitfalls. Last but not least, please do not establish KPTs and metrics like the ones we cited at the end of this chapter.

Hiring people, incubation, and mobility

In *Chapter 12, People Hiring, Incubation, and Mobility* we focused on the DevOps evolution's most valuable asset: people! We proposed that you should aim to enable *Π*-shaped profiles by balancing a broad DevOps awareness (the horizontal line) and deep specialization in two DevOps domains (vertical lines). When deciding how your Π-shaped profiles will be enabled, consider the evolution of the roles in the future to ensure that your profiles will be fit for purpose as time goes by. A lot of your efforts will go into hiring and incubation since your organization will likely not initially possess the skillset your evolution requires. When defining your hiring tactics, consider the parameters we have outlined. On the incubation side, remember to include your organization's leadership, be targeted and work-driven, and stay relevant. We also recommend investing in people's mobility within your organization, but please take precautions by consulting the areas that we outlined.

Site reliability engineering

I must admit that I wanted to give you even more *meat* in this chapter. I promise I will do this if there's a second edition of this book. *Chapter 13, Site Reliability Engineering in the FSI* was dedicated to SRE – *the purest distillation of DevOps*. The first thing you must do to start a scaled SRE adoption is to reconcile it with DevOps and provide clarity on the *DevOps versus SRE* dilemma. Kill the misconception from the start, making it clear that the two concepts do not conflict. As we proposed, use the *tenets (the common set of responsibilities across SRE teams)* to reconcile the two concepts and define the SRE's responsibilities. You can either use the ones we provided *out of the box* and adjust them or create your own. At the end of the day, *SRE is what you make of it*. The choice is yours. There are a few things to remember regarding the tenets: you must shift SRE left, monitor the balance, and understand that despite SRE being an operations-focused concept, it spans across the SDLC and provides gatekeeping authority using mechanisms such as PRR. As with DevOps, you need to apply SRE when it's relevant. We have cited several mechanisms from which you can draw inspiration. Consider the SRE eligibility parameters, distinguish between a tactical and an organic adoption, define an engagement model, and reconcile it with your ITIL adoption. By enabling the concept from a *people* perspective, there are several SRE professions you can define and get inspiration from the four we proposed. If you want some inspiration based on what *others have done* when deploying SRE, then take a look at the four use cases we listed at the end of this chapter. I urge you to not follow the path of the last one.

Final remarks

I have four final remarks before I say goodbye. Let's take a look.

Do not use DevOps to mask cost-cutting initiatives

I've seen this happen in several contexts and it never worked in the long run. You can optimize your operating expenses through DevOps outcomes, and you should aim for that. But having cost-cutting initiatives as your top DevOps priority without creating decisive efficiencies and adding end value is just wrong. Yes, it may make your balance sheet look better, but your daily operational reality will most probably get worse and be unsustainable in the long term. Also, your people are not of low mental capital. They will understand your incentives early on and plan their futures accordingly. The people *on the ground* care about building great solutions, not the cost/income ratio.

Manage uncertainty and the people exodus

There will be uncertainty during your evolution. DevOps will not be the only thing your organization focuses on and until you start making solid steps of progress and create a meaningful coalition (if you ever do), there will be a sense of uncertainty. This will inevitably cause a *people exodus* where people will resign and leave your organization. You know it will happen; you have probably seen it before. And you also know that it will be the very best ones that leave first. I have personally seen this happen again and again in the context of incumbents. It is an inevitable part of human nature to fight for survival when feeling that your future is at risk (do you remember Hobbes's metaphor of *brutish life* from earlier in this book?). A people exodus will heavily jeopardize the progress of your evolution. Therefore, through speed in your thinking and evolution, you must provide transparency, communication, people engagement, continuous demonstrated progress, and constant reassurance to keep your people motivated and engaged. Increased salaries and bonuses that you might use as retention mechanisms will not keep them around for long – they will only buy you a few months.

> **Note**
>
> Do not use uncertainty as a vehicle to get rid of *human debt*. I heard that as a saying once. The idea is that *if they (referring to the people with outdated skills) do not know whether they will have a job tomorrow, they will hopefully leave themselves, so we do not need to fire them and pay any compensation*. In the end, they do not leave because their skills are outdated, and they cannot find another job.

Balance "changing people" with "changing the people"

Once upon a time, I had a CEO who used to say, *I do not want to change people; I want to change the people*. The former *change* was indicating a *fire-and-hire* tactic, while the latter *change* referred to an *incubation tactic*. Focus on doing both strategically and thoughtfully. You will never be able to hire all the people and skills you need and, equally, you will never be able to effectively incubate everybody. Some you need to let go of and others will need to be incubated. However, I do urge you to bring new blood into your organization. At the end of the day, I believe that *if you already had the right people, you wouldn't need to run a formal evolution and would never need to incubate them. This would have happened already organically*. Think about it…

Manage your budget wisely

I know of two DevOps evolutions that ran out of budget in two different incumbents. One was terminated and the second one was compromised in terms of scope. I appreciate that life is uncertain, and I have mentioned that uncertainty aspect and its potential influence on your DevOps evolution in several parts of this book. But at the same time, I also think that if, all of a sudden and without a major event originating from the external environment, you realize that you do not have any more

DevOps funding, it would call into question just how *DevOps-serious* you are. If you find yourselves in that situation, it is a clear signal of a lack of true incentives, a *sloppy* business case, and naivety on what it takes to evolve DevOps in harmony at an enterprise level.

> **Busting the misconception about banks**
>
> For better or worse, I have spent my whole career working with banks. Some realities and myths surround banks. People say that banks are slow, bureaucratic, cannot implement DevOps and SRE, are heavily regulated, are old-school in mentality, are only profit-driven, are left behind in digitalization, and so on. And while those statements describe the reality of several banks, especially large ones, they are not unavoidable stoppers of DevOps evolutions. Banks have changed rapidly in recent years and as we have seen in this book, there are plenty of DevOps success stories out there driven by banks. It simply takes passion, emotional intelligence, and good brains.

Summary

Summarizing the summary is irrational and therefore I will omit it. So! That was it for this book on *DevOps in the financial services industry*. I hope that you enjoyed reading this book as much as I enjoyed authoring it. To be honest, I found it pleasantly challenging to fit all my DevOps stories and practices into a little bit more than 300 pages. Nevertheless, I am confident that you have found plenty of useful ideas, frameworks, and concepts that you can apply in your DevOps endeavors. Having said that, I would like to wish you the very best in your DevOps adventures. Enjoy, envision, and keep pushing! If you wish to have a *DevOps coffee* and tell me about your DevOps stories, you can find me on LinkedIn.

One last thing for you to remember before I go is that *where there is love, there is DevOps!*

Over and out!

Σπυρίδων

Index

Packt.com

Subscribe to our online digital library for full access to over 7,000 books and videos, as well as industry leading tools to help you plan your personal development and advance your career. For more information, please visit our website.

Why subscribe?

- Spend less time learning and more time coding with practical eBooks and Videos from over 4,000 industry professionals

- Improve your learning with Skill Plans built especially for you

- Get a free eBook or video every month

- Fully searchable for easy access to vital information

- Copy and paste, print, and bookmark content

Did you know that Packt offers eBook versions of every book published, with PDF and ePub files available? You can upgrade to the eBook version at packt.com and as a print book customer, you are entitled to a discount on the eBook copy. Get in touch with us at customercare@packtpub.com for more details.

At www.packt.com, you can also read a collection of free technical articles, sign up for a range of free newsletters, and receive exclusive discounts and offers on Packt books and eBooks.

Other Books You May Enjoy

If you enjoyed this book, you may be interested in these other books by Packt:

Go for DevOps

John Doak, David Justice

ISBN: 9781801818896

- Understand the basic structure of the Go language to begin your DevOps journey Interact with filesystems to read or stream data
- Communicate with remote services via REST and gRPC
- Explore writing tools that can be used in the DevOps environment
- Develop command-line operational software in Go
- Work with popular frameworks to deploy production software
- Create GitHub actions that streamline your CI/CD process
- Write a ChatOps application with Slack to simplify production visibility

Learning DevOps

Mikael Krief

ISBN: 9781838642730

- Become well versed with DevOps culture and its practices
- Use Terraform and Packer for cloud infrastructure provisioning
- Implement Ansible for infrastructure configuration
- Use basic Git commands and understand the Git flow process
- Build a DevOps pipeline with Jenkins, Azure Pipelines, and GitLab CI
- Containerize your applications with Docker and Kubernetes
- Check application quality with SonarQube and Postman
- Protect DevOps processes and applications using DevSecOps tools

Packt is searching for authors like you

If you're interested in becoming an author for Packt, please visit authors.packtpub.com and apply today. We have worked with thousands of developers and tech professionals, just like you, to help them share their insight with the global tech community. You can make a general application, apply for a specific hot topic that we are recruiting an author for, or submit your own idea.

Share Your Thoughts

Now you've finished *Industrializing Financial Services with DevOps*, we'd love to hear your thoughts! Scan the QR code below to go straight to the Amazon review page for this book and share your feedback or leave a review on the site that you purchased it from.

https://packt.link/r/1804614343

Your review is important to us and the tech community and will help us make sure we're delivering excellent quality content.

Download a free PDF copy of this book

Thanks for purchasing this book!

Do you like to read on the go but are unable to carry your print books everywhere? Is your eBook purchase not compatible with the device of your choice?

Don't worry, now with every Packt book you get a DRM-free PDF version of that book at no cost.

Read anywhere, any place, on any device. Search, copy, and paste code from your favorite technical books directly into your application.

The perks don't stop there, you can get exclusive access to discounts, newsletters, and great free content in your inbox daily

Follow these simple steps to get the benefits:

1. Scan the QR code or visit the link below

https://packt.link/free-ebook/9781804614341

2. Submit your proof of purchase
3. That's it! We'll send your free PDF and other benefits to your email directly

Printed in Great Britain
by Amazon

13868638R00208